To the Harbin Station

To the Harbin Station

The Liberal Alternative in Russian Manchuria, 1898–1914

DAVID WOLFF

Stanford University Press
Stanford, California
1999

Stanford University Press

Stanford, California

© 1999 by the Board of Trustees of the
Leland Stanford Junior University

Printed in the United States of America

CIP data are at the end of the book

To Woody
He taught us

Acknowledgments

THE HARBIN described in this book is almost gone, buried in the living debris of all that came later. The 1913 census estimated 110,000 inhabitants. By 1990 the figure had grown to nearly three million. Most of the physical city dating to the period of this book is now being torn down to make room for the architectural product of the PRC's recent economic growth. Children who experienced the 1917 Revolution in Harbin are all well over eighty. In the twilight of their generation, these former Harbiners live all over the world, for Harbin's history since the 1930's is one of fragmentation. And the records of this great urban experiment in intercultural interaction have followed their owners into the diaspora. To research Harbin, I too took a circuitous route.

At the beginning of the journey was the idea, and the idea came from Andy Wachtel, himself the grandson of *kharbintsy*. Conversations with the late Eva Naftali, whose remarkable memories of Harbin reached back until before the First World War, reminded me how close to the present my history ran. As the project took shape, at an important juncture, Marc Raeff gave me a very beneficial consultation. I was fortunate early on to visit with Rosemary Quested in England, where she is in retirement. She had traveled much of my road and generously gave me some good pointers. Numerous American, British, and French librarians aided before I arrived in Leningrad in the fall of 1988. Despite the soothing presence of Serafima Igorevna, a figure known to many generations of historians at work in the Russian State Historical Archive (RGIA), the triple taboo on foreign affairs, border questions, and Russian émigrés prevented me from getting access to the key documents. And then, almost magically, *glasnost* freed the materials central to this book from the vaults where they had lain sealed since the 1920's. For many files the last user had been the legendary historian B. A. Romanov, one of the fathers of the "Leningrad School." In Leningrad (now St. Petersburg), I owe thanks to Boris Ananich and Boris Mironov for many kindnesses and help in learning my way around "our house," RGIA. This kind of archival excavation is stressful, and I am grateful to Alanchik, Igor, Misha, Olya, Liza, Shurik, Katya, Lena, and Tanya for keeping me sane.

Glasnost also delivered to me the great naval fortress of Vladivostok. Soon after Vladivostok was opened to *Soviet* citizens without special permits in fall 1988, I began the search for an openness advocate at Far Eastern State University. In February 1989, I became the first long-term "capitalist" visitor (*kapstranchik*) to the university in several generations. I must thank Lena, Natasha, Tamara, and Volodya for making this both a productive and an exciting experience. I also would like to mention my debts to Amir Khisatmudinov, Viktor Larin, Pavel Minakir, and Vladimir Shishkin.

I arrived in China in May 1989 to find a most unusual state of institutional flux. In particular, there was a general lack of unanimity regarding the degree to which information on events both current and historical could and should be provided to foreigners. By the time the American consulate at Shenyang caught up with me in late June to let me know that all "nonessential personnel" were being evacuated from the PRC, I had had considerable access to three crucial collections that are, even today, not generally available. These were (1) the files of the Chinese Eastern Railway (CER) Land Department, confiscated in 1923 by the local Chinese government, when it took over the department from the Russian-dominated railway management; (2) the core archive of the Jewish community of Harbin; and (3) the largest remaining chunk of the CER library, buried in a basement since the Cultural Revolution. Each day as I finished work with these materials, I found my hands coal black. A true archival excavation! Many people cooperated to enable my access, often contrary to ruling ideological principles. I salute and thank them all.

In Japan, I recovered from the exhaustion of adventure travel, continued research, and gathered my thoughts together for a final assault on the doctorate. For being an exemplary *shido kyokan* and much more, I must first thank Hamashita Takeshi for inviting me to Tokyo University's Institute of Oriental Culture. Hara Teruyuki kindly brought me to the Slavic Center at Hokkaido University, where the rich collections added greatly to my knowledge of the region and my topic. Gratitude is also due to Enatsu Yoshiki, Eric Feldman, Toshi Hasegawa, Nakachi Mie, Nakami Tatsuo, Takao Chizuko, Wada Haruki, and the late Kobayashi Masayuki. At the University of Hawaii and the East-West Center, stacks of notecards were finally converted into linear text. I am grateful for Charles Morrison's invitation to spend a few months in paradise, for Pat Polansky's indefatigable bibliological aid, and for Bob Valliant's useful pointers. I learned most of all, however, from John Stephan's discriminating readings of my dissertation chapters.

Of course, there would not have been much to read but for my teachers. At Harvard, Louise Epstein, Bill Fuller, Ned Keenan, Nadya Kizenko, Sam

Levin, Steve Nielsen, Richard Pipes, Erich Schlaikjer, Vsevolod Setchkareff, Jessy Stern, and Andy Wachtel inspired and urged me on. At Berkeley, Suzanna Barrows, Catherine Evtuhov, and Yeh Wen-Hsin were influential in very important ways. Nicholas Riasanovsky has never wavered in his support for this topic, from earliest formulations to final pre-publication draft. As *Doktor-Onkel*, through him I have constructed an imaginary lineage that leads from Harbin to me as well as from Russia to Russian studies. Other Berkeley professors from Harbin, Boris Bresler and Gregory Grossman, also gave learned encouragement. Gail Lapidus was very generous to me in many roles, from dissertation committee member to professor to employer. Fred Wakeman has had a seminal impact on the way I read my sources, always searching for the zest in each moment of historical event. This book would never have been written without Reggie Zelnik, for I wrote each chapter, one by one, in order to elicit his multipage, single-space commentaries, as humorous as they were instructive in their attention to everything from the weighty and substantive to the smallest editorial detail.

Once upon a time, my brother Larry taught me how to write, and but for this I am lost. My sister Sharon has been an oasis of difference for many years. Lihui, at a crucial moment, reminded me of ultimate priorities. My friends Gary and Pete do not fit anywhere else, so they go here. My parents, Robert and Renee, though surely disappointed that such elephantine efforts have only borne a mouse, bear chief responsibility for all this excess education. I love them dearly.

Support for the research and writing described above came from UC-Berkeley's Slavic Center and Institute of East Asian Studies, the Fulbright-Hays Commission, the Hoover Institution, the International Research and Exchanges Board, and the Social Science Research Council. In early 1995, a sabbatical semester at Hebrew University's Truman Center gave me the opportunity to revise the manuscript for publication. Shortly thereafter, Stephen Kotkin's iron reading of my Introduction galvanized me to further significant improvements. The two anonymous readers, Josh Fogel and Tom Lahusen, provided clear and constructive critique, both substantive and editorial, that led to further rewriting and reorganization. At Stanford University Press, I am grateful to Muriel Bell and Norris Pope, who guided me smoothly through the process. David Deis and Vlad Shkurkin deserve thanks for assistance with maps and photos.

I alone am responsible for all errors that remain.

D.W.

Contents

Foreword, by Nicholas V. Riasanovsky   *xiii*

A Note on Conventions   *xv*

Introduction   *1*

1. Constructions   *14*
2. Interministerial Rivalry as a Way of Life   *49*
3. Manchurian Colonization: Policy, Results, and Feedback   *78*
4. War, Revolution, and Politics: Harbin, 1904–1908   *115*
5. Know Thine Enemy, Know Thyself: Russian Orientology in the Borderlands   *146*

Conclusion   *168*

Appendix: Some Notes on Russian Sinology in Beijing, Kazan, St. Petersburg, and Vladivostok, 1715–1899   *181*

Notes   *191*

Bibliography   *239*

Index   *251*

16 pages of illustrations follow p. 145

Foreword

IT IS A privilege and a pleasure to write a brief Foreword to Dr. David Wolff's first book, *To The Harbin Station: The Liberal Alternative in Russian Manchuria, 1898–1914*. I became acquainted with David Wolff and his work in the course of his graduate studies in the Department of History of the University of California in Berkeley—in particular, I was one of the formally assigned readers of his doctoral dissertation. Now, after successful completion of the doctorate and further research in several countries and many archives, the work is fully ready to be published as a book. Moreover, Wolff is pressing with new projects. More power to youth!

The twentieth century has established itself as an age of colossal developments and cataclysms, of the growth, clashes, and collapses of empires, of the rather sudden and enormous spread of communism to be followed by its demise in Europe, of the even more sudden and deadly rise of Nazism until its explosive extinction, of the unprecedented advances of science and technology, of the most murderous wars in human history. No wonder that very numerous scholars have devoted themselves to these and immediately attendant issues rather than to considerations of a lesser scope. Yet smaller topics also have much to offer. Such were, for example, individual cities, with a certain autonomy and character of their own, often found at a point where larger entities met. Thus one thinks of Danzig between the two world wars.

And one thinks also of Harbin. Founded at the very end of the nineteenth century as a Russian railroad town, but never legally part of Russia or the Soviet Union, it became associated with a whole series of Chinese central and local governments, with Japan as it expanded and established the puppet state of Manchukuo, with the Second World War and the great Chinese civil war, until it was totally absorbed into new China following the communist victory. Larger than ever with some three million inhabitants, Harbin is an important contemporary Chinese city, but its special position, nature, and role belong entirely to the past. The inhabitants, except for the Chinese, disappeared. Yet at one time, the population had been half, and some figures indicate more than half, Russian, with numerous Japanese, and substantial numbers representing many other nations of the world. Besides, "the Russians" included thousands of Jews, Poles, and individuals of other ethnicities. It was a truly cosmopolitan and vibrant society. Émigrés from Harbin have carried the memory of their former city all the way from Australia to Israel and from Alaska and Canada to Patagonia. Interestingly, in spite of the horrors many of them suffered from or witnessed, they still usually retain a soft feeling, and even nostalgia, for their unique city. This speaks favorably of human nature, but also perhaps of Harbin. I was born in Harbin in 1923 and lived there until 1936, and I can understand this general feeling of the émigrés, although my own memories include a flood, a cholera epidemic and dozens, probably hundreds, of corpses of Chinese soldiers killed by the Japanese and transported past our house to be buried.

What David Wolff has accomplished is to present a detailed, comprehensive, and thorough history of Harbin from 1898 to 1914. He seems to be equally in command, whether dealing with the crucial railroad, the soybeans or oriental studies in Manchuria, with the Russo-Japanese war of 1904–5 or with international diplomacy. All this is not as simple as it may seem. A historian must be qualified to use his sources, and Dr. Wolff is fluent in Russian, Chinese, and Japanese, as well as in several other languages. A historian must get to his sources, and here our author had the great good luck of finding and uncovering what he wanted, including many materials, notably in the Soviet (formerly Russian and Russian again) archives only now, and sometimes grudgingly, available to researchers. And Dr. Wolff has been able to handle his materials with intelligence and objectivity, whatever that last difficult concept may exactly mean.

What of the future? It is certainly to be hoped that Dr. Wolff will finish his history of Harbin with another book. Beyond that, his investigation leads in many directions. Perhaps because my field is Russian history, I am especially attracted by the story of Harbin as an enrichment and a nuance of late imperial Russian history, a point wholly appreciated by the author, even in the subtitle of the present work. Russian imperial government does deserve further study. But historians of China or of Japan are likely to have their own preferences. And the reader can easily see numerous possibilities for further research and writing when reading the present volume, and especially its conclusion.

Nicholas V. Riasanovsky
University of California, Berkeley

A Note on Conventions

BECAUSE sources for this study originated both within and outside of Russia, I was faced with a choice between Julian (Russian Old Style) and Gregorian (New Style) calendars. Despite a certain intuitive discomfort with the October Revolution coming in November, I opted for New Style in all dates. Old Style lags twelve days behind in the nineteenth century and thirteen in the twentieth. In cases where an event is referred to in the literature by its Julian date (e.g., the law of June 6, 1904) I have given both dates at the first mention. I then revert to Gregorian usage.

Russian transliteration follows the Library of Congress standard, except for Harbin, Moscow, Petersburg, Witte, and a handful of other proper nouns. Most Chinese names and words are rendered in pinyin. Japanese citations are romanized according to Hepburn.

The great river of Northeast Asia is known as the Amur in Russian and Heilongjiang (Black Dragon River) in Chinese. Both the Russian governor-generalship to the north and the Chinese province to the south of this waterway are named after the river. Thus, the Chinese refer to the Russian territorial unit as Heilongjiang and the Russians call the neighboring Chinese region Amurskaia. To clarify matters for the English reader I use Amur, the Russian word, for the Russian land areas and Heilongjiang for the Chinese. For the river I use both depending on which country's point of view is being expressed, but generally, Amur.

Similarly, although the city that stands in the center of this study is usually called Harbin, when special emphasis on Russian actions and attitudes is appropriate, a transliteration of the Russian pronunciation, Kharbin, is used. Conversely, when I wish to draw attention to a distinctly Chinese aspect of Harbin's development, I transcribe it into pinyin as Haerbin. Japanese *Harupin* is a matter for another day.

I have opted to leave the following traditional Russian measurements unchanged: the desiatina (= 2.7 acres = 1.09 hectares); the verst (= 0.66 mile = 1.06 kilometers); and the pood (= 16.4 kilograms = 36.1 pounds).

OPPOSITE: This circa-1901 map of Manchuria shows the *T* of the almost-completed railway running from the Russian Trans-Baikal to the Russian Maritime. The southern alternative for the East-West mainline appears as a dotted line, splitting from the actual railway at Hailar only to rejoin once back in Russian territory. Had this variant been constructed, "Harbin" would have mushroomed under a different name at a different Sungari crossing. Map drawn by David Deis after Pozdneev, *Opisanie*.

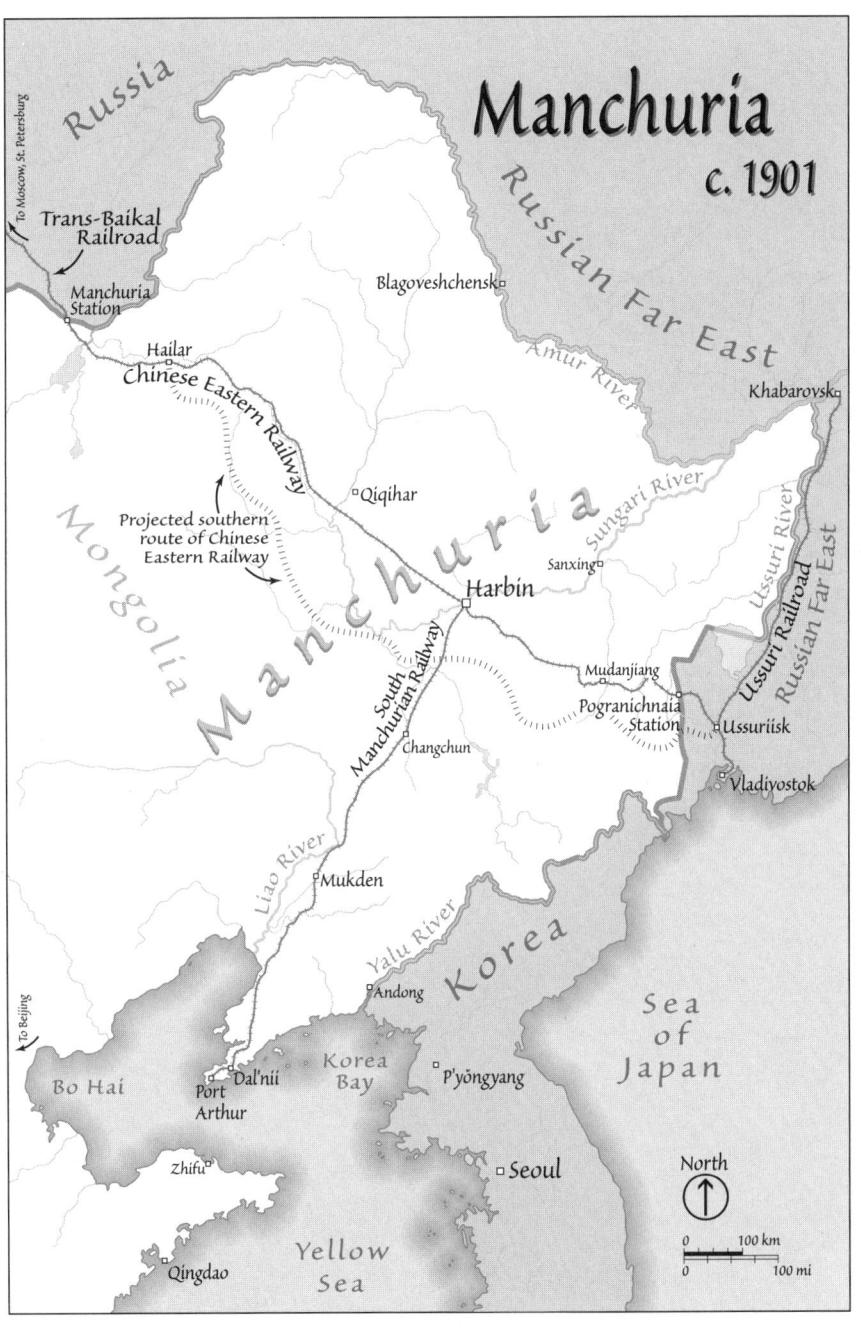

Here shall a city be founded.
—A. S. Pushkin, 1833

The builders' plan was wide in scope. Harbin, best of all, testifies to the grandness of their designs.
—Minister of Finance V. N. Kokovtsov, 1909

Introduction

NEAR THE projected intersection of the Chinese Eastern Railroad (CER) and the Sungari River, Russian engineers founded the city of Harbin. During the twenty-some years between the survey of the site and the profound dislocations of the 1917 revolution, Harbin grew from an abandoned distillery with a minor river portage into a bustling multiethnic urban center with over 100,000 inhabitants.[1] Chinese laborers learned pidgin Russian under the watchful eye of erstwhile Cossacks, now enlisted in the Trans-Amur Border Guards, who wondered if the dragon emblem pinned to their tunics would bring them bad luck in battle. Russian, Chinese, and Japanese merchants cooperated and competed under varying conditions of (non)parity and began the extraction for export of the region's great natural wealth. Local representatives of these three nations sparred and collaborated, while in their capitals opening moves were made in a new arena for the Great Game. The Russian and Japanese presence in Manchuria would last for fifty years. In tandem with the Russian colonial initiative, Manchuria changed from a largely unsettled wilderness into a wealthy agricultural zone on its way to rapid industrialization.[2] China's least developed border region became the vanguard of modern transformation, vying with the Yangzi valley as both a source of wealth and a contested sphere of imperial rivalries.[3]

Railroad-driven development was, of course, nothing new at the turn of the century as the age of steam reached out from its birthplace in Europe to encompass the globe.[4] As the last leg of the Trans-Siberian, the CER rivaled such gigantic projects as the Trans-Canadian and the Great Northern (U.S.). Just as these lines spawned major stations that soon evolved into such contemporary provincial capitals as Winnipeg, Calgary, Edmonton, St. Paul/Minneapolis, and Spokane, so the CER's principal urban legacy,

Harbin, would outlive its raison d'être after the dominance of rail transport had passed.[5]

Between the fin-de-siècle construction of the CER and the collapse of the Japanese Empire in 1945, competition among Russia, China, and Japan stimulated rapid demographic, technological, and economic development in Manchuria. Increasing prosperity and added value kept raising the stakes of regional dominance for all three powers. The result was recurrent armed conflict. The years 1895, 1900–1905, 1911, 1917–22, 1929, 1931–32, 1938–39, and 1945 saw large armies take the field within or on the borders of Manchuria. One might expect that the destruction and expense occasioned by regular hostilities and war preparations would have inhibited growth. Instead, even violent competition seems to have stimulated investment, both material and psychological, by suggesting further opportunities to each round's winner and by stiffening the losers' resolve not to lose all. Only in 1945 did the utter defeat of Japan put an end to the triangle.[6]

Although the centrality of railroad building makes this story an apparently ideal candidate for "railway imperialism," several caveats are in order before we can adopt a broadly "colonialist" framework.[7] The first is that an examination of the Manchurian case in the early twentieth century will leave us unclear regarding the identity of both the colonizers and the colonized. At the beginning, it was Russian capital and expertise invading Manchuria, but within a decade or so, both the Chinese and the Japanese had responded with railway endeavors of their own. In the course of fifty years, each of these three countries experienced periods of passing dominance, coupled with intolerance, during which citizens of the other countries were persecuted in the manner most resembling a crude version of "cruel colonialism." Thus, as a strictly binary hierarchical relationship, over any reasonably lengthy time span, the term colonialism becomes inappropriate.

A more general definition of colonialism, simply requiring "central" control (or the illusion of control) over "peripheral" space can be adopted, but even then we must allow for multiple, alternating centers. Therefore, it is the international competition into which the CER intruded that becomes the dominant trait. Although the Manchurian case belongs to genus "railway imperialism," it is also species "competitive colonialism." The latter is not a particularly rare breed, including such well-known "borderlands" as Alsace-Lorraine, Turkestan, Kashmir, and Texas. This type, unfortunately, often serves as a source of subnational violence and international strife. For that reason, it has been well studied, on a case-by-case basis.

The production of this literature faces three thorny research problems. The first is that the multilateral international scope of "competitive colonialism" has generated primary materials in multiple, often difficult, languages. Then, the volatile and violent nature of the borderlands themselves has scattered archival collections and libraries all over the globe. Some have been destroyed. Finally, since few borderland disputes are ever permanently resolved to the point where irredentism completely disappears, all the materials coming from the contending players must be evaluated carefully for bias. The same is true of recent secondary works.[8] In the borderland, the nation-state's urge to write its own history is revealed at its starkest, battling with other national and local narratives.[9]

The institutional emphasis of "railway imperialism" is useful in pointing out Russian Manchuria's central commonality with other places at some point in time, notably the rest of China, Thailand, southern Africa, India, Argentina, Mexico, and Canada.[10] It also highlights the CER's uniqueness as a railroad company run by a finance ministry that consciously and selectively introduced particular elements of Russian society and law to a new Russian-speaking colony centered on Harbin. The railroad technocrats, it seems, imagined themselves social engineers. The Russian Finance Minister S. Iu. Witte certainly did, claiming that the railroad was a "leaven" causing "cultural fermentation" wherever it passed.[11]

Furthermore, focusing on the railway heightens our consciousness of the proximity of the Russian Empire, just a border crossing away. Viewed from this angle, Russian Manchuria can be assigned to the subspecies "contiguous competitive colonialism." Following the CER tracks from Harbin to the Russian border, we also realize that the Russia we have entered is not at all like Moscow or St. Petersburg, over 4,000 miles away. In fact, in many respects the Russian Far East has more in common with Manchuria than with Russian Europe. Geology, biology, climate, and history link them as closely as one would expect from two halves of the same river basin. The unity and tension between the Russian Far East and Russian Manchuria is an important theme of this study.[12]

John Stephan tackles this question in his history of the Russian Far East when he explores the ties between identity as an *amurets* (those living on the Russian side of the Amur and Ussuri rivers) and identity as a *zaamurets* (those who had crossed the Amur River or its tributaries into Manchuria).[13] "Russian penetration of northeastern China after 1896," says Stephan, "sensitized Far Eastern merchants, professional people, journalists, and even military officers to divergences between imperial and regional interests." In this sense and for that period, one of the wellsprings of Far Eastern regionalism flowed from Harbin.[14]

Stephan begins the first chapter of his history by pointing out the "elasticity" in Russian of the term *dal'nii vostok* (Far East), with a semantic range extending "from a province to half the world." With the full-scale arrival of Russians at Harbin in 1898, the "Russian Far East" exercised its elastic prerogatives once again, stretching across the border into Manchuria. The vestiges of this presence can still be seen in the architecture of Harbin, in the Russian-language libraries and archival collections of Northeast China (often off-limits to foreigners), in the many senior Chinese professors of Russian studies originally from Harbin, and in the charming term for foreigners coined, and still used, in Manchuria to label Russians: "the old, hairy ones" (*lao maozi*). But for the most part, the Russian spirit has departed from the three-million-soul city that now stands on the banks of the Amur's largest tributary, the Sungari.

A historical analysis of Russian Manchuria thus contributes to ongoing debates regarding the nature(s) of colonialism, post-colonialism, borderlands, and regionalism. With the return to China of Hong Kong (1997) and the hundredth anniversary of Russian involvement at Harbin (1998), these issues have taken on a contemporary political relevance and stimulated yet another round of historical reevaluation. Rey Chow's comment that "the history of modern Hong Kong could always be written as some form of quest for a Chinese identity that was preempted and made impossible from the beginning, and most significantly by its inerasable colonial taint," is equally valid for Harbin.[15] Is the reabsorption of "colonial" Harbin by China really a good precedent for the desired outcome at Hong Kong? Beijing does unequivocally control Harbin, but much of the Northeast's economic dynamism, predicated on cross-border contact and cosmopolitanism at the local level, has been lost. Could this be Hong Kong's future too?[16]

A historical study of pre-1917 Harbin, the only demographically vital community in the CER railway zone, also sheds light on important questions of Russian urban history. As a haven of tolerance fostered by the highest circles of tsarist government in the final years of the empire, a contemplation of liberal Harbin forces us to reconsider the received wisdom that equates late Imperial Russian government with hidebound conservatism and visionless leadership. Somehow we must reconcile N. I. Bobrikov's suicidal attempt at forced russification in Finland and Mendel Beilis's trial at Kiev on the allegation of Jewish ritual murder with the enlightened Harbin model, which saw Jews and Poles peacefully at work in a wide range of urban activities, while their children, exempt from the *numerus clausus*, undertook to pass required courses in Chinese.[17]

The final decade of the nineteenth century was a period of great economic and cultural dynamism in Imperial Russia. Industrialization and urbanization proceeded at a brisk pace, and cooperative climatic conditions kept the countryside famine-free from 1892 until 1898. Just as the economic and cultural excitement of the Gay Nineties swept over America and Europe, in Russia, too, economic growth and brilliant cultural initiatives were the order of the day. For those who were prepared to turn a blind eye to the

Empire's social and political ills, worthy ventures could provide both a distraction from the many ominous signs and a field for energetic activity.

At the center of these exciting events stood the Ministry of Finance, captained for almost eleven years by Sergei Iulevich Witte. His was one of the longest ministerial tenures in late Imperial Russia. The only two fellow ministers to last as long bowed to Witte's primacy, allowing Finance to poach mercilessly on their administrative preserves.[18] Although his predecessor, I. A. Vyshnegradskii, had prepared the ground with a policy of fiscal conservatism, it fell to Witte to embark on a bold new course: deficit financing the path to industrial power. Prior to government service, Witte had been a railroad manager. Not surprisingly, this sector assumed central significance in his larger Empire-wide scheme. In his 1894 budget report, Witte called the Russian rail network "a very powerful weapon . . . for the direction of the economic development of the country."[19] The jewel in this iron crown was the Great Siberian trunkline.[20]

By 1895, with the exception of the stretch that was projected to parallel the Amur, work was under way along the whole 3,000-mile length from the Ural Mountains to the Pacific Ocean. A few hundred miles from Vladivostok, the eastern terminus, Qing China and Meiji Japan were battling for primacy in Korea. In April 1895 Russia, in company with Germany and France, prevented a victorious Japan from keeping the foothold on the Asian continent that it had wrung from Li Hongzhang, elder statesman and chief Chinese negotiator at Shimonoseki. In the same year Germany and France converted their claims on Beijing's gratitude into territorial acquisitions in North and South China, respectively. This set off a period that is known in Chinese historiography as "the mad rush to divide the melon" (*guafen kuangchao*). Throughout 1895 and into 1896, St. Petersburg held back on taking its due slice, leaving Beijing's Foreign Office to become increasingly nervous at the thought of what the Russians might be planning.[21]

What the Russians had in mind became clear in April 1896. Li Hongzhang, traveling to Moscow to attend the coronation of Nikolai II, was met in Alexandria by Prince E. E. Ukhtomskii, an intimate of the young Tsar and a proponent of Russian activism in Asia. A Russian steamer was put at their disposal, and, on the cruise north to Odessa, the two men gauged each other and exchanged preliminary views. On April 30 Li arrived in the Russian capital, where Witte wasted little time in suggesting that a Russian railway concession across Manchuria would be of mutual interest. This route would accelerate the completion of the final segment of the Trans-Siberian, the touchstone of Russia's eastward progress. The advantage for the Chinese side, a secret defense pact directed against Japan, combined with a 3,000,000-ruble bribe for Li himself, proved to have sufficient persuasive power to seal the deal.[22]

On June 3, 1896, a Russo-Chinese treaty of alliance was signed by Li, Witte, and the Russian Foreign Minister, Prince A. B. Lobanov-Rostovskii. The crux for our story was art. 4, which read:

> In order to facilitate the access of Russian land forces to places under threat, the Chinese government agrees to the construction of a railroad across the Chinese provinces of Heilongjiang and Jilin toward Vladivostok. The construction and administration of this railroad shall be granted to the Russo-Chinese Bank.

On September 8, 1896, a contract was signed in Berlin between the Chinese government and the Russo-Chinese Bank stipulating that the Trans-Manchurian railway would be constructed by the (as yet unformed) Chinese Eastern Railway Company (CER, Inc.). On paper, the Chinese government's participation in this venture, both administrative and financial, was extensive; in reality, Witte would be making all important decisions. Funding, much of it from France and Belgium, was channeled through the Russo-Chinese Bank, but the controlling shares rested securely in the vaults of the Russian Finance Ministry.[23]

Between 1897 and 1902, the Russian government poured over a billion rubles into Far Eastern development. Approximately a third was spent on the CER and its sibling enterprises. The dividend, Witte claimed, would be "control over the entire movement of international commerce in Pacific waters"; but only, he cautioned, if handled adroitly.[24] The Witte way, anticipating a later reformer's "wager on the strong," called for a group of colonists with enough capital, talent, knowledge, and willpower to extend Russia's "informal empire" from an urban base at Harbin throughout Manchuria. Minimal government support would guarantee the hardiness of the newcomers. The focus on people with the requisite commercial skills to develop export industries, whose need for freight carriage would support the CER, led stereotypically to the Jews as the "natural" social engineering tool to this end. It should come as no surprise that as Witte's brainchild, the CER provides an excellent example of the central contradiction embedded in the Witte economic development plan, a government-directed program with the ultimate goal of fostering private initiative.

The pivotal historiographic questions, however, remain without definitive answers. Had "Witte's way" continued, could the disastrous Russo-Japanese War of 1904–5 have been avoided? Was Witte's ultimate intention the outright annexation of Manchuria? Boris Romanov, whose brilliant study exposed the role and contents of Witte's General Chancellery (Obshchaia Kantseliariia) for foreign affairs, insists that Witte was just as imperialistic in his intent as those who favored less subtle means. Witte himself alternated from mute to hyperbolic regarding his long-range vision during the antebellum period. After the Russo-Japanese War, he and General A. N. Kuropatkin, both in disgraced retirement, indulged in mutual recriminations in the Russian and foreign press, with Witte continuing to emphasize the distinctiveness of his policy of "peaceful penetration." As corroborating evidence, one might cite Witte's moderate views on Turkestan, Finland, and the Baltic provinces, which failed to win out over the arguments of the Interior and War ministers.[25]

Nonetheless, it is hard, if not impossible, to tell what Witte really thought, for he carefully managed his own image and was not beyond mendacity.[26] This much said, one may feel safe in concluding that Witte's own comments, memories, and memoirs constitute a poor source on the great statesman's beliefs and intent. But whatever the final goals he envisioned, Witte's tactics were distinctive, resulting both in Finance Ministry opposition to annexationist suggestions right until the end of the tsarist regime and in the anomalous, "instant" urban development of Harbin. Most importantly, in 1903 the Japanese recognized the "Witte difference," identifying the Finance Minister's fall from power with a "victory of the expansionist party."[27]

As seemingly bright eastern vistas attracted the attention of other ministries, Witte defended his Manchurian domain against collegial trespass by citing international scrutiny and foreign financial participation, both by the Chinese in the CER and by European investors in the Russo-Chinese Bank.[28] Might not England be moved to unfriendly acts, if the Russian army's involvement in Manchuria became too patent? What right had the state comptroller or even the Interior Ministry to interfere with international investments on whose sanctity Russia's vital credit rating depended? With arguments along these lines, many an attempted intervention was thwarted. Some ministries, however, were necessary for the building and successful operation of the CER. The army, for example, was needed to guard the tracks and the settlements that sprang up alongside them. Diplomatic entanglements could be solved only with Foreign Ministry help. If amity was impossible, cohabitation was nonetheless unavoidable. These intragovernmental tensions became an integral part of Russian life in Manchuria.[29]

A corollary of excluding the full administrative structure of the Empire from the CER was that Russian laws, though officially on the books, were enforced selectively.[30] Colonization policies based on equal opportunity contrasted sharply with the ingrained prejudices of European Russia. Participatory politics were founded on the assumption that state and society shared common goals in Manchuria, the urgency of which gave local cooperation and paternalistic governance precedence over the antagonisms inherited from the metropolis. It is this emphasis on improved civil rights and political participation that leads me to apply the word "liberal" to Harbin.[31]

Although in this work, source accessibility for the period treated requires us to come at Harbin from a largely Russian perspective, central, regional, and local, it should be kept in mind that Haerbin (the Chinese transliteration) is a very different place, both historically and historiographically; it deserves its own archive-based monograph.[32] Various parts of this book will illuminate aspects of Chinese life in Harbin, but only in a very partial way. It should certainly never be lost from view that Harbin, with the largest number and concentration of foreigners in China, represented a special imperialist challenge to Beijing.[33] Within a few months of the October revolution, Chinese troops would take control of Harbin and the CER, only to find themselves constrained to hand them over to the Japanese army less than a year later as the Siberian-Manchurian intervention began.

Harbin, the provincial capital of Russian Manchuria, takes on a special meaning for the historian of the Soviet period. After 1917, with its Russian population doubled by a wave of émigrés, Harbin became the only Russian city in the world outside the Soviet Union.[34] Consequently, any Manchurian perspective on the Russian revolution and the Soviet Union must be based in the first instance on an account and analysis of Harbin's rapid transformation from frontier town, under government/company control, to a somewhat self-conscious, partially self-regulating community.[35] Not surprisingly, the dominant elements in this process are precisely those that are central to the burgeoning field of Russian/Soviet urban history; namely, the relationship between industrialization and urbanization; the role of the government in that relationship; ethnic, class, and occupational interaction; and the development of municipal self-government.[36]

In Harbin, these general Empire-wide processes were embodied in specific local dynamics. In order to uncover these two facets of the same set of events, I have adopted a literary strategy that intertwines a chronological history of Harbin's development with thematic discussions that allow the Harbin case to speak to central historiographic concerns. Since thematic strands develop along their own time line, the chapter on interministerial rivalry backs up into the 1880's, and the appendix on Russian sinology begins in the eighteenth century. In addition, a dual central-local focus requires occasional switches back and forth from policy formulation in St. Petersburg to implementation in the Russian Far East. What may at first seem like digressions are actually my narrative attempts at presenting multiple perspectives. Out of the struggle between central government intentions and the exigencies of local life, Harbin emerged.

That city was to be, for almost all of Russian Manchuria's existence, the area's social and administrative center.[37] Born as a communications hub in 1898, the capital of Russia's only colony grew rapidly within the liberal confines of Witte's policies, most of which were retained by the Finance Ministry even after Witte's departure from the scene. After the CER's completion in 1905, the Russian population became increasingly concentrated in Harbin, making it the only significant non-Chinese settlement in the railroad corridor from Trans-Baikalia to the Maritime province. Even more astonishing for a colonial city was the completeness of Russian Harbin's social structure, a fact that gave the young city, and by extension Russian Manchuria, an air of stability and permanence. In late 1903, for example, the French Foreign Minister received the following description from the French consul at Hong Kong, just returned to his post via the Trans-Siberian and Harbin:

> I was indeed struck, just as I had been on my first trip to Manchuria, to see all the classes of the Russian populace represented, from craftsmen and laborers to merchants and bankers. Russian and Siberian peasants are steadily replacing the Chinese element and Russian is spoken everywhere, even by the natives. That indeed is definitive colonization.[38]

The rapid pace of the CER's construction is unparalleled in the history of Russian railway building. It was also one of the most expensive projects of the late Imperial period, both per verst and as a single-line budget item. The heart of Chapter One is a narration of the planning, surveying, staffing, and building of the CER from Manchuria Station in the Transbaikal to Pogranichnaia in the Maritime province. The construction of the CER was one of Imperial Russia's last great infrastructure projects, and the fraternal corps of engineers, whose services had raised Russian railroad mileage from 6,970 in 1870 to 35,325 in 1900, was present in force.[39] Certain spots, such as the eastward descent from the Xingan Mountains, represented world-class technical challenges that stimulated the pride of Russian science and technology. Intimations of future departmental rivalries already appear here. I also detail the CER's gradual accumulation of the lands on which Harbin would grow and the railway's provision of the minimal requirements for retention of the Russian population. I hope that the spirit of the boom-town that it was comes across.

Chapter One concludes with a discussion of the ways in which the construction of the Trans-Siberian and the CER altered Russia's image abroad. For influential domestic personages, too, visions of grandeur in Asia played a key role in the self-delusions and miscalculations that led to the Russo-Japanese War. The chapter begins with contrasting "snapshots" of the Harbin to be of 1895 and the Harbin that was in 1909. By the latter date, something of a split personality had become apparent, as *kharbintsy* strained to reconcile an identity drawn from their Russian origins with the attractions of being an "international city." Although the French consul may have perceived Harbin as a typical Russian provincial city, others, in particular inhabitants of the Russian Far East, often struck a xenophobic note, labeling Harbin as "foreign." The need to avoid treatment as a "stepson" (*pasynok*) by disproving such allegations with "exact statistical data, so that the metropolis does not cut us off," became a central concern of Harbin's census-takers in 1913.[40]

In Chapter Two, I examine the impact of interministerial rivalry on Harbin's development. Though the Ministry of Finance's secret ownership of the majority of CER stock gave the Finance Minister sway in all matters affecting the company, five other tsarist ministries had at least a toehold in Manchuria. The most important of these was the War Ministry, which often viewed the physical protection of the railway as a minimal part of its mission and at times bid for full military control of the CER and all other Russian ventures in Manchuria. The actual balance of power between the War and Finance ministries shifted back and forth, largely in harmony with fluctuations along the war/peace spectrum.

The various administrative experiments aimed at defusing these tensions were largely unsuccessful, since the root cause of civil-military rivalry in Manchuria was a basic divergence of opinion over the ultimate fate of that region. Clearly, those who believed that Russia would at some point annex Manchuria possessed different views on both the desirable direction of development for the Russian presence there and the relations to be maintained with the Chinese "host." The resultant confusion between domestic and foreign policy was at least partially responsible for the incoherence in Russian diplomacy toward China and Japan that convinced the Japanese of Russian duplicity and finally drove them to war.

In undertaking competitive colonization against the Chinese in Manchuria, the tsarist government showed a flexibility and creativity not usually associated with the Russian Bear. By abandoning the strictures that hampered the development of civil society in Russia proper, the Finance Ministry succeeded in attracting some of Russia's oppressed minorities to Harbin. The best illustration of this policy was the Jewish community, which numbered over 5,000 in 1913. Polish residents were also numerous and active. As conditions for Jews and Poles in the western part of the Empire went from bad to worse, emigrants made the long trek eastward to form two of Harbin's most stable and influential communities. Along with a liberal nationality policy went a loosening of political and cultural control. In short, Harbin became the freest city in the Russian Empire precisely because it was not geographically within the Empire's official borders.

Initiatives first applied in Manchuria would later make their way back across Siberia to European Russia.[41] In Chapter Three, after analyzing the interministerial discussions that led to the adoption of these trailblazing policies, I use census data to examine the resulting composition of Harbin's population. Furthermore, to bring out more fully the qualitative effects of an enlightened minority policy, I chronicle the living conditions of the most numerous "Russian" minority in Harbin, the Jewish community (for, as Witte's successor, Finance Minister N. I. Kokovtsov, saw it, in China, even Jews could be Russians).[42]

In Chapter Four, I discuss Harbin's development during the Russo-Japanese War and the 1905 revolution. In the course of the unsuccessful Manchurian campaign, the army and the CER carried their earlier enmity to new heights. The generals complained that the railway's inability to deliver the goods made victory impossible; the CER countered that ignorant spear-chuckers had abused their rank to interfere with orderly and efficient technical operations. Fingerpointing was rampant even before the signing of the Portsmouth peace treaty. As the location of the army's rear headquarters and the CER's headquarters, Harbin was the center of these conflicts.

But the war also brought benefits to Harbin in the form of an economic and demographic boom. As the Russian treasury poured its largesse into the inflated goods and services Harbin offered to soldiers and officers alike, the city, the riverside Pristan district in particular, acquired a reputation for profound decadence. As the collection point for the war's wounded, Harbin experienced the full horror of large-scale modern warfare. The result was a pacifistic scar that gave the inhabitants an aversion to violent solutions. Too much Russian blood had been shed in Manchuria.

When the general railroad strike broke out in European Russia and spread to Manchuria in October 1905, the CER's Employee Strike Committee, headed by high-ranking company officials, decided to continue transporting the stranded army back to Russia. In fact, during the course of the strike, the volume of traffic increased. Both a workers' strike committee under Social Democratic influence and a radical committee on the West Branch of the CER found this apparent contradiction suspicious. The nationwide call for a return to work came just in time to prevent the Harbin-based ESC from losing control of the strike movement.

These political fine points, however, were lost on the military men. Proclamations coming off the army printing presses played on "stab in the back" sentiment to call for a violent settling of accounts with the railwaymen, revolutionaries, Jews, and other residents of Harbin. In the political space provided by the CER-army standoff, but under pressure from both sides, Harbin municipal and radical politics were born. In January 1906, the same repressive impulse that sent the punitive expeditions of Generals

P. K. Rennenkampf and Aleksander Meller-Zakomel'skii into Siberia made Harbin's new political movements grind to a temporary halt. After the military was withdrawn, however, Harbin reverted to its status as a haven for Siberian revolutionaries, with the CER housing employees convicted of revolutionary activities in 1905 in a detention center so comfortable that it was nicknamed "Prison El Dorado."

Chapter Five examines the young orientologist graduates of Vladivostok's Eastern Institute, their "practical school," whose center migrated from Beijing to Kazan to St. Petersburg before returning to the Far East, and the historical basis for Russia's (and Russian orientology's) claim to a special relationship with the Orient, bridging East and West. For many of these young men, education in Vladivostok was followed by employment at Harbin, where they would give "specialness" concrete form through local intercultural initiatives. (The prehistory of the Eastern Institute is discussed in the Appendix.)

In the liberal spirit of V. P. Vasil'ev, the founding father of the practical school and a veteran of the Great Reforms, these Eastern Institute alumni fulfilled the CER's need for research on and communication with the Chinese population, in the genuine belief that mutual knowledge could be the road to neighborly rapprochement. Through positions in the press, schools, and local institutions, the leaders of the Society of Russian Orientologists (SRO) made sure that Harbin's tolerance toward non-Russian ethnicities embraced the Chinese as well, even at a time when fears of the "Yellow Peril" had official support in the Russian Far East.[43] It is only a seeming contradiction that, at Harbin, the Chinese press and public institutions, imbued with modern nationalism, grew up in emulation of and competition with their Russian-sponsored counterparts.

The society's call for greater public participation in affairs of state reflected hopes for China's renewal and maybe for Russia's as well. Since SRO members served as the nucleus of Harbin's nascent public opinion, they were well aware that the CER and its Finance Ministry backers had already wagered on state-society cooperation as the best strategy for ensuring the colony's survival. What in Harbin was simply propaganda in support of the status quo would have been just another senseless dream within the Empire's borders. Nonetheless, the book's Conclusion examines a number of the Manchurian novelties that did indeed make their way back to influence the Empire in its final years, its Soviet successor, and twentieth-century Northeast Asia.

But in the summer of 1895, Lenin, still in his political infancy, was on his first visit to Western Europe, and the word Kharbin had yet to be spoken by Russian lips.[44] The rigors of exploration and discovery still lay ahead. Only after the completion of this preliminary phase could Harbin be founded. Even at the forced tempo with which Russia pursued its Far Eastern destiny, a short span would have to pass before a European city rose from the Manchurian wilderness. As our story begins, Harbin teeters at the brink of Russian history.

CHAPTER 1

Constructions

> An English merchant, a German investigator, and an American traveler were sitting under the tree before the English Club, looking out upon the charming Bay of Chefoo. What were they discussing? Russia, of course. In the Far East everybody is discussing Russia wherever you go, and the Manchurian-Siberian railway as the most conspicuous illustration of her activity. —U.S. Senator Albert Beveridge, 1904

> The engineer undid his collar,
> Off came carbine and canteen;
> Here we'll build a Russian city,
> Choose a name. Why not Harbin?
>
> Inzhener. Rasstegnut vorot
> Fliaga. Karabin.
> —Zdes' postroim russkii gorod
> Nazovem—Kharbin.
> —Arsenii Nesmelov,
> "Stikhi o Kharbine"

ON JUNE 7, 1895, THE *Telegraph* steamed out of Khabarovsk, threaded its way through the archipelago of alluvial deposits at the mouth of the Ussuri River, and headed up the Amur. Pre-departure prayers had been conducted in a driving rain, and this was taken, in accordance with Russian tradition, as an encouraging omen. Three days later, having taken on eleven Berdanka-armed Cossacks at the village of Mikhailo-Semenovskii, the boat left the clear waters of the Amur and entered the muddy yellow Sungari. Riverside marshes, distant hills on alternating horizons, and the smells of jasmine and peony continued unchanged, but now they were in Chinese territory. In addition to the crew and guard, on board were five men whose mission it was to explore opportunities for Russian trade along the Sungari and its tributaries. Two of them, Dmitrii Bogdanov and Nikolai Ivanovich Tifontai, were Khabarovsk merchants of long standing. They hoped to revive mercantile dreams of Manchuria's abundant resources and large market from fifteen years of dormancy. Multiple expeditions in the 1860's and 1870's had been thwarted by hostile Manchu officials. From the Russo-Chinese tensions of 1879–81 until 1895, no further attempts were even mounted.[1]

The exploring party had good reason to expect some success this time around. In May, S. M. Dukhovskoi, the Priamur governor-general, had asked Count A. P. Cassini, the Russian ambassador in Beijing, to request assistance from the Chinese Ministry of Foreign Affairs (Zongli Yamen). According to Dukhovskoi, the construction of the northern end of the Ussuri railroad and the increase in Russia's Far Eastern troop strength following the mobilization of 1895 had raised demand for Chinese grain, meat, and labor that could only be met by developing exchange between the lower reaches of the Ussuri and the Sungari basin. Although (possibly, because) Cassini's April overtures regarding Russia's construction of a Manchurian railroad had been immediately repulsed by the Chinese, Dukhovskoi's proposal was accepted by the Zongli Yamen and relayed to the governor (*jiangjun*) of Jilin province. Thus, the first fruit of Russia's pose as the Savior of Shimonoseki fell, not in Petersburg, but in the Far East.[2]

Four versts above the Sungari's only navigable mouth, the *Telegraph* stopped at the border checkpoint of Lahasusu, where its papers were examined. Things looked dark when the Manchu official stationed at Lahasusu declared that he had not received any notice of their arrival; but after a short wait, spent exploring the village and distributing some trinkets (miniature mirrors, small bars of soap, and the like), the party's permission to proceed up the Sungari was confirmed.[3]

This first success buoyed spirits on board the *Telegraph*. Clearly, the diplomatic hurdle was behind them. But the trading part of their mission still promised difficulties, the most serious of which was that profits had to be made based on Khabarovsk prices, often considered the most inflated in the Russian Empire. Fortunately, Tifontai (born Li Fengtai) was the ideal person for the task, both by nature and by training. Although rumor placed his origins among the myriad Shandong coolies whose poverty and land hunger drove them to Manchuria and farther north, by the early 1890's, Tifontai had already amassed twenty years' experience in border trade and a large fortune. In the late 1880's, he had petitioned the Priamur governor-general, Baron A. N. Korf, for Russian citizenship and been refused on the grounds of his Manchu braid. Otherwise, the requirements codified by the Second Khabarovsk Congress, christening and marriage to a Russian, seem to have been met. A second request made in 1894 to Baron Korf's successor, Dukhovskoi, was granted. Although Tifontai still balked at removing his braid, he overcame objections to his conversion by willing his worldly possessions to his son, born, christened, and raised in Khabarovsk. In the event of his son's death, the legacy, with the exception of a portion intended to support his two wives, would go to charitable works and church construction in Khabarovsk. *Priamurskie vedomosti*, the official organ of the governor-general's office, attributed the success of Tifontai's petition to his guarantee that his "descendants would be joined inseparably with native Russians." (The russification of his capital assets clearly also played a major role.) Once established as a Russian subject, Tifontai became eligible for government contracts and, thereby, to partake of the river of silver that would soon flow into Manchuria. At the outbreak of the Russo-Japanese War, his net worth would be estimated at 3,000,000 rubles. In 1895, however, Tifontai was making his first return to the land he had recently renounced and the first step toward expanded riches as a Russo-Chinese go-between in Manchuria.[4]

The boat steamed slowly upstream, allowing the topographer, Kokshaiskii, ample opportunity to complete the first detailed Russian mapping of the Sungari's channels and hazards. With depth gauge and bucket, he and Captain M. V. Grulev of the general staff also gathered data concerning the riverbed's contours and consistency, information that Grulev no doubt included in the materials he was compiling for a work of the "military-statistical" genre. Occasionally, the *Telegraph* put in for wood, and the passengers stretched their legs in the forest of Chinese sorghum (*gaoliang*) that lined the banks and marveled at the Manchurian wilderness. For one traveler, it was an awesome experience:

> You go ashore to examine this blessed steppe, to try and penetrate a little deeper. In some places, you can go no more than a hundred paces, at each step your foot sinking into a thick layer of last year's straw pressed down by the winter snows. A stubborn wall of vegetation bound by creepers refuses to part before you. With your rifle butt, you press it down and climb over. Behind you the wall rises again, and there you are at the bottom of a green funnel a *sazhen* [seven feet] deep, where only the guidance of the sun or a compass can keep you from walking in circles. Thorns tear your clothes, and blocks of wood hidden in the grass trip you. Ubiquitous gadflies, bumblebees, midges, and mosquitoes surround you in a dense cloud, driving you to flight. You feel all the impotence and helplessness of a lone man in the face of this powerful, unbridled nature.[5]

As a transitional region between northern, southern, European, and Asian habitats, Manchuria possessed a broad range of native flora and fauna from throughout the Eurasian land mass.[6]

About 260 versts above the mouth of the river, the landscape became dotted with low hills ascending up to a range of distant mountains. A few versts farther, and the Sungari was split into two navigable channels by a large island. Since the wide branch along the left bank had been filled with stones, the *Telegraph* had no choice but to take the narrow branch that led right under the silent guns of Bayantu fort. Fifteen versts farther brought the boat to an anchorage at Sanxing, a large right-bank town just below the confluence of the Sungari and the Mudanjiang.[7]

Sanxing in 1895 had a population estimated by the Russian visitors at 15,000, although the Chinese officials who received them claimed double that number.[8] In any case, with ten large trading companies and 60 stores, both Chinese and Muslim, this was the best marketing opportunity so far encountered, especially since the arrival of official permission from Beijing just four days earlier removed all apprehensions that trade with the Russians might later give grounds for sanctions. Tifontai swung into action with some key bribes and moved in with a local merchant. Meanwhile, Bogdanov, aided by the translator, Dobrovidov, invited the fudutong and other yamen dignitaries aboard for champagne and fruit. When the *Telegraph* moved on a few days later, the original capital investment of 15,000 rubles had already been guaranteed a 15 percent profit.[9]

Despite the crew's grumbling over the gritty tea made from Sungari water, the boat continued slowly upstream. Kokshaiskii continued his map-making labors with the assistance of Dobrovidov on Chinese names for the river towns and other landmarks. Later in the summer, Kokshaiskii and Dobrovidov would participate in a second expedition headed by N. G. Matiunin of the Priamur governor-general's administration and N. A. Zinov'ev, representing the Amur Steamline Partnership. Beyond their official responsibilities, both Matiunin and Zinov'ev were members of the Imperial Russian Geographic Society's Priamur section. By 1896, Bogdanov, Dobrovidov, Grulev, Kokshaiskii, Matiunin, and Zinov'ev would all publish accounts of their travels and studies, providing almost all of the material on the Sungari watershed to be included in Dmitrii Pozdneev's *Opisanie Man'chzhurii* (1897). For the twenty remaining years of tsarist power on the Sungari, this two-volume compilation, published by the Ministry of Finance, would stand as the standard work on North Manchuria in any language, transmitting the investigative fruits of 1895 to the next-generation specialists.[10]

At 430 versts from the Amur, the *Telegraph* turned right into the Hulan River, which led to the large city of the same name. With 50 large trading firms and a hinterland rich in grain, Hulan was the natural place to make a start on securing a food supply for the Priamur, which was after all the real goal of the voyage's official patron, Governor-General Dukhovskoi. After gaining the fudutong's approval, Tifontai placed an order for 3,000 *poods* (54 tons) of grain with a local merchant.[11]

Retracing its course to pass the military post at the mouth of the Hulan, the *Telegraph* reentered the Sungari. Moving upstream toward Bodune, the boat followed the river's curves back and forth on a westerly heading.

18   *Constructions*

The northern shore was deserted marshland. On the southern bank stood a half-dozen scattered houses nestled among alluvial sand and low-lying shrubs. On Kokshaiskii's map, this settlement is labeled "Khaabin." Some 200 meters west, but still on the riverbank, stood a "distillery" (*vinokuren. zavod*). From here, a path led south past a few more houses to a cluster of structures labeled "Khaabin-shao-go," meaning "Khaabin distillery." Kokshaiskii's caption reads: "From the settlement of Khaobin [*sic*], where there is a distillery, a road leads to the important town of Ashikhe, located on the river of the same name, 45 versts from the Sungari." Thus, as an insignificant fishing village, whose name's correct orthography and liquor factory's true location were open to question, Harbin was "discovered" and entered Russian history.[12]

Harbin "Discovers" Its Russianness

In the next fifteen years, this unprepossessing landscape metamorphosed into a large Eurasian city. Its nearly 44,000 "Indo-Europeans," mostly Russian subjects, made Harbin the largest foreign settlement in China. The inclusion of the 60,000 Chinese who lived permanently within the railway zone administered by the Russians and in neighboring Fujiadian made Greater Harbin the third-largest "Russian" city east of the Urals (after Tomsk and Irkutsk). Pre–World War One Vladivostok fell slightly short, but with reversed Russo-Chinese proportions.[13]

The orderly rectangular layout of riverside Pristan (*pristan'* means quay) belied the feverish economic activities of northern Manchuria's largest marketplace. Greater Harbin's 1909 volume of trade, with a value of 34,500,000 rubles, dwarfed that of other regional trading centers (Qiqihar 15,000,000; Jilin, 13,000,000; Mukden 13,000,000). By 1913, the Harbin total had grown to 58,000,000.[14] Where the two boats of 1895 had passed by almost without comment, 5,440 vessels docked in 1911. Goods came and went from forty foreign and 100 domestic destinations.[15] Beans, wheat, and meat for export flowed in by rail, ship, and cart from an ever more densely populated hinterland, to which Harbin's work opportunities and purchasing power had drawn millions of North China's impoverished and dispossessed.

A stroll down bustling Kitaiskaia (Chinese) Street past banks, department stores, hotels, and theaters led to the Officer Street viaduct, which bridged the elevation and social differences between bazaar and bureaucracy. Up on the ridge in New Town ruled and resided the representatives of Imperial Russia, and, after 1907, the other powers. As late as 1909, 95 percent of the land remained in the hands of the CER.[16] Large, indivisible plots and a strict building code made New Town into an architectural hodgepodge of expensive brick and stone buildings. The battle between neoclassical and art nouveau that raged in late Imperial Russia's cities was here compounded by all manner of whimsical Orientalia.

Also located in New Town was the railway station, its façade adorned by two pylons that may have been a stylized version of the Chinese "arch of virtue," the *pailou*. It was here on the platforms and in the station square that Harbin's heart pulsed. With the sound of wheel on rail for background music, arrivals and departures reaffirmed Harbin's double identity as Russia's urban ambassador to the Far East and "typical" Russian provincial city.

The vigor with which Harbin reaffirmed the second role is visible in the welcome offered to the grande dame of the Russian theater, Komissarzhevskaia, when her troupe arrived in Manchuria in the spring of 1909 after playing Irkutsk. All the spaces on the platform and inside the station building had been reserved by the upper echelons of the railway administration for itself and its military counterparts, so *le tout Kharbine* packed into the station square by the thousands. After being greeted by the town fathers, Komissarzhevskaia exited amidst applause to her waiting carriage, only to find that the density of the crowd would not permit her to leave the square. At this impasse, a group of young men came forward, unhitched the horses, hoisted the leading lady, carriage and all, to their shoulders, and bore her off through the cheering crowd to the guest house that the authorities had put at her disposal. Although *Charodeika* was not scheduled until the following evening, a state of entrancement had already been attained. Only Komissarzhevskaia's best would be worthy of the performance with which Harbin had greeted her.[17]

Fall 1909 found Harbin fulfilling its ambassadorial obligations. On October 24, Finance Minister V. N. Kokovtsov arrived on an inspection tour of the city and railroad, which (for reasons we will come to) fell under his jurisdiction. There he spent a day in conference with CER officials while awaiting the arrival of the Japanese elder statesman and former governor-general of Korea Ito Hirobumi. Although no agenda had been set for their discussions, the Russian ambassador in Tokyo, N. A. Malevskii-Malevich, lent credence to the rumor that Ito's month-long tour of Manchuria was preliminary to his appointment as viceroy of Japan's continental possessions. The new office's seat would be Dairen. This step might well require a new relationship with the Russians in North Manchuria. As the de facto capital of the region, Harbin was the natural venue for any such démarche.[18]

At seven o'clock on the evening of October 25, Ito changed trains in Changchun, transferring from the Japanese-controlled South Manchurian railroad to the Russian-owned Chinese Eastern. He was accompanied by high CER officials, as well as his own retinue. When his train pulled into Harbin the next morning at nine, the same "town fathers" who had greeted Komissarzhevskaia lined the platform—only this time, Kokovtsov, I. Ia.

Korostovets, the Russian ambassador to China, and A. N. Venttsel, the vice-chairman of the CER board of directors, stood ahead of the CER general manager, D. L. Khorvat. The theater aficionados had been replaced by an honor guard and a group of Japanese residents who had come to pay their respects. The Japanese consul, Kawakami Toshitsune, who had hurried back from a trip to the Russian Priamur to meet Ito, had asked the CER police to allow Japanese nationals onto the platform.

At 9:15, as Ito was inspecting the honor guard, a well-dressed young man stepped from among the Japanese group and emptied his six-shot Browning into the Japanese dignitaries. The military band made the attack inaudible to all but those closest to the action. Three bullets struck Ito in the head, chest, and stomach. He was carried back into his train compartment, received a morphine injection, and promptly died. Kawakami's wound was "serious, but not dangerous." Tanaka, a South Manchurian railway director, was struck in the leg. The assassin, a Korean militant named An Chonggun, calmly surrendered his empty revolver and shouted, "Long live Korea!" After an investigation by the Russian railroad police, which ostensibly netted three accomplices at Caijiagou Station (75 versts south of Harbin), An Chonggun was handed over to the Japanese. He was hanged in Port Arthur on March 26, 1910.

Ito's corpse started south at noon, accompanied by Korostovets, Khorvat, and General Ropp, the commander of the CER Railway Battalion. Honor guards met the train at each CER station where it stopped. The Russians left Ito's train at the CER terminus in Changchun. On October 27, a naval vessel transported Ito's remains from Dairen to Yokohama.[19] Although discussions about Manchuria's future had been preempted by the assassination, Ito's death had other diplomatic repercussions. In conjunction with an increasing recognition that Russian revolutionary refugees in Japan encouraged Japanese socialist and anarchist movements, the Harbin incident led to the conclusion on June 1, 1911, of a Russo-Japanese mutual extradition treaty for political criminals. This was the only such agreement the tsarist government ever signed with a foreign country.[20]

Standing at the center of late Imperial Russia's domestic and international concerns regarding the Far East, Harbin attained symbolic stature as the embodiment of all things wished from a successful expansion and all things feared from the "yellow hordes." In 1909, for example, when Russia, in connection with the Knox plan for the commercial neutralization of Manchurian railways, was forced to choose between the U.S. offer and firm Japanese opposition, Minister of Foreign Affairs A. P. Izvol'skii told the Special Conference on Far Eastern Affairs, "If we refuse the American offer, it is possible that it will cause a temporary chill," but "America will not declare war on us or send a fleet to Kharbin on this account. In this respect, Japan is far more dangerous."[21] A glance at the map reveals that for a Japanese fleet to reach Harbin, it would first have to subdue Nikolaevsk-na-Amure and Khabarovsk, the administrative and military capital of the Russian Far East. Although the surrender of these cities would in effect spell the complete loss of Russia's Pacific littoral, for the Foreign Minister the image of catastrophic defeat instantly conjured up the name Harbin.[22]

Surveying the CER Route: Engineers and Bureaucrats

Not all arrivals brought as much excitement as Komissarzhevskaia's and Ito's, but at least twice a day in each direction, through trains from the east, west, and south brought multicultural ingredients to the mixing pot that was Harbin.[23] Since over 100 versts of mainline, siding, and workshop track lay within the city limits, one was rarely out of sight and never out of whistle range of steaming locomotives. But in October 1897, the band of steel between Kaidalovo in the Transbaikal and Vladivostok was just a gleam in Witte's eye—and the source of considerable aggravation for a survey team under Prince S. N. Khilkov, which after three difficult months had almost finished tracing its section of the future railway, working east and west from a base camp in Bodune.

In late October, Aleksandr Iosifovich Iugovich, the chief construction engineer of the CER, had arrived from Jilin to announce that Khilkov should consider his work in the Bodune region completed and immediately move his men north to reconnoiter another possible route running from Qiqihar through Hulancheng to Ashehe. Although not announced as such, this meant the de facto abandonment of the southern route and the total devaluation of the survey work already completed by Khilkov's crew. It would also lead to several winter months of hard labor in frosts so severe that moustaches were welded to fur-lined sleeping bags every morning. But Iugovich had put Khilkov's dependability and industry to the test many previous times during the construction of the Riazan-Ural'sk railroad, where they had served in similar positions from 1892 to 1896.[24]

Certainly the knowledge that he could count on the subordinates whom he had brought with him from the Riazan-Ural'sk project helped the chief engineer to make his first important policy decision since arriving in Vladivostok on July 7, 1897. Despite strong pressures from St. Petersburg in favor of a more southerly route for the CER, Iugovich had already decided against it. The technical reasons were sufficient—an additional 150 versts of line (or triple the distance because of the mountainous terrain) and the lack of a usable pass through the Zhanguangcailing range. But Iugovich's exposure to the political and diplomatic sides of this question revealed additional pitfalls along the southern route, well outside the realm of engineering science. As the chief engineer's formative experience in CER activities and the immediate cause of Harbin's establishment, the routing decision deserves a short examination.

A related issue had already been broached on February 3, 1897, at a board of directors meeting of CER, Inc., barely a month after the company's incorporation. S. I. Kerbedz, vice-chairman of CER, Inc., and therefore the highest-ranking Russian,* called for immediate negotiations with the Chinese government for a wide-gauge railway branch to a port on the Yellow Sea. Iugovich, clearly envisioning the complications that such an extension could bring to his task, suggested a more cautious approach. Would it not be enough to seek a guarantee from Beijing that "should it at any time be agreeable to putting through a line from the Chinese Eastern Railway to one of the ports on the Yellow Sea, the Company should then enjoy a preferential right to build the line"? This proposal won the support of the board, but Kerbedz's interest in a southern line and/or a southern route continued unabated.[25]

When preliminary explorations had been unable to find a feasible crossing over the Zhanguangcailing range between Bodune and the Ussuri border, Kerbedz decided to call in a famous self-taught railroad surveyor named Tikhonov to appraise the situation. This invitation to a guest "expert" would hardly have sat well with the CER engineers, an exclusive fraternity made up wholly of graduates of the Institute of Transport or the Nicholas Academy of Military Engineering. Certainly, the fact that Tikhonov's honorarium of 25,000 rubles was one of the largest items on the salary sheet was deeply resented.[26]

Taking Kerbedz's meddling in stride, Iugovich, together with his handpicked assistant chief engineer, S. V. Ignatsius, had simply gone on to complete preparations for their departure, using a room in Petersburg's Evropeiskaia Hotel as construction headquarters.† In the main, these "preparations" consisted of gaining full authority to finish the job once on site. The board assented, confirming Iugovich as CER, Inc.'s representative "on the works, in Siberia and in the Priamur." He also received full control of

---

*The chairmanship of the board was reserved for a high-ranking Chinese official, whose sole function was to run interference for the CER in Beijing. After the execution of the first incumbent, Xu Jingcheng, in 1900, the position remained vacant until 1917.

†Sergei Vladimorovich Ignatsius, besides being an eminent engineer in his own right, had served for the past five years as the director of technical affairs for the Riazan-Ural'sk's board of directors. This probably qualified him to help his friend Aleksandr Iosifovich strengthen his position vis-à-vis the CER board, in particular, the micromanaging Kerbedz. His more standard railroading credentials (he was graduated from the Institute of Transport Engineers in 1883) may have helped redress recruitment problems caused by Iugovich's unusual curriculum vitae. In any case, Iugovich valued his assistant highly, labeling Ignatsius "most chief" (*glavneishii*) engineer. Nilus, *Istoricheskii obzor*, pp. 29–30.

all materials and orders in the Far East, including Japan and China. Finally, to help with the recruitment of necessary personnel, the chief engineer was empowered to issue five-year passports.[27]

Although it had been decided that a formal division of labor between the Board (*pravlenie*) and the local administration (*upravlenie*) would not be drawn up until the CER became operative (originally estimated for 1902), the company's statutes provided preliminary guidance. According to points 18 and 19, the board's functions during the construction phase were limited to (1) hiring personnel, (2) financing, (3) ordering materials and equipment from Europe and America, (4) getting the products of the above three activities to the work site, and (5) defending the enterprise from encroachment and criticism.

Though these tasks in the broad seemed to allow the board to tread heavily on the chief engineer's turf, the extraordinary powers of oversight granted to the Finance Ministry by point 27 guaranteed arbitration in case of dispute by Witte himself or his point man on CER affairs, P. M. Romanov. For example, the appointments of both Iugovich and Kerbedz were subject to Finance Ministry approval.[28]

On May 7, 1897, Iugovich and Ignatsius departed for Marseilles and points east, accompanied by Mrs. Iugovich and the CER's newly appointed head doctor, M. I. Poletika. After a short stop in Shanghai to discuss financial questions with the Russo-Chinese Bank office (the main branch in the Far East), Iugovich proceeded to Beijing, where his arrival coincided with that of Prince E. E. Ukhtomskii, the chairman of the bank. By observing the fabulous reception arranged for the prince (who had just transferred the first million of the infamous Li Hongzhang bribe to intermediaries), Iugovich was able to get some idea of Chinese protocol. As chief engineer, he was presented to the Foreign Ministry and granted the privilege of an audience with the Emperor, upon whom he made an "excellent impression."[29]

More important, he either witnessed or was informed of the complete failure of Prince Ukhtomskii's attempts to obtain permission for a southern line or at least a southern route. In fact, the Chinese vehemently rejected both ideas. Even the ostensibly friendly Li Hongzhang said: "We let you into the courtyard; [now] you want to slip into the rooms where our wives and children are." It may have given Iugovich some pleasure to see Ukhtomskii retreat to the position adopted at the February 3 board meeting by requesting assurances that the right to build a railway connecting the Chinese rail network and the CER would not be granted to any country other than Russia. On June 10, the chief engineer left Beijing.

In late June, four days after Iugovich arrived in Vladivostok to give final instructions, Prince Khilkov and his assistant, A. I. Shidlovskii, departed with their survey team for Khabarovsk, where they rented the steamer

Strongman (*Silach*) to take them to Bodune. The owner was the same Dmitrii Bogdanov whose adventures began this chapter. For the rest of the summer, Iugovich himself idled on Vladivostok's Golden Horn (harbor) trying unsuccessfully to get the navy to clear away its minelayers (*minnyi gorodok*) from the waterfront site that had been temporarily put at the CER's disposal. He also made preparations for the official commencement of construction scheduled for August 28. Article 3 of the construction contract between the Russo-Chinese Bank and the Chinese government had stipulated that work must begin within a year of signature, and begin it would.[30]

The groundbreaking ceremony took place at Sanchakou near the Poltavskaia border station. To regale and accommodate the 80 Russian and Chinese dignitaries who attended, Iugovich spent 45,000 rubles. Highlights of the event included the Ussuri cossacks' ataman general, D. I. Subotich, throwing out the first clod and the debut of the CER flag, a colorful mélange of Russian and Chinese colors and symbols. Colonel (later Major-General) D. L. Khorvat, who would succeed Iugovich in 1903, was also present in his capacity as head of the Ussuri railway.[31]

Within a few days of fulfilling this final ceremonial responsibility, Iugovich and Ignatsius left for a five-month, 3,000-verst tour of CER survey sites. September was spent studying successful trailblazing farther north in the Zhanguangcailing and Tikhonov's failure along the southern variant. From these observations, Iugovich must have drawn his own conclusions, for within days of reaching Bodune, he ordered the termination of survey activity in the area, and he had the earthworks at Sanchakou halted at the first conceivable pretext, a frost on October 17. This was the first and last construction on the southern route. But if by action there was no mistaking Iugovich's view on the eventual choice of route, in an October 23 telegram to Romanov we find him nevertheless discussing the plans for a Sungari bridge at Bodune. He was not yet ready to tip his hand to Petersburg.[32]

Iugovich left Bodune on November 15 to inspect the western reaches of the railway from Qiqihar to the Transbaikal border. Four days after his return on January 2, Prince Khilkov arrived in Qiqihar with the news that the Qiqihar-Hulancheng-Ashehe survey had been completed. At some point during the last six weeks of 1897, Khilkov's party had chosen the point at which the longest of the CER's bridges would span the Sungari, 45°45′N, 126°38′E. Already marked for drastic change, the site of the future Harbin settled in for the last winter and thaw that would escape the historical record. Meanwhile, the Russian engineers in Qiqihar celebrated Christmas on January 6 (December 25 o.s.). On the same day, Iugovich was fêted by the jiangjun En Ze, who was (by now needlessly) worried that the southern route would deprive his provincial capital of importance and revenue.[33]

At a January 24 meeting in Ninguta, Iugovich gave Tikhonov one last chance to find a crossing. Once more, Tikhonov disappeared into the mountains. (This time he was accompanied by the few members of the newly arrived CER guard who had managed to pass unscathed through ports of call at Constantinople, Port Said, Aden, Colombo, Singapore, and Nagasaki; on reaching Vladivostok, the bulk of the guard had been promptly hospitalized for a variety of venereal diseases.) Shortly after, Tikhonov admitted defeat and co-signed the telegram to the board scrapping the southern option on geographical grounds. Since by then a Russian squadron had already occupied Port Arthur, brightening the prospects for a southern branch and consequently dimming interest in the CER mainline's route, there was no noticeable reaction from Petersburg to Iugovich's choice. It was routinely approved.[34]

The Birth of Russian Harbin

The chief engineer had experienced and learned a great deal during his first year in office. His sometimes less than harmonious relations with ministries, companies, admirals, generals, and Chinese officials led him to conclude that CER construction had to be insulated from outside interference. The only way to accomplish this was to move his headquarters out of reach into the Manchurian interior. The Sungari crossing, to which materials and supplies could be shipped during the navigation season, seemed a logical choice.

Iugovich could in any case cite several clear advantages to leaving Vladivostok: (1) building from the center, as well as from the extremities, would speed up construction; (2) work would proceed faster because of the lack of distractions (life on the CER in the early years was described as "semi-Robinsonian," *polurobinzonovskoe*); (3) the esprit de corps would be better since the leadership was experiencing the same deprivations as the workforce; and (4) the administrators would be in a better position to cope with the unpredictable problems that might arise with Chinese officials and local inhabitants.[35] In early February, shortly after his return to Vladivostok, Iugovich ordered Shidlovskii to take a small party back to the Sungari crossing that he had helped survey only a few months earlier. His mission was to prepare housing, offices, and storage for those who would arrive by boat later in the spring.

On March 20, 1898, Shidlovskii's party, of 75 men, one woman, and one child, left Vladivostok for Nikol'sk-Ussuriisk. After a few days spent buying supplies, the pioneers departed in a thirty-cart wagon train carrying 100,000 rubles in silver bars. Passing the abandoned earthwork at Sanchakou, the group made good time as far as Ninguta, covering 250 versts in six days. Then bad luck struck. The spring thaw arrived just as they began to cross the Zhanguangcailing. In the following two weeks, daily progress was cut to ten–twenty versts as the wagons slowly made their way along mountain trails that had suddenly become channels for rapid torrents. Finally, they came out on the Jilin-Ashehe road and quickly completed their journey, arriving in Ashehe on April 22.

After hooking up with a small party from Khilkov's survey team, which had wintered in Qiqihar, Shidlovskii and a small group continued on toward the Sungari. Reaching a precipice two versts from the river, the Russians stood dumbfounded. Before them lay the sparkling surface of a flooded swamp speckled with tiny islands on which stood isolated groups of two or three Chinese-style houses (*fanz*). At the Sungari's bank, a narrow elevation supported a small fortress (*yingpan*) belonging to the Chinese riverine customs and a few more *fanzy*.

Shidlovskii had been ordered to find lodging as close as possible to the river, but that was clearly not an option, as it had seemed to be the previous winter, when the swamp had been frozen solid and masked under snow. It was also his misfortune that 1896 and 1897 had been unusually wet years. After finding the way down to the flatlands and the water-covered road to the fortress, Shidlovskii examined the riverbank and returned to camp thoroughly troubled. No time remained to alert Vladivostok. The construction administration would arrive in approximately two weeks. Lodging had to be found somewhere.

It was at this point that one of the Chinese guides pointed out an abandoned liquor (*khanshin*) factory at Xiangfang some eight versts from the river. It was a "distillery" unlike any the Russians would have been familiar with, of a piece with the many such concerns George Lensen describes:

> Plants in which *hanshin* was distilled were scattered all over Manchuria. Like the residences of officials, they were surrounded by walls of unfired brick mixed with chopped straw, about seven feet high and five or six feet wide, and constituted veritable fortresses. The walls were provided with loopholes and towers; the gates were of heavy lumber, reinforced with iron.[36]

The distillery-fortress at Xiangfang however, had not withstood the local bandits, known as "Red Beards" (*honghuzi*). After the pillage, production had been discontinued. Shidlovskii found the wooden buildings in various states of decomposition, but the gray brick structures were still in good shape. With slight repairs, they would be habitable. Space to add buildings within the circumference of the outer walls was plentiful. The party's translator, Chuprov, was sent to Ashehe and soon returned with the two owners. After long negotiations, the buildings and adjacent lands were purchased for 8,000 *lan* (approximately 320 kilograms of silver).[37]

The next step was to hire Chinese laborers to help the twenty Russian workers who had been brought along from Vladivostok to construct office and living space. Along the raised embankment to the west and east of the yingpan, tents and storage barracks made of straw mats sprang up. Behind them, on the draining flatlands, the poppies began to bloom. For the last time in Harbin, the local villagers put on their harvesting thimbles to collect Manchurian opium, the quality and portability of which had made it a much appreciated currency throughout the region. Seasonal workers could be sure that earnings carried home in drug form would increase in value as they moved south.

On June 9, the steamer *Blagoveshchensk*, carrying Ignatsius, Khilkov, and the core construction crew came up the Sungari. After passing the mouth of the Ashehe River, they began to scan the left bank for signs of Shidlovskii. Eight versts farther on, the lookout sighted the Russian flag flying above the tent city to the east of the yingpan. Thus was Harbin found and founded.[38]

Alienated Land

So when is Harbin's birthday? Possibly, in September 1897, when Iugovich decided that the southern route was unfeasible. Or the day when Khilkov's surveyors determined the location of the Sungari crossing. Or maybe in February 1898, when the decision was taken to move construction headquarters out of Vladivostok, since that facilitated the rapid growth of Harbin that would follow. The problem is, no single day can be fixed to any of these events. From the standpoint of property rights, Shidlovskii's purchase of the distillery represents the first tangible russification of Haerbin into Kharbin. Unfortunately, here again no date is certain, although April 25 or 26 seems likely. Logically, the arrival of the construction administration on June 9 would favor that choice, since the city of Harbin could hardly predate its raison d'être.

Like so many other phenomena, the birthday options are different when viewed from the capital. The charter adopted on December 16, 1896, for example, required a route that avoided "cemeteries and graves, as well as towns and villages." Once communicated to the survey parties by an order dated April 8, 1897, this provision guaranteed that the site at which the tracks bridged the Sungari would be an essentially new settlement, not a buildup of an existing one. And, finally, from an official point of view, we might accept the date on which Harbin's location was approved by the Finance Ministry. In my examination of the Siberian Railway Committee's archives, I came across a copy of the 80-verst-per-inch map prepared for Pozdneev's *Opisanie Man'chzhurii*. It was dated December 30, 1898, and on it Harbin's location had been penciled in. If not approval, this record at least reflects the capital's recognition.[39]

Each of these dates is a defensible birthday, but a study of the Russian acquisition of the soil on which Harbin grew would no doubt focus on Shidlovskii's purchase as the critical moment. This would be a true kharbinets choice, for it gives preference to the town over the railroad and to local over capital-city considerations. However, like the determination of Harbin's location, this Manchurian event has a European prehistory. On September 8, 1896, in Berlin, Xu Jingcheng, the Chinese minister to Germany and Russia, signed the contract for the construction of the Chinese Eastern Railroad with L. Iu. Rothstein and Prince Ukhtomskii, representing the Russo-Chinese Bank. Clause 6 of the definitive French text read: "The land really necessary for the construction, use, and protection of the line, as well as the land near the line necessary for procuring sand, rock, lime, etc., will be given to the Company." To encourage the timely transfer of these lands, clause 3 stated that the Russians had to complete construction within six years "from the day when the route will be definitely decided and the necessary land placed at the Company's disposal." As insurance, Li Hongzhang was scheduled to receive his second million-ruble payment when the railway route was approved by the Chinese government.[40]

As the historian E. Kh. Nilus notes, these rights were doubly significant from the Russian point of view:

First, the very extensive real estate hereby provided, either *gratis* [Chinese state lands] or "*au prix courant*" [private domains], represented China's only substantial investment in the enterprise. Second, by becoming a Manchurian landowner, the CER was but a step from becoming a Manchurian landlord. With the issuance of leases, the CER automatically took upon itself many new obligations to the tenants. This process converted the CER from a railroad into a multifaceted colonial enterprise.

According to Vice-Chairman [A. N.] Venttsel, "The Chinese Eastern Railway Company must not be considered merely a carrying enterprise since its activities greatly exceed the limits of operating the railway line only. It is also entrusted with the administration of a vast Concession Zone."[41]

Only months after receiving these land rights from the Chinese government, the company granted Iugovich full power of attorney to enforce them. Moreover, in the letter it sent him to that effect just before his departure from Marseilles, the board also empowered him to settle criminal and civil cases arising out of and at the site of construction. The result of Iugovich's efforts was a long strip of land enclosing the railway in a sheath thirty-three sazhen (220 feet) wide. This was almost in conformity with practices on the Siberian trunkline, where the upgraded specifications codified in 1896 called for thirty-five sazhen. At each station, this Belt of Alienation (*polosa otchuzhdeniia*) bulged out a bit. At Harbin, the swelling took on proportions more appropriate for city planning than station building.[42]

On July 7, 1898, less than a month after the *Blagoveshchensk* arrived, the fudutong of Ashehe promulgated a decree fixing the levels of compensation that the Russians would have to pay to landowners in and around Harbin. The items involved were houses, acreage under cultivation, and gravesites; and the prices were scaled to the amounts paid in the Beijing-Hankou railway's land expropriations.[43] Under these guidelines, 2,235 desiatinas were purchased at Harbin by July 1900 to flesh out the 200 desiatinas of Shidlovskii's original purchase, already known as Old Harbin. Two-thirds of the final product, an irregular polygon of land roughly four versts square, lay in the riverside flatlands, the future Pristan. The remainder, perched on the precipice from which Shidlovskii had viewed the flood, would become the heart of New Town.[44]

During the 1900 Boxer siege, the Russians retreated to the right bank of the Sungari, abandoning the plot at Old Harbin. New Town was evacuated by all but armed defenders. The Boxers never captured it. After the siege was broken, an additional 280,000 rubles was budgeted for acquiring "defensive" land at Harbin. A supplement of 70,000 was also allotted for buying out local landowners. How much of this fund was actually used is unclear, but by 1901 ditches had been dug to demarcate an area more than twice the size of the original. The riverside plot had expanded to the west and inland, swallowing up Old Harbin. The move toward consolidation, however, was somewhat offset by purchases made on the left (north) bank of the Sungari.[45]

In December 1900, Iugovich, Kerbedz, and I. I. Khodorovskii, another board member, conferred in Harbin and decided that the motive for land purchases should still be limited to immediate necessity. This paved the way for an agreement signed on May 28, 1902, by Iugovich and the Jilin diplomatic bureau (*jiaosheju*). By clause 6 of this act, Harbin, which had been the first purchase site in Manchuria, also set the precedent for limiting its own growth. The Russians bound themselves to make no further extensions to "Harbin-Central Station" (Haerbin zongchezhan). In exchange, the Jilin bureau reaffirmed the CER's permanent right to the 4,000 desiatinas it had recently purchased from thirty-one local landlords. At 5,660 desiatinas, right-bank Kharbin reached its maximum area. Although the agreement did not touch on private property, the Russians' vow of self-restraint may well have helped procure Chinese cooperation in the CER's first auctions of long-term land leases to private individuals and firms. To inspire confidence in the solidity of CER land tenure in China, the publicly invited tenders were sent through the Jilin bureau. The first auctions were held on June 9, 1902, four years to the day on which Ignatsius and the construction crew had arrived. In Harbin, the CER had changed roles from purchaser to leaser of land. It was time to settle down.[46]

Railwaymen: Russian Engineers and Chinese Labor

Not surprisingly, the very first to settle down were the builders, both Russian and Chinese. As we have seen, many of the technical personnel were recruited personally, through professional networks established by mutual employment on other projects during the 1890's railroading boom. As one engineer put it, "Railroad building in Russia during the last half-century has produced a special category of construction specialists, living their own peculiar way of life and usually bound to each other and their leaders by internal soldering [*vnutrenneiu spaikoiu*]."[47] The CER had hoped to supplement the group obtained through Iugovich's Riazan-Ural'sk connection with a large contingent from the Ussuri railroad, which was virtually complete when the company began its recruitment efforts in 1897. But enlistment was light. Many in the Ussuri's upper echelons planned to stay on as part of the operations staff; and others, having collected their bonuses, were ready for a rest. Recruiting Ministry of Transport personnel proved equally difficult. Many potential employees, both in the Far East and in European Russia, reacted cautiously to the CER's generous offers, concerned not so much with moving to terra incognita as with losing their status in the ministry.[48]

To calm these fears, an Imperial edict dated January 28, 1898, allowed engineers serving on the CER to keep their Ministry of Transport ranks and, in general, to enjoy all the "rights of actual state service." This was extremely important for those worried about pensions and promotions. Earlier decrees had extended similar benefits to doctors and telegraphers who signed on.[49] To soften the hardships of the six-week sea voyage from Odessa to Vladivostok, employees salaried above 2,000 rubles a year received a 500-ruble travel allowance, sufficient for a first-class cabin. (In recognition of the fact that six weeks between decks was an unreasonable hardship, the cut-off salary for *intelligenten Beamten*, white-collar workers, was lowered to 1,500 rubles in 1899.) Others had to make do on 150 rubles.[50] From Vladivostok, the new arrivals proceeded by train to Khabarovsk, where they filled the CER Hotel to bursting while waiting for the CER river fleet to transport them to Harbin.[51]

For many, these perquisites and guarantees were not necessary. Double salaries, the promise of further raises, and the sheer excitement of pioneering in exotic Manchuria were enough. Large advances underwrote extravagant farewell parties in Vladivostok. One observer reported that "everywhere the gay and energetic cry went up: 'We are going to the Manchurian [*Idem na Man'chzhurku*]'".[52] For many, like the veteran railroad builder E. P. Ia., the recruitment process was a face-to-face affair:

One or another engineer with whom we were acquainted would invite us. We trusted and followed him. As sections were completed, the builders, headed by their engineer, would move to new construction sites. We lived like migrating [*pereletnye*] birds and were little interested in regulations. We loved our work. Of course, somewhere in Petersburg at the Board there were staff lists and budgets, but we received our pay from the section heads and asked no further.[53]

A variation on this theme is the case of F. I. Rozanov, who arrived in the Far East in 1890 to establish a settlement for forced labor outside of Vladivostok. After six years on the Ussuri line, he had saved 3,000 rubles and decided to seek his fortune as a private contractor. Within the year, a brick factory on the Transbaikal railway had delivered him into bankruptcy. In need, Rozanov contacted his old boss on the Ussuri, N. N. Bocharov, now head engineer on the CER Fourth Section (Xingan). Presumably as a result, Rozanov was hired to found and direct the operations of the CER brick factory at Harbin. Men with engineering degrees remained in short supply throughout the construction period, so technicians (*tekhniki*) with less theoretical background but compensatory experience on either the Ussuri or the Transbaikal were often entrusted with positions up to and including subsection chief (*nachal'nik distantsii*).[54]

Manual labor was largely reserved for Chinese coolies, who were transported en masse from Zhifu and Tianjin. For this, both precedent and procedure had been established during the construction of the Transbaikal and Ussuri sections of the Trans-Siberian, whose workforces were over 21 percent and 40 percent Chinese, respectively (the latter figure includes Koreans). On the CER, the proportion hovered between 70 percent and 90 percent.[55]

The CER planners preferred Chinese labor because of its seemingly limitless availability and inexpensive unit price. A CER overseer at the Harbin workshops, I. Levitov, made some comparisons, based on the mixed group under his orders. Russians, he calculated, needed sixteen rubles for a summer wardrobe and 28.5 rubles in winter, compared with just two and nine rubles for the Chinese. Food costs showed a similar gap: where the Russians required between ten and thirteen rubles a month, the Chinese minimum was a remarkable two rubles. In light of these disparities, it was in no way surprising that the Chinese were willing to work for from 50 kopecks to 1.2 rubles a day. The most unskilled Russians, with far higher subsistence costs, could not afford to work at a daily rate of less than 1.2 rubles. A separate review of housing conditions was not impressed with the Chinese laborers' lodgings, but noted that even Iugovich's office in Harbin was "in a building whose exterior, lack of the most primitive comforts, and cold [rooms] remind one more of a backwoods post station than the office of an administrator heading the construction of a 2,500-verst railroad."[56]

Still, cost was a less important consideration than the speedy completion of the railway, an accomplishment that could clearly be achieved only by hiring workers in force. As early as January 1897, D. D. Pokotilov, Witte's and the Russo-Chinese Bank's main agent in Beijing, forwarded information to D. M. Pozdneev, secretary of Witte's "General Chancellery," regarding the costs, conditions, and necessary lead time to hire coolies from Zhifu. Russia's consul at Tianjin, Shuiskii, reported that recruitment was complicated by wild rumors that, once on board ship, Chinese laborers would have their braids cut and faces chalked, so they could be sent to India to fight the English.[57] At Harbin, the first batch of 15,000 arrived in late 1898 from Tianjin and Zhifu. A June 1899 report from Iugovich announcing the arrival of a 31,000-man contingent from Tianjin put the total Chinese labor force at 49,000.[58] A year later, when the Boxer Rebellion (or the "Chinese disorders" as the Russians called them) broke out, the count was 75,000. The presence of 57 percent of these coolies on the West branch reflects the engineering challenges of construction in that sector, just as their near absence on the East branch testifies to the essential completion of Harbin's tie to Vladivostok.[59]

Almost all of these workers were hired through Chinese compradores, who arranged their transportation, accommodations, and work assignments.[60] After receiving earnest money, the workers were brought to port and shipped in dehumanizing densities to Yingkou, Port Arthur, Dal'nii, or Vladivostok.[61] Once on site, relations with the CER engineers would be handled by a work-group representative. The compradores made no performance guarantees and provided no mediation services. In general, necessary communication was of a fairly simple nature, possibly prompting U.S. Senator Albert Beveridge's comment that Russians "picked up" Chinese in less than a month. More likely, Beveridge, ignorant of both Russian and Chinese, did not recognize the Russo-Chinese mixed dialect commonly used on both sides of the border. The Ussuri engineers would have been familiar with it already, and others would have acquired it quickly.*

In attempting to inculcate the Chinese workers with new work methods and ethics, the Russian engineers were once again on their own. In one case, the successful introduction of piecework for embankment construction was followed by a complete rejection of the wheelbarrow. The Chinese

---

*Beveridge, *Russian Advance*, p. 253. This dialect dates back to the 18th century and has several interesting traits. For example, verbs do not conjugate and tend to be used in the form most common in spoken language, usually the imperative. Words often start in Russian and end in Chinese, allowing the listener to pick up on either end, e.g., *bazashir* = *bazar* + *shi*, *subutang* = *sup* + *tang*. But as in any language with a broad enough temporal and geographic range, etymological mysteries remain. The most common phrase in the Russo-Chinese borderland, for example, was *shibko shango*, meaning "very good"; both sides thought it came from the other's tongue. There is a large literature on the dialect, and somewhere the materials from the 1929–30 Soviet Academy of Sciences' ethnolinguistic study still await analysis; but a good place to start is Shprintsin, "O russko-kitaiskom dialekte."

preferred baskets, since they were lighter when empty and easier to repair with ubiquitous willow branches. Some disagreements hovered uneasily between the sinister and the absurd. For example, when bones were discovered in a garbage dump near Harbin, the rumor spread among the coolies that human fat was needed to grease the locomotives. Work stopped, and things reached a boiling point. In a final attempt to avert violence, hunters were sent out to kill a bear. Doctor Poletika dissected it in front of a large Chinese audience and successfully matched the bones to those of the reputed human sacrifice. The tensions died down. In Harbin, where the workmen's barracks lay in the very center of the city they were building, housing for 1,000 men actually held many more. An 1899 account of Harbin describes an "anthill," overrun with competing Chinese labor cooperatives.[62]

Also in 1899, engineers on one of the sections near Qiqihar sent to Blagoveshchensk for Chinese with railroad-building experience on either the Ussuri or Transbaikal works. These "model" workers were then distributed evenly along the line to serve simultaneously as examples, teachers, and translators for the Tianjin and Zhifu laborers. Employment on the CER probably saved these men's lives because on July 17 of that year, Cossacks drove most of Blagoveshchensk's Chinese population into the Amur to drown. Until the Boxer storm had been pacified by Russian military occupation, the Russian engineers took refuge at Harbin, which endured a short siege, while the Chinese hirelings awaited the outcome of the crisis. Russians working near the border retreated to Russia proper.[63]

When construction was renewed in the fall of 1900, the labor situation changed in several ways. First of all, the source of coolie labor was different. During the next three years, there is no mention at all of laborers arriving from Tianjin. This was certainly due in good part to the opening of Port Arthur and Dal'nii harbors, which made transport from Zhifu cheaper. But it is also possible that the Russians preferred not to draw their manpower from an area that had been occupied by the Allied Expeditionary Force, and so avoid a complication that might have disrupted the "special" (and ostensibly friendly) relationship between Russians and Chinese in Manchuria. Whatever the reasons, the results were numerically impressive. In 1901, 814 boatloads from Zhifu brought 81,598 coolies to Port Arthur, 25,717 to Dal'nii, and 23,983 to Vladivostok.[64]

By December 1901 Harbin's Chinese population had swelled to an estimated 12,000, with the result that the city's riverside neighbor, Fujiadian, which had fully 1,220 innkeepers (*ludian*) among its 4,000 permanent residents, seems to have functioned mainly as a housing area for the overflow of Harbin's Chinese workers.[65] Demand from this enlarged laboring population and the Russian army of occupation drove up prices. Disruptions in distribution and uncertainties about the harvest contributed to inflationary pressures on food and other commodities. Labor costs rose swiftly. The unskilled, who had been paid 20 kopecks a day in spring 1900, received 60 in the fall. A carpenter's daily wage of 30 kopecks had risen to 75.[66]

Fearing total dependence on Chinese labor, the board ordered the engineer in charge of the West Branch, N. N. Bocharov, to the Transbaikal in search of Russian workers. In the meantime, the Chinese, without demur, returned to work, and construction continued. In the early months of 1901, a Russian workforce of 4,500 arrived.

[These workers] were not enlisted in the best circles. Quite the opposite. The police, whose cooperation we had requested, tried to dump into distant Manchuria [*splavit' v dalekuiu Man'chzhuriiu*] the most restless urban elements. These were the dregs of such cities as Irkutsk, Blagoveshchensk, Chita, and Verkhneudinsk [now Ulan Ude]. Constant misunderstandings, dissatisfaction, increased demands, drunkenness, fights, and debauchery began to occur. Truly, it seemed no easier than [dealing with the] Boxers.[67]

In spring 1901, a commission from the board assigned to examine workers' complaints found that almost all the petitioners had been justifiably fired because they were not "capable of conscientious labor."[68]

Still, this by no means applies to the entire Russian workforce. In June 1901, aside from the "rabble" that had been foisted on the CER, 4,100 Russian "workers and craftsmen" were employed in areas requiring special skills. One example is the paymasters' *artel'*, which was hired from a larger Moscow cooperative on April 3, 1897. Three weeks later, nine paymasters were among the first survey crews that left Odessa on the *Vladimir*. In 1900, during the Boxer commotion, this group was credited with not losing track of even a single kopeck from the millions of CER rubles in cash and silver that were disbursed along the railway.[69]

Specialist labor was also brought in to build the Sungari bridge at Harbin. Just over 3,000 feet long, this would be the longest bridge in Northeast Asia until the completion of the Amur bridge at Khabarovsk in 1916. The whole project was entrusted to a famous expert on caisson work, A. N. Lentovskii. He, in turn, brought in 350 Russian craftsmen with bridge-building experience. The 1899–1900 construction of the Sviato-Nikolaevskaia cathedral, which dominated Harbin's central square (until torn down by Red Guards in 1966), serves as another case in point. Groups of Russian carpenters, trained in the woodcarving style of Siberian *rez'ba*, were brought in to finish the detail work. As it turned out, many of them had to be evacuated during the Boxer siege of Harbin, and Chinese craftsmen were then tried and found superior.[70]

Harbin as Company Town, 1898–1904

Recruitment was just the first of the construction administration's problems. Now Russian parties arriving by the thousands and Chinese by the tens of thousands had to be welcomed by the CER to "uncivilized and unexplored" Manchuria, where "unpropitious climatic and natural conditions" reigned side by side with "bands of bandits."

In such a situation it [was] necessary for the company itself to concern itself with the creation of all necessary conditions for construction, beginning with the building of living space and the guaranteeing of food supplies for the employees and workers and ending with the organization of the Guard, telegraph and postal communications, police, judicial, and medical-sanitary units, etc.[71]

These were minimal conditions for survival. The creation of a stable community of Russians in Manchuria would also require the satisfaction of "spiritual" needs, such as religion, education, and some unifying conception, an "imperialist ideology" perhaps of the Russo-Chinese task in which the newcomers were engaged.

By the summer of 1900, approximately 5,000 Russians were living in Harbin. In early July, when Boxer aggression shut down construction, 3,000, many of them women and children, floated down the Sungari to safe haven at Khabarovsk. The rest withstood what appear to have been uncoordinated and halfhearted attempts to take Harbin. The governor-general of Qiqihar had been ordered by Beijing "to take Harbin by trickery or by force." His failure meant death, a reported suicide, for him, and continued life for Harbin.[72]

The Russian population soon shot back up. The number of employees alone reached 7,000 in early 1901, only to double by the next year as the pace of construction accelerated. In May 1902, the Finance Ministry reported 15,000 CER employees on the books, with 18,000 dependents accompanying them. That figure did not include the CER guard (25,000 men) and the officers' families (5,000). Though only a small percentage of these troops were based at Harbin, over a third of the railwaymen were domiciled there. Of the 20,000 inhabitants Witte found at Harbin in October 1902, probably three-quarters of the Russian families collected their paychecks from the CER. Before the Russo-Japanese War, Harbin was a company town.[73]

And the CER took care of its own. At the beginning of May 1898, the Ministry of Finance informed the Siberian Railway Committee of its plan to build 385 square sazhens (18,480 sq. ft.) of living quarters at the central construction site. Some 5,000 miles away, the engineer Shidlovskii was busily turning this figure into an underestimate. By May 1899, the ministry reported that 4,000 square sazhens of temporary housing had been erected at "Settlement Harbin." The location, nine versts from the Sungari crossing, indicates that this was the Xiangfang (Old Harbin) distillery.[74]

By 1900, the first urban development plan had been approved, and the construction of permanent housing began in "Sungari," as New Town was originally known.* Some 1,500 square sazhens were complete before the Boxers struck in July. The following year, building starts increased, reaching 7,500 square sazhens of permanent housing in Sungari and 10,000 of temporary lodging at "[Old] Harbin." In 1902, this building fever produced an instant city: 60,000 square sazhens of homes for CER personnel were completed, and the core of New Town filled in the muddy spaces between the three largest projects, the CER administration headquarters, the St. Nikolai church (later cathedral), and the grandiose train station.[75]

The Vologda-style woodwork of the church stood at New Town's main intersection, from which radiated roads to Old Harbin, the CER headquarters, the station (with Pristan beyond), and the graveyard.[76] But the dominant style was art nouveau. Most of the important public buildings in New Town exhibited features common to this fashion so recently derived from the decorative arts of London, Paris, and Vienna. In Harbin, unlike the European capitals, this innovation was not submerged in the accumulated architectural heritage.

Harbin's "modernness" struck visitors from the moment of arrival. At 10,000 square sazhens, the Harbin Station dwarfed all the stations of Siberia. Dal'nii, the only other CER station designated as first class, was only a fifth the size. Friedrich von Nottbeck, visiting from Berlin, expressed a fondness for the "light, pistachio-green New Station built in the modern style," and the Austrian Alexander Spaits was struck by the station's "largeness, cleanliness, and, above all, the modern [Viennese] Secession style." In fact, after the station, Spaits found the rest of Harbin somewhat disappointing.[77]

After lodging, the most urgent need was a familiar diet. Originally, the CER administration fed its employees with a combination of direct tariff-free imports made by a food supply committee and subcontracts issued to private individuals. But the line between these two categories came to be blurred as employees' wives, traveling back and forth between Harbin and Khabarovsk, indulged in semiclandestine trade and barter in order to supplement their husbands' incomes. In late 1900, with the increased demand for Russian bread by both civilians and soldiers, the CER allocated

---

*This part of town is now called Southern Ridge (*nangang*), referring to its position relative to the Sungari. Before the Russian arrival, it was known as the Qin Family Ridge in honor of a pioneer peasant family in the area. In the Chinese historical literature, the pre-Russian name is often emphasized to counter claims that Harbin occupied an uninhabited space. For example, Zheng Changchun "Haerbin nangangde youlai," p. 138, claims that "over 200 households" (*erbaiyu hu*) lived in the space between New Town and Old Harbin.

380,000 rubles for the building of a flour mill along the Sungari embankment. It was completed the next year, with a second installation following in 1902. By June, D. D. Pokotilov, of the Russo-Chinese Bank, was able to report that production had reached 800 poods (14 tons) a day, and that "the first experiments with producing flour from local grain [had given] such good results that, according to those experienced in these matters, this branch of Russian industry in Manchuria [had] a brilliant future." Supplies of horned cattle from Mongolia were described as "endless," and the first Harbin slaughterhouse opened on May 14, 1902. The cost of living in Harbin was still considered quite low compared with the Russian Far East, although the days when an empty bottle could be traded for two chickens and 100 eggs had receded into the realm of myth.[78]

By 1901, market forces had already begun to take over many of the CER's paternalistic tasks. The mills were sold to private entrepreneurs at a profit. The food supply committee was scaled down, continuing to exist only as a brake on inflationary prices. Although estimates vary, expenditures in Harbin certainly reached the tens of millions, and as one Irkutsk paper remarked, "the grass is greener" (*slavny budny za gorami*). By 1902, the Finance Ministry cited this influx of "a public of all sorts, estates, and professions" in calling for the establishment of local police to look after "the whole town that has arisen next to the administrative center . . . at Harbin."[79]

In 1901–2, much of this urban growth took place in Pristan, where the completion of a 350,000-ruble embankment along the Sungari meant that flooding would no longer be a common occurrence.[80] In the course of 1903, the space between Pristan and New Town filled up, and the CER engineers constructed a viaduct to bridge the ravine between the ridge and the lowlands. Further recognition of Harbin's duality came with the official extension of road building to include Pristan, "the town market, where a settlement of 10,000 has already arisen."[81] The same quarry, brick factory, sawmill, and Nobel Brothers' warehouse that had provided materials for railroad construction now supplied private demands.[82]

Although the CER administration had taken notice of Pristan's growth, there was no assumption of equality between the "administrative center" and the "town market." At the first auction of leases on land conceded to the CER for the duration of its 80-year contract, the price differential clearly reflected a certain evaluation of both contemporary status and future prospects. Land in New Town was divided into four categories, with the minimum bids for the highest fixed at ten rubles per square sazhen, and the lowest at two. Old Harbin's lack of promise was expressed by a one-ruble minimum, and bidders needed just one more ruble to buy the very best real estate there. But noblesse oblige, so landowners in New Town faced further hurdles in the form of more stringent building regulations. Where owners of the top category in Pristan were required to invest six rubles in construction per square sazhen within a two-year period, their New Town counterparts had to invest fifteen. In addition, before construction, landholders in New Town's top two categories had to submit detailed plans to the CER for approval. The only acceptable materials were brick and stone. Pristan's building code had just one requirement: "no inflammable roofs."[83]

Hard work in the frontier boomtown alternated with hard play. According to one critical commentator, not only had the "Manchurians" placed themselves "beyond good and evil," they had even coined a variant on a common Russian folk saying to describe their special situation: "A hundred rubles is not money, fifty versts is no distance, and a Chinaman is not a man."[84] The spirit of the old Chinese liquor factory that was the builders' first headquarters spread quickly throughout Harbin. At first, the CER forbade the import of alcoholic beverages from Russia proper, but this merely led to smuggling under various guises and the purchase of cheap, but impure, Chinese products, known universally as *khanshin*. Workers and Cossacks used to the high tariffs imposed by Russia's imperial liquor monopoly were amazed by the five-kopeck-a-bottle price tag and "drank themselves crazy, into delirium tremens. Then, they died." To cope with the problem, the CER administration invited a certain Popov of Blagoveshchensk to set up shop in Harbin to purify the "foul khanshin" of residual poisons before reselling it at fifteen kopecks a bottle. By 1902, P. S. Smirnov had grabbed the import market on genuine Russian vodka. In December 1903, the U.S. consul at Niuzhuang, Henry Miller, found eight large distilleries operating in Harbin to satisfy a daily consumption of 1,000 Russian buckets of vodka (2,707 gallons).[85]

Drunkenness was not Harbin's only sin. The same critical commentator observed that just as Monaco had become the world's gaming house, so Harbin and Port Arthur had become the world's whorehouses. As one might expect in this frontier town, women accounted for just a small proportion of the population, still representing only about 13 percent of the total as late as May 1903 by the official census. But Chinese prostitutes are known to have been on the scene as early as 1899, and the census-takers probably had no way of registering the Chinese female population. Nor is there any way of knowing how many of the Russian females (who accounted for perhaps 36 percent of their community in the city by my calculation) may have practiced the world's oldest profession.[86] In any case, many of the men so impressed by cheap liquor were also intrigued by similar bargains in human flesh. The CER's medical personnel had been able to contain the incidence of venereal disease until 1900. But as the growth of Harbin and the CER accelerated after the Boxer Rebellion, so did the spread of syphilis and gonorrhea. Table 1, showing the figures for 1897–1902, illustrates this

TABLE 1 *Reported Cases of Venereal Disease in Harbin, 1897–1902*

	Syphilis		Gonorrhea		
Year	Hospitalized	Walk-in	Hospitalized	Walk-in	All cases
1897	4	12	4	52	72
1898	50	228	60	498	836
1899	171	195	239	994	1,599
1900	249	419	194	773	1,635
1901	453	1,635	409	2,895	5,392
1902	795	2,027	885	3,463	7,170

SOURCE: Poletika, *Obshchii meditsinskii*, pp. 52–54.

trend clearly. Although it is impossible to tell how many of the cases shown represented either simultaneous infections with both venereal diseases or repeated treatments for the same individuals, we can safely conclude that at any given moment a significant proportion of Harbin's population carried and spread the unfortunate consequences of intercultural intercourse.

The CER doctors, who by 1901 numbered twenty-seven, investigated what was plainly now a serious problem and found that almost all Chinese women in Manchuria had gonorrhea. Attempts to teach basic hygiene to Harbin's prostitutes failed, reportedly because the girls refused to take baths in the superstitious fear that cleanliness would lead to a lifelong loss of happiness. Hopes that the situation might be improved by opening a Japanese whorehouse with semiweekly examinations were disappointed when these services proved almost as expensive as in Vladivostok. Workers and enlisted men continued to frequent the Chinese "dens" (*pritony*). Illness of all kinds was common in the unfamiliar conditions of wilderness Manchuria, with 38,776 hospitalizations during the five years of construction. Four of five patients were Russians.[87]

The CER was as interested in the spiritual well-being of its employees as it was in their physical health. A church with a capacity of 500 figured in the budget for 1898. Consecration took place on October 13, 1899. Since the intended devotees were, in large part, members of the Protective Guard, the officiating priest came from the military and naval clergy. The CER believed that manual laborers would also feel a religious need, since churches were originally planned for the eight stations with depots and/or workshops. When the Protective Guard became the Frontier Guard in early 1901, the War Ministry refused to continue providing spiritual guidance to subordinates of the Finance Ministry, and new priests were assigned from the Beijing Ecclesiastical Mission. With two hundred years of experience servicing the needs of the Russian Orthodox community in China, the mission was ideally suited for the job. As the number of guards and workers rose, the CER clergy complement increased from one to ten, four of whom served in Harbin.[88]

Despite its name, the Beijing Ecclesiastical Mission had no proselytizing goals. In fact, it appears that no efforts were ever made to convert the Chinese in Manchuria to the Russian faith. But the CER was not prepared to tolerate other Christian sects. On February 18, 1901, the Catholic Vicar Apostolic of North Manchuria, Monseigneur Lalouyer, wrote to the French consul at Zhifu that the Russian authorities at Harbin had forbidden both the propagation of the faith and the provision of medical services by missionaries. Diplomatic representations in Petersburg aimed at loosening this regime proved futile. Both the doctors and the engineers of the CER found the limited medical knowledge with which the men of God attracted converts to be both an impudent affront to Science and a further barrier between the Chinese and modern medicine. Among the proponents of a Russian cultural mission in Asia, European missionaries came in for a particularly heavy dose of contempt. Prince Ukhtomskii, for example, in his book on the Boxer uprising, blamed "missionary-fanatics playing in politics" and the "defense of sham [*mnimo*] Christian but in fact direct commercial interests."[89]

By 1899–1900, enough families of CER employees had arrived to necessitate the opening of primary schools capable of accommodating 80 pupils. In the 1901 CER budget, schools and churches shared an allotment of 62,000 rubles. By 1902, each of Harbin's neighborhoods had its own school. Iugovich's request for a *progimnaziia* (middle school), described as an important aid to the recruitment of reliable, long-term employees to cultureless Manchuria, received Witte's approval in early 1900. Put on hold by the Boxer siege, this project was upgraded in 1902 into a plan for men's and women's *gimnaziia* (high schools) capable of preparing students for the entrance exams of Russian universities. The following year, in line with his plans for strengthening the Russian economic presence in China, Witte converted the all-purpose *gimnazii* into a commercial school, complete with a museum of commodity science (*tovarovedenie*) and a chemical laboratory. For the chief engineer's early emphasis on education, Iugovich scholarships were established to honor his departure from Manchuria. The dedication read: "Let your name be known to future representatives [*deiatel'*] of our region [*krai*], even as they sit on the school bench. May it serve them as an example of glorious service to the motherland and unreserved devotion to duty."[90]

Although the word motherland has patriotic connotations, the emphasis on "region" draws a clear distinction between Russia and Russian Manchuria. This ambivalence prevented patriotism from crossing over into chauvinism. Like the railroad and its churches, the CER educational institutions undertook the propagation of an "enlightened" China policy. The Pedagogical Committee considered one of its tasks as part of the "Russian cause in Manchuria . . . to inoculate the students with appropriate views regarding the Chinese by introducing the necessity of correct relations with them into the academic regulations." Although in most respects a liberal institution, abjuring corporal punishment and endorsing coeducation, the Commercial School had no tolerance for racial intolerance. In the first year of operation, 1905–6, this point was made abundantly clear by the highly publicized suspension of a student for teasing and throwing stones at Chinese. The immediate clarification of this issue was essential as the school prepared for the admittance of its first Chinese students the following year.[91]

Other auxiliary enterprises provided by the CER designed to improve the quality of daily life "in the distant borderland" included bathhouses, fire brigades, a technical extension school for employees, a hotel, a theater, and parks. On June 23, 1903 (o.s.), the *Harbin Messenger* (*Kharbinskii vestnik*) began triweekly publication under the auspices of the CER's commercial section. As its sponsorship would suggest, its primary purpose was "to support the development of commercial relations between Russia and China." The accomplishment of this task depended on several subordinate goals, including the study of Far Eastern economies in general, and "of the relationship of the CER to trade and industrial tasks of the territory it crosses" in particular.[92]

Additionally, in order to satisfy the "spiritual needs" of the local Russian population, information regarding Russia's "cultural tasks in the Far East" would be provided. The importance of correct and humanitarian personal relations for the development in Manchuria of Russia's imperial ideology was clarified by the publication in the next issue (June 25) of Iugovich's orders regarding the polite handling of all Chinese by CER agents and the appointment of Chinese police at all large stations to explain the rules of railway conduct to the Chinese public.[93] The Russians meant to show Manchuria and the world that they were not like other Europeans in China. In the process, they would draw a line between the rest of Russia and themselves.

Delusions of Grandeur: Propagated and Perceived

Because Japan's determination was soon to turn Russia's Far Eastern bravado into a bloody blunder, historians have justifiably devoted their energies to describing Russian moves in Asia as a series of miscalculations regarding Russian power and Japanese intentions. Others, considering the Russian revolutions that followed, have focused on the bankruptcy of a political system that disregarded a broad variety of domestic problems dangerously close to reaching critical mass as the state pursued an exotic imperialist adventure. In the eyes of most contemporary observers, however, the forces of the Tsar had made enormous and inexorable progress from 1896 to 1903. The 1896 defense treaty, the 1898 acquisition of ice-free Port Arthur, and the 1900 occupation of Manchuria were seen as the initial phase of a grand undertaking. The tenor of public expectations is shown by the fact that between July 1901 and April 1902, journals in Europe, Asia, and America published seventeen putative Russo-Chinese secret agreements.[94] None of these ever existed.

The well-balanced tools of this eastward drive were perceived to be cunning, brute force, and a superior understanding of the "Oriental mind." The Russian government, though disavowing the methods and the attendant Gendarme-of-Asia image, basked in the glow of its purported success. Count Cassini, who was posted to Washington after his tour in Beijing, helped to publicize the glories of Russian Manchuria (and his humble part in their making):

Through the pacific channels of diplomacy my government acquired privileges which, accepted in good faith, have been exercised in a spirit of true modern progressiveness, until now the flower of enlightened civilization blooms throughout a land that a few years ago was a wild, and in many parts a desolate, seemingly unproductive waste. Before the signing of the treaty which I had the honor to negotiate on behalf of my Sovereign, . . . no white man could have ventured into that province without danger to his life. . . . Russia built a railway into and through Manchuria. She built bridges, roads and canals. She has built cities whose rapid construction and wonderful strides in population and industry have no parallel, certainly in Europe and Asia, perhaps even in America.[95]

The argument for a special affinity was most eloquently voiced by Prince Ukhtomskii:

Asia—we have always belonged to it. We have lived its life and felt its interests. Through us the Orient has gradually arrived at a consciousness of itself, at a superior life. . . . We have nothing to conquer. All these peoples of various races feel themselves drawn to us, and are ours, by blood, by tradition, and by ideas. We simply approach them more closely. This great and mysterious Orient is ready to become ours.[96]

The key weapon in this civilizing mission was the railway. Already by 1900, the Trans-Siberian had become a myth of international proportions, attracting long queues to the Russian exhibit at the Paris World's

Fair. Visitors looked out of immobile first-class cars to see painted landscapes of Europe and Asia scrolled past them. An influential French account of developments in Northeast Asia, Leroy-Beaulieu's *La Renovation de l'Asie*, describes the Trans-Siberian as "a great work that does honor to a great country, and any other country except maybe England and America would have, without doubt, solved the problem that faced the Russians less felicitously." Henry Norman, in his preface to the first English edition of Leroy-Beaulieu's book, added: "Whether from the point of view of intercommunication, of commerce, or of diplomacy and arms, no single development so significant and so far-reaching in its consequences has occurred in the modern world."[97]

Even the Russians who knew best the drawbacks and costs of the project allowed themselves to be carried away by the Trans-Siberian's scope. The governor-General of the Priamur N. I. Grodekov compared it to the Suez Canal, and Witte labeled it "one of those world events that usher in new epochs in the history of nations."[98]

As the final leg of the line, the CER, approached completion, attention and anxieties focused more tightly on the rapidity of construction. An English visitor to Manchuria, Henry Whigham, wrote: "I do not believe there is any other instance on record of the creation of a railway system in an entirely new country of such a length in such a time; and, when the difficulties in the way of construction are considered, the execution of the great enterprise seems to belong properly to the region of fairy tales."[99]

Here the reality was as striking as the impression. The Ussuri railway, running 717 versts from Vladivostok to Khabarovsk, had taken six years to complete. Despite the one-year delay during the Boxer Rebellion and the need for repairs, the 2,400 versts of the CER were finished in the same time span. The costs had been high, but defensibly so. The key factor, as already indicated, was Chinese labor. Whereas the Ussuri branch had employed a maximum of 17,000 laborers (1897), the CER, at the height of construction, employed around 130,000.[100]

The use of cheap Chinese labor for the furtherance of Russian imperialism inspired the seemingly contradictory visions of Yellow Russia (Zheltorossiia) and Yellow Peril (Zheltaia ugroza). The first viewpoint foresaw and welcomed the creation of a Russo-Chinese ethnic reservoir dammed at the extremities by Lake Baikal and the Yellow Sea. In imitation of the right to establish manufacturing industries in China, newly granted to foreigners by article 6 of the Treaty of Shimonoseki (1895), export-oriented factories in Manchuria and Siberia could be capitalized by a Russian syndicate and run on Chinese manpower. As the CER official I. S. Levitov saw it, "with the labor of the yellow race so cheap, this step will be easy for Russia to take. Only in this way will Russia be able to enter the arena of worldwide production." The flip side of this prediction saw Chinese masses, under Japanese leadership, gradually blotting other races off the Eurasian continent. The completion of the CER, providing modern transport for Chinese outward migration, heightened a fear of the East that has been an important theme in Russian culture since the Mongol invasion.[101]

The Japanese, on their side, were well aware of the danger that an epidemic of "yellow peril fever" (*kyoonetsu*) would represent for an Asian country anticipating war with a white nation. On December 30, 1903, six weeks before the surprise attack on Port Arthur, the Japanese cabinet issued a set of "guidelines for policy toward Qing [China] and Korea in case negotiations with Russia rupture," making "the prevention of the reappearance of yellow peril fever" a high priority. After all, should France and Germany feel compelled to "intervene" on racial grounds, Japan would face a reprise of the shameful debacle of 1895.[102]

Prince Ukhtomskii, the companion, confidant, and chronicler of Nikolai during his visit to the East in 1891, simply saw these variants as two possible futures, where the Chinese would become either "the most dangerous of neighbors or the most devoted [*kovarneishii*] of subjects." Even the Japanese, he argued, "instinctively sense in us a part of that spiritual world that both mystics and pedantic scholars name vaguely as "the East." Since the "haughty" (*nadmennyi*) Europeans would inevitably reject Russia, the country must either follow its age-old calling to be "a world power linking West and East" or follow the path of "inglorious . . . decline." And for Ukhtomskii the crucial *trait d'union* between Russia and the East could be none other than unsullied Autocracy, the "White Tsar" of immemorial myth. The whole formula was given geographic specificity by calling all of Russia east of Trans-Baikalia "Our Asia." This was where the historic rapprochement would take place.[103]

This picture of a developing Russo-Chinese preserve in Manchuria was viewed with alarm in the United States. The tremors caused by the 1900 closing of the free port at Vladivostok grew more pronounced as Russian exclusionary policies took hold. On December 5, 1903, the U.S. consul at Niuzhuang, Henry Miller, reported: "The United States trade in Manchuria with the Chinese amounted to several millions of dollars per year, and was almost entirely imports. It had grown very fast, . . . before the railway construction began."[104] The threat seemed all the greater when the first results of transport on the CER suggested that the railroad would be a financial success. Since construction was still incomplete, army and railroad service loads predominated, but the remaining capacity was over-subscribed. With the beginning of regular service in July 1903, there was slight improvement. In 1903, the annual totals for civilian passengers, private freight, and total income on the CER increased by 34 percent, 51 percent, and 65 percent, respectively.[105]

The possibility of some kind of Russo-Chinese union was just as frightening for the Japanese. One point of concern was the barriers the Russian bureaucracy in Manchuria was erecting to keep Japanese residents out, although, in practice, well-placed bribes could overcome these obstacles.[106] This paled in any case next to the object of paramount dread, the railroad.

In 1890, Yamagata Aritomo, the most influential of the Japanese elder statesmen in military affairs, had formulated the twin concepts of "line of sovereignty" (*shukensen*) and "line of advantage" (*riekisen*). The latter has often been considered the theoretical underpinning of Japanese foreign policy during the next 50 years, a period characterized by a search for security through expansion. Originally Yamagata was merely contemplating the fate of Korea, laid open to Russian aggression by the completion of the Trans-Siberian railway.

In addition to inspiring this seminal doctrine, the Trans-Siberian provided a subject of passionate debate among the Japanese leaders and public over the next decade. As the railway neared completion, and Russo-Japanese relations deteriorated, the Japanese military and Foreign Ministry began to examine the new structure's carrying capacity. Japanese victory in a Manchurian conflict would be largely dependent on the Russians' inability to transport troops from Europe to Asia; growing mobility obviously decreased Japan's chances. In a very real sense, railway construction became a countdown to war.[107]

Still, for some, like the English writer Putnam Weale, the Russian success in Manchuria was no success at all. Weale made his sympathies clear by dedicating his book *Manchu and Muscovite* (originally published in 1904) "To the Gallant Japanese Nation." His conclusions that "Russian Manchuria is something of a myth made possible by gigantic bluff," and that "travellers who have no knowledge of the real Far East are responsible for the absurd tales which I every day read in the home Press," are fleshed out with withering attacks on the specifics. On a visit to Harbin, the station was a "crush," Russian engineers showed an "insensate love for open-cuts," the mattresses of Russian Manchuria had "to be seen to be believed," and the nightclubs' clients wore "the most impossible combinations of colours." Amidst the vituperation, Weale nonetheless admitted that "in the whole of Manchuria proper—excluding, of course, the leased territory—Harbin [was] the only place that [had] any importance or real significance."[108]

Harbin at the Center

Already by the summer of 1900, the Chinese had reached a similar conclusion. When hostilities with Russia began, Beijing sent the Qiqihar governor-general a telegram identifying the main target of the campaign:

> Judging by telegraph reports, Harbin lying in the heart [of North Manchuria] serves as the cause of the troubles. This place is the most vital point for the Russians, regarding which all chances of receiving additional aid are considered. Therefore, we order . . . you to find means to take Harbin either by trickery or by force.[109]

The dynamic Russian recovery from the siege of Harbin not only increased the acreage of the city but also inaugurated "the bloom of private enterprise and commercial animation in Harbin." The clearest indicator of the private sector's active and optimistic outlook on Harbin's prospects is the real estate market. The first auctions for 80-year leases of CER land (the length of the railroad concession) were held on June 9, 1902. Bidding was brisk, and the CER averaged 12,000 rubles per desiatin for lands that had been purchased from the Chinese for an average of 60. One hotly contested half-acre plot opposite the unfinished Pristan station was bid up from 783 to 7,826 rubles. By mid-1904, all of these values had "doubled and even tripled."[110]

In trying to define this boomtown at the edge of the Mongolian steppe, writers compared it to a number of cities, both Russian and foreign. Appellations derived from Russian cities were "Manchurian Petersburg" and "Moscow of Asia." Paris, Vienna, and Birmingham were the expectations of certain travelers, who, after exposure, switched metaphors to Port Said and "modern abortion." Weale, ever spiteful, suggested that Harbin might become the "Sedan of Russian Far Eastern dreams," and Charles Repington thought that an eventual victory at Harbin might have for the Japanese the same significance as the capture of Moscow for Napoleon. By 1903, Japanese diplomats had no doubt either of the importance of Harbin as the "only big city in central Manchuria."[111] The most common expectation, however, and the most durable when faced with reality, was "that Kharbin resembled one of those huge American cities that grow up in a night." "Mushroom" and "boomtown" were words that often appeared in descriptions of the city. The railroading element made Chicago a frequent reference; for some, the Sungari brought the Mississippi and St. Louis to mind.[112] Certainly, rapid growth, geographic similarities, and the frontier setting were key factors in identifying Harbin with America, but even more important were the behavioral transformations that reliable witnesses claimed were overtaking the Russians in Manchuria. The Russians, it seems, had discovered the work ethic.

In reviewing the construction period, the historian Nilus gloated that "to the amazement of foreigners, jealously following Russia's successes in China, the clumsy Russian bear unexpectedly showed itself capable of truly American tempo and work style." Further details of this metamorphosis were added by the influential American senator Albert Beveridge in *The Russian Advance*, originally serialized in the *Saturday Evening Post*. On his visit to Manchuria in 1901, the author met with key figures in Russia's newly minted Far Eastern empire and found them capable, energetic, and industrious, "very much like an ambitious young American building his fortune in one of the great cities of the United States." The CER railway administration was taking advantage of pristine conditions to "establish modern methods" and eliminate "fixed and forfeited ancient abuses." Further exposure to American and German enterprise in the Orient meant that "Russia herself [would] catch the spirit of modern things and fall in step with modern methods in her entire commercial economy, but first of all in her railway administration." But most of all, Beveridge was impressed by Witte, whose Lincoln-like eyes were "in every financial center of the world," whose perspicacity was systemizing an "almost Orientally disorganized" Russian Empire instinctively bent on world conquest. After all, had not Konstantin Pobedonostsev himself stated that "Russia is no state; Russia is a world?"[113]

All of this should be taken with a large grain of salt. The one certainty, however, is that this vision of potent transformation fueled Russian self-confidence and foreign fears. After the mushrooming of Harbin and Dal'nii, there was no reason to doubt reports in the *North China Herald* of August 28, 1903, that Russia had decided to throw up yet another city, this one on the Amur, from which to govern the Chinese Northeast. The source for this rumor was claimed to be an imperial memorial by the Mukden governor-general Zengqi.[114]

On the Russian side, the ostensible success and importance of the Far Eastern venture made present participation and future profit a plum to be coveted and fought over by the various tsarist ministries. Although all might agree with General A. N. Kuropatkin's ranking of Russian interests, in which only Korea was subordinate to Manchuria, the attractiveness of the project led to contentiousness out of all reasonable proportion. The fact that Witte's patronage made this one of the last budget items to reflect the economic downturn that had begun in 1899–1900 added bullish glamor to generally bearish financial horizons. Only in 1902 would investment in the Far East begin to taper off.[115] At a juncture when intractable social and economic problems were approaching crisis proportions, the Empire could ill afford endless rounds of interministerial bickering over a secondary matter.

Of more immediate importance, the exaggeration of the Oriental enterprise's value undermined the attempt to reach a modus vivendi with Japan.

No one wanted war, but placing limitations of any kind on Russian activity in Manchuria was anathema. Witte's fall and the rise of Admiral E. I. Alekseev were certainly the product of several political and personal dynamics within the Empire's highest circles, but the battleground on which these momentous personnel changes took place was Far Eastern policy. Interior Minister V. K. Pleve's alleged remark about Russia's need for a "short victorious war" to forestall revolution is often viewed as a callous attempt to manipulate Russian society's patriotism. This attitude certainly existed, but we must not lose sight of the fact that this planned diversion was merely the latest manifestation of an escapist trap in which all the ministers and the Tsar himself had already been floundering for years, distracted by the glory of a Far Eastern empire that was not to be.

CHAPTER 2

Interministerial Rivalry as a Way of Life

> I reminded the Sovereign of the day on which he made me
> a minister. At that time I told His Highness: "You bring me
> great tidings [*velikaia novost'*], Your Highness. You are showing
> great confidence in me, but in my heart I feel no joy. I have
> not felt that joy, Your Highness, during the difficult five and a
> half years that I have been a minister. It has been unbroken,
> laborious, nerve-racking work. Beyond the heavy load of my
> own office, much energy has gone into battles with the Grand
> Dukes and the [other] ministers...."
> The Sovereign nodded his head in agreement and said:
> "Yes, I know." —War Minister A. N. Kuropatkin, 1903

HARBIN WAS founded amid universally high expectations that would not be spoiled by either Boxers or economic recession. Many Russian ministries, aside from Witte's Finance Ministry, wanted to share in the apparent success of the Far Eastern venture and the bright prospects of the new city. What happened when they clashed, both in the capital and in Manchuria, is described in this chapter. Although the discussion is confined to the pre-1905 period, bitter interministerial conflict in fact continued right up to 1917.[1] In describing Petersburg-centered implications, I follow a line of analysis pioneered by B. A. Romanov, Andrew Malozemoff, and David McDonald, and then continue by using Russian archival materials to detail the rough-and-tumble of bureaucratic competition.

Japanese diplomatic correspondence reveals that Tokyo followed the internecine conflict closely and considered it an important predictor of chances for a negotiated settlement in Northeast Asia. To make the situation comprehensible to his superiors, the Japanese ambassador to Russia described the situation as similar to the interplay of feudal lords (daimyo) during the Tokugawa period. In August 1903, the rise of Admiral E. I. Alekseev and A. M. Bezobrazov, together with the fall of Witte and Foreign Minister V. M. Lamsdorff, was immediately interpreted as a "victory for the expansionists" (*kakuchoha no shori*). In a last-ditch effort to stave off war, Foreign Minister Komura Jutaro had transmitted Japan's draft terms to the Russians on August 3. The sudden change of personnel responsible for the negotiations left the Japanese less sanguine about the eventual outcome and less patient for results. Like the Japanese diplomatic corps, we too can shed light on the enduring mystery of how the Russians stumbled into the Russo-Japanese War by examining interministerial conflict.[2]

This approach, however, still does not allow us to penetrate to the grassroots, where the regulations hammered out by a handful were lived out *in situ* by thousands of subordinates. Chapters Three and Four will complement the "top-down" view by showing how interministerial rivalry shaped policies that, in turn, influenced Harbin's demographic composition and political identity. In reading this chapter, it should be kept in mind that most of the events described are taking place simultaneously with the railroading activities highlighted in Chapter One.

Conflicts between administrative organizations are a common bureaucratic phenomenon. In the Russian case, however, bitter decades-long struggles between entrenched institutional interests were compounded by Imperial favoritism. The Tsar was the touchstone in all policy matters, the sole recourse in carrying through unpopular programs. In the late nineteenth and early twentieth centuries, when the complexity of the state's interests and apparatus increased drastically, the last Romanov monarchs lacked the requisite leadership skills for successful management. K. P. Pobedonostsev could only advise his pupil to "*cherchez des capables*," but a further criterion, subservience, often clashed with competence. Nikolai was no judge of men. Ministerial appointments became a toss-up between talents and toadies.[3]

Since the coming of the railroad made the War and Finance ministries the key competitors in the Russian Far East, William Fuller's work *Civil-Military Conflict* provides a solid foundation for understanding the central dynamics of this opposition as it was played out along the Neva. Fuller argues persuasively that "it was military professionalism, solicitude for the army, and anxiety over military weakness which underlay the conflict." The last two concerns were particularly strong in Petersburg, where the annual battle of the budget took place. The first concern, by contrast, echoed Empire-wide, as officers discussed the army's proper role and contrasted it with actual conditions.[4]

Army commanders were particularly incensed that their men were often "borrowed" by civil departments for various policing and guarding functions. Harmful effects on regimental housekeeping, training, and esprit de corps were often cited. War Minister P. S. Vannovskii wrote: "While I recognize the necessity of using troops to suppress disorders, I will never agree to their use in a police capacity or to their subordination to policemen."[5] This emphasis on the chain of command suggests the presence of what Fuller calls "institutional imperialism: the belief that the soldiers belonged to the army and that the army should therefore fully control what was done with them."[6]

The most widely spread and "hotly detested" transfers were to guard duty. Complaints came from "every district headquarters in the Empire." Many of them were directed at the so-called Separate Corps of Frontier Guards, which not only "borrowed" enlisted men, but also "stole" officers with the lure of higher pay. That is exactly what the CER's Protective Guard did, starting in 1898. And the practice continued when, in 1901, that military unit was shifted to the Finance Ministry's control as the Trans-Amur District of the Frontier Guard. The controversy regarding the defense of the CER was thus more than a question of Far Eastern policy; it was a point of tension between civil and military throughout the Empire. Fuller has also pointed out that by the beginning of the twentieth century, the army was "willing to assume all the responsibility, or none of it."* After five years of split authority and accompanying strains, the 1903 subordination of the Priamur governor-generalship, the CER, and the Guandong Leasehold to the Viceroyalty of the Far East would finally give the local military forces carte blanche in the region.

A close examination of the 1897 seizure and 1898 lease of the Liaodong peninsula allows us to evaluate the seminal work of B. A. Romanov. His central contention that Witte's policy of "peaceful penetration" was just as aggressive as the plans of the military and Bezobrazov factions stands up well. In large part, the seeming clarity of this dichotomy turns out to be a web of lies and half-truths with which Witte and his publicists endeavored to fend off blame for the Russo-Japanese War.

Additionally, Witte, like other European leaders, operated in an international psychological environment peculiar to the heyday of imperialism. Pragmatism strengthened with vague strains of Social Darwinism rationalized enormous rapacity. The rise of such technologies as the railroad, telegraph, and telephone produced an illusion of long-distance control. The reality was just the opposite: local leaders commanding massive dis-

---

*Fuller, *Civil-Military Conflict*, p. 104. It is probably not coincidental that some prominent proponents of increased military professionalism had extremely abrasive experiences as members of the CER guard's officer corps. Both the future Octobrist A. I. Guchkov and the Transamur border guard commander E. I. Martynov were recalled from service in Manchuria, Guchkov after challenging Harbin's town architect to a duel, and Martynov after accusing the CER general manager of high treason. Nilus, *Istoricheskii obzor*, p. 507; Khorvat "Memoirs," chap. 2, p. 11. All the same, the creation of the viceroyalty was not a victory for the War Ministry, which found itself excluded from decision making on Far Eastern policy. Deep unhappiness over that policy provoked the exchange between Kuropatkin and the Tsar quoted in the epigraph to this chapter.

cretionary power. Though Ukhtomskii might consider it inappropriate "to fear distances," putting his faith in the "hourly accomplishment of new discoveries and perfections [in technology]," the primitiveness of administrative structures on the periphery encouraged the power-hungry to think in terms of miniature kingdoms.[7] In Northeast Asia, Witte, Alekseev, and Kerbedz all succumbed to this tempting vision.

Where the three parted was on methods. For example, regarding the all-important question of how to protect Russian interests in Manchuria without incurring international censure and diplomatic isolation, Lamsdorff and Witte were prepared to fulfill Russia's obligation to evacuate regular troops after establishing "a defensive system against which no political objections could be raised and after enveloping the area in a network of influences that would make Russia absolute mistress [of the situation]." The army of occupation would be replaced "by a kind of militia that, as frontier guards of the Finance Ministry, would be no less than an army of occupation made up of activated army reserves [*réserves actives de l'armée*]." The French ambassador, Count de Montebello, to whom these remarks were addressed in March 1901, could rest assured that the Russian ally would take care to avoid potential casus belli. The accretion in the Finance Ministry's Manchurian role had simply been worked into the diplomatic solution.[8]

Two weeks earlier, Admiral Alekseev had written to War Minister Kuropatkin suggesting a completely different approach to the problem.

In recognizing our agreement with China concerning the construction of the Manchurian Railway, they [foreign powers] recognized our right to defend this [railway] with the means most suitable for it. The actual manner of defense, *i.e.*, the replacement of the [CER] guard by [regular] troops, is an internal matter, a military-technical [matter] so to speak, which cannot arouse serious objections.[9]

Here we already see characteristics of Alekseev's diplomatic efforts as viceroy in 1903. One is the confusion of internal and international spheres. The other is a complete disregard for (or ignorance of) the finely tuned usages of nineteenth-century European diplomacy. Immediate questions of local control predominate over larger *Weltpolitik* perspectives. Although from a more general analytical standpoint these two options are equally grasping so far as China is concerned, Romanov overstates his case when he equates the effects.[10] Mixed signals before the creation of the viceroyalty and Alekseev's unstatesmanlike negotiating style thereafter quickly convinced the Japanese that for their immediate needs, diplomacy offered only dead ends.

The Tsar, His Ministers, and Far Eastern Policy

From the very beginning of his reign, Nikolai had been uncomfortable with his ministers. On his accession in 1894, he is said to have told his cousin, the Grand Duke Aleksandr Mikhailovich: "I am not prepared to be a Czar. I never wanted to become one. I know nothing of the business of ruling. I have no idea of even how to talk to ministers." This attitude appears to have continued unabated throughout Nikolai's reign. In August 1903, in a moment of candor, the Tsar admitted to War Minister Kuropatkin that, "although it might seem strange, . . . psychologically," he would have greater confidence in Kuropatkin as a general than as a minister.[11]

In greater or lesser degree, all ministers suffered from Nikolai's lack of trust. In this, as in so many other respects, Witte's prominence made him first among equals.* During his tenure as Finance Minister from 1892 to 1903, Witte amassed an ever-widening circle of activities. Theodore Von Laue, a sympathetic biographer, explains this expansion:

> By the nature of his [Witte's] "system," . . . he could not accept a clear-cut boundary between domestic and foreign policy, between economics and politics. The logic of industrialization required that all government activities be directed toward this central goal. Thus the Minister of Finance was driven to trespass upon the domain of the Minister of Foreign Affairs. This, of course, was incompatible with the essence of autocracy. Every minister was supposed to stay within his jurisdiction and leave the central direction of affairs to the Tsar. As Nikolai, however, did not provide such leadership, his ministers were increasingly engaged in a wrangle for ascendancy. By virtue of his office (not to mention his temperament) Witte was fighting in the midst of it, and not always by fair means.[12]

Throughout the 1890's, as the Trans-Siberian extended ever farther eastward, so did Witte's influence.

The creation of the CER inaugurated the terminal stages of both the Trans-Siberian and Witte's power. Clause 28 of the CER statutes reveals the basis on which the Finance Ministry formally crossed into Manchuria. It seems that Witte's creation, the Russo-Chinese Bank, had "refused" to administer the railway company unless it was subordinate to Finance. Witte, modestly took up this new responsibility with a long but carefully qualified sentence:

> Although the very varied and complicated affairs now under the Finance Ministry's direction, and the new extent and always growing activity [of the ministry],

---

*The special rancor Nikolai harbored for Witte comes across clearly: "I have never seen such a chameleon, a man of such changeable convictions. . . . Because of that almost no one trusts him any longer; he has finally undone himself in everyone's eyes, except perhaps for the foreign Yids." Nicholas II, *Secret Letters*, p. 211.

are a considerable burden for the Finance Minister and do not correspond entirely to his views, in light of [the bank's stance], State Secretary Witte does not consider it possible to oppose the growth in Finance Ministry activity, if the Trans-Siberian Railway Committee considers this indispensable.

Since the Finance Minister was the dominant voice on the committee, as well as in the bank, it is hard to take his disclaimers seriously. Witte chose his own path.[13]

At the end of the path waited the Manchurian imbroglio and the Finance Minister's downfall. On August 29, 1903, two weeks after the establishment of the viceroyalty, Witte was shifted to a largely ceremonial job, chairman of the Committee of Ministers, and worse still, from his point of view, asked to help out in "dismembering" the Finance Ministry. (In a pun on the names of the Finance Minister's most implacable enemies, Witte was said to have left office "spit upon and disfigured" [*oplevannyi i obezobrazhennyi*].) The CER and the frontier guard were two institutions that the Tsar immediately proposed to move elsewhere. In his diary entry for that day, Nikolai wrote, "Now I rule."[14]

When ministerial opinions and vested interests collided, the sovereign was forced to choose among them, a mental effort that he himself thought sufficient "to make a horse bolt."[15] Nikolai's distaste for interministerial rivalry makes research along these lines real detective work. Post-1917 memoirs are painfully biased. Contemporaries, fearing the Tsar's annoyance, often denied or played down such conflicts. Fortunately, the phenomenon was too ubiquitous and ran too deep to be completely covered up.

Civil-military tensions in the Far East had already caught Nikolai's attention by the mid-1890's. On Khorvat's appointment as manager of the Ussuri railway in 1895, he had been granted an Imperial audience at which the Tsar had commanded him to "set in order the relations between the local civil and military elements that, as was often the case in Russia, left much to be desired." As general manager of the CER from 1903 to 1920, Khorvat would have ample opportunity to observe this phenomenon. Similarly, Alekseev's appointment to the Far East in 1899 was originally viewed as a means of "ending daily discord between the governors of the principal ports in these parts, . . . Port Arthur and Dalien [Dal'nii]."[16]

On March 1, 1903, the Tsar told Kuropatkin that he found the situation in the Far East "alarming, not so much on account of the Japanese, as because of the local discord [*rozn'*] between the representatives of financial and military organs." In April, at a conference attended by all the principals in Far Eastern policy, Nikolai suggested "uniting all the functions of state authority in the East in order to put an end to the existing painful dissension between department representatives." Kuropatkin, Lamsdorff, and Witte immediately assured the Tsar that "differences of opinion" among them were never "expressed in the form of lack of coordination between departments" since they always acted "by the direct instructions" and "under the immediate guidance" of the Tsar himself.[17] It is difficult to believe that Nikolai found these protestations very convincing. The thread of autocratic thought that would lead to the creation of the viceroyalty four months later had already begun to unravel.

On December 16, 1896, the chairman of the Department of State Economy, D. M. Sol'skii, addressed a special ceremonial meeting of the Trans-Siberian Railway Committee held at Tsarskoe Selo with the Tsar in attendance. The occasion was the throne's approval of the CER company charter. Chairman Sol'skii lauded Nikolai in no uncertain terms:

> Your Imperial Highness's mighty personal influence, together with Your strong, yet kind and approving word, impelled China to submit to Russia's demands. Thus, it is directly to You Sire that the Fatherland will owe the completion of an enterprise that at once testifies to its [the fatherland's] present strength and serves to guarantee its great future.[18]

Bureaucratic competition between aspiring mouthpieces of this unitary Imperial "word" soon imperiled Russia's Asian projects. The war that followed revealed its true military and economic weakness, social discord on a grand scale, and a most foreboding glimpse of the future.

Civilian and Military in the Russian Far East

Until the late nineteenth century, most of Siberia was little more than an armed camp, where military personnel and methods kept a tenuous grip on vast expanses of wilderness. Since communications to and from St. Petersburg took months, governor-generals wielded broad discretionary powers encompassing activities delegated to different specialized organs in European Russia. Because these Siberian satraps commanded the army units in their purview, they were of necessity all military men with field experience.*

After 1882, part of western Siberia was absorbed into the civil administrative structure of European Russia. The rest was incorporated into a new unit, the Governor-Generalship of the Steppe, embracing the area southward from Omsk as far as Lake Balkhash. It too was civilly adminis-

---

*The Russian word for governor-general, *general-gubernator*, has shades of meaning slightly different from its English equivalent. In English, the "general" refers to a breadth of function, often encompassing the jurisdictions of subordinate governors or lieutenant-governors. In Russian, a stronger hint of military rank is present. Both Ushakov's and the Soviet Academy of Sciences' dictionaries (but not Dal') use the word "*voenno-administrativnyi*" to describe the *general-gubernator*'s role. Fuller, *Civil-Military Conflict*, p. xxii, points out that vast territories in the Caucasus and Central Asia were under direct military rule as well.

tered. The Governor-Generalship of East Siberia, however, with its seat in Irkutsk, remained a largely military affair. The Priamur Governor-Generalship, removed from Irkutsk's jurisdiction in 1884, was even more so. Greater distance from Petersburg worked in favor of broader local powers; and the increasing possibility of armed conflict with either China or Japan favored militarization.[19]

This is not to say that civil tasks were neglected. Rather, they were analyzed and rationalized in terms of strategic goals. For example, Governor-General N. N. Murav'ev's positioning of the newly formed Trans-Baikal Cossack Brigade into settlements along the Amur and Ussuri rivers had a triple thrust. First of all, these armed villages, of which there were over 100 by 1861, became by their very presence a border guard. Second, by planting them twelve to eighteen miles apart, a line of communication was established running all the way to the Pacific coast. Regular, if seasonally dependent, civilian postal service began at about the same time. Finally, local agriculture was intended to provision Russian forces downriver, in particular, the Pacific Fleet Headquarters in Nikolaevsk-na-Amure. Unfortunately, the even distribution along the border, necessary for both frontier defense and communications, did not always correspond to soil fertility or flood-free locations. The result was the failure of autarkic provisioning and local hardship on a grand scale.[20]

Although existence within the constraints of strategic thinking could be burdensome for the local population, in the Far East most of the inhabitants were used to life by *diktat*. Until the 1880's, the majority of Russians in the Amur and Maritime provinces were subject to military rule, either as Cossacks or as regular troops; and many of the permanent settlers were retired reservists, who might be called to arms at any time. The tendency to see regional demographic requirements through a strategic prism continued into the twentieth century. In 1901, the fallout from the Boxer uprising included a plan to quadruple the Amur Cossack population and sextuple their Ussuri counterparts.[21]

Into this zone of garrison towns and Cossack settlements came the railroad, bringing with it an alternative to the military monolith. The opening of the Suez Canal (1869), the declaration of the Vladivostok free port (1872), the establishment of regular service from Odessa to Vladivostok by the Volunteer Fleet (1879), and the Amur "gold rush" of the late 1880's had already given civilians a greater part in the population and vital affairs of the Russian Far East. Nonetheless, it was the Tsarevich Nikolai's ceremonial shovelful on the Ussuri railway in 1891 that heralded irreversible change and divided authority.

On March 29, 1891, Alexander III forwarded a rescript to his son, Nikolai, who was traveling in Japan. In this letter, the Tsar described royal participation at the Ussuri railway groundbreaking ceremonies as "a further proof of my sincere efforts to ease communication between Siberia and other parts of the Empire [and] to show this region, so near to my heart, my lively concern for its peaceful prosperity." On June 5, the Minister of Communications, A. I. Giubbenet, announced his joy at being the executor of "such a great structure" and called on his subordinates to push their "knowledge, zeal, and energy" to the limit "for the sake of overcoming the difficulties presented not only by the vastness of the task, but also by the hardships of a distant and sparsely populated region." For the Petersburg planners, the Far East was part of the problem and would be treated as such.[22]

Whatever undesired administrative changes the railroad might bring, there could not be any question of opposing its expansion. The Siberian military authorities were responsible for defending the Empire's eastern borders, and, in the long run, this could only be accomplished by a rail connection to the west, where the main forces of the Russian army were located. Even worse, areas that had little or no rail service were condemned to stagnation. The great Siberian metropolis of Tomsk quickly sank to the second tier when by-passed by the trunkline. It was rumored that municipal leaders had haughtily refused the surveyors' requests for payoffs.[23] Likewise, the upper and middle stretches of the Amur languished for an additional fifteen years when the decision was made to lay the transcontinental tracks across Manchuria.

Thus, in his 1896 recommendation to the throne, the Priamur governor-general, S. M. Dukhovskoi, argued against the Manchurian route, not only as a strategic error, but also as a setback to development along the Amur:

It will be an extremely heavy blow for the Priamur if the ray of light that shone upon it is extinguished. Colonization, gold mining, and the powerful rise of Russian life will all suffer a reverse.... Will it not be a historic error to continue the Great Siberian Railway for two thousand versts through a region that will long be foreign to us?

At this point, the Imperial reader penned "No" in the margin, and that was that. Furthermore, Dukhovskoi, afraid that his opinions would not even be taken into consideration, cited the necessity of his office's cooperation to complete whichever of the two routes was chosen in requesting "access to all discussions" of this matter.[24] All of his successors would have ample opportunity to complain of other ministries ignoring or outflanking the governor-general's office while operating in the Far East.

Two years later, in his report for 1896–97, Dukhovskoi was already searching for a way to moderate the administrative side-effects of railroad construction by the CER. First, he noted that recent developments had "multiplied our contacts with Manchuria." In 1896, 4,000,000 poods of grain and 40,000 head of cattle had been imported into the Priamur. The Far Eastern Military District's mobilization in 1895 and the ban on livestock export imposed by Chinese officials in 1897 had highlighted the Russian Far East's increasing dependence on border trade. Soldiers and railroad laborers could not be provisioned in any other way. Workers, both Russian and Chinese, were also flowing freely back and forth across the Amur and Ussuri.

These new ties, Dukhovskoi continued, needed "constant regulation." To this end, he suggested the establishment of "a special organ for all trade and administrative questions related to the [CER] construction." Dukhovskoi noted that he had already sent memorandums to the Foreign Ministry and the War Ministry explaining the diplomatic and military advantages of this scheme (but he apparently did not broach the subject with the Finance Ministry, which almost certainly would have rejected the plan as an unnecessary dilution of CER authority). In conclusion, the governor-general wrote, "now the whole life of the Priamur senses the approach of a turning point and awaits an indication of the new direction."[25]

Bureaucratic Infighting and Russian Diplomacy, 1897-99

In 1897, civil-military tensions made their debut in Manchuria proper. There, in contrast to Siberia, the railroad and its Finance Ministry backers arrived first. The 1896 Russo-Chinese defense treaty and CER construction contract provided the legal basis for the civilian presence. As one would expect, the embryo of local civil-military conflict was conceived in a Petersburg rivalry. Surprisingly, it was neither the army nor the navy that rose to contest Witte's monopoly in Manchuria. Instead, it was the Foreign Ministry, under M. N. Murav'ev, that by-passed Finance in making the "next step," expanding Russian influence from North to South Manchuria. The lease of Port Arthur would provide the military with an ice-free port, a beachhead in China, and a base for civil-military conflict throughout Manchuria.

Witte had tried to preempt any such move. At the February 1897 CER board meeting, where Kerbedz had pushed for a branch line to the Yellow Sea, P. M. Romanov, the "director of the chancellery of the minister of finance [later assistant minister], a man who, as Witte's closest collaborator, knew all of the ministry's intrigue in the Far East from the ground up, a member of the boards of the Chinese Eastern Railway Company and of the Russo-Chinese bank,"[26] announced that exactly this issue had been on the agenda during the Witte-Li negotiations in May 1896. However, no agreement had been reached.

Again, in the summer of 1897, Prince E. E. Ukhtomskii, chairman of the Russo-Chinese Bank, had broached the topic during a visit to Beijing. The

Chinese reception was decidedly chilly. This initiative had been taken after Murav'ev had returned from Copenhagen to take up his ministerial duties, and there is strong evidence that Witte misled him regarding the goals of the Ukhtomskii mission. When confronted by Murav'ev with the failure of the approach and the detrimental consequences that had followed, Witte provided weak rationalizations, which ultimately boiled down to the claim that he had merely been executing the Tsar's instructions.[27]

Murav'ev would soon have his revenge. On November 26, 1897, a ministerial conference was called to discuss a memorandum he had penned, the gist of which was to urge the immediate occupation of Port Arthur as a counterbalance to the German landing at Jiaozhou in China's Shandong province. The head of the Naval Department, Admiral P. P. Tyrtov, pronounced himself against the move: he believed that a location on the Korean coast would be more suitable for Russia's needs; and that the future would offer another chance to take an ice-free port. War Minister Vannovskii deferred to his naval colleague. Witte argued in several different directions, but the thrust of his arguments was that outright seizure was not the optimal method. Instead, "economic interests" could persuade the Chinese to cede a port without compromising the useful cover story of Sino-Russian friendship. Witte was satisfied that he had made his case when the conference concluded with a decision against occupation.[28]

A few days later, the Tsar overruled the decision and ordered the Pacific Fleet into Port Arthur.* According to Witte's memoirs, this fateful change of mind was abetted by Murav'ev, who fed Nikolai rumors that the British fleet was about to snatch the prize. Murav'ev, Witte claimed, was "jealous of Lobanov-Rostovsky's success" negotiating the treaty with China in 1896. Earlier in his memoirs, though, Witte discounted Lobanov's role by scoffing at the late Minister of Foreign Affairs' total ignorance of the Far East and so, in effect credited himself with the 1896 coup.[29]

The historian B. A. Romanov, noting the tug-of-war between Witte and Murav'ev, comments sardonically:

Witte was so far unreconciled to this intrusion of the Russian empire's minister of foreign affairs into the sphere of its foreign policy in the Far East that he could see nothing besides unscrupulous self-seeking on Muravev's part in the discord that had arisen. In this sphere of purely personal attitudes Witte now got back from

---

*The Tsar was quite pleased with himself, writing to the Dowager Empress on March 30, 1898, as follows: "Of course you already know, dear Mama, the glad news of the occupation of Port Arthur, which in time will be the terminus of the Siberian railway. At last we shall have a real port that does not freeze like Libau. Wladivostok unfortunately is frozen for three months each year. Above all I am thankful that this occupation was peaceful, without the loss of any Russian blood! This gives me real joy. . . . Now we can feel safe out there for a long time!" Nicholas II, *Secret Letters*, p. 130.

Muravev as good as he had given in the spring of that year [Ukhtomskii's mission]: the next move in Manchuria, then unsuccessfully made by Witte behind Muravev's back, had now been made by Muravev behind Witte's back.[30]

Persistence, however, was one of Witte's strong points. When the Chinese came looking for a loan to pay off the Japanese indemnity, he was ready with conditions that went far beyond the securing of an ice-free port and rail access to it. Chinese acceptance would have spelled Russian railway and industrial monopolies in both Manchuria and Mongolia. Had Witte carried off this coup under peaceful guise, the Finance Ministry might well have reestablished its predominance in Far Eastern affairs. The Chinese, however, panicked, and English bankers arranged the loan.

Still lagging a few weeks behind German initiatives, the Russian Foreign Ministry regularized the Empire's fait accompli possession by signing a lease for the whole Liaodong peninsula on March 27, 1898. Witte, out of options, fell into step with the other ministers. His official reaction to the final settlement was to rejoice "like any Russian," although in his memoirs, he claims that he went along with this policy error only in an attempt to soften its disastrous consequences. Murav'ev also tried to paper over the rift with Finance by expressing "heartfelt gratitude" for the "invaluable sympathy and cooperation without which it would not have been possible to bring to a favorable issue so difficult a matter."[31]

Nonetheless, the damage was done. Witte's hopes for exclusive control of Far Eastern affairs had been dashed. Despite strong rearguard action by the Finance Ministry, diplomatic moves initiated in 1898 by Murav'ev made concessions to Japan and then England, largely at the expense of Witte-controlled enterprises. Article 3 of the Nishi-Rosen agreement signed on April 25, 1898, recognized the primacy of Japanese commercial and industrial activity in Korea. These were the very spheres that the Finance Ministry had counted on in its plan for economic penetration. In anticipation of that step, Witte had positioned his own nominee as the financial adviser to the Korean throne. This arrangement was now annulled, even though Witte claimed that the step would be "detrimental to Russia's prestige in the Far East." The Russo-Korean Bank, a structure analogous to the Russo-Chinese Bank right down to their interlocking directorates, folded after four months of existence. Its Seoul branch had only been open for seven weeks.[32]

A year later, in a Russo-British agreement and "supplementary note" signed on April 28, 1899, the Russian government committed itself to refrain from soliciting railroad concessions in Britain's sphere of influence, the Yangtse (Changjiang) Valley. The only potential Russian competitor, of course, was the Russo-Chinese Bank, firmly under Witte's control. Interministerial strife over the issue had stalled the agreement for nine months and was visible enough for the British ambassador to Russia, Sir Charles Scott, to note that the crux of the matter was the relationship between the bank and the Russian government. In a complicated three-sided compromise, Murav'ev had his way in the matter.[33] By 1899, it had become clear that Witte's grandiose plans for Russia in the Far East would be played out on a more limited stage, Manchuria.[34] To make matters worse from his point of view, the Finance Ministry and its "private" commercial offspring no longer had sole control of even this arena. Ever since the disembarkation at Port Arthur on March 27, 1898, Russian Manchuria had become a very contentious place.

If we keep in mind that the diplomatic agreements with Japan and Britain were considered necessary to consolidate the Port Arthur seizure, it becomes clear why Witte so vehemently opposed that move under auspices other than his own. Russia's sharpest political infighter was fully aware that both the maintenance of his personal position and the successful realization of his policies were largely dependent on his ability to win out over his fellow ministers. Defeat on one issue could undermine a whole series of related positions. Thus, for Witte, losses in Korea and South China rapidly followed his defeat over Port Arthur. In an institutional setting where all depended on the Tsar's vacillating favor, a catastrophic drop in prestige set off by secondary matters could quickly destroy a career. In analyzing policy formulation in such a system, the rational examination of substantive issues is often insufficient to produce an explanation.

Witte's desire to have the Finance Ministry as the sole agent of Russian policy in Manchuria solves another riddle that has puzzled historians who have paid no heed to the internal dynamics of Russian government in their analysis of Far Eastern events. In discussing the Finance Minister's negotiations in 1896, Romanov states: "If Witte's testimony is to be trusted, the only hitch in his negotiations with Li Hung-zhang—though he did not regard it as such, and took every precaution to render it fictitious in actuality—was his inability to obtain the railway concession in the name of the Russian government directly." Nowhere does Romanov elaborate why the de jure private status of the CER was favorable to Witte.[35]

Interministerial rivalry is the key to that question. Again and again, Witte staved off his colleagues' competitive initiatives by flashing the bogey of international repercussions that might attend formal Russian government meddling in Manchuria. This argument also worked in reverse against criticism by foreign powers. The Russian government could disavow CER actions as private in nature. Witte did not consider the arrangements a "hitch" because they provided a beneficial legal framework for avoiding the pitfalls of interministerial life. With his background in the private sphere, we might even suspect that Witte had angled for just such a result.

Rivalry at the Local Level: The Birth of Dal'nii

As Witte maneuvered to keep his prerogatives from being curtailed in Petersburg, his CER subordinates had their hands full trying to contain the expansive efforts of the newly arrived military forces. In the first instance, this shaped up as a battle for control of Dal'nii.[36] In April 1898, when the CER company's ranking official in Manchuria, Kerbedz, arrived in Port Arthur, he was laboring under the impression that both commercial and military vessels under the Russian flag would make use of the port. Rear-Admiral F. N. Dubasov, the commanding officer of the Russian Pacific Fleet, was quick to disabuse him of that idea: the military rejected the notion of a mixed port for fear of "inconveniences and constraints." Together with Iugovich, Kerbedz then proceeded to scout out the shoreline of Dalian Gulf for other likely spots. On May 29, they wired the Ministry of Finance that the portion of Victoria Bay known as Horse Anchorage appeared to be the best choice. A sixteen-verst rail branch could connect the port with the projected location of the Harbin–Port Arthur trunkline. Five days later, Rear-Admiral Dubasov and his staff made a personal inspection and approved the site. Within the week, Witte had obtained an Imperial order awarding the construction of the new port to CER, Inc. On June 24, the exploitation of Dal'nii, upon completion, was also promised to the CER. In order to handle the transport of building materials to the new site, the CER was permitted to establish a seagoing fleet. Witte was commanded to inform the Foreign and War ministries of these arrangements. In effect, this announcement would be a declaration of interministerial war.[37]

On August 26, 1898, Minister of War Kuropatkin wrote to Witte suggesting that the whole leasehold, including Dal'nii, should be under the military. What basis could there be for a CER presence? P. M. Romanov replied tersely that it was necessary. In any case, he added, the Siberian Railway Committee would soon take up the question. Witte, when asked, was more informative. In order to attract Asia-Europe trade from the Suez and Trans-American routes, the Trans-Siberian had to be exploited rationally, even perfectly. Only the joint management of the natural economic ties between the CER and its endpoint port, Dal'nii, could deliver that result.[38]

Clearly, this answer did not satisfy Kuropatkin, since another suggestion from the War Minister followed on October 18, 1898. Would it be possible to organize a joint committee similar to the one used to administer Vladivostok's commercial port? Witte's response was effectively no.

In Vladivostok, he pointed out, the opinions and needs of the Ministry of Communications, Volunteer Shipping Fleet, the city, and the CER had to be harmonized. So far, Dal'nii was a vacuum, but the Ministry of Finance would, of course, be attentive to the future needs of other departments.

General Kuropatkin was still not happy. On February 8, 1899, the Siberian Railway Committee met, and the question of Dal'nii's affiliation floated up again. This time, the War Minister stated that he merely wanted to make sure that Dal'nii would be subject to the general rules and regulations of the leasehold, that is, under the military. Certain statements made by the Finance Minister suggested that the new city had a special status. This point of view could lead to "misunderstandings and conflicts between various authorities." Besides, the main port of a region should be subordinate to that region's chief leader. Witte replied with more empty assurances of his solicitude for the army's needs, and the committee as a whole, a bastion of Witte strength, noted that only Dal'nii's construction and exploitation were on the agenda at present. Long-term administrative arrangements would be discussed elsewhere.

In fact the jurisdictional fault lines Kuropatkin had predicted had already begun to sully the pristine map of Russian Manchuria. On July 13, 1898, General Volkov, the officer in charge of billeting at Port Arthur, wrote to the Russo-Chinese Bank claiming that the bank's local branch was taking up too much space. He had already reduced the living quarters of some of the bank's merchant sub-lessees, he announced, and he might now have to confiscate some of the land occupied by the bank as well. The Russo-Chinese Bank replied that its complaint at this arbitrary behavior had already been forwarded to the Finance Ministry.[39]

Up in North Manchuria, CER predominance gave ample opportunity for retaliation. On September 19, 1898, the War Ministry asked Witte if the CER would help set up a land mail service from the Priamur to Port Arthur via Harbin. A month later, the CER replied that it was too busy; such distractions would slow the progress of railway construction. No direct communications between Port Arthur and Harbin were established until May 1899, when telegraph facilities were completed. The CER did, however, find enough manpower and funds for a "pony express" run, to pick up employee mail in Vladivostok.[40]

In the middle of this sniping, the CER company carried on with its development of Dal'nii. V. V. Sakharov, the engineer who had built the Vladivostok commercial port, was appointed to head the project. Nominally, he was Iugovich's subordinate, but the chief engineer's already excessive burdens, Dal'nii's distance from Harbin, and the lack of communications guaranteed Sakharov virtual autonomy. His main link to Petersburg was Kerbedz, who visited South Manchuria five times during the construction period. As a military engineer, his chances of maintaining good-neighborliness with Port Arthur were somewhat improved. By May 1899, a Ministry of Finance report boasted that Dal'nii "had been gifted with everything necessary for quickly becoming one of the most important points in world trade." The CER was no less kind than nature. In four years, almost 20,000,000 rubles were invested.[41]

Like Harbin, the CER, and the whole Russian presence in Manchuria, Dal'nii made a positive impression on most foreign observers. On October 30, 1902, the French ambassador to Russia, Bompard, wrote to the Foreign Minister, Théophile Delcassé, breathlessly evoking a Britannic nightmare: "What is Dalny becoming, this great commercial port and large American-style city, head of the line for all the Asia traffic on the seas of China, this port that the Russians wish to make so considerable that Hong Kong will be deserted?"[42]

The army viewed these grand developments and grandiose designs askance. On April 26, 1902, a War Ministry representative on the Siberian Railway Committee, Ivan Ivanovich Chevalier de la Serre, bemoaned the imbalance in the government's spending patterns:

Even in Dal'nii's neighbor, Port Arthur, for lack of credit, the War Ministry must strongly limit its needs and postpone completion of works for many years to come.... What is more important there? Dal'nii's future is hazy; its value for Russia is problematic. The role of Port Arthur is completely defined. The very existence of Dal'nii depends on the strength of our position in Manchuria, and in particular on the completeness and strength of Port Arthur.[43]

In fact, so bright did Dal'nii's prospects appear that Kerbedz conceived the idea of transferring CER operational headquarters from Harbin to the new port. In early 1902, he submitted a proposal to unite the CER railway, port, and steamship operations under a director-in-chief (*glavnyi direktor*). This official would exercise broad local powers through a twelve-section chancellery. The director's seat would be Dal'nii. Part of the proposed geographic redistribution would involve moving the CER workshops from Harbin. Iugovich immediately condemned the move as unsound railroading. Harbin's geographic position as a railway hub was far superior to Dal'nii's.

Put forward at a March 5, 1902, CER board meeting, Kerbedz's proposal found favor with neither the directors nor Witte. In fact, dissatisfaction with the secretive and high-handed way in which the vice-chairman had been handling affairs on the local level had already prompted the appointment of an accounting commission under I. I. Khodorovskii. No wrongdoings were discovered, but Kerbedz's lack of economy and "absolutism" (*samovlastnost'*) came under attack. This final plan, which could easily be interpreted as an attempt to carve out a small personal kingdom with its capital at Dal'nii, was the last straw. Within a few months, Kerbedz was replaced by A. N. Venttsel, a less ambitious man.[44]

Harbin Between Civilian and Military

The concern for Dal'nii momentarily overshadowed Harbin's development. But the CER was all the while busily cultivating the forces that, it was hoped, would prevent the army from expanding its influence into the company's north Manchurian redoubt. The defense treaty of 1896 had specifically stated that, in peacetime, Russian troops would have the right of transit across Manchuria "with stops allowed only for reasons associated with the needs of the transport service." Clause 5 of the CER construction contract further stipulated that the Chinese government would "take measures to ensure the security of the Railway and its personnel against any and all attack." Nonetheless, the CER put its own construction on the "absolute and exclusive right of administration over its lands" vouchsafed by Article 6 of its own statutes to draw a distinction between the Chinese task of ensuring protection from "extraneous attacks" and policing functions handled by Russian armed agents within the right-of-way. Witte's "explanatory notes" to the statutes claim that this distinction was based on the practices of foreign settlements in China.[45]

On May 22, 1897, the CER board approved the formation of a protective guard (*okhrannaia strazha*), whose men would be hired members of the army reserve. After a commission chaired by P. M. Romanov had met with War Ministry representatives, the potential service pool was extended to regular army officers and Cossacks. In addition, the army agreed to provide weapons, to continue "service rights" for men serving in the guard, and to free them from mobilizations and other military duties. The next month saw an agreement on the guard's subordination to the Maritime military court and provisions for reintegrating officers into the regular army after their tour with the guard had ended. (These two arrangements were based on rules promulgated in 1880 during the Russian tutelage of the Bulgarian army.) A final report was composed by War Minister Vannovskii and approved by the Tsar on July 22, 1897.[46]

Colonel A. A. Gerngross was transferred from the Transcaspian Military District to head the new unit and ordered to recruit thirteen additional officers and a veterinarian. Infantry was also drawn from Gerngross's old unit. Together with Cossack cavalry from the Kuban, Orenburg, and Tersk detachments, five squadrons (*sotnia*) totaling 720 men were formed. On November 14, 1897, they departed from Odessa for Vladivostok aboard the Volunteer Fleet's *Voronezh*. By this date, the board had already decided to send a further contingent of ten squadrons; they left Odessa aboard the French transport *Les Alpes* on April 20, 1898.[47]

Right from the start, these forces were placed at the disposal of Iugovich, a man without military qualifications. He, in turn, had to answer to Kerbedz and Witte, both equally ignorant in the ways of war. Even at peace, misunderstandings were inevitable. For example, in addition to the protection, escort, reconnaissance, pony express (*letuchaia pochta*), and police duties originally assigned to the guard, Kerbedz wished to include day labor. After considerable confusion and disagreement, this practice was discontinued as harmful to military discipline and to the chain of command. In Manchuria no less than in European Russia, the officer-elites greatly resented nonmartial tasks. The guard would continue police duties until June 14, 1904, when the gendarmerie, subordinate to the Interior Ministry, took advantage of the war to make a belated appearance in Harbin.[48]

One sore point for officer and trooper alike was their new uniforms. It was not a matter of the outfit in general, which was basically identical to the uniform of the Empire's border guards, except for the color of the trim on the buttonholes, piping, and sheepskin hats—yellow instead of green. (The choice of color may have been an oblique reference to the guard's role as affiliates of Zheltorossiia, Yellow Russia.) What angered the officers was the lack of epaulettes. Although mere straps as shoulder decoration made immediate recognition of rank a little more difficult, the truly embarrassing moments occurred when the guard officers were on leave. Within the Empire, their unfamiliar outfit was often mistaken for that of a foreign army. Worst of all, some officers had been refused entry to restaurants and other public establishments when they were misidentified as students.[49]

For the lower ranks, the most controversial matter was the dragon emblem that ornamented all rifles, swords, headgear, and regimental flags. Many of the Cossacks were deeply religious and considered the wearing of this "evil creature" (*xieezhi wu*) a blasphemous act. The most offended group was the Ural squadron, many of whom were Old Believers. During the Boxer engagements, one junior officer from the Urals, Lieutenant Kazarkin (Kazhaerjin), was seriously wounded. After his arm had been amputated, one of his dragon pins was discovered stuck into the detached appendage. This was interpreted as divine retribution for sins undetermined. Despite sermons against these superstitious fears by A. Zhuravskii, the guard's chaplain, many of the men stopped wearing their dragon-infested sheepskin hats (*papakhas*).[50]

Despite these minor frictions, there was never any problem in recruiting for the guard. Soldiers in the regular army were paid two rubles and seventy kopecks a year. In Manchuria, the lowest ranks received twenty rubles a *month*, and junior officers received up to forty. Because many men were eager to sign up for this lucrative tour of duty, stringent health requirements and political reliability checks were used as selection criteria. The exotic locale was an additional lure for promising young officers. Among them were several men of future military renown in the Russo-Japanese and First World wars, including A. I. Denikin, A. I. Guchkov, L. G. Kornilov, P. I. Mishchenko, and N. G. Volodchenko.[51]

After the South Branch of the CER was completed and came under the guard's purview, the number of men increased rapidly. The original 720 rose to 2,000 in 1898 and to 5,000 in 1899. With the outbreak of hostilities in China proper, the Tsar authorized a further augmentation to 11,000, though this contingent had not yet arrived when the Boxer storm burst on Russian Manchuria. In fact, numerically, the guard was catching up with the regular army in the Guandong (Kvantun) leasehold. Estimates in the period just prior to the invasion range from 12,000 to 13,500 men. In South Manchuria, the military authorities had living proof of this competitive buildup before their eyes on a regular basis. Because the construction headquarters for the South Branch was located in Port Arthur, protective guard troops being posted to that sector landed there. During 1899, detachments arrived in March, June, and November.[52]

The Boxer Uprising and Military Dominance in Manchuria

In July 1900, Russian troops crossed the border into Manchuria to protect Russian lives and property endangered by the growing wave of violent antiforeign incidents known generally as the Boxer Rebellion.[53] During the next two years, the three Manchurian provinces would remain under Russian military occupation, a state of affairs that by its very nature gave the War Ministry predominance over Finance in all interministerial conflict. Witte could never prevail when events moved toward the rough end of the war-peace spectrum. His only viable strategy would be positional maneuvers aimed at preserving the CER's autonomy, coupled with steady pressure to end the occupation.

To begin with, Witte made concerted efforts to head off a full-scale invasion. Apart from the obvious preeminence the army would gain in wartime, he was concerned about the potential costs of such a move. To avoid inciting the Chinese, the Finance Minister prevailed over colleagues who would have put Russia in the forefront of the Allied expedition preparing to march on Beijing. As Rosemary Quested rightly points out, the policy of distancing Russia from the Allied forces had a historical precedent. Similar tactics during the Second Opium War and the occupation of Beijing (1856–60) had been rewarded by the bloodless annexation of the Amur's left bank and the Maritime province. Other preventive measures included the dispatch of more guards to the CER right-of-way and the appropriation of 300,000 silver taels with which Iugovich baited requests to the jiangjun of the three Manchurian provinces to prevent railroad wrecking.

To make sure that jingoist generals would not jump the gun, Witte tried and probably succeeded in having the decisive word on whether to invade North Manchuria, in particular, the CER zone. On July 3, Iugovich tried to dispel wild rumors circulating in Harbin by publishing a telegram from Witte claiming that fears of the Boxer unrest escalating into a war were groundless. Two days later, however, alarming news from Mukden forced the chief engineer to perform a *volte-face*. He requested the intervention of regular troops, and Witte, fearing that the railway would be totally destroyed, and its employees slaughtered, gave in.[54]

Fortunately for the Russians, the Boxer attack was halfhearted or, as George Lensen suggests, merely incompetent. He cites the example of a "fierce encounter [that] lasted for ninety minutes and cost the Russians one dead and one seriously wounded. . . . Only the aimlessness of the heavy Chinese fire preserved the Russians from annihilation." The siege of Harbin lasted eight days, most of it passed in anxious waiting for both the much feared attack and the fervently desired rescue.[55]

Despite some intimidating bombast, Shou Shan, the jiangjun of Heilongjiang province, was unable to muster enough manpower and resolve to overwhelm the 840 infantrymen and 750 cavalrymen who remained in Harbin after the bulk of the guard had escorted CER employees out of harm's way via the railway. Shou's most serious problem was that his Jilin colleague, Chang Shun, would not cooperate. In fact, Chang made efforts to help the Russians and thwart the Boxer representatives who, arriving from Fengtian, made claims on his support. On the night of August 1, 1900, while Shou prepared a *coup de grâce* for Harbin, Chang rounded up all the Boxer leaders in Jilin and had them quietly beheaded. On August 3, the Russian armada that had been pushing its way upriver arrived to end the siege and begin the occupation.[56]

On November 12, 1900, an interministerial conference attended by the Ministers of War, Foreign Affairs, and Finance attempted to sort out jurisdictions by confirming an agreement called "The Fundamentals of Russian Governmental Control" that had been drafted by Kuropatkin and amended by Witte. As Romanov rightly emphasizes, this document served a

twofold purpose: (1) to serve as "regulations for this control," the government's instructions to itself, as it were, respecting modes and limits for the exercise of the authority that had virtually fallen to it in the occupied country, and (2) to formulate a program respecting which it was "imperative" to endeavor to see that the basic positions, "insofar as they touched China, should enter into our forthcoming agreement with China."[57]

From this point, right up until the Japanese initiation of hostilities in February 1904, interministerial relations and foreign affairs in Russian Manchuria became fatefully and increasingly intertwined. But in October 1900, a clear separation of the army and the CER was still possible. The "Fundamentals" stipulated the railroad's supremacy in the right-of-way and full military authority everywhere else. Four of the five clauses that "marked off a position of independence for the Chinese Eastern Railway" were Witte's additions. In a separate communication, however, Witte did encourage his engineers to aid the military, since "we all serve the same Tsar."[58]

Clause 5 of the agreement laid the groundwork for a future attempt to shoehorn the army out of Manchuria by maintaining the integrity of the protective guard. This article defined the guard as a "special army division . . . subject to its own commander" and subordinate to the army's authority only during "use in combat." At Witte's suggestion, the separation of command lines was further formalized by renaming the railway guard. On January 22, 1901, the Protective Guard officially became a Separate Corps of Frontier Guards (Otdel'nyi Korpus Pogranichnoi Strazhy) within the Trans-Amur Military District, subordinated to the Ministry of Finance. At the same time, its maximum strength was increased to 25,000, and six batteries of artillery were attached.[59]

This name change was motivated by more than a mere wish to elevate the status of the CER force. A 25,000-man protective guard was estimated to cost 12,000,000 rubles a year. By phasing out the high salaries in favor of the lower pay offered ordinary border guards, the annual outlay was kept to 8,700,000 in 1903. Colonel Gerngross, the commanding officer of the original unit, had received 15,000 rubles a year; his replacement, *General Diterikhs*, was paid only 4,200.[60]

Although Iugovich's control of this force had become somewhat tenuous, the frontier guard's subordination to the Finance Minister continued to guarantee the "unity of leadership in all CER matters." Witte also felt great personal pride in his entry into the ranks. In his report on his Far Eastern trip, the Finance Minister's pleasure in reviewing his troops and ordering them into battle with Chinese bandits (*honghuzi*) shines through. A year later, when he had been deprived of Imperial favor and his ministry, Witte still derived a certain "consolation" from the Tsar's permission to continue wearing the uniform of the Border Guard-in-Chief. The dragons did not bother him in the least. But in 1901, what Witte found most satisfying about the frontier guard was that it gave him an army of his own making with which "to avoid depending on the military ministries."[61]

While this unit was being assembled, Harbin hosted two regular army corps under General N. I. Grodekov, who had been placed in charge of the occupation in North Manchuria. Because he concurrently served as

Priamur governor-general, Grodekov kept residences in both Harbin and Khabarovsk, moving back and forth for nearly two years. His stays in Harbin provided Iugovich with numerous unwelcome distractions. Until the evacuated *kharbintsy* returned, "the Cossacks had the place to themselves, and they gave free rein to their insatiable greed and dissipation. There was not left, it is said, a single store, not a single house, where the guard did not play the master. The guard did a fine job of guarding."[62]

As in Port Arthur, the lack of decent housing presented numerous opportunities for petty rivalries between the army and the CER. Witte, not wishing the occupation forces to feel too much at home, refused Kuropatkin's May 1901 request for help in preparing winter quarters. He claimed that simultaneous construction by two ministries would drive up the cost of labor and materials. When the army proceeded anyway, the results helped to fuel the building boom that was swiftly transforming Harbin from an outsized bivouac into a European city.[63]

The occupation forces at Harbin were a great temptation to Kuropatkin to increase military influence over the CER. On August 16, less than two weeks after the liberation of the city, Grodekov appointed Colonel Chevalier de la Serre, an engineer himself, as the military's representative to the railway, but within a week his functions were limited to "checking on the exact execution" of a status quo allowing almost complete CER autonomy. And when Witte caught wind of a plan to subordinate the CER to Grodekov in case of war, he trotted out the well-worn diplomatic, technocratic, and administrative reasons for the CER's independence: (1) any impingement on the CER would violate the Russo-Chinese Treaty of 1896; (2) the experts on railroading in Manchuria were all employees of the Finance Ministry and the Siberian Railway Committee; and (3) such a development would encourage overlapping authority (*dvoevlastie*), leading to conflict, in particular between Grodekov and Alekseev over control of the South Branch. In April 1901, Kuropatkin tried again by appointing a military "railroad transport manager" under an 1890 regulation, but Witte had read the fine print and knew that such "managers" were only allowed on "operating" railroads. He informed Kuropatkin that the CER was not yet in operation.[64]

In 1902, amid widespread rumors of peculation on the CER, Witte successfully employed similar lines of argumentation to stave off an audit of the company's financial records by the government's auditor-in-chief, General P. L. Lobko. Lobko (and others) suggested that the 58,000,000-ruble write-off that the CER had taken as "Boxer-related damage" might be a cover-up for large sums corruptly siphoned from the Imperial treasury.[65] In written arguments addressed to D. M. Sol'skii, whose commission would decide the issue, Witte equated this proposed dilution of his powers with previous requests to turn over the frontier guard to the War Ministry, and the telegraph facilities to the Interior Ministry. Not only would such a move violate the private status of the CER, possibly incurring diplomatic consequences; it would also cultivate divided authority. The latter phenomenon, Witte added, was harmful in Russia's interior, worse on the fringes, and completely unacceptable for "such a large and complicated Russian enterprise operating within a foreign state."

Then Witte went further, indicting for immaturity not only the governmental organs with which he was required to spar daily, but the whole nature of Russian society:

The matter has gotten to the point where the heads of the other ministries confidentially communicate to the Minister of Finance rumors about colossal embezzlements on the Chinese Eastern Railway as received from these ministries' [local] agents.... The very fact that such rumors appear shows how difficult it is in Russia to carry out a difficult and serious matter in spite of Russian society's penchant for slander. In other countries, where society and the press are better educated, they are able to differentiate a serious matter from an ordinary one; they are able to devote sufficient attention to a matter concerning the patriotic interests of that country; they are able to provide necessary support in a timely fashion. Among us, neither the press nor society has matured to that point. It is impossible to expect such support. This [unsupportiveness] emerged in full during the construction of the CER, making it all the more difficult for that department charged with managing this matter, and that individual who heads the department.

Witte's play for bureaucratic sympathy was a resounding success. Lobko's draft reforms dated July 2/June 19, 1902, called for audit personnel on the CER to be taken out of the hands of CER, Inc. A one-letter amendment submitted by Witte reversed the sense of the draft, thereby confirming the full independence of CER activities. Witte's version was then approved.*

If preserving sole control in Russian Manchuria had not been a core component of Witte's plan right from the start, the actual construction of the railroad and its auxiliary institutions quickly highlighted the importance of doing so. The dynamics of the tsarist government constrained Witte's most important successor, Kokovtsov, to the same task. Moreover, when the enduring interministerial rivalries crossed into foreign policy,

---

*RGIA 1273: 1, 171, pp. 4–43. The wording of Lobko's draft was changed from "Emy [Finance Ministry] *ne* budet prinadlezhat'" to "Emy *zhe* budet prinadlezhat'"; "will not have" became "will have." This struggle with Lobko over the CER was only one aspect of the auditor-in-chief's frontal attack on the Witte economic system. It climaxed in a State Council plenum in December 1902, where Lobko demolished Finance's inflated claims for the national economy. RGIA 1273: 1, 272, pp. 144–45; Von Laue, pp. 219–21. If the CER had something to hide, Witte did well to keep it from Lobko's inquisitive malice.

the results could be at best confusing, at worst catastrophic. The following examination of the never-completed evacuation and the establishment of the viceroyalty will illustrate these pitfalls.

The Scuttling of the Russian Evacuation

On April 8, 1902, a Russo-Chinese convention was signed that provided for a phased withdrawal of Russian troops from Manchuria over the next eighteen months. The first evacuation, from the region west of the Liao River, was completed before the October 8, 1902, deadline. As the regular army troops abandoned and prepared to abandon their positions, Witte's agents, the CER, the frontier guard, and the Russo-Chinese Bank moved in to resume the hegemony they had enjoyed before July 1900. But the military would not let itself be so easily supplanted.

On February 28, 1902, the bank's representative in Mukden had remarked on the company's stagnation in Manchuria "in view of our relation to the Port Arthur authority." Admiral Alekseev, commander of the Guandong garrison and the Pacific Fleet, allowed his suspicion to extend as far as demanding that the bank's telegraphic code be revealed to him. Nevertheless, by September, with the first stage of the evacuation pending, the bank had recovered somewhat and was participating in three large mining ventures.[66]

The CER guard was also leaning southward. In 1902, it added three new priests to its ranks, two for Harbin and one for the 1,000-man garrison at Tieling, 65 versts north of Mukden. The request for religious personnel noted that the "largest quantity of Trans-Amur [Military] District units is located on the southern line." On March 31, eight days before the second phase of the evacuation was to clear the remainder of Fengtian and the whole of Jilin province of the Russian army, the commander of the guard "asked permission to occupy this position simultaneously with the departure of the Russian troops, before the Chinese should have time to occupy it." At Mukden, the Chinese administrative center for Manchuria, railway guard barracks were under construction, even as the army prepared its evacuation. This may well have played a role in Alekseev's decision to order the reoccupation of the city.[67]

These local actions by the CER, its railway guard, and the Russo-Chinese Bank were the opening moves in Witte's plan for recovering his ministry's dominance in the Far East. All he had to do was sit back and watch the army fulfill its international obligations, and then move in to pick up the pieces under cover of his enterprises' de jure private status. The move was as legally unimpeachable as it was transparent. As early as August 1902, the

Japanese consul at Niuzhuang saw that "in the name of railway protection, soldiers could be stationed at Mukden forever."[68]

As it turned out, by then a constellation of enmities had arisen to bring the Finance Minister down. Grand Duke Aleksandr Mikhailovich, out of familial concern, accused Witte of garnering too much power at the expense of the Tsar himself. The newly appointed Interior Minister, V. K. Pleve, claimed that Witte's system was, at least indirectly, encouraging the malcontents of Russian society. Considering that his predecessor had been assassinated in April 1902, Pleve had every reason to take the matter personally. Finally, A. M. Bezobrazov, who had Nikolai's ear for a while, noisily denounced Witte's misguided Far Eastern policy. Clearly, the only issue that might be regarded as one of substance was the final one. Pleve himself later affirmed that "the whole matter" revolved around Witte's plan "to organize a separate state [*osoboe gosudarstvo*] in Manchuria."[69]

On his return from the Far East in October 1902, Witte immediately sensed a new coolness in the air. One of the Tsar's first acts was to remove the merchant marine from the Finance Ministry's trade section and hand it over to Aleksandr Mikhailovich to manage. This was the Grand Duke's first administrative job. Witte characterized the move as "cutting off a finger" and suggested that the creation of a pig-breeding administration would be a logical next step. By the spring of 1903, Nikolai had still not returned Witte's report on the Far East, an unmistakable signal that Finance Ministry input was no longer desired in this sphere of activities. But at that point, with the army abruptly having given up any pretense of making the necessary preparations for the second stage of the Manchurian evacuation, Witte had already effectively conceded the game.[70] Recognizing that a full withdrawal was more and more unlikely, thus making the maintenance of the frontier guard's integrity and strength moot, he had agreed on March 20 to modifications in the "Fundamentals" of November 1900. The different chains of command for wartime and peacetime were maintained, but the commander of the Priamur and Guandong forces was now to be in charge of the frontier guard's peacetime military training (a provision that supports Fuller's thesis of "professionalism" as a core issue of civil-military conflict). The guard's independence was further limited by a requirement to report all information of "military significance" to the regular army commander. Included in this category were all agreements with Chinese military and civilian authorities.[71]

A month later, on April 23, 1903, Kuropatkin told the Tsar that Witte was "quickly getting used to the idea" (*bystro gotovitsia k mysli*) that the frontier guard would be converted into a general military force subordinate to the War Ministry. The creation of the Trans-Amur Railway Brigade, a militarized unit of lower- and mid-level railroad employees, was mentioned as a step in this direction. Shortly afterward, the arrival of this new civil-military hybrid in Manchuria was used as an excuse to cut the frontier guard's effective strength from 25,000 to 20,000.[72]

By midyear, Witte was no longer in a position to resist creeping militarization. On July 7, Kuropatkin and Alekseev decided to move the headquarters for the Second Siberian Corps to Harbin and to remove the Trans-Amur District from the frontier guard. Later in the month, Alekseev's request for twelve desiatinas of land for military needs at Dal'nii was approved. By November, the area had expanded to 80 desiatinas.[73]

The historian B. A. Romanov, like the French, British, and Japanese diplomatic observers in Manchuria at the time, believed that the frontier guard would offer a screen behind which a withdrawal of regular army troops could take place without forfeiting Russian control or violating diplomatic propriety. Instead the occupation forces under Admiral Alekseev's command just stayed put. What the Japanese then interpreted as stalling tactics in preparation for annexation or war may actually have been no more than unwillingness on the part of the regular army to abandon the field of victory to the Ministry of Finance and its front organizations.[74]

The Far Eastern Viceroyalty and the Coming of War

On August 12, 1903, Alekseev was named viceroy of the Far East with sole authority for Russia's military, economic, and diplomatic affairs east of Lake Baikal. One of his first diplomatic initiatives was to terminate negotiations with the Chinese to make sure that Beijing would be unable to force an evacuation by suddenly approving the supplementary compensations and guarantees that Russian diplomacy had, so far, been unable to obtain. In a conversation between the Tsar and Lamsdorff about the continuing occupation, Nikolai stated that Alekseev "had always been of the opinion that we should not evacuate Manchuria. In response to Lamsdorff's comment that, not long ago, [Alekseev] had expressed a different opinion, the Tsar answered: he was not yet viceroy then."[75]

Malozemoff has argued that this new office and the Special Committee for Far Eastern Affairs that oversaw it, "merely retarded the normal course of events," since "supreme control was still retained in the hands of those who had held that control before—the Tsar and his ministers."[76] That is simply wrong. With Witte's "promotion" to chairman of the Committee of Ministers on August 29, the Finance Ministry fell silent regarding the Far East. Furthermore, through the fall of 1903, with time running out, Foreign Minister Lamsdorff found himself left out of the diplomatic negotiations for which his office would bear ultimate responsibility. In October, according to the Japanese ambassador, Lamsdorff refused to discuss Far Eastern affairs "on account of the creation of the [viceroyalty]. He says he does not seem to have anything to do with Russian government." Lamsdorff also complained that Admiral Alekseev was deliberately delaying negotiations in preparation for war. He repeatedly offered to resign his ministry.[77] As Malozemoff himself states: "The delays continued. The Japanese became anxious."

Most crucially, the Japanese perceived the connection between these vicissitudes of interministerial politics and the unlikelihood of a negotiated settlement. At the beginning of 1903, in a long memorandum to Foreign Minister Komura, the Japanese ambassador in Paris had thoroughly analyzed the upper circles of the Russian bureaucracy as conveyed to him by knowledgable French informants. A September follow-up by Kurino in St. Petersburg evaluated the most recent changes and judged them a "victory for the expansionists." During the Port Arthur conference in July, both Bezobrazov and Alekseev had been identified by reports from Japanese sources in the Far East as proponents of war.[78]

Though the French ambassador to Russia pointed out to his Japanese colleague that the main difference between the civil and military factions was merely the speed at which they wished to expand Russia's influence, for Japan, with the Trans-Siberian railroad nearing completion, time was exactly what counted most. When Tokyo was informed by Ambassador Uchida in Beijing that, according to his British ally there, Alekseev would be in charge of negotiations, the natural assumption was that the process would be "very much protracted and the conclusion will be very remote." In addition, Japan's previous experiences in negotiating with the viceroyalty's foreign affairs office had shown that St. Petersburg would not always back up Port Arthur's word.[79]

In a second report on the same day (September 9), Uchida set out the stated view of the U.S. ambassador that

although he had become accustomed to bad faith on the part of Russia, he was never so struck with her audacity. He was of the opinion that Russia's method was simply to gain time in order to strengthen her hold of Manchurian provinces; that she would be complete master of those provinces, if she continues to stay there another year as she demands anew. . . . Russia will dominate over all Manchuria with her troops stationed on the railway lines, and along the whole length of that grand Sungari.

By October, rumors of war had begun to spread throughout Manchuria.[80]

The effects of the changes at the top went much further than souring the negotiations with Japan over Manchuria. They were to have equally dramatic effects in Manchuria itself, where the brunt would fall on the Chinese. Alekseev wished to establish totally new relations both with Petersburg and with the Manchurian lands of his Far Eastern domain. From September 23 until November 17, 1903, a commision co-chaired by Generals Volkov and I. P. Nadarov prepared the statutes for the administration of the viceroyalty. The two principles that were to guide them had been telegraphed from Petersburg by Pleve as vice-president of the Far Eastern Committee. The first was independence from the ministers. The second was a separate budget. The viceroy was to be cut loose from all restraining ties to the Petersburg bureaucracy.

At the local level, Alekseev found definitive solutions for the interministerial rivalries that had plagued him and his brothers-in-arms. The CER was to be placed under the "supervision and care of Russian state organs," which is to say, the viceroyalty. To make sure that the railway would find neither aid nor comfort elsewhere, all local offices representing the Foreign and Finance ministries were to be eliminated. To simplify Russo-Chinese relations in Manchuria, the statutes called for enforced isolation from the Beijing government.

In place of the Russian and Chinese central organs, Alekseev planned to establish the office of general commissar to oversee the military commissars who had been attached to each of Manchuria's three provincial yamens since 1900. The broad discretionary powers of these officers allowed them to interfere with the jiangjun's affairs at will. Elevation to the status of a governor-general made the general commissar

> the direct superior of all [Russian] administrative personnel and institutions in Manchuria as well as the armed forces under their charge. . . . The general commissar must take all measures to obtain the broadest guarantee of [Russia's] political and commercial interests in Manchuria. . . . He has full influence over Chinese officials, their appointment and administration; [he] gathers information on the taxable resources of the region and their expenditure; [he] encourages just and humane judicial procedures, communicating to the Chinese people the principles of humanity and respect for Russia.

The goal of this final and lofty measure was "to gradually change them [the Chinese] into true servants of our Fatherland," almost an echo of Ukhtomskii's call for reeducation.[81]

Since breaking with Beijing also meant dispensing with the services of the Russian embassy there, the general commissar was to be given ambassadorial privileges. On November 2, the Chinese Foreign Ministry informed the Japanese ambassador that the "Russians have now prohibited all telegraphic communications between Fengtian and Beijing," and that the Russian ambassador refused to discuss Manchurian issues "on the ground that

Fengtian is now under control of Admiral Alexieff and the [Russian] minister has nothing to do with it."[82]

New as this structure was, its origins in interministerial rivalry are evident. The raison d'être for the general commissar was given as

> the need to unify the actions of our representatives, . . . since the Chinese authorities are in constant communication with each other . . . and capably make use of our weaknesses and mistakes, especially differences of opinion [*raznoglasiia*] between representatives of the separate authorities. Therefore, all matters touching Manchuria, whether political, military, or commercial must be handled exclusively through the general commissar.[83]

Possibly, Alekseev had in mind the reoccupation of Mukden in October 1902, when the jiangjun of Fengtian province had immediately sent a wire to Khorvat asking the CER general manager to intercede. The Chinese knew well where the lines had been drawn. Antagonism toward the CER is also visible in the choice of Mukden as the general commissar's seat "and by no means Harbin, the center of the CER right-of-way." As a further slap at the soft, civilian types who dominated in Harbin, the whole right-of-way was to be placed under the management of the frontier guard's commanding officer. The guards would also govern.[84]

In late December, Admiral Alekseev recommended that negotiations with the Japanese be terminated on the grounds that their terms were becoming "even more exigent" (*pritiazatel'nye*). Continuing discussions, he feared, might lead to a rupture.[85] Clearly, diplomacy was not Alekseev's forte. It would be unfair and unprovable to blame the viceroy for the outbreak of the Russo-Japanese War. Nonetheless, he had striven hard to be the wrong man in the wrong place at the wrong time. With Admiral Alekseev at the diplomatic helm, there could be no last-minute rescues. This sinking ship would soon be followed to the bottom by the rest of Alekseev's command, including the Russian Pacific Fleet, Port Arthur, and a whole panoply of imperialist dreams.

CHAPTER 3

Manchurian Colonization: Policy, Results, and Feedback

> Behold, these shall come from far:
> And, lo, these from the north and from the west;
> And these from the land of Sinim.
> —Isaiah 49:12

FROM THE very beginning of the Trans-Siberian railway's construction, Witte had highlighted the decisive importance of colonization to the venture's eventual success or failure.[1] In analogous fashion, the question of settlement was intimately related to the building of the Trans-Manchurian CER. But as discussed in Chapter One, the laying of the line took precedence, and demographic accretion was left to the steady influx of employees, guards, and workmen, and those who supplied their daily needs. A cooperative relationship with the Chinese partner and heightened Japanese sensitivities demanded extreme caution in pushing policies that might be viewed as steps toward annexation.

After the suppression of the Boxer uprising in Manchuria, three years went into developing a migration policy. This process was characterized by a lack of coordination with the locality under discussion and interministerial conflicts. Two clear options emerged from these discussions, one associated with the army and calling for "traditional Russian" colonization by Cossacks and soldiers, and the other a Ministry of Finance plan to lure Dukhobors with promises of religious tolerance. In the end, events overtook bureaucratic lucubrations. Chinese migration, both spontaneous and government-sponsored, began to fill in the Manchurian vacuum. Even more important, the Japanese victories of 1904–5 took the edge off of the Russian appetite for expansion.

Nonetheless, the Finance Ministry's antebellum plan formed the basis for postwar policy. Initiatives in ethnic tolerance and a "wager on the strong" attracted sizable groups of Georgians, Latvians, Ukrainians, Poles, and Jews to Manchuria. At a time when "territorial" (i.e., other than Palestine) solutions to the Jewish problem were an object of serious discussion, Manchuria's growing Jewish community presented itself as an alternative to Zion. In 1905, when the up-and-coming leader of the Polish Zionist organization (Poalei Tsion), Ber Borokhov, published an article entitled "On the Question of Zion and a Territory," in which he analyzed the various options for a Jewish homeland, Manchuria was among them, along with Palestine, Uganda, Angola, Morocco, and Canada.² At the same time, a preference for urban development confirmed Harbin's demographic dominance over the rest of the CER right-of-way. While enlightened social policy brought an unusual mix of Russian subjects to the banks of the Sungari, the circulation of millions of gold rubles acted as a magnet to attract a slightly larger number of Chinese. By 1913, these subpopulations had melded into a single unit, by headcount the largest city in Eastern Siberia.

Not only in Harbin would the colonization policies of 1902-3 leave their mark. The principles elaborated for Manchuria were later applied in Siberia (1904) and European Russia (1906). A growing spirit of experimentation made Manchuria a test case—a program whose implications could be discussed all the more freely because the region was officially beyond the Empire's borders. In addition to specific colonization measures, a mechanism for balancing the needs of Siberian settlement with the ability to control the sources of outmigration was tried first in the Manchurian arena. Since the key figures in the making of the Stolypin Reforms had strong Siberia-related backgrounds, they were bound to be receptive to ideas originating in the eastern reaches of the Empire. In this respect, an examination of Manchurian settlement uncovers a missing link in late Imperial Russia's rural reforms.

First Plans, 1898-1902

There is little material in the archives on the colonization of Manchuria before the Boxer rebellion. Surely, both those who considered the CER primarily a trade conduit and those who emphasized its political importance could foresee that only a stable population of Russian citizens could realize these goals. As Nilus, indulging in prophetic hindsight, states:

It must have been clear to both the Russian and the Chinese government of that time that the completion of the grandiose construction plan here in Manchuria would be followed by Russians settling en masse, bringing with them culture, language, and customs, together with social and family ways—all so alien to the Chinese elements [*stikhii*] surrounding them.³

As discussed in Chapter Two, from 1898 till mid-1900, Petersburg, intent on mending the diplomatic bridges damaged by the occupation of the

Liaodong peninsula, avoided issues that might further rile Russia's competitors in Europe and Asia. The Nishi-Rosen agreement left Japan predominant in Korea; and the discussions with the British in the following year clarified spheres of influence in North China. Silence also ruled at the local level, presumably because the engineers had their hands full with recruitment and construction tasks. Nevertheless, the two most important figures in pre-1904 Manchuria policy, Witte and Kuropatkin, had already begun to toy with conceptions that would later blossom into alternative views of that region's demographic relationship to Russia proper.

In early 1899, Witte composed a memorandum in which he cited "especial steadfastness, energy, love of hard work, and the spirit of mutual solidarity" as the qualities that settlers must embody in order to compete successfully with the Chinese. The Minister of Finance found that Dukhobors fit the bill. But there was a competitor for their labors. Canada had offered to provide communal lands, and Tolstoy had donated the royalties from his novel *Resurrection* to cover travel expenses for members of the sect who wished to settle along the Canadian Pacific railway. According to Witte's data, around 4,000 had already left Russia, but from 5,000 to 10,000 remained in the Caucasus. An additional 300 families still lived in Kharkov province. The offer of thirty desiatinas (2.7 acres) a family (as compared with a fifteen-desiatina-per-male standard for Siberian colonization), it was hoped, would lure the bulk of these religious dissenters to Manchuria instead of North America.[4]

On March 13, 1899, P. M. Romanov wrote to Iugovich to ask if he was ready to settle a party of 300 families (1,300 people) along the CER, with an additional 1,000 families to follow. Iugovich replied on March 27 that the original party could be located at Harbin, Kuanchengzi, Qiqihar, and other large stations, but that land prices in those areas had already risen to 60–70 rubles per desiatina. In a follow-up telegram of April 5, he stated that settling the whole 1,300 families would be difficult because of passive resistance by the Chinese authorities, angered by the protective guard's recent "uncontrolled" behavior. The Qiqihar yamen, it seems, had decided to resist the CER's demands by pressuring the railway's Chinese contractors. Iugovich concluded this pessimistic missive on a bright note by mentioning that the two "Chinese bureaus" for which he was presently negotiating would solve many of these problems by allowing him to operate outside the purview of the Qiqihar and Jilin jiangjun.[5]

Since no further correspondence followed on this question, we can safely assume that the issue was left hanging until the general post-Boxer reevaluation of Manchurian colonization. The exchange is nevertheless worth noting as a signal of things to come, namely, the readiness of Petersburg to put forth unorthodox approaches to the problems of Manchuria; the difficulties of accommodating these plans to local realities; the central role of land availability and price as a limiting factor; the tendency for events in turbulent Manchuria to overtake not only developmental processes, but even the normal delays of bureaucratic decision making. Policies died of planning obsolescence.[6]

In contrast to Witte's creative vision of using social and cultural gradients within the Empire to build a demographic bridge to the China market, Kuropatkin saw only a bridge to be defended. Just a few weeks before Russian troops would pour into Manchuria, in a discussion with Count de Montebello, the French ambassador, the general insisted that he, personally, was only in favor of peaceful methods of penetrating China. After all, he explained, "if Manchuria became Russian territory, how would we prevent our new subjects from invading our territories, where we wish to remain Russians of pure race?"[7] The primary concern here was the Yellow Peril, a phobia whose grip on the Russian popular and official imagination had recently begun to tighten. With regard to migration, the Chinese Northeast would need both guarding and guarding against.

The Boxer tide briefly swept back the Russian presence in Manchuria, bottling it up in Port Arthur and Harbin. The sieges were short and loose, but for Russian policy the whole affair had the rousing effect of a swim in the Amur, no doubt a vicarious shiver transmitted by the thousands of Chinese residents who were herded into the river during the "Blagoveshchensk Utopia" in July 1900. A few weeks after the armies of General Grodekov had subdued and occupied Heilongjiang and Jilin provinces, the governor-general wrote to Kuropatkin recommending aggressive colonization as a means of defense. He suggested taking a strip of land five kilometers wide on each side of the CER and filling it with armed settlers. This measure would guarantee the railway workers' security and should be carried out without delay, lest the Chinese preempt the move.[8]

Reaction was immediate. On November 16, two weeks after Grodekov submitted his report, Witte ordered Iugovich to enlarge the right-of-way wherever possible in order to "distance untrustworthy elements from the [rail]way" and "settle the [rail]way with Russian elements." The next day, Witte informed Kuropatkin that the army's request had already been transmitted to the local level.

In Harbin, Witte's command provoked a bureaucratic reflex, the calling of a special conference. By early December, Iugovich, huddling with the CER board members S. I. Kerbedz and I. I. Khodorovskii, had concluded that the realization of Grodekov's plan would be impracticable, ineffective and prohibitively expensive. Not only were the available lands within five kilometers of the east-west mainline infertile and, therefore, unsuitable for colonists, but their very emptiness meant that there was nothing nearby to defend. On the heavily populated South Branch, purchases would be expensive and strongly resented by the Chinese. The estimated bill for land appropriation was 275,000,000 rubles, almost as much as the total construction cost for the CER. Kerbedz's report on the conference added that an anonymous "some" considered the settlement of Manchuria by Russians "inconceivable." On March 4, 1901, another of the CER board members, A. N. Venttsel, reported to the Russo-Chinese Bank's Beijing agent, D. D. Pokotilov, that the Finance Minister had reversed his decision to expand the right-of-way. The inability to coordinate local and central information had led to Petersburg's issue of an infeasible order, but Witte was probably not too unhappy to see a plan under army auspices fall by the wayside. In tandem with the unbridged gap between real estate realities and projected settlement, bureaucratic rivalry had claimed its first post-Boxer victim in the area of colonization policy.

Since the primary focus of interministerial attention in 1901 was the question of whether Manchurian occupation would be followed by annexation or withdrawal, even the Tsar's personal interest could not rescue the colonization question from the backburner. On August 16, the soon-to-be-assassinated Interior Minister, D. S. Sipiagin, notified Witte that the Tsar had marked the following passage on Manchuria in Governor-General Grodekov's 1898–1900 report on the Priamur:

No less important for success is the question of the selection of settlers. In this respect, I would consider it advantageous to make use of *raskol'niki* and other categories of sectarians, like, for example, the Dukhobors, some of whom emigrated recently to North America. In the absence of a permanent Russian population such individuals do not represent a danger from the point of view of religious propaganda and, in addition, they are already proven colonizers, steadfast in the defence of their nationality (*narodnost'*) and capable of overcoming the most difficult conditions of settlement.[9]

Witte responded by relating the unencouraging results of the special conference held the previous winter in Harbin.

By early 1902, the annexation option had been rejected, and attempts in Beijing to extract compensation for a future evacuation had failed. With his mercenary trump card, Li Hongzhang, dead, Witte turned to the local authorities in the hope of obtaining concessions. On February 26, he asked Iugovich to cooperate with Pokotilov in negotiating the Russo-Chinese Bank's concession rights to gold, iron, petroleum, nickel, coal, and timber in Manchuria. Iugovich was unwilling to involve himself in activities beyond the scope of railroad construction, broadly defined; only coal and timber, he thought, were of any concern to him. Nevertheless, possibly remembering Witte's November 1900 land fever, the chief engineer suggested the purchase "in generous quantities . . . of large sections of land in proximity to stations that would subsequently have commercial importance." Both the "revenue from increment in property value" and the "political" influence of owning future Chinese and Russian settlements were cited in support of this move.[10] Twelve days after Iugovich wired his proposal to Petersburg, Witte received the Tsar's consent to use funds remaining in the Li Hongzhang bribe account for a new purpose, the expansion of CER land holdings. By May 1902, 40,800 desiatinas had been taken along the line, giving the settlement question a new lease on life.[11]

Civilian and Military Preferences: Dukhobors vs. Cossacks

By summer, two independent and far different proposals on Manchurian colonization were under consideration in Petersburg. In late June, Governor-General Grodekov, this time writing to Interior Minister Pleve, presented his blueprint for Manchurian settlement, together with a report on the related views and actions of the CER compiled by two investigators sent from the Priamur.[12] In keeping with views he had expressed earlier, Grodekov argued that on the South Branch, land should be taken only at major stations. As he had previously told Kuropatkin, the local populace so deeply resented the economic changes the railroad had worked that further incursions would lead to "bloody and continuing clashes."[13] Furthermore, in keeping with past practice, the land should nominally be received by the CER. Only uninhabited plots should be taken to limit Treasury expenses.[14]

The settlers, according to Grodekov, should number 35,150 males, of whom 5,550 would be Transbaikal Cossacks. These latter would be given forty desiatinas each in the strip from the Transbaikal border to the Xingan Mountains. They would be under the direct orders of their ataman, the military governor of the Transbaikal. Thus, the Russian military authorities in the Far East would acquire jurisdiction over a new zone contiguous to their other areas of responsibility, a de facto control of Manchuria west of the Great Xingan range, and a commanding tactical position halfway from the border to Qiqihar, the seat of the jiangjun of Heilongjiang province. The recruitment and administration of the "reliable" settlers for the remainder of the mainline from the Xingans to the Ussuri border would be placed under the control of the Resettlement Administration of the Interior Ministry. This plan would at one stroke give Pleve a foothold in Manchurian affairs and allow the army to maintain much of its influence in North Manchuria, even after withdrawing its occupation forces.

Grodekov's proposal is in most respects a refinement of positions expressed previously by himself and his predecessor, General Dukhovskoi. In the almost two years since he had urged immediate settlement on Kuropatkin, Grodekov had merely sharpened his knowledge of local conditions in order to make his plan more specific and, therefore, more persuasive to a new potential supporter in Petersburg. The idea of concentrating land appropriation and migration nearer to the Russian border had been brought up by Dukhovskoi in his January 1896 proposal to track the CER through Mergen in preparation for the annexation of the nearly 80,000 square miles of wilderness delimited by the bend in the Amur-Argun' waterway. To strengthen his case, Grodekov cited the alarm of Lieutenant-Colonel Bogdanov, military commissar in Qiqihar, at the speed of Chinese colonization, especially within the fifteen-verst swath bordering the CER right-of-way.[15] This line of argument, despite fresh expert testimony, was simply a renewal of the general's earlier warning that the Chinese would outcolonize the Russians in the areas nearest the railway.

The most novel aspect of Grodekov's dispatch was the inclusion of a report compiled by two of his subordinates, V. V. Perfil'ev, future governor of Kamchatka, and the agronomist Kovalev, on their fact-finding mission to northern Manchuria. The purpose of their trip, as shown by the title of their report, was the "clarification of the conditions for settling a Russian population in the CER trunkline's right-of-way." Grodekov had clearly lost faith in the ability of the CER and the Finance Ministry to make this information available to all concerned, both in the Far East and at Petersburg, and had ordered his agents to make the rounds of the CER construction sites collecting opinions and impressions.

Meanwhile, despite Iugovich's belief that the colonization of Manchuria by Russians was an unlikely proposition, in accordance with his orders (and his own February suggestion), he had instructed his subordinates to buy land at all the major stations.[16] It was an order that pleased N. S. Sviagin, head of the East Branch, who informed the chief engineer that he was in favor of Russian settlement, but, without official encouragement, had been unwilling to take land in quantity. The only exception had been at the site designated as the future bordertown Pogranichnaia, where slightly more than 4,000 desiatinas had been taken. According to him, all the section heads on his branch had commented on the flood of Chinese settlers that had descended on the barely functional railway. Maoershan (100 versts east of Harbin), Wujimi (120 versts), Imianpo (150 versts), and Shitouhezi (200 versts) had all grown from nothing or "at most a few buildings" into sizable hamlets. Prince S. N. Khilkov, in charge of the Sungari section (including Harbin), added that the railroad itself contributed to this phenomenon:

From the masses of Chinese, up to 50,000 of whom are currently working on the line, many will remain near the line forever. Basing themselves on such temporary worksites as wood-cutting [operations], brick factories, and stone mines, the Chinese gradually begin to cultivate kitchen gardens and build permanent *fanzy*, and in this way settle down for good.

The arrival of many Koreans along the section from Shitouhezi to the Russian Ussuri border was also noted. Lieutenant-Colonel Bogdanov continued to air his forebodings by claiming that colonization within fifty versts to the east of Harbin was already impossible because agricultural development had reached the saturation point. He estimated the population density at eighty men per square verst.[17]

This fear of superior Chinese adaptability found an echo at CER board meetings held on June 15 and July 2, 1902. At least two members who had been in Manchuria recently, P. M. Romanov and Kerbedz, should have been at least as well-informed regarding local conditions as Grodekov. Recognizing the lack of arable land along the railway and the competitiveness of Chinese agriculture, the board sat down to discuss a document entitled "On Schismatics and Sectarians as a Colonizing Element." This report, prepared by the Finance Ministry's General Chancellery, came down in favor of the religious dissenters. Witte's own comments on it provided clear guidance to the board members on what course they should take.

According to Witte, the very fact that a foreign country was the settlement target ruled out "normal measures." The lack of a land fund and of tax control compounded the dilemma. Nonetheless, colonization had to be encouraged, and attracting sectarians with secret (*neglasnyi*) measures seemed a desirable experiment. Not surprisingly, the board agreed with its boss, adding as an additional advantage that sectarians would not even need a special "invitation," since it would be sufficient to "guarantee them that of which they are at present deprived within Russia's boundaries, namely, full religious tolerance. Even now, as can be seen in the papers, a movement exists among Volga sectarians to emigrate to the Chinese [rail]way." Still, they were not to be universally welcomed, the board cautioned. Care must be taken not to recruit people who planned to make their livelihood from agriculture; only those planning careers in trade or industry should be included. Other desirable elements were nonsectarian artisans, workers, and merchants, whose activities would eventually provide freight for the railway. The board was ready to offer these men inexpensive household plots.

Moreover, following the precedent of Grodekov's decree of April 2 inducing regular troops to stay on after their tour of duty by offering them the chance to claim their expense-paid discharge trip back to Russia anytime within five years, the CER directors decided to extend the same offer to its border guards. Finally, the board concluded that every effort should be made to keep the Chinese out of the right-of-way. No detailed prescriptions were provided, however. In fact, the Finance Minister would soon be arguing that such an "elemental" movement was unstoppable, and that any attempt to do so would merely feed the Chinese government's fears of Russian encroachment, leading to redoubled official colonization efforts.[18]

Thus, by mid-1902, two colonization plans had emerged. One emphasized Cossack and soldier settlements, and the other sectarian migration and the attraction of traditionally urban groups. The two continued to be debated during the remainder of the year. For one strong proponent of the military solution, M. M. Manakin, the goal of "peaceful conquest" (*mirnoe zavoevanie*) was best attained by the "traditional, homegrown Russian [*prisushchii k Rossii*] means of broadening the borders by the promotion of Cossack settlements and posts, of a Cossack line." For that reason, he said, he favored the War Ministry's idea over the Interior Ministry's version.[19] On the other hand, many supporters of the Dukhobor idea, most notably Pleve, were attracted by the possibility of killing two birds with one stone. Not only would the Manchurian colony find loyal and hardy settlers, but at the same time the Empire proper would be rid of a social and religious nuisance.[20]

Witte pushed his advocacy to new heights in October 1902, after he finally experienced the full 8,000 versts of the Trans-Siberian. Transit through Manchuria and a stop in Harbin were reflected in his report to the Tsar. Stylistic requirements and *amour propre* smoothed away the vacillations of land acquisition and colonization policy observed above. First, Witte claimed that "from the very beginning," his farsightedness had produced an order to alienate twice the amount of real estate accrued by the Russian railways. "Then, in November 1900," he had suggested further enlargements to the chief engineer. (He took care not to mention the impractical nature and later annulment of this order.) "Further, this March, I once again" called for large-scale appropriations near major stations. (Iugovich receives no credit for his own idea.) As others have noted, the Witte line, running on rails of steely mendacity, often triumphs over historical reality.[21]

Turning from land acquisition to the logical next step, Witte postulated the axiom of Manchurian colonization that would remain in effect right up until 1917. "Next, regarding the conditions of Russian colonization in the right-of-way zone of the CER, it must be noted that these conditions are completely exceptional, having nothing in common with those within the Empire. Therefore, the principles on which migration is based within Russia cannot be extended to colonization in the CER region." In place of the existing system of Siberian migration, Witte suggested a "wager on the strong." Since limited lands and indomitable Chinese competition had ruled out a rural approach, Manchurian settlement must be left to "private initiative. Then, desirable individuals will come here—the most energetic, steadfast, and adaptable; namely, those of the trade and industrial class, searching for enrichment at their own risk." In colonizing, the CER did not want to be saddled with the kind of rabble that had been foisted on them as construction workers in 1900.

Even with all the interest in this matter, by the time a special conference was convened on February 7, 1903, to discuss additional conditions to be requested of China in exchange for fulfilling the evacuation commitments Russia had made in 1902, there had been little headway. In rejecting the idea of asking China to forbid its subjects from settling near the CER, Witte simply stated that all efforts were being made to appropriate land and prevent "disorderly settlement by random elements." Colonization rules, he added, were already being worked out for submission to the appropriate authorities. War Minister Kuropatkin replied that he was glad to hear this, since it had been reported to him that Russian subjects still encountered difficulties in acquiring land in Manchuria.[22]

A few weeks later, on February 26 and March 5, a joint committee, formed by the Finance and Interior ministries and chaired by P. M. Romanov, hammered out the "Rules Pertaining to the Settlement of Russian Subjects on Manchurian Lands Belonging to the CER."[23] This document reflected the principle Witte had expounded in his 1902 report that private initiative and urban development should be the basis of Russian life in China. Except in special cases, only the trade and industrial classes would be allowed to rent land. Moving expenses would not be subsidized, and a minimum worth was established for receiving land from the CER. City dwellers would receive no more than one desiatina. Away from the major settlements, the maximum would be fifteen desiatinas. A. V. Krivoshein, the assistant chief of the Siberian Resettlement Department within Pleve's ministry, backed the "no incentive" approach, since sweetening Manchurian settlement might undermine efforts to attract colonists to the Maritime province, one of his responsibilities.

The Romanov committee intended these guidelines to also cover all those who wished to stay on in Manchuria after their contracts with the CER, the army, or the border guard expired. Witte's sectarian gambit was approved, but with a major change. In light of the defensive role that settlers were expected to play, all groups objecting to the use of weapons were ineligible. Among others, this eliminated the Dukhobors, whose travails and travels had been the original inspiration for the plan. The CER and Finance Ministry would supervise all land and colonization operations, but according to the final clause (15), any changes in incentives or significant policy reinterpretations had to be cleared with the other ministries concerned.

Many of these plans came to naught, but one important provision, passed by unanimous vote, did survive: the decision to suspend all migration rules within Manchuria. Although a loose passport regime was soon established there to monitor arrivals, no papers were ever required from the place of origin. Witte had recommended this bureaucratic reform for all of Siberia after his 1902 trip; that would not come to pass until June 19, 1904. Here, as elsewhere, Manchuria represented a field of experimentation for reformist policies that still faced stiff resistance in Russia proper. In discussing the Manchurian case, so far away as to be almost theoretical, key figures in later Imperial reforms, such as Krivoshein, tried out new concepts and approaches. Khorvat, who had just been appointed general manager of the CER, sat in on the conference and began to grasp Petersburg's developmental vision of the colony whose local administration he was to dominate for seventeen years.

In the spring and summer of 1903, the final details were worked out. An additional 4,800,000 rubles was budgeted to purchase 141,000 desiatinas judged necessary for colonization. To help with surveying, the Ministry of Agriculture and State Domains lent a seven-man team, headed by the Amur Migration Detachment's director, Counselor S. P. Kaffka, to Khorvat, newly arrived in Harbin. By the end of the summer, 500 farmsteads had been mapped out. A. A. Rittikh, later director of the Agriculture Ministry's Department of State Domains, was invited to manage the overall colonization effort on the CER.[24]

Sectarians who chose to farm were to receive plots of five to ten desiatinas on the West Branch of the CER between the Transbaikal and Qiqihar. To obtain a land deed, a family had to prove that it possessed over 400 rubles.[25] On June 25, 1903, Witte forwarded to Pleve a draft of the "Highest Proclamation" (*Vysochaishii Ukaz*), a document that would liberate sectarian emigrants to Manchuria from over 200 years of persecution and prejudice:

Now, in consideration of services in settling the State's borders performed by Old Believers and the followers of several other faiths, as well as their steadfastness in preserving their Russian nationality in foreign surroundings, We, ever-graciously (*vsemilostiveishe*), grant the same rights, both civil and religious, enjoyed by Our Orthodox subjects to those [sectarians] migrating in accordance with the rules for lands along the CER confirmed by Us on May 23 [the Romanov conference].

The religious rights embraced all aspects of worship, both ritual and spiritual. The construction of distinctive chapels, churches, cemeteries, and monasteries was expressly permitted; the public wearing of clerical vestments was to be allowed throughout Manchuria; and children of sect members could be educated in their own schools. In return, the grateful recipients were to imbue themselves with "loyalty to Throne and Fatherland."

A few days later, Pleve replied that "Proclamation" sounded too solemn. "Command" (Povelenie) would be more appropriate. Although, he added, one could argue that there was nothing new in all this, since the law of May 15, 1883, already stated that limitations placed on sectarians applied only within the Empire, "in essence, the principle of full equality between the Schism and Orthodoxy is proclaimed here." In conclusion, he cautioned Witte that Orthodox children should not attend *their* schools, and that the "command" should be kept secret (*"vo vseobshchee svedenie ne opublikovat'"*).[26]

The plans for the settlement of military personnel also made progress. On February 9, 1903, even before the Romanov conference, Iugovich had chaired a meeting in Harbin to come up with some appropriate numbers. The group concluded that 2,500 military families could be accommodated at the stations where border guard brigade headquarters were located, 1,000 in Harbin, and 500 each at Bohedu, Handaohezi, and Liaoyang. After a long silence, a CER board meeting on July 1 reduced the number of families to 500, 300 at Harbin and 50 on each of the CER branches (their math was not the best). Start-up costs were to be covered by an appropriation of 250,000 rubles.

After being cleared with Admiral Alekseev in Port Arthur, settlement regulations and housing norms for the border guard were forwarded to Witte and approved on August 12. To encourage enlisted men on active duty to bring their families to Manchuria, "soldier cantonments" (*soldatskie slobodki*) were to be located at the four stations listed above. Basic housing and up to half an acre (50 square sazhen) of arable land were to be provided. On expiration of their service period, guard families would have the option of moving to one of three "soldier settlements" (*soldatskie poselki*), located at Harbin, Hailar, and Pogranichnaia. Once there, they were to receive up to 600 square sazhen (six acres) and 300 to 450 rubles for start-up costs.[27]

The deed was easier said than done. On August 26, General N. M. Chichagov, in charge of the Transamur Border Guard, wrote to Witte as his commanding officer complaining that the Russian authorities in Manchuria had refused to distribute the necessary lands to the 3,400 families he had recruited. Repeated requests had been ineffectual, making it ever harder to convince "Russian pioneers of the special care of our administration." Finessing through the Finance Minister's strong ego, Chichagov suggested that Transamur Cossack colonies could be named "Witte settlements" (*Vittevskie poselki*). This proposal was obsolete before the letter reached Petersburg, since as of August 29, these decisions were no longer in Witte's hands.[28]

In fact, neither of the programs worked out by the Petersburg planners fully came to pass. Though thorough and creative, both the past and the future stood against them. By 1903, construction had already brought a population of 83,000 to the railway zone, 44,576 of whom were recorded as kharbintsy in the census of May 28, 1903. But only 15,579 were Russians, and approximately a third of these were women. Most of the adult Russian males were employed by the railroad. In large part, the modalities of daily life had already been established in Harbin. What had been a tabula rasa when the colonization deliberations began was no longer so.[29]

An even greater disruption of planning occurred a few months later, when the surprise attack on Port Arthur drove long-term development off the priority list. Clearly, all Manchurian questions would need to be reconsidered in the light of postwar eventualities. Although the Russo-Japanese War brought immediate disaster to Imperial Russia, Harbin profited immensely. Standing between the hundreds of thousands of troops quartered in southern Manchuria and the Russian homeland, Harbin became the focal point for massive influxes of money and materiel. According to the German military attaché who lived there for several months in 1905, it was the only "happening" city in Manchuria (*"wo 'etwas los war'"*). What exactly was happening prompted the Reuters correspondent to compare Harbin to Port Said, that carrier of all images vicious and immoral.[30]

Demographically, this meant that the troops were soon followed by a large number of men (and women) who set about satisfying the demands that arise in such situations in exchange for Treasury funds, which flowed even more freely than during the construction of the CER. It has been claimed that during the course of the war, the civilian population of Harbin (with Fujiadian) rose to 250,000. By the time the tide ebbed, the construction of the CER had been completed, and most of the prewar employees had returned to European Russia. Little demographic continuity exists between pre- and postwar Harbin.[31]

In the broad, if not in detail, the proposals of 1899–1903 did have a long-range impact. The principles agreed on by the February 1903 joint conference established a policy tradition that would carry on after the war. Just as important, the presence of the local administration in the person of Khorvat guaranteed that these doctrines would be followed up at the local level. Although Russia's Portsmouth obligations prevented the aggressive development of such measures as the soldier settlements, the spirit of creative colonization based on initiatives for which Russia proper was not yet deemed ready would provide the Manchurian colony with elements of dynamism, even after expansionism emanating from Petersburg had been replaced by passivity.

Colonial Demography: Harbin, 1913

With the end of the war, Harbin was no longer riding the crest of Empire. Instead, the near-bankruptcies of the CER, its owner the Russo-Chinese

Bank, and the two companies' erstwhile supporter, the Russian government, brought an end to almost ten years of official largesse. The army's evacuation silenced the booming grain mills, Manchuria's largest industry. Political uncertainties stifled credit and brought Harbin's economic life to a standstill. Russians who had come for profits went home. Chinese who had fled from the battlefields of southern Manchuria returned to their fields and ancestral burial grounds. The town's population fell precipitously, to around 25,000.[32]

Fortunately, for Harbin, by 1908 the revival of the grain trade under a consortium organized by the Russo-Chinese Bank, together with the debut of soybean exports from northern Manchuria, had pulled the city out of the doldrums.[33] The explosive growth of European demand for soybean derivatives guaranteed that the tariff closure of the Maritime province to Manchurian flour in 1909 would have little negative impact on the city's rapid development. International trade was also aided by the official opening of Harbin to foreign residents on January 7, 1907, although demographically this element was almost invisible. According to the 1913 census, 1.1 percent of Harbin's residents were Japanese (including a large group of prostitutes), and the share of other foreigners, representing twenty-one countries, was a mere 0.67 percent (434 people). The statistician in charge of analyzing the census materials, V. V. Soldatov, described Harbin as "a composite Russian-Chinese population with a minor admixture of Japanese subjects." Consequently, a demographic examination limited to Harbin's Chinese and Russian subjects provides an almost complete picture of that city in 1913.[34]

Table 2, showing the changes of population within the CER beltway between 1912 and 1913, indicates that Harbin was the only demographically dynamic location. For Russians and Chinese alike, turnover at Harbin explains the bulk of the population change: fully 96 percent for the Russians and a marginally less impressive 84 percent for the Chinese. Although interesting developments in Russo-Chinese trade took place at the border stations of Manzhouli-Manchuria and Suifenhe-Grodekovo, the social history of Russian Manchuria is, in the main, the urban history of Harbin.

Witte, in his 1902 report on his visit to Siberia and Manchuria, had insisted on the necessity of excluding foreigners from the CER right-of-way because of their "independent interests, generally contrary to our own." Chinese, by contrast, were to be welcomed as the future clients of the railroad. As noted above, ten years later, though the official restrictions were gone, there was still only a handful of foreigners. The degree to which the Chinese, who made up slightly more than a third of Harbin municipality's population in 1913 (35 percent), had been integrated is much harder to measure. Perhaps it will be easier, if we begin by breaking the city down into more manageable neighborhood-sized portions.[35]

TABLE 2 *Harbin and CER Beltway Population, 1912–13*

Area	1912	1913	Net change
CER beltway[a]			
Russians	70,117	66,898	−3,219
Chinese	27,398	45,334	17,936
Combined total	97,515	112,232	14,717
Harbin only			
Russians	46,478	43,391	−3,087
Chinese	8,453	23,537	15,084
Combined total	54,931	66,928	11,997

SOURCE: RGIA 560: 28, 138, p. 66.
[a] Includes Harbin.

Most descriptions of Harbin before the Russo-Japanese War describe three separate settlements, Old Harbin, New Town, and Pristan. Old Harbin, the abandoned distillery and the construction camp that grew up around it, had never pretended to permanence. Although successive temporary needs kept the area full until the war ended, it was doomed to decline. The removal of the Alekseev church to Mojiagou (near New Town) in 1912 was symptomatic of demographic shifts confirmed by the 1913 census. The population of Old Harbin had fallen 48 percent from its May 1903 level. Kharbintsy always had a weakness for their town's alcoholic origins, but when plague struck in 1910–11, nostalgia was put aside. Old Harbin remained outside the barriers with the rest of infected China, even though its population was proportionately more Russian than either New Town or riverside Pristan.[36]

New Town, with a 17.2 percent Chinese population, was 0.8 percent more sinicized than Old Harbin, but here the numbers are misleading. As befitted the administrative center of Russian Manchuria, Chinese had little impact in New Town. Most of them lived in the peripheral areas called Districts I and II in the census. These two zones lay to the southwest and northeast of the city center. Only one-half of 1 percent of New Town's real estate was in Chinese hands. In addition, the occupations of New Town's Chinese were not vital to the success of this part of the city. A survey carried out in February–March 1911 found that 35 percent were employed as either "boys" (*boiki*) or cooks, and another 38 percent had unskilled and semiskilled jobs (*chernorabochie*, etc.). Run by and for its 17,000 Russian residents, New Town was the measure of Russia's expansion and local control.[37]

Pristan was altogether different. Here Chinese held 14 percent of the private land and accounted for 43 percent of the population. About 40 percent of the residents were tradesmen, storekeepers, or skilled workers. Where there were just twenty-seven businessmen (tradesmen or storekeepers) in New Town, 1,994 of Pristan's Chinese residents alone were so engaged. It was here that Russo-Chinese transactions would begin to turn Manchuria's economic development into a classic case of staple export-driven economy.

Although the four census districts employed by the Russians in 1913 showed an even distribution of Chinese subjects, running from 41.1 percent to 44.4 percent, that result is misleading. A street-by-street count conducted in the 1911 survey revealed a very high concentration of Chinese in two adjacent subdistricts officially separated by the border between Districts I and II in 1913. In fact, over 70 percent of Pristan's Chinese population lived in the strip between Kitaiskaia (Chinese) Street and Vodoprovodnaia (Water Pipe) Street. The fourteen-row town bazaar was completely within the Chinese quarter. Symbolically enough, the legations of the Chinese diplomatic representatives (*jiaosheju*) from Fengtian and Jilin provinces stood opposite the marketplace; and the Heilongjiang legation was only a block away.[38]

Other statistics bear out this ghetto-like situation. Pristan, for example, was the most densely settled area of Harbin, with 42.1 people per acre. New Town's density was just 16.6. The area between Novogorodnaia and Kitaiskaia streets, the heart of Chinatown, had 96.0 people per acre. Although according to 1910 statistics, Petersburg's two worst wards were 200 percent more crowded, and six others were over 100 percent more densely populated than Pristan, multistoried housing in St. Petersburg greatly reduced the crush. Few buildings in Pristan were taller than two stories.[39]

In a 1913 article, the head of the city's statistical bureau, V. V. Soldatov, wrote:

What the sanitary conditions of Harbin are, we all know quite well. We know that Pristan stands on a swamp, and that the soil is infected and fouled by excrement and refuse. We know what disgusting water, mostly drawn from the subsoil, is drunk by the Pristan population. It is thanks only to the salutary climate that Harbin's death rate is still not too high.[40]

Despite this restrained optimism, crowding and the lack of even the most elementary sewage system did have their fatal effects. In late October 1910, isolated cases of pulmonary plague (*legochnaia chuma*) began to appear in Fujiadian and in the "Chinese quarters of Harbin itself." By mid-January, the epidemic was in full swing. In just five months, it claimed 60,000 victims in Manchuria, at least 6,000 in Fujiadian, and 1,556 kharbintsy. In Harbin, only 40 Europeans died.[41] A comparison of maps showing the distribution of plague cases in the early stages of the epidemic and then again in its twelfth week indicates how quickly death homed in on Pristan's squalid Chinese ghetto.[42]

In spite of this drastic Malthusian corrective, by 1913 Fujiadian was clearly taking Old Harbin's place in the urban trinity.* With a higher population than either New Town or Pristan, Fujiadian was a source of labor and trade that had to be taken into account. In late December 1910, when it became necessary to quarantine Harbin off from even more virulent Fujiadian, concerns were voiced regarding the disastrous effects on business. A few years later, Soldatov claimed that no true picture of the "economic unit called Harbin" was possible without a thorough census of Fujiadian, Harbin's Chinese counterpart.[43]

Data on the daily traffic flow between Fujiadian, Pristan, and New Town also indicate their increasing integration into a single urban unit. An average of several seasonal samplings in 1912–13 showed that in a twenty-four-hour period, 4,744 people traveled between New Town and Fujiadian, 21,946 between New Town and Pristan, and 29,346 between Fujiadian and Pristan. Even assuming that most of this traffic owed to local commuters, as the nearly equal numbers in both directions would suggest, on an average day over 28,000 kharbintsy went to another part of the city. Harbin's well-being was becoming ever more dependent on the symbiotic relationship of its constituent parts, both Russian and Chinese.[44]

Where did all these kharbintsy come from? Shandong, that mighty reservoir of impoverished humanity, sent just over half. Adding on Zhili (16.6 percent), Jilin (8.1), and Fengtian (5.9) provinces accounts for over four-fifths of the total. Only 357 men and women claimed that they had lived in Harbin for more than twenty years, that is to say, from before the Russian arrival. The oldest living native Haerbinren were in their seventies. Possibly some of them were the original settlers who founded the fishing village in the nineteenth century. What a tale they could have told, if anyone had thought to ask them.[45]

Russian citizens can be divided into three sets by origin. The largest group in 1913 had come from European Russia. If we include the Caucasus under that rubric, they accounted for 54 percent of the Russian total. Emigrants from Siberia and the CER right-of-way accounted for another 28

---

*That rise was by design. In 1907, with the opening of Harbin as a treaty port, the Chinese authorities decided to promote Fujiadian, the seat of the newly appointed *binjiang guandao*, as a counterweight to Russian-controlled Harbin. In connection with this, the third character in Fujiadian's name was changed from the word for "store" to the somewhat more impressive word for "pasture." These two characters are homophonic, so the pronunciation remained unaltered. Zhao Tian, "Fujiadiande lailongqumai," p. 136; *Haerbin shizhi*, pp. 9–10.

percent. The remainder were native kharbintsy. Harbin's birthrate of 57.4 per 1,000 was just barely outstripped by Russia's most reproductive provinces, Riazan (58.1) and Samara (57.7). The statistician who calculated this rate called it "unconditionally monstrous." Women made up only 41 percent of the Siberian group but were a majority (51 percent) of the "Europeans."[46]

All of this detail the historian owes to the March 9/February 24, 1913, census conducted by the Harbin municipal administration. On its election in February 1908, a study of the city's population had been one of the first issues broached. But the matter had been dropped for lack of funds until the plague epidemic put it back on the agenda. The lack of demographic data had forced the Plague Commission to improvise its own emergency census, thereby proving this measure to be the sine qua non of urban planning. On November 14, 1911, the city government allotted funds to undertake a census and to found a municipal statistical bureau to analyze the results.[47]

The contents of the census questionnaire reveal both the concerns and the expectations of the local compilers. If we take the census questions posed in the 1897 Empire-wide poll as a base set, the addition of three new questions on past, present, and future residence (items 5–7) suggests the municipal government understood that mobility was one of the city's central characteristics. A series of supplementary queries dealing with citizenship, ethnic identity, religion, and languages, both native and secondary (items 9–15), hints at human variety not fully captured by a simple Russo-Chinese dichotomy. Questions on unemployment and employability probably reflect an increasing awareness of these ills in Russian society as a whole. The sole categories from the 1897 census to disappear completely in Harbin's case are the "estate" (*soslovie*) and "registration" (*pripiska*). Neither vertical social structure nor traditional methods of local control were welcome on the Manchurian frontier.[48]

The importance attached to these questions as a means of defining local character is clear from the care with which they were worked out by a joint committee of municipal leaders and possible end-users of the census data (e.g., schoolteachers, the town architect, and the CER commercial agent). These conferences occupied the better part of three days (January 25, 27, and 29, 1913), with the most heat being generated by arguments for and against an extensive surveying of language skills. The second half of the first session was spent pruning back this section of the questionnaire, only to see a concerted counterattack in the second session reinstate almost all of the cuts.

The most powerful and eventually decisive argument in favor of reinstatement was presented by the *gymnasium* teacher V. A. Vasil'ev:

It is important both from a national [*gosudarstvennyi*] point of view and from the point of view of local interests to prove that Harbin is a Russian city. In the metropolis, the idea has taken hold that Harbin is a foreign [*inorodcheskii*] city that has lost touch with the metropolis. Therefore, [Harbin] is looked on as a stepchild [*pasynok*]. We must disprove this idea with exact statistical data, so that the metropolis does not cut us off, so that Harbin . . . will have a State Duma representative, and so that repressive economic laws will not be applied to Harbin. The census will establish which language is predominant, thereby showing to which culture the city belongs.

The spokesman for statistical science, Soldatov, added that his field considered the language question more essential than the already approved poll of ethnicity (*natsional'nost'*).[49]

Not all committeemen subscribed to Vasil'ev's desire for rapprochement. Some argued the necessity of presenting the census as a purely local initiative on the grounds that residents would only place their trust in investigators "under the supervision of local public organizations." Bureaucratic surveys by those "alien to the region" (*chuzhdye mestnomu kraiu*) would inevitably meet with suspicious informants and, consequently, distorted information. In ambivalent Harbin, fears of alienation and abandonment coexisted with the knowledge that the embrace of the Imperial motherland could be more smothering than protective.[50]

Together with this vested interest in identifying Harbin as a Russian city, the census preliminaries reveal a genuine curiosity about the Chinese population. The statistician Soldatov was not only convinced of the need to survey Fujiadian for a complete picture of Harbin as an economic unit; he was also excited at the thought of making the first "scientific" census of a Chinese city. Unfortunately, the Chinese saw these activities as merely an extension of Russian municipal authority, a contentious matter ever since the administration's establishment in 1908. Permission to poll Fujiadian was denied. Nonetheless, special attention was paid to the Chinese population within the CER right-of-way. A separate questionnaire was composed, and Chinese students from the Harbin commercial schools were employed as census-takers.[51]

The Jewish Community: An Eastern Zion?

One of the most interesting facts to emerge from the census data is the presence in Harbin of a sizable Jewish community. In Siberia, only Irkutsk had more Jews (6,100 in 1909). But that community's representation among Russian passport holders was much smaller. Harbin's 5,032 Jews constituted 11.5 percent of the Russians, compared with just 5.6 percent for Irkutsk.[52] This group vies with the Poles for the honor of providing Harbin with its earliest minority organization.[53] The Polish residents, however, were a smaller group (5.9 percent). More important, most were dependent for their livelihood on either the CER or the army. For that reason, an examination of Jewish life will be more revealing of social conditions in prerevolutionary Harbin outside official circles.

Harbin's first Jewish residents officially constituted themselves as the Jewish Minority (*natsional'naia*) Community on February 16, 1903. From the beginning, the elected Spiritual Directorate (Dukhovnoe Pravlenie) sought and received police approval. At the first few meetings, this body focused its attention on the need for a place of worship. The rental of a building was soon arranged, and the directorate called on N. D. Dunaevskii of Odessa to collect funds in European Russia for a Harbin synagogue. By August 27, community representatives were attending the directorate's sessions. On November 11, this organ debated the desirability of appointing a delegation to meet with Admiral E. I. Alekseev during an upcoming visit to Harbin. The intended goal would be to obtain permission to build a permanent prayer house.[54]

From the beginning, questions of religious observance were a foremost concern in the absence of qualified religious practitioners. Many of these issues were resolved with the arrival in August 1904 of Harbin's first rabbi, W. Levin. For example, on January 7, 1904, a sitting of Jewish leaders had decided to assess a communal tax of five kopecks per chicken on kosher slaughtering but put off a decision on the number of kosher butchers to be allowed in Harbin until the rabbi's appearance. As it turned out, Rabbi Levin was also skilled in the art of circumcision, putting an end to such a painful delay as that of little Vol'f Romanovich, the first child listed in the Jewish community's birth register (*metricheskaia kniga*), who was born on January 10, 1904, but had to wait for his circumcision until an itinerant *mohel*, Abram Naer, visited in early June.[55]

Rabbi Levin left in 1906, suggesting that his duties may have been related to the influx of Jewish servicemen during the Russo-Japanese War.[56] One source corroborates this interpretation by calling the first house of worship the "soldier" synagogue. Whether for this reason or because of the new economic opportunities provided by the opening of hostilities, statistical data indicate rapid growth. There are no total population figures available for the Jewish community before 1913, but the birth register offers several vital statistics whose gist is sufficiently clear (see Table 3).

An increasing demographic base of support led naturally to a wider spectrum of community services. A new synagogue and a primary school emphasizing Jewish studies were completed in 1907. By 1910, the synagogue was running enough of a profit to support the school, whose enrollment had risen from eighteen to 200 students. Among the other institutions

98 *Manchurian Colonization*

TABLE 3 *Births, Marriages, and Deaths in Harbin's Jewish Community, 1903–14*

			Deaths	
Year	Births	Marriages	Male	Female
1903	20	9	8	1
1904	12	3	26	3
1905	19	10	45	2
1906	53	34	42	25
1907	107	31	18	14
1908	116	39	28	14
1909	124	45	33	16
1910	114	54	19	10
1911	115	38	28	13
1912	99	55	35	16
1913	117	63	35	31
1914	132	64	29	26

SOURCE: Birth register (*metricheskaia kniga*) of Harbin Jewish Community. HLJ 83,1,487.

established before 1914 were a burial brotherhood, a Hebrew school, a cemetery, a *mikvah* (ritual bathhouse), an old-age home, and a Torah study group. The Jewish Women's Charity Committee was founded in 1907, and a library was built in 1912. In 1911, statutes for a committee to aid Jews migrating to Palestine were rejected by the CER's Civil Management Special Council because a notary's seal had not been affixed. Probably, the repair of the technical oversight resulted in a reversal of that decision.[57]

The termination of the war and the recession that followed hurt the Jewish community as much as other kharbintsy, but where others might have been tempted to step back across the border into Siberia, an 1899 ban on new Jewish settlement east of the Urals eliminated this option for Harbin Jewry. The only choice was to stay or return to the Pale of Settlement, where poverty and pogroms had probably generated the original impulse to come to Harbin. In fact, the statistics in Table 3 suggest that Jews were arriving in relatively large numbers just when tens of thousands of war speculators were leaving. Hundreds of Jewish soldiers who discovered Harbin while awaiting repatriation soon returned from European Russia with their families.[58]

The upswing caused by the rising export of soybeans put an end to hard times for both Harbin as a whole and its subpopulations. Jewish merchants played a special role in this process, since it was one of their number, Roman Moiseevich Kabalkin, who pioneered the export trade. Kabalkin, who had already made his name and fortune in European Russia as a grain trader with no fear of novel methods, served for fourteen years as a consultant to the Riazan-Ural'sk railway, the chief source of engineers for the CER. This association led to an invitation from the chief of the CER Commercial Department, K. P. Lazarev, to help develop freight traffic between Siberia and Manchuria. To this end, Kabalkin founded R. M. Kabalkin and Son, Inc.

His relationship with the CER and his experience in Siberian trade probably served Kabalkin well during the wartime profiteering. Afterward, his knowledge of world grain markets made him an early advocate of the soybean. Legend describes Kabalkin wandering in the Harbin marketplace, pointing out heaps of beans to his son and calling them the "gold of Manchuria." Although Kabalkin had suggested the export of bean oil to the CER as early as 1903 and sought Petersburg's permission as early as 1907, European export by another of his companies, Natanson and Co., did not start from Vladivostok until January 1909. The Japanese beat Kabalkin to the punch—Mitsui Bussan's first shipment left Dairen in November 1908—but his eventual inability to compete resulted less from the two-month headstart than from the unwillingness of the Russo-Chinese Bank and CER to extend necessary credit. Both companies, the only major sources of Russian capital in the Far East, were already committed to Manchuria's grain mills as the key to Harbin's industrial future. This would prove to be an expensive miscalculation for Russian trade prospects in the region.[59]

Even after the Russo-Asiatic Bank (the Russo-Chinese's successor from 1910) came around to a position of support for Kabalkin, he faced different hurdles in the form of anti-Semitic regulations in Russia proper. For example, during his second export season, in 1909–10, he was almost expelled from Vladivostok. Only intervention by Khorvat kept him from being forcibly separated from the shipment he was loading. The issue arose anew the following year and was settled, but once again only on a temporary basis, by the Council of Ministers. In 1913, Prince G. G. Kugushev, the director of the Russo-Asiatic Bank's Harbin office, raised the matter with a visiting Duma member, V. I. Denisov, pointing out how the exclusion of Jews from Kamchatka had delivered the fishing industry into Japanese hands. Nonetheless, Kabalkin's plan to build an oil-pressing mill at Vladivostok was vetoed by the Priamur governor-general, N. L. Gondatti. Yet another attempt to expel Kabalkin in 1915 gave this harassment a chronic air.[60]

Another important role model for Harbin Jewry was Lev Shmulevich Skidel'skii, whose wealth derived from lumber and other interests was almost as great as gossip hinted. He was Harbin's only millionaire and seems to have been shrewd enough to sidestep the crash of the ruble that destroyed so many Russian fortunes after 1917. Although he seems to have been relatively inactive in the public sphere, sheer wealth guaranteed that anecdotes would circulate. For example, a charity collection received 100 rubles from Skidel'skii's son and heir, Salomon. When Lev Shmulevich decided to give only twenty-five, he was chided, "But your son . . ." "I don't have a rich father," he shot back.[61]

Money led to influence in the public sphere. Since membership rosters did not specify people's religious affiliation, it is impossible to determine the exact representation of Jews on the Harbin exchange founded in 1907 and the municipal assembly elected in 1908. Seven of the thirty-two original members of the exchange who were still involved in 1910 (22 percent) and ten of the forty men who were elected as representatives by the 1,696 voters in February 1908 (25 percent) were clearly Jewish. A few weeks later, these forty men selected four of their number to serve on the municipal council, an executive organ. Two of the four were Jewish.[62]

For all this, Harbin was still a late Imperial Russian town, and this ensured the presence of at least a modicum of anti-Semitism. As elsewhere in the Empire in late 1905, the search for a scapegoat on which to blame both military defeat and internal disorder led unerringly to the Jews. The humiliated officer corps appears to have been the source of these slanders. An appeal written by a lieutenant-colonel named Alekseev (not a relative of the ex-viceroy) and printed on the Rear Headquarters' press in Harbin warned the "free citizens of Harbin" that the Jews would use the new freedoms to invade all areas and institutions. It concluded with an open invitation to violence: "crush the vile enemy in time. Crush him so that he never rises again."[63]

In response, the Jewish community began to look into the purchase of weapons for a self-defense force. First inquiries were made in Shanghai, but shipping problems ruled that out; civil transport from South China to northern Manchuria had not yet been reestablished. The community's representatives then turned to Rear Commander I. P. Nadarov with a request for arms. Whether Nadarov acceded to this entreaty, as one source claims, he plainly found the Jewish community's fears convincing, for on December 10, 1905, he telegraphed to General Kuropatkin asking for reliable troops with which to keep the tensions between strike committees and reactionaries from developing into pogroms.[64]

A separate and very interesting case of anti-Semitism occurred in 1911. In that year, the journal *Vestnik Azii* (Herald of Asia) quoted Harbin's Chinese Chamber of Commerce as saying in a report to Beijing's Ministry of Industry, Agriculture, and Trade:

Jews have been Russian subjects for several centuries, but only those with over 1,500 rubles' worth of real estate are permitted to live in large cities. Since they lack specific occupation, the Jews chose Manchuria as their refuge. Let's look at Harbin. Every day more arrive, making up 70 percent of the European population. But this European element is, by nature, a swindler.... Their further spread threatens the Chinese government and, unless measures are taken, future danger will be difficult to avoid. The approaching review of the trade treaty is the most convenient moment to raise the Jewish question. In each article providing the Russians with privileges, we must include a note that that article does not apply to Jews. Only in this way will we succeed in limiting the rights of the Jews. We think that even the Russians will agree with the necessity of these inclusions for several articles of the above-mentioned treaty.[65]

Although anti-Semitism in pre-1917 Harbin seems never to have reached the level of violence, this quote implies that the Chinese had discovered Russian men of influence who were not well-disposed toward the Jewish community. It also raises the question of Harbin's role in the spread of anti-Semitism from Europe to Asia. Authorities in Petersburg were also reading exaggerated reports of Jewish influence in Harbin. On November 7, 1915, Colonel Gorgop, the commander of the Harbin gendarmerie, informed his superior that Harbin was "mostly Jews" (*v bol'shinstve evrei*), who controlled the municipal government.[66] Nonetheless, these were clouds in generally sunny skies. In Harbin, there was little overt prejudice and no pogroms.

One of the most important advantages Harbin offered its Jewish residents was the absence of the *numerus clausus*. In 1908, what had previously been an administrative rule limiting Jewish admission to secondary and higher education hardened into Empire-wide law. The next year, despite the opposition of the Minister of Education, Stolypin raised the quota of Jewish students allowed in state secondary schools to 5 percent in the capitals, to 15 percent in the Pale of Settlement, and to 10 percent elsewhere. The downside was that these restrictions were extended to private schools. Enforcement was also stepped up.[67]

School enrollment statistics for Harbin show a very different situation. The men's and women's commercial high schools, founded and funded by the CER, were the closest Harbin had to "state" schools. In 1913, 14.7 percent of the combined student body was Jewish. The percentage in private schools was much higher (25 percent), and the overall rate for secondary education was 20.1 percent. Since the 402 students enrolled represent most of the Jewish children of high school age, we can safely assume that education was available to all who qualified. In privileged Harbin, dire tidings from European Russia of legal restrictions and blood libel cases occasioned no more than long-distance commiseration and secret relief.[68]

TABLE 4 *Age Structure of Harbin Population by Ethnic Group, 1913*
(Percent)

Age group	Russians	Poles	Jews	Chinese	Japanese
0–1	2.9%	1.5%	2.1%	0.3%	1.0%
2–5	12.1	6.7	11.9	2.5	5.0
6–10	9.3	4.8	11.9	2.1	1.3
11–15	6.7	3.9	11.2	2.3	1.4
16–20	6.1	4.2	10.0	8.6	17.3
21–25	25.7	42.8	8.3	17.0	22.6
26–30	11.2	10.9	10.0	22.8	19.6
31–35	8.7	7.6	9.7	18.5	16.2
36–40	8.1	5.9	9.2	11.5	8.1
41–45	3.8	4.6	5.2	7.3	4.0
46+	5.4	4.1	10.5	7.1	3.5

SOURCE: *Stat. op.*, p. 66.

The Harbin census data on language use provides a potential explanation for why some Jews would prefer to "emigrate" within the Russian realm in these years when nearly 2,000,000 had opted to leave the Empire altogether. In answer to the question, "What language do you usually speak in the home?" 62 percent of the Jews replied Russian, and only 32 percent Yiddish. In contrast, according to the 1897 census, 97 percent of all Russian Jews declared Yiddish as their mother tongue. Perhaps, for the Jewish "Russianists," a location outside the official boundaries and prejudices of the Russian state, but within a Russian-speaking cultural, social, and economic world, was the best solution. If other new arrivals had chosen Harbin for similar reasons, this would go far toward explaining the impressive cultural life, quite atypical for a frontier boomtown, that flourished in Harbin.[69]

Not surprisingly, a thriving ten-year-old community exhibits unmistakable signs of demographic stability. With 91.5 women for every 100 men, the Jews had by far the most normal male-female ratio among Harbin's ethnic groups. The ratios for Russians and Chinese in 1913 were 66.8:100 and 19.0:100, respectively. Table 4, showing the age structure of the various groups, tells the same story. The Russian, Polish, Chinese, and Japanese accord exactly with the vision of a young frontier town. The Chinese figures indicate the increasing capability for hard labor in a slightly older age category (26–35). And we see a younger median in the Russian and especially the Polish populations because of the many enlisted men in the 21–

to 25-year-old group. The prevalence of young prostitutes accounts for the strength in the 16–20 Japanese age group. The Jewish community's balanced distribution is a triumph over the local environment, for Harbin's child mortality rate was exceedingly high.[70]

This feat of social hygiene appears even more impressive if we consider that 90.6 percent of Harbin Jews (4,559) lived in Pristan, and that the bulk of them (82 percent, or 3,738) resided either within or adjacent to the Chinese ghetto (District II). Still, if, as seems likely, Jewish domiciles were clustered around the synagogue and primary school located side by side on Artilleriiskaia Street between Pekarnaia and Konnaia, a long block (approximately 300 m) would have put some distance between Harbin's healthiest and the unsanitary dangers of the Chinese quarter. The logical hunch that Jews would gravitate toward their religious and cultural center is supported by data on enrollments in the free municipal preparatory school named after Tolstoi. It opened in 1908, to celebrate the eightieth anniversary of the author's birth, at a location only four blocks from the synagogue. In the inaugural year, 27.6 percent of the students were Jewish.[71]

As of March 31, 1911, roughly fifteen months after Khorvat approved the new regulations of the Jewish spiritual community (January 6, 1910), there were 609 registered members. Since the age- and sex-distribution data given above suggest that approximately one in four Jews was an adult (over age eighteen) male, that figure is well under the 1,000 we would expect to be registered from the 1913 census data. What might account for the shortfall? One possibility is rapid growth in the intervening two years. Certainly, there was an upward trend, although probably not sharp enough to explain the whole difference.[72] Another possibility is that some of the males in the 18–40 group were enlisted men and therefore ineligible for membership in the spiritual community. Such an explanation would mean, then, that Harbin's Jewish families were larger than the census would predict. A third possibility is that some Jews in Harbin either had too little interest in religious matters to join or did not have enough discretionary cash to cover the three-ruble annual membership fee.[73] Probably all three factors played some part.

In Defense of Difference: Jews, Poles, and Politics

The continuation of peace and prosperity for Harbin Jewry was contingent on both a supportive policy at the center and its active enforcement at the local level. There was no lack of anti-Semitic officials who were appalled by the CER's tolerance. Even in the construction phase, central figures in the "East Asiatic Industrial Company," a group that would later become famous as the Bezobrazov clique, were complaining that "instead of bringing our own best powers into play, we left the work to Jews and Poles whom S. Yu [Witte] commissioned to be our color-bearers." The alarm was sounded that the "Russian cause" in the Far East was in danger of falling "prey to the Jewish consistorium and the tricks of European diplomacy."[74]

In 1900, Witte was still too strong for these fulminations to find an outlet. The belief in laissez-faire migration that had motivated the Finance Minister's unsuccessful opposition to closing Siberia to the Jews kept Manchuria open to all, although in this period the only unbaptized Jews in the right-of-way were government contractors. Even these men occasionally faced difficulties in traveling to Manchuria because of an 1860 law, aimed at preventing the flight abroad of Siberian gold, that forbade Jews to come within 100 versts of the Chinese border. On hearing that the Transbaikal governor was enforcing this rule, Witte immediately ordered him to desist. In January 1903, Iugovich published an order "for whomever needs guidance" stating that Jews were allowed into the CER Beltway. A simultaneous statute forbidding Jewish exiles and their offspring to settle in the CER right-of-way cannot be considered prejudicial since the July 17, 1902, passport rules made the same distinction for Russians and Chinese. In contrast, Jewish residence had already been forbidden in the Guandong leasehold. An American citizen was arrested in Port Arthur simply because it was suspected that he was a Russian Jew. The CER itself appears not to have employed any Jews before World War One.[75]

Iugovich was succeeded in July 1903 by a man who had been present at the February conference that had confirmed the use of religious toleration to encourage Manchurian settlement and so was unlikely to oppose the extension of that inducement to Jews. In fact, during his long tenure as general manager of the CER, D. L. Khorvat appears to have been a steady supporter of a liberal minority policy and a proponent of urban colonization. On June 1, 1906, he approved the land grant in Pristan on which the Jewish community would build its synagogue, school, and hospital. On the other hand, Khorvat was not particularly keen on Jews as civic leaders and seems to have made use of his two appointments (out of six members) to the municipal council to balance the Jewish overrepresentation.[76]

Khorvat's first year on the CER was also a transitional year for the tip of the bureaucratic iceberg. Although Witte was already weakened, it was not until August 29, 1903, that he was kicked upstairs to become chairman of the Committee of Ministers, where he could do little more than watch as his Finance "superministry" was dismantled.[77] Almost immediately, the pioneering colonization policy that had taken so long to establish came under attack.

On January 26, 1904, an assembly called the Preliminary Conference for Discussion of Questions Regarding Russia's Financial, Industrial, and Economic Undertakings in the Far East met under the chairmanship of Count A. P. Ignatiev, a member of Bezobrazov's inner circle. The unspoken but obvious goal was the consolidation of Witte's two main undertakings in the Far East, the Russo-Chinese Bank and the CER, under the control of A. M. Abaza's Far Eastern Committee. The means were to be privatization and russification.

Work stalled through several meetings until the conferees brought the new Minister of Finance, V. N. Kokovtsov, aboard in order to get at his ministry's data on the targeted enterprises. On May 23, Kokovtsov made a presentation proving conclusively that neither of his corporate charges could be touched because of their international commitments. The Finance Minister suggested three other steps that might be considered instead: (1) the manipulation of customs dues, transportation tariffs, taxes, and credits; (2) the removal of various formalities hampering the organization of other companies; and (3) the renunciation of "intolerance toward foreigners and Jews." "We should not fear," he added, "that foreigners will get rich, since our Russians are either too satiated or too poor." Capitalists would not "seek their fortunes in the Far East" as long as the Moscow dry-goods trade brought a 24 percent profit. Even Abaza was forced to admit that "as soon as Russian influence begins, . . . the spirit of enterprise declines."[78]

Once having begun in this vein, Kokovtsov provided steady steering for the next decade. His long tenure as Finance Minister offered the continuing sanctuary within which Harbin's Jewish community grew, safe from the storms that swept over their brethren in Russia proper. Neither Kokovtsov nor Witte before him was especially pro-Jewish, but they did both have a well-developed rationale for tolerance in Russian Manchuria. It was this that made Harbin so different from the metropolis (or the Pale) for minorities fleeing the routinized anti-Semitism of their "homeland."[79]

Although the Finance Ministry's tactics for defending unorthodox approaches in Manchuria called for deciding as many questions as possible on the spot, far from the critical eyes of powerful central government figures, interministerial rivals at the local level sometimes succeeded in drawing St. Petersburg's attention to the distant periphery.[80] Between September 14, 1910, and January 13, 1911, Kokovtsov received requests for clarification regarding three "progressive" organizations that had been allowed to form in Harbin. The questioners, the assistant manager of the CER responsible for civil administration, a vice-minister of the Interior, and an assistant minister in that same ministry, wanted to know more about the Society of Residents and Voters of Harbin (Obshchestvo obyvatelei i izbiratelei g. Kharbina), the Polish Association (Gospoda Pol'ska), and the Jewish community's new school, respectively. The final letter asked also for background information on the status of Jewish residence in Harbin.[81] Two internal memorandums (*spravka*) provided both the logic and the language from which Kokovtsov would draw his replies, all addressed directly to P. A. Stolypin as Interior Minister. As a series, the documents construct step by step a coherent argument for why Harbin had been and should continue to be liberated from the most egregious strictures of Russian social and political life.

Major-General M. E. Afanas'ev had confirmed the bylaws of Harbin's Society of Voters on September 6, 1910, but then, thinking better of it, he had written to the board of the CER on September 14 to ask if this was an appropriate decision. The fact that the CER was under close scrutiny in Petersburg probably motivated him to seek confirmation in the capital of what seemed routine by Harbin standards. The resultant spravka prepared for Kokovtsov admitted that the Petersburg version of this organization had been closed as an anti-government center, but insisted that since Harbin had no Duma representation, such activities could not serve as a springboard to higher-level opposition. Furthermore, the writer said, "In view of the oncoming battle of nationalities [*natsional'nosti*] in Harbin caused by the international situation there and taking into account the [strong] organization of the Chinese element, any measure contributing to the rallying [*splochenie*] of the local Russian population on the basis of local interests [could] it would seem, only be welcomed."[82] Since no query had come from outside the ministry, no external correspondence ensued.

The second inquiry, a November 10 note to Vice-Minister S. F. Veber of the Finance Ministry from Vice-Minister P. G. Kurlov of the Interior Ministry, had clearly hostile intentions. Kurlov began by describing the Polish Association as an organization established in Harbin in August 1907 for the express purposes of encouraging the "cultural rapprochement and unification of Poles living in Manchuria" by means of meetings, theater and concert performances, public lectures and discussions, libraries and reading rooms, charity, and education. Did not these aims, he asked, contradict the "basic tasks of Russian government policy" presented in the Senate ukase of September 17, 1909? (That ukase, targeted mainly at the Poles in the Ukraine, had been used to shut down a Polish cultural organization, Osvita, in Kiev.)[83]

Kokovtsov got back to the Interior Minister on the first query on December 17, 1910. Following his spravka closely, he advised his colleague that the parallelism between the Society of Residents and Voters in Harbin and like-named organizations in the metropolis was only superficial. The recent suppression of these groups in European Russia on grounds of excessive electioneering should not be extended to Manchuria, where local politics operated on a basis similar to other international settlements in China, rather than the Russian model. More generally, if the Russians were to maintain their position in Harbin vis-à-vis the Chinese, "a rallying [*splochen-*

nost'] of the Russian population" was needed. To this, Kokovtsov added: "In my opinion, organizations proposed by the local inhabitants that would contribute to the uniting of patriotic [*otechestvennyi*] elements by asserting national [*natsional'nye*] interests in the sphere of local administration . . . lead toward this goal."[84] Of particular interest here is the association of the national interest with the development of local institutions based on local initiative, a policy conception that goes against the conventional view of the Russian Imperial state ideal as top-down, centralizing, and devoted to standardization.[85] It seems reasonable to assume that Kokovtsov wrote this memorandum without extramural prompting in order to set a precedent for more controversial issues to follow.

Less than a month later, Assistant Interior Minister S. E. Kryzhanovskii wrote to tell Kokovtsov that the Jewish community of Harbin had just opened a new school. His source, the Russian-language Zionist weekly *Rassvet* (Dawn), claimed that the festive inauguration had "brought into the daily lives of Harbin Jews thrown together from all corners of Russia a bright light [*svetlyi luch*]." Kryzhanovskii's desire to know "how Jews are permitted to live in Harbin" probably represented an intention to put that bright light out.[86]

By February 3, 1911, the request for an explanation of Gospoda Pol'ska's existence was already three months awaiting, but, probably because of the extreme sensitivity of the Polish issue at that time (the western zemstvo crisis in the Duma was building toward its dramatic climax), Kokovtsov decided to handle the Jewish issue first. He had already received a spravka on the Polish question, however, and with some light editing, he was able to apply it to the Jews of Harbin. As in the previous letter, the Finance Minister began by emphasizing Manchuria's atypicality. "Those conditions that make necessary the application of constraining measures [*stesnitel'nye mery*] to the Jews in Russia," he stated, "have no place in our Far Eastern colony." The next passage, which establishes a *Staatsraison* for nondiscrimination, is lifted verbatim from the internal memorandum:

Really, in our Far Eastern colony, where by virtue of political conditions a fierce battle on the basis of international rivalry holds the first place, those peculiarities and aspirations of separate peoples [*narodnosti*] that are meaningful at home do not play such an essential role. Under the conditions of this rivalry, narrow national [*uzkonatsionalisticheskie*] differences, tribal and religious discord among separate elements of the nation, are wiped away. The participants in this [international] conflict, by the very nature of things, are fully conscious that they are representatives, not of one or another particular people [in the internal memorandum on the Poles, "particular people" reads "region"] of a given state, but of that state in its entirety, and that their interests are directly bound to the realization of the interests and consolidation of the influence of their fatherland [*otechestvennyi*].

Consequently, any group that encouraged "the feelings of communality, initiative, and solidarity [aided] the Russian task in the Far East."[87]

Having provided the theoretical underpinnings for the Polish case to follow, Kokovtsov went on to the matter of the Jewish community. "Whatever your opinion of the Jewish element from a governmental point of view," he told Stolypin, "it is necessary in all fairness to recognize the enormous significance of the Jews for Manchuria, where their energetic commercial activity in the course of these last years has solidly established grain exports and guaranteed their [the exports'] future." Moreover, the continuing arrival of new Jews was bringing needed capital. For these reasons, he was convinced that any curtailment of Jewish rights in the CER zone would have a very unfavorable effect on the Russian position in Manchuria.

When, on May 10, 1911, Kokovtsov addressed the long-pending Polish question, he preferred to take a low-key approach, wary presumably of a vexatious question that had already proved to be a ministerial nemesis. Except for noting the assurances he had received from CER and police authorities regarding the harmlessness of Gospoda Pol'ska and the continuing scrutiny it would receive, Kokovstov merely took the occasion to repeat in broad general terms the message of his previous missives:

I have already had the honor of pointing out the desirability and full allowability of the unhampered functioning of analogous organizations in the CER's Belt of Alienation on the grounds that, by force of the international competition there, the manifestation of the Russian State idea in Manchuria should take other forms than those within the Russian Empire, and that social undertakings arising on the CER's territory should be viewed differently than from the Imperial point of view.[88]

The Interior Ministry replied to Kokovtsov's arguments tersely, but in agreement. Harbin's location outside of Russia was held to be an acceptable reason for special treatment. Even the Polish case elicited the admission that "so far" there was no need for "repressive measures."*

Implicit in Kokovtsov's articulation of the principles of government desirable for Harbin was an assumption that Russian success in Manchuria was conditional on a relationship between state and society fundamentally different from the status quo in European Russia. In the Far East, social organization and initiative were regarded, by and large, as allies of the state. Furthermore, it was in the interests of the state for ethnic strife to be kept down in an arena of international competition. In essence, the Jews of Harbin were hailed as the Cossacks of the twentieth century, where cavalry

---

*Nonetheless, by November 1913, the Ministry of the Interior was once more asking the Finance Ministry if Jews were really allowed in the railway zone. The February answer was yet again "Yes." RGIA 560: 28, 290, pp. 66–73.

raid had been replaced by trade war and stockade had given way to stock exchange.

The Manchurian Experiment and the Stolypin Reforms

As we saw earlier, Harbin's liberal colonization policy had taken from 1899 until 1903 to jell. That leisurely pace, a lack of coordination with local authorities, and interministerial rivalry were characteristics not limited to this issue. Quite the contrary, they were the hallmark of late Imperial bureaucracy. The Manchurian question, though in many ways exceptional, attached to much broader issues than the mere matter of settlement along the CER. A closer look at the context in which the Romanov joint conference of February–March 1903 took place will show how the study of a geographically peripheral city such as Harbin can uncover new facets of well-studied central policy questions in late Imperial Russian history.

In the aftermath of the multiple economic and social crises of 1899–1902, the view that rural reform was necessary hardened into nearly unanimous conviction. On February 15, 1902, Nikolai appointed Witte to the chairmanship of the newly founded Special Conference on the Needs of Agriculture. Eight days earlier, an editing commission in the Interior Ministry had been assigned to reexamine the peasant's legal status. The final result of these parallel endeavors was a "full articulation" of "new perceptions of rural society." After several years of back-and-forthing, the recommendations written up in reports by A. A. Rittikh and V. I. Gurko were codified and put in train. After 1906, they came to be known to the general public and posterity as the Stolypin Reforms.[89]

Although the emphases were slightly different, the editing commission and the special conference had essentially identical research agendas. Even with overlapping membership, these two bodies were sure to become entangled in the traditional conflict between Finance and Interior. The accession of Witte's "sworn enemy" Pleve to the helm of the latter ministry led to an escalation on all fronts. Battlefields included S. V. Zubatov's police unions, the noble and peasant land banks, and factory-inspection and minority policies. According to Witte's biographer Theodore Von Laue, "the entire gamut of domestic issues" was involved, but "chief among them the direction of peasant reforms."*

This then is the atmosphere in which the joint conference of February–

---

*Von Laue, *Sergei Witte*, pp. 224–25, 229, 252, 259. Eventually Pleve, by denouncing Witte as "an accomplice of revolutionaries," helped to undermine the Tsar's confidence in the Finance Minister. Pleve's success was short if sweet. He was killed in July 1904, when real revolutionaries lobbed a bomb into his carriage.

March 1903 was convened. As discussed above, the Finance Ministry's delegates were largely guided by the CER board's discussions of the previous summer and Witte's even more recent observations in the Far East. The novel Manchurian measures, however, were drawn not only from Witte's suggestions regarding the CER, but also from his comments on Siberian colonization in general.[90] Since Manchuria was officially outside the Empire, a free discussion of unorthodox approaches could be pursued unimpeded by the taboos of autocracy. Indeed, given that many of these policies were later extended to Siberia and even European Russia, "Manchuria" might well have played an Aesopian role. A plan for limited local experimentation before wholesale reform was making the rounds in 1902. Although this plan never materialized, the use of Far Eastern initiatives as an empirical base for wider applications can be viewed in the same vein.[91]

A good example is the law of June 19 (June 6, o.s.), 1904, the posthumous child of the Siberian Railway Committee. Approval of this measure in draft form was one of that Witte stronghold's final acts before expiring on January 23. The new law eliminated the division of settlers into legal and illegal and drew a new line between the "encouraged" and "other." "Encouraged" settlers were people who applied for resettlement aid in much the same way as permission to migrate had been sought previously. Criteria were flexible and open to recurrent redefinition.

Selection as an "encouraged" migrant meant more fertile lands, start-up payments in cash and kind, and a better deal on tax breaks and military exemptions. Most important was the guaranteed right-of-purchase of a private plot and a share in the communal lands at a fair price, underwritten, if necessary, by a government loan. The downside of "encouragement" was that it had to be reciprocated by fulfilling conditions meant to ensure preparedness for an ordeal in elemental Siberia. A group of prospective migrants, for example, might be required to send an advance "scouter." Such requirements, it was hoped, would reduce the return rate. "Encouraged" migrants were in a somewhat improved position compared with their "legal" predecessors.

Settlers in the "other" category did not need any permission to migrate but shared only a couple of the "encouraged" group's advantages, namely, the right to purchase railroad tickets at colonization rates and tax breaks. The best virgin lands remaining in Siberia, located in the Priamur and Turgai regions, were off-limits for the "others." Clearly, as Witte had argued in his 1902 report, only the "energetic, steadfast, and adaptable . . . searching for enrichment at their own risk" would undertake migration in the face of these handicaps. The removal of the "illegality" stigma from Siberian settlement was similar in its result to the suspension of the rules prohibiting internal migration that the joint conference enacted for Manchuria alone.

The lack of support for the "others" was analogous to the "wager on the strong" Witte had called for in his 1902 report. Both the Manchurian and the Siberian version adumbrate the basic thrust of the Stolypin Reforms.[92]

The grant of religious tolerance for schismatic migrants to Manchuria was also ahead of its time. European Russia would have to wait until Easter 1905 for the Tsar to proclaim freedom of worship within the Empire's bounds. Of equal importance to this measure itself was the fact that it received enthusiastic support from both Witte and Pleve. As Donald Treadgold has pointed out in his work on Siberian migration, Witte's priority was populating Siberia, whereas Pleve was concerned mainly with the "improvement of the life of the population of places of departure."[93] Resettling sectarians satisfied both goals.

The law of June 19 extended this double-edged approach to the wider arena of Siberian colonization. The "wager on the strong" would allow those with sufficient resources and resourcefulness to make their way to new opportunities. Exclusion from the best agricultural regions would inevitably drive a portion of these migrants into Siberia's cities. It was, after all, urban and industrial development that interested Witte most of all. During the thirteen years that this law remained in effect, Siberian cities did in fact grow much more quickly than the surrounding countryside.[94]

On the other hand, the designation of "encouraged" settlers put a powerful and subtle tool of social engineering in the hands of the government. Whether economic policy required the pruning of the impoverished and landless from the left bank of the Dnieper or ethnic concerns demanded that Russian peasants be discouraged from leaving the western borderlands, the law of June 19 could do the job without prohibitions or coercion.

It could also be applied on the receiving end, as in 1907, when the Agriculture Ministry suspended the application process and simply declared that all migration to the Priamur region would be considered "encouraged." Most of the human wave was absorbed by the Maritime province, with a record 61,722 arrivals. In August, after the migratory season had passed, the normal procedures were reinstated. In 1908, the number of settlers plunged to 21,501. Clearly, the system worked. Here again a technique pioneered in the joint conference's discussion of Manchuria had grown into a demographic implement whose Empire-wide utility both Witte and Pleve could agree on.[95]

The fact that the two men who would be most responsible for carrying out the Stolypin Reforms, A. V. Krivoshein and A. A. Rittikh, were at the heart of this ill-natured exchange of opinions provides a clear line of transmission from Manchurian affairs to Siberia to European Russia. Krivoshein was the Interior Ministry's delegate to the 1903 joint conference and served from 1896 to 1905 as vice-director and then director of the ministry's Siberian Resettlement Department. Later, as the head of the Chief Administration of Land Settlement and Agriculture (1908–15), he was in charge of implementing the policies he had helped frame some years earlier, but they now carried Stolypin's name.

When the Russo-Japanese War broke out, Rittikh had been slated to manage the whole colonization effort in Manchuria. His previous post in Vladivostok as head of Far Eastern migration and his unswerving loyalty to Witte were probably the necessary qualifications. Extensive exposure to Siberian affairs was bound to affect Rittikh's later work, when, in late 1903, as Witte's special assistant for agriculture, he compiled an influential summary of the voluminous materials collected by Finance's special conference. This local bias was already visible earlier in 1903, when Rittikh completed a study of peasant dependency on the commune. His conclusions called for flexible solutions specific to individual regions. After 1905, as director of Agriculture's Department of State Domains, he became "the executive manager of the [Stolypin] reform throughout its duration."[96]

Because of this tendency toward competitive borrowing, historians have needed either good imaginations or strong biases to find significant differences between the final results of the special conference and the editing commission. George Yaney has even argued that "the enactment process evolved out of an interministerial conflict, not an ideological one. The main issue in the enactors' minds was not the nature of the reform but who was to control it." Furthermore, by his lights, in the course of these "elaborate rhetorical exercises," Witte was dragged into agrarian reform: "Let me remind the reader," Yaney announces early on, that Witte entered government service with the purpose of building and organizing railroads. . . . He acquired his sense of social responsibility from the interministerial controversies in which he had to engage in order to build railroads."[97] Although I agree with Yaney that internal bureaucratic dynamics played a central role in the development of ideological positions on the peasant question, and that Witte's primary interests did not lie in this field, an important qualification is necessary.

First of all, by 1902 Witte's "railroading" had expanded in many directions. There was no area of governmental activity for which he did not have his experts and his opinions. By the turn of the century, it was no longer possible to dismiss Witte as a bureaucrat-industrialist with limited horizons. Nonetheless, a certain set of pragmatic principles deriving from his railroad-building program strongly influenced his views on other matters.

This "ideology," for instance, gave urban development a higher priority than rural development. Witness the arguments for increasing Siberia's urban/industrial population Witte made in his November 1902 report; or the hidden benefits for cities in such ostensibly rural legislation as the law of June 19. The favoring of economic methods over military coercion was another trait of Witte's approach. As discussed in Chapter Two, though the Finance Minister knew well the art of arguing strategic needs to garner support for his policies, he was consistently against the use of force. He feared both the high financial costs and increased military authority at the expense of his own.

Even more fundamental was Witte's belief that his industrial program must eventually give way to private enterprise. In 1900, Nikolai contracted typhoid fever, and the Romanov crown seemed on the point of passing to his brother, the Grand Duke Mikhail Aleksandrovich. As tutorial materials for the heir apparent, Witte prepared his *Lectures on the Economy and State Finance*, a simplified credo. Here he stated: "Not to stifle independent action, but to develop its strength by creating favorable conditions for its application, that is the true obligation which in our time the state must discharge toward our ever more complex national economy." A few pages later, Witte affirmed his belief in technology as the most effective catalyst in this process. "The railroad is like a leaven, which creates a cultural fermentation among the population. Even if it passed through an absolutely wild people along its way, it would raise them in a short time to the level prerequisite for its operation."[98] Unfortunately for Witte, the bread did not rise in time to save him from the wrath of all those whom his "system" had transformed into his enemies.

This belief in independence and stimulation is also visible in Witte's work on peasant reform. As Yaney notes, the "attitude in the MVD's [Interior Ministry's] central offices in 1902 [was] quite different from Witte's." Finance's policy decidedly allowed far more freedom of expression and broader participation. Even more telling, on being appointed to chair the special conference, Witte immediately told the Tsar that the peasant's greatest needs were "freedom and independence of action." It is possible, to be sure, that this was simply a ploy to avoid changes that would directly affect Witte's principal tasks or to encroach on the jurisdiction of the Interior Ministry. But this statement is also consistent with Witte's long-term views on the role of the human factor in the economy. It was a similar conception that formed the economic rationalization for the "wager on the strong." In 1911, Krivoshein would name voluntarism as the fundamental principle of the government's peasant program. The Witte system has a strong parental claim on the Stolypin Reforms.[99]

Kokovtsov had served a six-year stint in the Finance Ministry (1896– 1902) before he inherited Witte's position. His testimony at the "Preliminary Conference" in 1904 and his correspondence with Stolypin in 1910–11 certainly show a minister concerned to defend his Manchurian bailiwick from the encroachment of others. Turf war was a crucial facet of ministerial interaction. Nevertheless, Kokovtsov's long-term defense of Harbin as a haven of economic, social, and political laissez-faire attests to the presence at the highest bureaucratic levels of an alternative view of what state-society relations in Russia could be. It also shows the enduring nature of the Witte legacy, at least within the ministry that had been his power base.

CHAPTER 4

War, Revolution, and Politics: Harbin, 1904–1908

Conversations in numbers, dreams in multiplication tables, thoughts in arithmetic calculations. Such was Harbin before the war, and such it remains. Only now the pioneers have been joined by new arrivals who have rushed here from every corner of Russia with a sole goal—to snatch a large sum [*tsapnut' krupnyi kush*] while avoiding the military courts and get away in time, in one piece [*s tseloiu shkukoi*]. Armenians, Georgians [*imeretiny*], Germans, Jews, Russian kulaks, and even gypsies all rush into the mad hurly-burly, thinking in thousands at the least, without fear of sums reminiscent of the [vast] distances from Earth to Mars. —V. I. Nemirovich-Danchenko, 1904

The mood of Harbin is reflected in the newly formed [army divisions]. I would never have recommended the choice of such an infectious pit [*zaraznaia iama*] as Harbin for the formation. You'll see that the influence of Harbin will remain in these divisions. —General A. N. Kuropatkin, 1905

IN EARLY 1905, as national attention alternated between growing civil discontent in European Russia and a series of military defeats in the Far East, the tsarist regime became increasingly concerned about the physical and moral state of the Manchurian army. If these military forces had proved incapable of upholding the autocracy's primary functions, national defense and international prestige, were they still willing and able to suppress domestic threats to the Romanov dynasty? With the conclusion of the Portsmouth peace treaty in September, it became clear that, for the moment, the nearly 400,000 regular troops east of Lake Baikal were more interested in repatriation than revolt. The disposition of the 600,000 reservists was less sure. Now a logistical question overshadowed all others: how to bring home this potential dynastic bulwark along the Trans-Siberian without allowing it to be infected with the revolutionary sentiments that had prompted recurrent railway strikes since October? For both the demobilized and the recalled, the Chinese Eastern Railway would be the first leg of the journey. With the bulk of the soldiers still dug in north of Mukden in anticipation of the next Japanese offensive, Harbin would be the departure station for the long trip home.

The dynamic process by which army and railroad would interact at the major depots of eastern Siberia was initiated at the Harbin Station, but the Imperial regime was only interested in a straightforward answer to the simple questions of loyalty and transport. This narrow focus and the 10,000 versts of separation never allowed Petersburg to comprehend the complications involved, in many ways more a product of prewar life in the Russian Far East than of the All-Russian revolutionary moment.

Soviet historians, in particular, M. K. Vetoshkin, the sole member of the Siberian Union of Social Democrats to participate in the CER strike, have been most keen to shape that and other events to fit the Party's historiographic line. Unfortunately, the use of a potential counterbalance, a non-Soviet memoir written by the chairman of the CER Employee Strike Committee, requires equal caution. The author, Anton Ferdynand Ossendowski, turns out to be a confirmed adventurer and liar who places himself squarely at the center of all events, both historical and imaginary.

After the war, the general passivity of Petersburg toward the Far East left initiative to the region itself. What these Russian communities of the borderland would make of this opportunity depended largely on political and social polarizations dating from wartime experiences and the conflict's immediate aftermath. A sense of abandonment by the center would also strengthen local identity. Along the CER, the restraint shown by both management and labor during the strike had successfully averted bloodshed. Without bitter memories of 1905, the new structures of local politics could avoid the spiraling recriminations and paralyzing enmities that characterized state-society relations in Russia proper. In the postwar years, as the pendulum swung widely to the peace side of the spectrum, army influence at Harbin sank to an all-time low. The recently established branch of the gendarmerie (1904) would take over five years to come into its own as an organ of effective local control. The responsibility for law and order in Russian Manchuria rested with the Finance Ministry and its proxy, the CER.

Neither of these was organizationally prepared for the task. Nor did they possess the appropriate corporate ethos. The political prisoners of 1905, sentenced by military tribunal, became house guests in a comfortable prison with a liberal "home-visit" policy. On release, they were reincorporated into the CER family. The local police warned revolutionaries of impending arrest in time to make their getaway. The patriarchal general manager of the railroad, General D. L. Khorvat, eschewed the powers that would have both allowed and required him to take repressive action against the political, social, and criminal activities of a city that may well have been Imperial Russia's freest. CER management's empathy toward CER strikers reflected strong institutional loyalties, especially when they were attacked by the army, as well as the same liberal political orientation that supported religious and ethnic tolerance.

Railroad Justice

To discuss the birth of politics in Russian Manchuria requires that we first examine the legal basis of life on the CER and the legacy of Harbin's yearlong service as Rear Headquarters. In June 1897, P. M. Romanov chaired a special conference attended by three consul-generals on home leave from diplomatic posts in China. Their goal was to work out the concrete means by which Article 7 of the CER statutes was to be carried out. According to this article, "crimes, lawsuits, etc., on Chinese Eastern Railway territory will be settled by Russian and Chinese local authorities on the basis of the existing treaties." The group concluded that the resolution of judicial problems among Russians involved in CER construction should be left to the "tact and management" of Iugovich or his representatives. Once the CER began operating, investigators and justices of the peace would be assigned from the Chita and Vladivostok circuits to live and work on the CER. Then the legal system would operate just as if the right-of-way lay within the Empire's boundaries.[1]

Under no circumstances were consular officials to become involved, since foreign powers might then use the pretext of equality among most-favored nations to require the Chinese to open Manchuria to non-Russian diplomatic representatives. Additionally, although Russia's five treaties with China provided the legal basis for extraterritoriality,* that was not the answer here for purely practical reasons:

The principle of extraterritoriality . . . would hardly be sufficient by itself to define the legal structure for tens of thousands of Russians settled in a vast, compact territory, bringing with them to Manchuria their own juridical way of life, social ties, and organizations; creating whole cities with a multitude of industrial, commercial, and cultural undertakings.[2]

Unfortunately, Iugovich and the man on whom he relied in these matters, Harbin police chief Kazarkin, lacked professional legal training and could do no more than mete out rough-and-ready justice of the frontier variety. One early inhabitant of Harbin, F. Z. Vasil'ev, described these

*The Russo-Chinese treaties in effect were the treaties of Kuldja (1851), Aigun (1858), Tianjin (1858), Beijing (1860), and St. Petersburg (1881).

methods: "For example, someone would come to the police chief complaining that he had been insulted or not repaid a debt owed. The police chief would summon both the accused and the plaintiff and without further trial suggest that they make their peace or pay up the debt; otherwise, they would both get a week in jail."[3]

By 1899, with 12,000 CER employees and 5,000 border guards working on the railroad, this jerrybuilt justice system was swamped. Both Iugovich and Colonel Gerngross, the commanding officer of the frontier guard, registered their complaints with the CER board and asked that the engineers and officers be freed from the inappropriate and excessive law enforcement duties that were distracting them from their primary tasks.[4]

A first step toward siphoning off some of the burden was taken by the Foreign Ministry in June 1899, when a new position was created to handle all legal matters arising in Qiqihar and Jilin provinces that did not involve the CER or its employees. The opening of the Niuzhuang consulate, decided in July 1899 and slated for 1900, offered similar services for southern Manchuria. Further ameliorative moves were delayed by the Boxer uprising and the Russian invasion that followed. Only on July 22, 1901, when a special conference brought together Witte, Lamsdorff, and Vice-Minister of Justice S. S. Manukhin, was the overall legal situation on the CER reconsidered.

According to the memorandum Witte presented for discussion, the number of employees in the CER right-of-way had dropped to 7,000, but this had been offset by a rise in the frontier guard effective to 12,000. Witte's proposed solution was to phase in the investigators and justices of the peace from the Chita and Vladivostok circuits immediately. Until such time as the line was complete, however, Iugovich would remain the sole legal recourse in all CER-related matters. The new officials needed to gain local experience, Witte argued. Until then, the vital task of establishing the railroad link with Russia's only ice-free port should not be exposed to any unnecessary interference.

Manukhin objected to this approach for various reasons. First, the proposed division of labor would still leave the bulk of the cases in the hands of the chief engineer, thereby defeating the whole purpose of the special conference. Second, the piecemeal implementation of Witte's plan would still not form a sound judicial structure. Third, by keeping Russian cases out of the Foreign Ministry's hands, the CER would be violating the principles of extraterritoriality. If these were to be the results, why introduce a reform at all? Despite these cogent arguments, with Lamsdorff's support Witte had his way.[5]

As a result of this conference, a twelve-point description of jurisdictions in the CER zone was promulgated as an Imperial ukase on August 2,

1901. Point 12 stipulated the nonpublication of the edict, probably because points 9 and 10 gave the CER and its employees the status of governmental institutions and officials, respectively, before the law. This was at odds with the CER's ostensibly private status. The preapproved ukase would come into force only "at a time to be determined by the Ministers of Justice and Finance."[6] The special conference had already decided that Witte would take charge of choosing the correct moment. Witte's fencing off the CER from the Justice Ministry, of course, is merely a variation on the interministerial rivalry theme detailed in Chapter Two.

Later in 1901, three justice-of-the-peace courts (*mirovye sudy*) were established. The East Branch, including Harbin, was covered by a judge based in that city; a second judge at Khailar handled the West Branch; and the South Branch fell under the jurisdiction of Yingkou. Because of the distances involved, all three judges were often on the road. By early 1903, the unworkability of the system had become clear. In the face of a threat from Manukhin to request that the Tsar place all judicial matters on the CER under the Port Arthur circuit, another interministerial conference was called. In attendance were Witte, Kuropatkin, Manukhin, and the deputy Foreign Minister, Prince Obolenskii-Neledinskii-Meletskii.

The overall weakness of Witte's position in 1903 is clearly reflected in the minutes of this meeting. First, the Finance Minister agreed to a proposal by War Minister Kuropatkin to place both the frontier guard and the newly formed railroad brigade under military justice. Then, in response to Manukhin's attacks on using railroad affiliation as a criterion for removing cases from the authority of the Russo-Chinese diplomatic bureaus (*jiaosheju*), Witte volunteered to shift all accusations against Russians, even by Chinese, to the justice-of-the-peace courts. However, here Kuropatkin and Obolenskii stepped in and forced Manukhin to retreat. The "timing" on changes in the bureaus' competence was to be left to the Foreign Ministry. For the moment, the status quo would be maintained.[7]

At about the same time, the CER board was taking note of the fact that the East Branch court, presided over by Justice K. I. Kaido of Vladivostok, was overburdened. In 1902, it handled 300 preliminary investigations, 150 full investigations, 2,000 cases, and 1,000 notarial acts. The source of this flood was Harbin, "the most important hub [*uzlovoi punkt*]." The board's first thought was to add two more justices of the peace along the CER, one covering New Town and short distances east and south of it, and the other Pristan and the West Branch as far as the Nonni River. In July 1903, however, Witte decided to add only one position devoted exclusively to Harbin's legal well-being as a whole, a decision that probably reflected a recognition of the increasing integration of the city's constituent parts.[8]

In 1903, the caseload for the East Branch judge rose over 50 percent, to

1,330 criminal and 1,833 civil cases. This was in addition to 351 investigations and 207 other "legal findings." To try and stanch this overflow, the Vladivostok circuit court appointed an investigator to assist Judge Kaido. The outbreak of war did not help matters. The first half of 1904 alone saw 1,438 criminal and 1,718 civil cases.[9]

On February 8, 1904, the Japanese navy attacked Port Arthur. On February 10, war was declared, and on February 12 the Port Arthur circuit court adjourned to Harbin for the duration of hostilities. On its arrival there two days later, Khorvat informed the refugees that no housing was available: they would have to continue on to Chita. But he was able to preserve the CER's prerogatives for only a few months. On April 23, an Imperial command subordinated all judicial bodies on the CER to the Port Arthur circuit court, thereby eliminating the complicated patchwork in favor of the straightforward extension of Russian law into the right-of-way. On June 24, the Port Arthur court triumphantly reestablished itself in Manchuria. The traditional enmity between North and South Manchuria expressed itself in Harbin's indifferent reaction to Port Arthur's surrender. A Hungarian visitor reported in 1905 that many kharbintsy believed that the loss of Dal'nii would help open their city to world trade and other international currents.[10]

Ironically, the unwelcome court system in Harbin would be the last Russian institution to bear the name of Port Arthur. The circuit was rechristened the Frontier Court (Pogranichnyi) on February 15, 1906, more than a year after the Port Arthur fortress's capitulation.* The organization of judicial institutions in Russian Manchuria continued to be a pawn in interministerial power plays after the war. The resultant division of labor offered opportunities for the unscrupulous and the politically savvy to take advantage of the freewheeling lifestyle of a frontier town and an unsophisticated electorate. Not a few benefited from the fact that many Russian statutes were inapplicable within Chinese sovereign territory (in the domains, for example, of customs, excise taxes, and building codes);[11] and perhaps even more were encouraged into criminal activity by the CER authorities' shortsighted belief that the court system was less important than the construction, operation, and commercial well-being of the railway.

---

*In fact, Harbin courts would eventually be the last practitioners of the legal code elaborated in 1874 under Alexander II. On Sept. 23, 1920, a Chinese presidential decree deprived Russians of extraterritoriality, and on Oct. 1, Chinese troops closed the frontier court. Nilus, *Istoricheskii*, p. 565.

Harbin at War

No statistics are available on criminality in wartime Harbin, but impressionistic contemporary accounts leave little doubt that the rule of law broke down. Rosemary Quested cites oral "informants" in stating that local control over the civilian population lapsed badly. Maurice Baring claimed that Harbin was inhabited almost exclusively by "ex-convicts and Chinamen." After a week in the city, he came to the conclusion that police authority seemed "non-existent."[12]

Closer examination of the violations offered as examples reveals that all were crimes of greed. V. I. Nemirovich-Danchenko, the co-founder and co-director of the Moscow Arts Theater, spent the summer of 1904 collecting materials for *Na voinu*, his contribution to the voluminous memoirs of the Russo-Japanese War. With a discriminating eye and trenchant prose, he traced the transformation from engineering and commercial center to the capital of covetousness. Although possibly less visible to the European eye, many Chinese fortunes were also made in 1904–5.[13] Nemirovich-Danchenko divided this hunting pack into several subspecies: "merchants, entrepreneurs, swindlers, fishers of muddy waters, knights of the 'Look sharp!' [*ne zevai*] order." Common characteristics were "twelve-handedness" and the ability to present an expression of "ecstasy and adoration" whenever anyone connected with the quartermaster corps came by. In that quarter lay the golden eggs.[14]

During the course of the war, the 700 officers and 20,000 soldiers assigned responsibility for provisioning the Russian army bought over two billion pounds of food and fodder. By September 1905, rations were being distributed to 950,000 men and 250,000 horses. Because of Manchuria's qualities as a first-rate granary and Mongolia's abundance of livestock, what resulted was the best-fed Russian army ever seen in the field. Sadly, victory did not follow victuals. The stocks assembled in Harbin and stored in the new "Commissary Suburb" (Intendantskii Gorodok) sustained not only Russia's Manchurian army, but also the Maritime province. While contributing to the rapid growth of North Manchuria's agricultural economy, these gargantuan purchases enriched thousands of middlemen. For many temporary residents of Harbin, it was indeed a short, victorious war.[15]

The lure of mammon also seduced those who came to Manchuria with other plans. One of Nemirovich-Danchenko's new acquaintances was a "15% journalist" who devoted the rest of his hours to this "once in a lifetime" opportunity to make a fortune. Even officers on leave from the front sometimes found themselves embroiled in ventures whose duration and charms gradually converted them into deserters. As General Sylvestre, the head of the French mission to the Russian army, noted in his highly critical final report on the war: "Each evening there are two or three hundred [officers] at the circus, even on days following the saddest news. From time to time the commandant of the place [Harbin] conducts a raid and sends back to the army the officers he picks up. After the battle of Chaké about a thousand were found and sent back to the front."[16]

Entrepreneurs who failed to land big contracts for provisioning the army could still get rich by catering to the desperate pleasures of officers intent on blotting from memory the boredom of the trenches and the fear of death. Colonel P. M. Zakharov, the head of military communications for the Manchurian army, estimated that every day 150 to 200 officers arrived in Harbin after five to six months of unrelieved service in the field. Before the war, Harbin and Port Arthur had been labeled "the brothels of the world." With the evacuation of civilians from Port Arthur, Harbin held that dubious honor alone. Restaurants drew crowds by day, and nightclubs (*kafe-shantan*) operated into the morning, serving Shanghai's contribution to the war effort, a noxious ersatz champagne that the Chinese had baptized into pidgin-Russian as "*shipi-shipi.*" One memoirist recalled that when it was rumored that a new battle was being prepared, "Harbin was filled with mad debauch. The champagne flowed in rivers, the courtesans were doing a splendid business. The percentage of officers fallen in battle was so great that all expected certain death, and so bade good-bye to life in wild orgies."[17]

In sharp contrast to the gallows gaiety concentrated in Pristan were the sober spirits of another group returning from the battlefield to settle in a band along the railroad between New Town and Old Harbin. From its founding in 1904, this section was called the Hospital Suburb (Gospital'nyi Gorodok), for Harbin was the central collection point for the wounded and dying. By July 1904, twelve army hospitals and two Red Cross facilities had been established. But the second half of the year saw a series of bloody battles, and when the U.S. army's medical observers visited in January–February 1905, 84 hospitals with a capacity of 30,000 were functioning; approximately 20 percent were under the supervision of the Red Cross. Most large buildings, including barracks, schools, workshops, hotels, clubs, and theaters, had already been requisitioned. Continuing defeats and retreats guaranteed that hospital construction in Harbin would continue unabated, never quite catching up with demand.[18]

Ferdynand Ossendowski, an employee of the CER Commercial Section, recalled many years later:

How well I remember one sad morning! I had left my house early and was making my way across the Place in front of the Cathedral on the way to my laboratory. The sun was just coming up, and the shadows of the night still lingered in the angles of the roofs behind the massive corners of the church and in the hedges and bushes around the Place. No passers-by were visible; one heard no rattlings of the droskies over the protruding stones of the awful pavements of the city. But, as I turned out of the Place, I heard something which brought me to a halt to listen. From somewhere, as though up out of the earth, there was borne in upon me a long wail, full of pain and despair growing ever more distinct and increasing in volume. . . . As I passed beyond the hedges, my eye was struck with long rows of white tents with the Red Cross flag above them, which had come as ghosts during a night when such a mass of wounded had been brought in that the hospitals, numerous as they were, could no longer hold them. It was from these tents that the wail of the wounded rolled out to crush the soul.[19]

Though far from the front lines, the recklessness and sorrow of war became a formative experience in Harbin's history.

In addition to the medical corps' hospitals and the quartermaster's storehouses, Harbin gained other new structures from the military buildup. Across Mojiagou stream from the Hospital Suburb, the Rear Command laid out and built a new cantonment for a 60,000-man reserve force. On either side of a main artery stood 50 officers' huts. Behind each of these were three dugouts (*zemlianki*) designed for 200 men apiece. Maximum occupancy was 350. In a pinch, Harbin could house 105,000 troops. New support facilities like bakeries and bathhouses sprang up as the army tried to keep pace. With the retreat from Mukden in March 1905, the chances of a Japanese attack on Harbin increased, and twenty-three defensive works in and around the city were hastily put in order. They never saw action. The concentration of troops and casualties in Harbin also demanded new sanitary measures. These included waste dumps, sewage disposal, well drilling, and street improvements. The necessity of better communications among military sites led to the construction of various viaducts and a summertime pontoon bridge across the Sungari.[20]

Although postwar Harbin would inherit these structures of very unequal peacetime value, in 1904–5 the army was only taking care of its own. Even though CER employees now worked under the military, they did not receive any supplies from the quartermaster. Khorvat was forced to form food committees to save his railwaymen from the inflated prices of the local market. Baring described prices in Harbin as "exalted beyond dreams of Ritz." In addition to requisitioning office and service buildings, army big wigs commandeered the company housing and service cars of CER engineers. Since the line had been placed under martial law within hours of the Japanese attack on Port Arthur and subordinated to the viceroy's railroad section on February 27, 1904, there was little Khorvat could do but comply. All the same, he was not prepared to suffer in silence. In October 1904, he reported to the CER board that the situation on the CER was barely tolerable, because of the large numbers of individuals giving commands and orders. These managers are the heads of the [military] railway administration, military communications, etc., but those held responsible [for their actions] are the [CER] board and management. Our rolling stock has become housing for [military] staff and hospitals for the wounded. . . . The stations are overcrowded. Harbin and Mukden are traffic jams [*probki*]. The [military] chiefs only blame and abuse the railway personnel. . . . It is impossible to correct the present situation. War is not the moment to establish a legal order [*pravoporiadok*]. The agents of the CER, both young and old, have decided to bear with it, but we ask that we not be reproached for the confusions [*neuriaditsy*], which are not our fault.[21]

The only positive result of these tensions was a rise in CER corporate solidarity. In March 1905, a new social group, the Railway Club, dedicated to giving employees a way to spend their free time with "utility, comfort, and satisfaction," opened in spacious quarters directly across from the huge CER administration building. Forty-one of the club's 61 "elders" (*starshiny*) were elected, and the others were appointed by Khorvat from the top ranks of the CER hierarchy. The board provided a start-up loan of 15,000 rubles. On August 24, Khorvat issued an order ending the use of "thou" when addressing subordinates. On October 6, the statutes of a CER consumer society were confirmed. All of these events point to management's genuine concern for the well-being and human dignity of its employees.[22]

As military defeats multiplied, competition for resources became merely an aggravating factor in the heated crossfire of mutual recriminations. The CER complained that army commanders had taken over tasks beyond their technical capacities. When the rear commander, General N. P. Linevich, was approached regarding the need for more efficient scheduling, he is reported to have said: "Laissez là les graphiques, marchez avec votre conscience et votre coeur. J'ai confiance en eux." Although well-intended as encouragement, Linevich's remark backfired. Ignorance of and disregard for railroad science could not help irritating professional engineers. Khorvat complained in his memoirs that Viceroy Alekseev threatened to deport anyone who followed standard procedure and blew the train whistle during switching. According to Ossendowski, in mid-1905 many high officials of the CER signed a telegram condemning the army's conduct of the war. The text, addressed to General Kuropatkin and the central government, was drafted in the Railway Club. In return, military men accused the railroad of losing the war by preventing a speedy concentration of forces. The CER responded that the army was making unreasonable demands; that Kuropatkin's call for forty-eight trains a day, for instance, was simply not possible on a single-track line. In reference to such untutored statements, Khorvat remarked sneeringly on Kuropatkin's talents as a "theoretical general." Besides, the carrying capacity of the Transbaikal railway was lower than the CER's. Since at this stage all supplies and troops were coming from Europe, the Manchurian railroad was definitely not the narrowest point in the bottleneck.[23]

Relations between Alekseev and Khorvat seem to have remained cooperative, despite the viceroy's reputation in Harbin for incompetence. In early 1904, a new suburb adjacent to Old Harbin was named Alekseevka, and in July of that year, Alekseev wrote to Finance Minister Kokovtsov in glowing terms of the "energy, knowledge, experience, and devotion" that made Khorvat worthy of promotion to the rank of major-general.[24] But with the viceroy's departure three months later, even this frail tie between the railway and the military was broken. Harbin, with its triple image of greed, debauch, and disease, was hardly calculated to please the "honest soldier" Kuropatkin, who was now in sole command. To make matters worse, the official CER organ, *The Harbin Herald* (*Kharbinskii vestnik*), published remarks that were interpreted as an insult to the former Minister of War.

In October 1905, when these two bêtes noires of the high command, the CER and Harbin, commingled in celebrating and developing the newly granted freedoms in Manchuria, loyal officers were more than ready to crush the festivities. General Kuropatkin went so far as to suggest that repression was justified since political guarantees for Russian citizens went only as far as the Chinese border. Harbin should be treated like an "armed camp." Instead, even the most resolute reactionaries swallowed their bile for fear of triggering a soldiers' revolt of "unheard-of proportions" that might engulf city, army, railway, and possibly, all of Imperial Russia in violence.[25]

In the Shadow of the Reservists: Peace and Politics

The conclusion of the Portsmouth peace treaty in August 1905 drastically changed the situation in Harbin. Over 100,000 of the approximately 1,000,000 men awaiting evacuation from the Far East were garrisoned in the city.[26] Dissatisfaction with the officer corps that had led them to defeat combined with inactivity to induce an extremely virulent and contagious form of homesickness. The officers, for their part, paid little attention to maintaining the morale and discipline of their troops, since they themselves were thoroughly demoralized by the sudden armistice that had cheated them of victory. Vengeful brooding joined drinking, gaming, and whoring as favorite pastimes in Harbin.[27]

General Linevich, who had replaced Kuropatkin as commander-in-chief after the battle of Mukden, dispatched the first trainful of soldiers to European Russia on October 27, 1905.* Four days later, the train reached the

---
*Kuropatkin stayed on in Manchuria as commanding officer of the First Manchurian Army, Linevich's previous position.

Russian border at Manchuria Station to find its passage blocked by the general strike that marked the zenith of the 1905 strike movement in Russia proper. Although CER operations were not affected, the Transbaikal and Siberian lines were paralyzed. The troop trains in transit pulled into the nearest stations with stockpiled provisions and waited. In Harbin, the only organization to echo the all-Russian strike was the Central Telegraph Office, which went out on October 29. The army quickly moved in military personnel to serve as replacements, and the strike was over by November 2. The text of the October Manifesto in which the Tsar acceded to an array of reforms arrived in Manchuria the following day.[28]

The next week seems to have been a time of joyous political experimentation as the population of Harbin tried out its new rights. Assemblies, circles, councils, commissions, and committees were formed at a frenzied pace as "the principles of political freedom proclaimed by the Manifesto were immediately put to use by the citizens in the fullest measure, with the greatest enthusiasm and pleasure. Demonstrators appeared in the streets with red flags, the squares and other public places rang with heated political speeches, the sound of the Marseillaise could be heard."[29] The Railway Club quickly established itself as a central locus for discussion and debate. On November 8, a crowd of 7,000–9,000 jammed the Borovskii circus to endorse calls for the formation of a temporary revolutionary committee. Meetings in the CER workshops seconded this proposal, but the new organ did little more than lure those with political ambitions out of the closet. The Bolshevik M. K. Vetoshkin disparagingly labeled the committee members "ultra-moderates."[30]

Moderate they might have been, but they were also very active. In 1906, V. P. Lepeshinskii, the head of the CER administration's chancellery (*pravitel' del*), was brought to trial and sentenced to two years' imprisonment for his part in the activities described in this chapter.* In a newspaper article denouncing this mockery of justice, Lepeshinskii listed his political activities during the war and in the period just after the issuance of the October Manifesto. A comparison will help explain what the CER management meant when it informed the board in Petersburg that the "city has changed its physiognomy significantly."[31]

Lepeshinskii began by stating that he had always had his doubts about the outcome of the war.[32] Since many units of the Rear Headquarters were

---

*Like most of his fellow activists in Harbin, Lepeshinskii had brought his political orientations with him from European Russia. He had in fact been arrested before (in Odessa in 1879) and had also lost a position in the administration of the Southwest railway in 1883 for political reasons. Presumably, his railway connections and experience were what earned him a position on the CER and a high one, at that: though an exact ranking is difficult, pravitel' del was certainly one of the top 10 positions on the railroad.

housed in the CER administration building, he had had plenty of opportunity to discuss these views with the officer corps. As a result, the headquarters commander, I. P. Nadarov, fearing an infectious pessimism, had eventually forbade his men to talk with Lepeshinskii. In addition, Lepeshinskii said, he had joined other CER men in sending protest telegrams back to the Russian newspapers and government. One had backed the first zemstvo congress's call for civil liberties and a representative assembly. Another, drafted after the battle of Mukden, called for an end to the bloodshed. A third complained about tense relations with the army. Finally, in the line of duty, Lepeshinskii had investigated transit permit abuses.

After October 17, he had shifted to a different course. "I considered it necessary for every citizen to develop his own political worldview [*mirosozertsanie*] and actively participate in the building of public and state life," Lepeshinskii wrote. Turning to specifics, he noted that personally, he had adopted the Kadet platform and considered presenting himself as a Duma candidate, should Harbin be granted a seat; that he had joined "all kinds of public organizations," though only legal ones; and that, as a senior member of the Railway Club, he had initiated and pushed through a proposal to allow "public meetings and gatherings" in the CER auditorium. Finally, he saw fit to mention his refusal to accept overtime pay for his work during the war. He wanted no blood money.

A review of Lepeshinskii's article shows that, in the earlier period, the political impulse focused tightly on the capital cities as center and sole recourse. After October 17, much of this energy was redirected into local activities. In a certain sense, this represented a narrowing of scope. Simultaneously, the original tendency to remain within the CER professional circle broadened to embrace a new constituency, the town of Harbin. Both of these changes paralleled the transition from negative words to positive deeds. A strong current of pacifism underlay the whole process.[33]

An outbreak of disorders in Vladivostok on November 12 created consternation at Harbin, where it became clear that discontent among the rank and file might combine explosively with the revolutionary breakdown in discipline. Communication, the necessary substitute for compulsion, had been neglected when the soldiers had been left out of the manifesto celebrations. The army staff had decided not to have the Tsar's decree read to the troops, and when the Harbin civilians revealed the truth, the officers averred that the new freedoms did not apply to men under arms. Doubts and distrust resulted. Rumors circulated that the second half of the manifesto had been suppressed. Back home, the Black Partition was allegedly allotting land to people who were present; those who were absent would receive the dregs. The decision to make the Thirteenth Corps, the last arrival in Manchuria, the first to leave seemed strikingly unjust to the rank and file. How could they know that Linevich had warned the War Minister that this move would be deeply resented, but that his concerns had been brushed aside because regular troops were needed both to guard the Trans-Siberian and to put down unrest in European Russia?[34]

Despite a ban on liquor sales, the ready availability of high-proof, low-price *hanxing* obscured good judgment, lessening the chances that the dark cloud of hate and hurt would be dispelled. In the matter of chronic inebriation, the officers' example was followed carefully, though the lower ranks could hardly afford the *shipi-shipi*. In this atmosphere, the voice of sober reason did not carry far. Lieutenant-Colonel Levandovskii's recommendations that officers be required to educate their men regarding the manifesto, and not with machine guns, and that drunkenness and "disgraceful behavior" (*bezobraziia*) be punished severely regardless of rank, elicited no discernible response.

Salutes became rare, although sometimes left-handed ones drew laughter from onlookers. V. V. Veresaev witnessed the following incident at the Harbin Station, where thousands of soldiers waiting for trains home had quartered themselves. In the buffet, an officer sat eating while a soldier went among the tables selling souvenirs of the Orient.

"How much is the fan?" asked the colonel. . . .
"Two rubles, your Highness."
"Too expensive," said the colonel indifferently and returned the fan.
"Too expensive? Are you paid so little?" retorted the soldier, looking threateningly at the colonel.
The colonel stood up, acting is if he was leaving anyway and headed for the exit.
"Too ex-pen-sive!" screamed the soldier after him. "You won't even let a soldier earn a kopeck. Have you really made so little money here, you bastard?"[35]

In the shadow of the unruly soldiers, local citizens formed a committee to "defend the unassailability and security of person and property." The bloody, reactionary pogroms that had followed the manifesto in Russia proper must also have prodded Harbin to take defensive measures. This modest organizational step was almost immediately extended into an attempt to establish a municipal administration to handle such matters as "hospitals, schools, bridges, lighting, water supply, etc." Khorvat agreed that Harbin should become a "self-administrating town" under the terms of the Municipal Act of 1892, though it would have to be modified slightly to accommodate the city's peculiar legal position. In the interests of urgency, these modifications would be taken up by the first municipal council, which would serve the double function of administrative and constituent body.

With the discussion of voter qualifications, however, the more divisive aspects of politics began to take precedence over unanimous enthusiasm. An electoral commission wanted to limit suffrage to property owners, merchants, and industrialists, but the defense committee insisted that the municipal council must not be monopolized by the "representatives of capital." Harbin's two private papers, *The Harbin Leaflet* (*Kharbinskii listok*) and *The New Territory* (*Novyi krai*), took opposing positions. The *Leaflet*, edited by P. V. Rovenskii, adopted the more egalitarian view. Rovenskii, an exile to Siberia since his arrest in 1880, had established his paper only months before, in January, as the city's sole counterpoint to the CER-owned *Harbin Herald* (*Kharbinskii vestnik*). The *Herald* itself had been founded in 1903 to replace Rovenskii's first *Harbin Leaflet* when it was closed down by gendarmerie order. In light of the difficulties he had encountered in obtaining CER permission to publish, it is not surprising that Rovenskii was an early and active proponent of Harbin's complete independence from the railway.

On November 5, Rovenskii printed a special run of 12,000 copies of the October Manifesto on red paper, with the intention of transmitting the news to the soldiers. The next day, he was visited by a military censor, one Anosov, who wanted to know why he had published without approval. When Rovenskii pointed to the manifesto's abolition of censorship, Anosov informed him that the manifesto was "not law." An argument ensued, and at the end of the conversation, Rovenskii refused to shake the officer's hand. Anosov, with hand outstretched, counted to three and then hit Rovenskii. This incident and the ensuing lawsuit drew further attention to civil-military tensions. A few days later, the *Leaflet* analyzed General Nadarov's order forbidding military men to participate in political meetings and parades on the basis of Article 39 of the Military Service Code. Rovenskii argued that these assemblies were not equivalent to the "disorders" (*besporiadki*) described in the article but in fact closer to the "popular fêtes" (*narodnoe gulian'e*) permitted by the same ordinance.

Rovenskii's competition, *The New Territory*, was still considered a Port Arthur product, although by 1905 its evacuation had taken on an air of permanence. Its owner and editor, P. A. Artem'ev, had army connections and support. His paper stood in firm opposition to Rovenskii's radical ideas and lent its pages to Anosov to express his views about the "sharp practice" (*shulerstvo*) and "cheating" (*moshenichestvo*) of the *Leaflet*'s editor. A full political spectrum was beginning to emerge, but within the context of civil-military antipathy.[36]

Late November saw the appearance of another important organization, the CER Employee Union. Its slogan was, "In unity—strength," and its program, as set out in its "temporary statutes," called for a fundamental reexamination of the value of labor; the protection of members, both as employees and as private individuals; the satisfaction of a wide range of cultural needs; and cooperation in realizing by legislative means the general political program endorsed by other Russian railroads. The union also espoused freedom of conscience and national self-determination. Since only members would enjoy these services and protections, a clear line was drawn between CER employees and other kharbintsy.[37]

On November 28, a competing group, the Organizational Bureau, published a leaflet exhorting telegraph workers to form their own union. The CER Employee Union was too bourgeois to represent the special needs of the 1,500 telegraphers in Manchuria, the leaflet declared. Although the oppressors might "trim their sails to the wind" (*derzhat nos po vetru*), the proletariat had to avoid joining unions that included management. Accordingly, the bureau was going to hold a founding Congress in early January and was requesting that delegates be selected, five from Harbin and twenty-one from other stations along the CER. The rush of events that followed buried this announcement and its promoters. In 1905, one month was a very long planning horizon.[38]

The far left made its political debut in Harbin on November 27, when a recent arrival from Chita, M. K. Vetoshkin, rose before a gathering of 300–400 CER workers in the railway workshops' library. Taking much the same stance as the Organizational Bureau a day later, he cautioned against trusting the CER Employee Union, since in his view it was dominated by the bourgeoisie. Instead, the workers should prepare for an armed insurrection. Alluding to the thousands of disgruntled soldiers, he later reminisced with pyromaniacal glee: "There were lots of combustibles."

After the meeting, Vetoshkin announced that he had been sent by the Siberian Union of Social Democrats to establish a Harbin branch. Then and there, he began to form workers' groups. As it happened, Harbin already had a Social Democratic Committee, which was less than enthusiastic about a man who seemed "poorly informed regarding local conditions, but imbued with *Sturm und Grand* [sic] ideas and sentiments." An attempt to verify his credentials by telegram was balked by the severing of communications with Siberia the next day. Negotiations with the cocksure Vetoshkin failed, and there was nothing the committee could do but stand by as Harbin's only Bolshevik flirted with fire.[39]

On the very night of Vetoshkin's incendiary speech, a wing of the CER administration building burned to the ground. For lack of firefighting equipment, the only way to save the rest of the structure was to remove all the wood from the connecting corridors and pull up the roof. Although the investigation that followed did not produce any conclusive evidence, arson was suspected. Further blazes on December 11, December 25, and January 1, all originating within the building, strengthened that suspicion. The fact that Rear Commander Nadarov had removed the military guard from the building shortly before the first fire and that soldiers had looted the burning building led to accusations by the CER. In the middle of the bone-chilling Manchurian winter, seven of the CER's ten sections found themselves homeless. Nadarov assured Khorvat that some barracks would empty out by spring.[40]

On November 28, the day after the first fire, a nationwide postal-telegraph strike reached Siberia, cutting off Harbin from the rest of Russia. For the next six weeks, communication would remain fitful. With ties to the center cut, the rumor mill began to grind out fantastic and frightful stories. By December 1, as General Linevich confided to his diary, "Anxiety in Harbin [had] reached its apogee. The town's residents passed sleepless nights guarding their apartments from the expected attacks. Many took counsel regarding the removal of their families, generally considering the international ports of China and Japan to be the most convenient [sites]." Worse still, a whole battalion at Harbin had refused to mount guard duty and, what with all the reserves around, Harbin was "nothing but disorders." The situation was very tense.[41]

The CER "Strikes"

On December 4, 1905, a military tribunal at the Central Asian railway's Kushka Station handed down the death penalty for several strike leaders. Sympathy strikes followed immediately on many lines. The Central Bureau of the All-Russian Union of Railroad Employees and Workers informed the Minister of Communications, K. S. Nemeshaev, and the Minister of War, A. F. Rediger, that unless the imprisoned strike leaders were released, a general strike would begin on December 7. At the last minute, the government gave in. But because of the ongoing postal-telegraph strike, CER workers only learned of the Kushka incident on the same day it was resolved. On the morning of December 7, the employees' union voted to go out on strike. The prosecution of the strike was handed over to a hastily formed committee (the Employee Strike Committee, or ESC), which remained in session in the Railway Club until two in the morning. For the seven days until the call-off message arrived, the workers demonstrated their professional solidarity. But this was no ordinary work stoppage: over 90 percent of the trains operated as usual, and the soldiers that constituted the CER's most important freight item actually increased in number.[42]

The contradiction is only superficial. No attempt was made to hide it. The very first point of the strike announcement to all CER employees reported the decision to continue the evacuation and provisioning of the troops. Only private passenger, baggage, and freight service was eliminated. Since this kind of service had been comparatively tiny throughout the course of the war, total traffic figures were barely affected. Point 6 was a request to the Samara Committee, the nationwide coordinator, for confirmation of this plan. The strike's goals were taken directly from the Russian version: the outlawing of capital punishment, military field courts, and "reinforced protection" (*usilennaia okhrana*). Below this list of three, the ESC added, "We will communicate additional demands as we receive them from Russia."[43]

The decision to continue transporting the reservists back to Russia proper stemmed from two impulses. Populist sympathy for the innocent victims of autocracy's war of aggrandizement blended with the urge to use these armed men to free Russia of the "autocratic-police-bureaucratic regime." To this end, even before forming the ESC, the CER Employee Union's Organization Bureau proposed that the soldiers be brought over to "our ideas." In addition, the fear of a reservist pogrom persisted. Now that the railroad was in the strikers' hands, there could be no doubt who would suffer "the unbelievable calamities and horrors" first, should the schedule be retarded. On December 10, the ESC reemphasized the need for "all efforts to support unobstructed military transportation, delays of which will cause immeasurable harm to the popular, common cause [*obshchee i narodnoe delo*]." Emotional bonds to both their railroading colleagues and the "Russian people/soldiers" reinforced the hold of Russia proper on the hearts and minds of the Manchurian expatriates.[44]

On the second day of the strike, Anton Ferdynand Ossendowski was elected chairman of the strike committee. Soon after the war broke out, Ossendowski, a Pole by birth, a chemist by training, and an adventurer by inclination, had been made head of a CER laboratory that experimented in the use of local resources to manufacture fuel and lubricants. His inventiveness gained him acclaim and decorations from the army. Unfortunately, his creativity compromised his veracity; in his autobiography, he styles himself, not chairman of the ESC, but "President of the Revolutionary Government of the Russian Far East." The day after Ossendowski won office, the possibility of electing a vice-chairman was broached, but nothing seems to have come of that. Approximately 50 representatives, five from each of the CER's services, became members of the ESC.[45]

The ESC conceived its mission as roughly parallel to that of the CER. Consequently, it assumed responsibility for many functions beyond the mere running of trains. For example, it commandeered the telegraph service and fired two employees who protested the action. Only telegrams concerning the technical operation of the railroad and the evacuation of troops were accepted. Even then, they had to be in the clear (coded messages were strictly forbidden) and to pass through the telegraph office's censors. Private telephone service was shut down. Even army headquarters was cut off from St. Petersburg for several days until communications were reestablished via international lines.[46]

The ESC also assumed the CER's role as employer of much of the labor force in Manchuria. Not surprisingly, it succeeded where Khorvat failed in preventing a strike at the Zhalainuoer coal mines. The ESC simply requested the miners to postpone the strike for the "attainment of common political goals." Later support for the miners' demands was promised in return. On the third day of the CER strike, the company's in-house newspaper, *The Harbin Herald*, was declared the organ of the ESC.[47]

To ensure continuing smooth leadership for the duration, the ESC kept all administrators in place and simply exercised oversight. Employees and workers were ordered to respect the pre-strike chain of command, except in cases where management instructions "clearly opposed the basic principles of the strike." Very few administrators seem to have resented the role of the ESC enough to endanger their jobs. In fact, a December 10 circular from the ESC stated that "the heads of all branches have joined the strike movement."[48]

But what seemed pragmatic to the strike leaders constituted an insensitivity to issues of social class for others. The ESC strike call did not reach the West Branch's Zhalantun Station until four o'clock on the morning of December 9. As it happened, the delegates of the CER Employee Union had only just arrived there for a congress. In reaction to the news, the assembled representatives discussed and approved the strike, then reconstituted themselves as the West Branch Strike Committee and forwarded a telegram to Harbin announcing the creation of this new organization. The ESC did not bother to reply. That highhanded attitude bruised West Branch feelings.

The next day, the ESC issued telegram no. 4330, signed by "Shol'p," announcing that, since all military loads were still being carried, the strike actually had a "narrow" character. The West Branch considered this an attempt to "belittle" the strike. Verification of telegram 4330 was requested and received. Rumors that CER management had joined the ESC increased suspicions. The revival of local traffic on December 12, ostensibly to satisfy protests by Chinese authorities, signaled a de facto return to the status quo ante. The strike continued in name only until December 14, when the resumption of normal operations on the Ussuri and Transbaikal lines made further pretense unnecessary.

On December 15, Bohedu Station sent out a circular conspicuously not addressed to the ESC. The end of the strike was noted and accepted, since the Moscow Committee had indeed called it off. The rest of the text was a strongly worded attack on the ESC: "We consider the actions of the Harbin Employee Strike Committee and its departures from the program of the Russian railway strike to have been unsteady, and in certain cases deliberately unconscientious. We consider the relations of the committee and management suspicious." The circular went on to congratulate the Worker Strike Committee (WSC) in Harbin for being the first to unmask the ESC. On December 16, Anda Station condemned the ESC for its "bureaucratism" and "carelessness." The whole West Branch took exception to the ESC decision that the CER would not participate in any future strikes for fear of compromising the evacuation of the army. Further cooperation would not be possible until Harbin received an infusion of "democraticism" (*demokratichnost'*).[49]

The strike group that had earned the Bohedu workers' praise—the WSC—was even more adamantly against the ESC's approach. Under Vetoshkin's leadership, the group had already attracted enough support by the beginning of the strike that the ESC was obliged, in its first announcement, to recognize the workers' right to their own strike committee. On December 8, the WSC, which had established its headquarters in the Pristan CER workshops, reported that it considered the strike only a means for promoting a general armed uprising. Two days later, the workshop representatives to the ESC walked out and sent a telegram to the depots and workshops of the largest Siberian stations demanding that they stop the flow of returning soldiers so the men could be recruited to the cause.

In Harbin, a concerted effort to this end took the form of leaflets run off on the ESC printing press to which the WSC had obtained access; and a call for a general strike. The latter measure, with its inclusion of hairdressers, cabbies, whorehouses, circuses, theaters, and liquor stores among the should-be strikers, was tantamount to a declaration of war on the officer corps' way of life (which had been hard hit in any case by the blockade on private freight). On December 14, when the strike was lifted, the WSC accepted the turn of events with good grace, while vowing to intensify propaganda among the troops. Vetoshkin concentrated on refining his organization in preparation for a takeover of the CER by the workers.[50]

The Army Strikes Back

The launching of the strike was hardly likely to damp down the fears of violence in an already nervous population. One of the ESC's first concerns was to organize a defense force against the anti-Jewish and anti-intellectual pogroms rumored to be in the offing. Publications coming off the military press called the railroad employees "the present enemy." In response, the strike committee dispatched telegrams to Witte and Kokovtsov requesting their vigorous intercession with the War Ministry. During the ESC's December 9 session, the local defense committee born in the turbulent aftermath of the October Manifesto asked for the strikers' recognition in order to shore up its capabilities. In a short report, the would-be organizers of Harbin's security said that discussions with representatives from the town's constituent communities had revealed that only the Jews had already made plans. On the same day, the ESC purchased 82 rifles from a Mr. Bobov. Its requests for weapons from army stocks were refused. Vetoshkin was also looking for weapons with which to arm a workers' militia. Ossendowski was inseparable from his Browning.[51]

Despite suspicions that pogroms were being organized, public paranoia still focused on the danger of an elemental, chain-reaction riot by the reserves. On November 16, Linevich informed the War Ministry that he was changing the schedule to accommodate more reserves. Troops would now return to Russia in the same order in which they had arrived. In the week starting November 6, only 687 reserves were among the 25,700 men moving west on the Trans-Siberian from Manchuria Station. This was a paltry 2.7 percent of the total. The rate climbed to 19.8 percent in the next two-week period and jumped to 34.5 percent in the succeeding two weeks; 19,744 reservists boarded trains for home between November 29 and December 13. In absolute terms, moreover, the number of soldiers leaving Manchuria increased 200 percent from one fortnight to the other. The ESC, once in charge, tried to boost the reserves' confidence in the system still further by posting evacuation schedules and sticking to them. For the period from December 6 to December 11, the freight traffic column was eloquently empty. This served as a graphic illustration to all reservist readers that the strikers were trying to get them home as quickly as possible.[52]

Both Linevich and the CER employees recognized that they were sitting on top of a volcano. The logical choice was cooperation to defuse the situation. Later on, when Linevich was accused of "negotiating" with the strikers, he insisted that he had met only once with members of the ESC: when they came in to complain about slanders being heaped on them by General M. I. Bat'ianov, commander of the Third Manchurian Army. Ossendowski, on the other hand, mentions a visit by one of Linevich's aides-de-camp bringing the commander-in-chief's blessings to the strike committee. These stories are not necessarily mutually exclusive. Both sides would have been compromised by public stances of reciprocal support, but an urgent common task dictated an uneasy modus vivendi.[53]

Not all generals were so reasonable. In late November or early December, the following appeal began to roll off the press at Rear Headquarters:

Free citizens of Harbin! We were not given freedom because Jews, various foreigners, and Russian traitors, servants of the Jews, demanded it. . . . Crush the vile enemy in time. Crush him so that he never rises again. . . . Look carefully who celebrates most in the red-flagged crowd: the Jew and scoundrel Rovenskii, brazenly [*boiko*] distributing his rotten, forged [*podlogaia*] paper, *The Harbin Leaflet*; the Jewish thiefs, Zazulinskii, Gabriel', Fride, rascally Jewish doctors and the shame of the Russians, the villain Lepeshinskii.[54]

The Social Democrats and the Jews were equated. Their goals were the conversion of all that was national to cosmopolitanism and the transformation of Russia into a republic "over which clever Israel will rule." Similarly, Veresaev quotes officers as saying: "All Jews! This was all done by Jewish money."[55] No wonder Harbin's Jewish community had taken self-defense measures so quickly.

Other ranking officers abandoned this traditional scapegoat in favor of poisoning relations between the enlisted men and the railway workers. On December 9, during a military review of the Order of St. George at Yaomen, General Bat'ianov had delivered himself of the words that had brought the infuriated ESC members to their face-to-face with Linevich:

> Gentlemen, listen to the words of a man who has served 50 years and has little [time] left to live. I have served four Tsars, and I tell you that Russia became rich and powerful thanks to the Tsars, not the people. . . . We are sitting here and waiting to depart for Russia; I myself have ten children, and we're all bursting to get home, and yet we are held here. The reason for this is the railway strike; the employees demand a raise; they don't have enough. What does the peasant get? Now railway battalions are being formed, and when we occupy the railway, then we'll drive the employees and their families and children into the cold.[56]

Bat'ianov went on to suggest that the correct way to handle such matters had already been demonstrated in Tomsk, where about 600 employees of the Siberian railway had been killed in a pogrom on November 3, 1905.

The ESC responded to this instigation of a pogrom by drafting protest telegrams to Linevich, Khorvat, Witte, Kuropatkin, the Samara strike committee, and all Russian newspapers. It also passed a resolution denying Bat'ianov the right to use the railway on his return trip to European Russia. A general meeting of CER employees called for a similar boycott of the Rear commander, Nadarov, and those of his staff officers who were printing anti-CER propaganda. Less realistically, they called on the ESC to relieve Nadarov of his duties. Even Khorvat saw fit to respond to the extent of joining his voice to that of the ESC in demanding that Linevich publish a statement averring that the CER was not among the railways delaying evacuation. Linevich, however, was unwilling to make any kind of public statement.[57]

On December 15, Nadarov escalated the conflict by giving an aggressive speech to the officers of the Harbin garrison. In it, he called the railroad strikers "enemies of the Army," but recommended that all other channels be exhausted before resorting to violence. The version that circulated on the CER telegraph had Nadarov saying that, if necessary, he himself, "sword in hand," would lead the troops against the "seditious railwaymen, their wives, their children, and their aged." The circulated version added that, "fortunately," Nadarov's officers were left uninspired by this tirade. Instead of violence, they had called for negotiations to satisfy mutual needs.[58]

The local branch of the gendarmerie under Colonel Glinoetskii was also accused of instigation. In a telegram to Witte, the central railway union in Moscow, and various Russian newspapers, the ESC berated the gendarmes for aggravating a delicate situation by "openly and impudently crying out 'Long live blood' and 'Down with freedom' in public places." Now that the war was over, the strike committee argued, this 250,000-ruble "luxury" [the gendarmerie] should be scrapped. The frontier guard could do the job just as well.[59]

Harbin came in for its share of the High Command's wrath: Kuropatkin called the city "the disease's breeding ground" (*ochag zarazy*), explaining that its civilian population, "unscrupulous [*nerazborchivoe*] in profiteering," was now also "unscrupulous in exciting the most extreme doctrines leading to anarchy among the lower ranks and officers." Linevich's views on Harbin were not dissimilar. The commander-in-chief had taken several prophylactic measures to protect his troops from political propaganda, but "proclamations" still reached the enlisted men because "revolutionary frenzy [*ugar*] seized a large part of the urban population, and almost all of the employees and workers on the Railway. . . . At present the town of Harbin is a nest of every kind of revolutionary and agitator." When Rovenskii met with the general to protest the closing of his paper, Linevich simply said, "I have but five years more to live, and I will not allow the corruption of my army."[60]

Kuropatkin singled out the Social Democrats and their "leader, the student Ivanov" (Vetoshkin), as "especially harmful," but since the organization in which their influence was dominant, "the workers' group" (the predecessor of the WSC), was located in Pristan, there was still some distance between them and Harbin's two strategic centers, the CER administration building and the main railway station. The precipice separating Pristan and New City limited the access points between the two sections and made it easy, in case of need, to interdict communications between them. Contact between the CER, based in New Town, and the army was less susceptible to quarantine, but Nadarov tried. In addition to forbidding soldiers to attend political meetings, he requisitioned the Railway Club and put an end to the public role Lepeshinskii had given it.[61]

In short, in the minds of the top army commanders, the CER, Harbin's civilian population, and the local revolutionaries blended into a largely undifferentiated but clearly hostile unit. Both the language and the activities of the military reflected such a "bunching." From its very inception, political life in Harbin was intimately tied to the civil-military conflict, the brunt of which had previously been monopolized by the sole administrative authority, the CER.

General Nadarov, it seems, took the boycott seriously enough to avoid entrusting his return trip to Vladivostok to the railway. When he was replaced as commander of Rear Headquarters by General N. I. Ivanov, he made his way to Jilin on horseback. That precaution was probably superfluous. On January 15, 1906, Bat'ianov left Harbin for Siberia without incident. Although the CER Employee Union announced (mistakenly) that the general had been appointed "dictator of Siberia," and the First Manchurian Workers' Congress, meeting in the Harbin workshops under Vetoshkin's leadership, called desperately for someone to stop "His Black Hundred Highness" (Ego Chernosotennoe Prevoskhoditel'stvo), a single battalion stationed on the train platform sufficed to cow any potential resistance.[62]

A week later, it was the two trains of General P. K. Rennenkampf's punitive expedition that stood on a siding at Harbin Station. Vetoshkin, notified by the depot workers, excused his inability to prevent their departure by claiming that Rennenkampf remained in Harbin for only a few late night hours, too short a span to muster the workers' militia. Military correspondence, however, shows Rennenkampf leaving Front Headquarters at Laoshaogou on January 19. He exited Harbin three days later. Since only 120 versts and several hours separate those two stations, the troop trains almost certainly stayed awhile in Harbin. Rennenkampf reportedly had enough time at least to consult with the new Rear commander. Assuming that was the case, the two most likely explanations for Vetoshkin's failure to act are that his claim to command 1,000 armed workers was an exaggeration or that at the critical moment he lacked the revolutionary will to move. In any event, on January 22, 1906, Rennenkampf left for Transbaikalia, where he shot all of Vetoshkin's closest comrades and brought the striking railway workers to heel.[63]

Rennenkampf's departure coincided with the first anniversary of Bloody Sunday. From early morning, workers streamed into the workshops to prepare for a demonstration march. About 500 got in before 11:00 A.M., when the Cossacks and soldiers who had been sent to surround the whole quarter prevented new arrivals from entering. When the procession was ready to sally forth, the military blocked its path. General Fok, the detachment's commanding officer, politely informed the workers' spokesmen that if they insisted on leaving the workshop precinct, he was under orders to open fire. Participants could still leave freely.

The demonstration, however, took place, and the military authorities took an active part in it with its preparations, machine guns, and artillery. They aroused the whole town and forced even the most indifferent strata of the population to start talking about the 9th [n. s. 23] of January. Our organization was also very thankful to the reactionary, provincial [*poshekhonskii*] staff for demonstrating its dread [*boiaz'no boiazn'*] today.

Linevich reported to the throne that the infamous anniversary had passed "without any demonstrations." That night, the workshops were raided, and the arrests began.[64]

Prison El Dorado: The CER Protects Its Own

Three days after the demonstration, General Ivanov sent a list of ESC members to the Harbin gendarmerie for investigation. That night, Ossendowski returned to his home to find the chief of police, A. I. Zaremba, waiting for him. He had come to suggest to the former chairman that he leave town before the gendarmes closed in. Three days later, on January 29, Ossendowski and twenty other CER employees were arrested. Khorvat states in his memoirs that he protested this harassment of his subordinates, only to have the shadow of Petersburg's suspicion broaden to include him too. In particular, Khorvat had argued for Lepeshinskii's release, because in keeping the general manager up to date on all developments in the strike committee, he had rendered a signal service. According to Khorvat, Lepeshinskii was an "honorable and reasonable man of rather liberal views" and was "useful" to him "as an informant who truthfully answered all [his] questions about what was going on among the leaders of the revolutionists." The fact that Khorvat had treated with the strike committee on a daily basis and without visible animosity was now turned against him.[65]

After an on-the-spot inquiry, the CER board member S. I. Kazi concluded that Khorvat had actually been in full control of operations throughout the strike. The ESC, by "absorbing [*sderzhivaia na sebe*] the wave of the strike movement," had served as a screen" for the rightful administration. According to Kazi, the whole CER strike had "a platonic character," merely "expressing sympathy for the nationwide railway strike." What Kazi probably intended as a vindication of Khorvat turned out to be quite close to the earlier West Branch accusations. General Linevich agreed that Khorvat had indeed maintained control, but General N. M. Chichagov, head of the frontier guard, wrote to Witte stating just the opposite.[66]

The truth lies squarely in the middle. The general manager was well-liked by his staff, who had punningly nicknamed his domain Schastlivaia Khorvatiia (Happy Croatia). The fact that he was able to work smoothly with his top assistants, even if they called themselves a strike committee, should come as no surprise. Nor does it compromise Khorvat's fundamental monarchism or the ESC's anti-regime liberalism. Besides, in December

1905, no one cared all that much as long as the reserves continued funneling into Harbin and out of Manchuria.

A closed-door military tribunal tried the strikers from March 30 until April 5, 1905. A long list of accusations had to be dropped for lack of evidence, but in the end, all but two of the defendants were found guilty of printing and distributing leaflets "calling for revolt." The evidence presented by the prosecutor was a set of proclamations printed in the name of the Social Democratic party that Vetoshkin had produced with the connivance of A. P. Kozlovskii, his "Menshevik" rival, who sat on the ESC's three-man editorial subcommittee. Considering that the group was charged with political crimes, the sentences were comparatively light. Kozlovskii fared worst, drawing three years in a fortress. After all, he had betrayed both the old order and his fellow strikers, who were shocked to find that they had harbored a Social Democrat in their midst. Lepeshinskii received two years, and Ossendowski one and a half.* According to Ossendowski, the intercession of Witte, Kerbedz, Linevich, and Khorvat had saved them from the death penalty.

There was one further cause for celebration. We returned to our cells as prisoners of a higher social class than the others in the military gaol. Imprisonment in a fortress had in the Russian code a special name, "honourable custody,"... and carried with it certain privileges, such as the right to wear one's own clothes, to receive food and books from home and to have a walk each day in the prison yard.[67]

The one hitch was that Harbin had no fortress. Khorvat solved this problem by requisitioning a large house, installing bars on the windows, and building a tall fence around the premises. The cells, "large and clean and well-lighted," were called "Dunten hotel rooms" (*Duntenovskie nomera*) in honor of the Harbin commandant who was responsible for both security and comfort. A feigned toothache would get you a night at home. Rovenskii, in his memoirs, remembers cheerfully how he, "already condemned to exile, met New Year 1907 at home with family and illegal friends." In leaving the "Hotel on Main Street" (Bol'shoi prospekt), he had been required to give his "word of honor" to be back by seven the next morning. Ossendowski called it "prison El Dorado," and set to work on scientific studies; these would earn him a prize from the Society for the Study of the Amur Dis-

---

*RGIA 1068: 1, 19, pp. 22–27. Interestingly, the editorial subcommittee that Kozlovskii bypassed was drawn exclusively from the CER Commercial Section. Other members were N. N. Tychino and L. I. Kamenev. Only Kozlovskii was sent back to Russia proper to serve his prison sentence. The others stayed in Harbin. This trial seems to have sensitized the authorities in Harbin to the special dangers of printers and print shops. Between June and December 1906, four more SD presses were confiscated, the last one even before it had been set in operation. GARF 533: 1, 522, p. 13.

trict in 1907. During this scholarly sequestration, he also published articles in *The Harbin Herald* about the natural resources of northern Manchuria.[68]

Of course, real revolutionaries felt rather uncomfortable in "El Dorado," at least until they got used to the comforts. A. I. Berger, arrested in June 1906, was shocked to discover that the "uniformed, well-brought-up citizen with the intelligent look" sitting next to the interrogator was a fellow prisoner. Afterward, he met the rest of the "hegemons, . . . who had taken the prison into their own hands," realizing that they were all "mid-level employees, engineers, lawyers, etc.; what we call the bourgeoisie." The large percentage of haughty Poles inspired the ethnic label "fraternity of Polish nobles" (*panibratstvo*). One evening, Berger witnessed Novakovskii chasing a singing miner off the veranda so that Tychino and his visiting wife could sit "intimately" (*intimno*) and privately. When one of the working-class inmates scolded this lapse in revolutionary morality, Tychino called him a "bore" (*kham'e*). In the end, Berger arrived at the same conclusion that the West Branch had reached a few months earlier: "There was no boundary between the strikers and the administration."[69] Nevertheless, the activists continued to pursue their goals as best they could. Berger was gratified by the successful propagandizing of the guards, some number of whom had already had a first dose in Japanese prisoner-of-war camps. Many were Poles, and the hegemons had reached them by playing their "national [heart]strings" and by talk of religious oppression against Catholics. When one soldier was transferred, Ossendowski made an eloquent speech and presented him with an inscribed silver cigarette case. Berger was "stunned by this scene." Sometimes the soldier on watch would come on duty drunk, throw down his rifle, and offer to aid escape attempts. After serving his time, Berger eventually helped two comrades to make use of these offers. By that time, he had developed an appreciation for a jail where it was easy to visit friends inside on a regular basis and where "the whole guard knew me well, like an old acquaintance."[70]

On release from prison, many of the "criminals" were to resume their previous CER positions after a seemly interval had passed. Lepeshinskii's reinstatement in 1909 raised eyebrows both in Irkutsk, seat of the appellate court for the Frontier district, and in Petersburg.* On January 28,

---

*The army had insisted on Lepeshinskii not serving his sentence in Harbin, since he had personally irritated many top commanders. The CER dragged its feet about giving him up. Three weeks after his sentencing, he was still in CER housing and drawing his salary. Only General Grodekov's complaint to the Interior Ministry got the wheels of justice turning again. In jail in Irkutsk, Lepeshinskii got low marks for behavior by refusing to appeal for mercy, by assuming a leadership role among the "politicals," and by placing articles in local papers with an anti-government orientation. GARF 102: 119, 281, *chast'* 11, pp. 21, 26 (1910).

1910, Finance Minister Kokovtsov sent a confidential note to Justice Minister I. G. Shcheglovitov explaining that no other "worthy candidate" for the head job in the CER Chancellery could be found. The fact that after almost four years as acting pravitel'del, V. N. Vuich returned to his position as Lepeshinskii's assistant strongly suggests that the job was intentionally kept open.

Before his reinstatement, Lepeshinskii worked for nearly two years as the secretary of the Harbin municipal council, where he proved his "usefulness and tact." He also proved his popularity in Harbin, as the seventh-highest vote-getter in the elections of early 1908. As in the past, he no doubt kept Khorvat well informed regarding council views and plans. According to Kokovtsov, "These qualities were especially valuable in view of the fact that the Harbin public administration is not only a municipal self-administrating community [*obshchina*] in the narrow sense of the word, but above all the nucleus and conduit [*iacheika i provodnik*] of our national state idea in Manchuria." The Irkutsk authorities saw things differently. For them, the Lepeshinskii affair represented "the beginning of the revolutionary movement in the area [Russian Manchuria]." Here the mechanism by which the experience of 1905 was transmitted to and transmuted into the development of Harbin municipal politics is laid bare.[71]

The gendarmerie in Petersburg continued to insist that having an ex-convict in charge of the chancellery would inhibit "secret communications" with the CER, and on November 22, Stolypin told Kokovtsov that Lepeshinskii's "revolutionary orientations" made him "unacceptable." Kokovtsov replied that Lepeshinskii had already been transferred to head the railway's commercial section, but Stolypin was still not satisfied: he did not think a "politically compromised" person should be on the CER "at all" (*voobshche*). In 1911, A. A. Bratanovskii replaced Lepeshinskii in that high visibility post, but in October 1913, when the Duma member V. I. Denisov met with a commission from the town stock exchange to discuss Harbin's economic prospects, who was on it but Lepeshinskii? The CER did not abandon its own.[72]

The Legacy of Liberal Politics at Harbin, 1906–1908

Far from being eradicated, the revolutionary movement flourished in Harbin. A 1907 report compiled by the chairman of the Irkutsk Judicial Chamber claimed that "political crime [had] recently made itself a comfortable niche [*prochnoe gnezdo*] in Harbin, as shown by the existence of various criminal parties and the most serious projects of the revolutionaries." Unfortunately for the gendarmerie, Harbin's 1907 opening as an international settlement made it increasingly difficult to crack down. The political activists realized full well that Harbin was an "international open field" (*mezhdunarodnaia cherespolositsa*) and made use of their Harbin branches as safe houses for work in Siberia.[73]

In addition, the dominant Russian authorities in Manchuria did not seem to consider the crushing of illegal political activity to be of primary importance. On May Day 1907 (May 14 n.s.), a crowd of nearly 1,000 gathered in the municipal park to listen to speeches. When a police order to disperse was ignored, a volley was fired into the air. The audience at the season opening of the summer theater, which stood alongside the park, came rushing out. Among the spectators was the Russian consul, V. F. Liuba, who requested that the detachment leave the park immediately. The police retreated to the accompaniment of "hissing and whistling." In the ensuing bureaucratic correspondence, the police chief accused Liuba of playing the crowd. Liuba, in response, wondered whether the police were trying to provoke an international incident.[74]

The CER was no better. The temporary (still) gendarme administration in Harbin knew well in advance that a one-day strike and mass demonstration was planned for May Day 1908. Despite some preventive arrests on the eve, by ten in the morning boats began ferrying groups across the Sungari to a field near the edge of the right-of-way. Proclamations circulated, the crowd sang the Marseillaise, and a troop of young women marched with red flags. At noon, as the crowd swelled to around 10,000, speeches began. In addition to the usual nameless young revolutionaries, two town worthies stood up to stir the gathering: Iosif Isaakovich Ifland, a Jewish merchant who had just been elected to the municipal council, and David Danielli, the director of the Harbin free library. Added excitement came when the anonymous "chairman" announced that two police informers were in the crowd. One escaped. The other was beaten badly.

By June 23, the correspondence on this embarrassing incident had made it to the top of the bureaucratic pyramid. Prime Minister Stolypin sent Finance Minister Kokovtsov a short memo asking why the meeting had not been suppressed. When Kokovtsov replied on July 7, it was to rush to the CER general manager's defense.[75] To begin with, since the CER was located on Chinese territory, neither a state of "martial law" nor a state of "reinforced protection," or even of "extraordinary protection," could be declared there; and though Khorvat did in fact have the authority to call out the frontier guard, those troops could be used only in cases "of extreme necessity." Furthermore, the location of the crowd near the edge of the right-of-way meant that Chinese and other foreign subjects might be present. Had such bystanders been injured in any repressive action, a diplomatic incident would have been sure to result.[76]

That point made, the Finance Minister then proceeded to the practical handicaps that would have made a strong reaction by Khorvat difficult even had he been appropriately empowered. The pontoon bridge, which had become a seasonal feature in Harbin since the war, was not yet up, so it would have taken several hours to send a detachment across the river via the railroad bridge. (Kokovtsov did not say why water transport was ruled out). Besides, with only 400 troops on hand, how could a crowd of this magnitude be dispersed? The points are clear. First, Harbin was an international city where Russia did not have as free a hand in domestic matters as within the Empire. It is the same argument used by the revolutionaries. Second, the administrative structures maintained in Harbin did not offer the same options for government activity as in Russia proper.

When Kokovtsov's letter arrived, the follow-up to Stolypin's June 23 note had already been drafted by Assistant Interior Minister Kharlimov. It showed clearly where that ministry thought the blame should be placed. After reiterating the massive nature of the demonstration and the complete lack of countermeasures, the draft concluded by pointing out "that such connivance [*popustilel'stvo*] by the local authorities, on the one hand, [would] inevitably strengthen the revolutionary movement in Harbin, and, on the other hand, [would] complicate in the extreme the battle with manifestations of this movement in the parts of the Empire nearest to Harbin." Since Kokovtsov's arguments were juridically unassailable, Kharlimov's attack on the political trustworthiness of the CER was never sent. But no one was fooled.[77]

For radical politics, the memory of cooperation between apparent enemies in 1905 was still alive. When the gendarmes were preparing to search the quarters of one career revolutionary, B. Z. Shumiatskii (alias Silin), the Harbin police gave the Social Democrat a half-hour warning to "clean up" his apartment and go into hiding. An examination of another party member's home turned up pictures of radical comrades. The police chief, who had made the discovery, made sure no one was watching before returning the photographs to the suspect with the suggestion that he should put them somewhere "a little farther." This scene is strongly reminiscent of Zaremba's visit to Ossendowski.[78]

On December 7, 1907, a one-day strike caught CER management by surprise. An investigation into the causes came up with the rather implausible explanation that a letter received two months earlier had triggered the preparations for the work stoppage. Since the letter had discussed the impending trial against the Second Duma's Social Democratic faction, Soviet authors have accepted this view without demur. Possibly, the latest cause célèbre from the center played a motivating role, but the choice of the same day on which the 1905 strike had begun could hardly be coincidental. The CER investigators concluded that this "proves the ease with which strikes take place on a signal from without." The CER had no interest in discussing the traditions of protest that had been born in 1905 and that, nurtured at all levels of the company hierarchy, had continued to grow within.[79]

IN 1895 the Russian merchant vessel *Telegraph* cruised up the Sungari, a Chinese tributary of Northeast Asia's mightiest river, the Amur. A topographer on board traced the channels and banks, including a few buildings in a swampy area called "Khaabin." Twenty years later a Russo-Chinese city of more than 100,000 had emerged as the central place in North Manchuria, imperial Russia's only colony outside Russian borders. The *T*-shaped Chinese Eastern Railroad (CER) laid the infrastructure for modern development in Manchuria (railway, telegraph, telephone, roads, research, education, press, and so on) from its headquarters at Harbin, founded at the point where the railway forded the Sungari. The largest elements for the great bridge were floated upriver from Khabarovsk, the *Telegraph*'s home port.

In 1897, Russian and Chinese officials inaugurated work on the CER, while the new company's emblem, a dragon clutching a winged wheel, flew rampant above them. Several hundred thousand Chinese coolies would construct this final leg of the Trans-Siberian and its branch south to Port Arthur. Chief Engineer A. I. Iugovich constructed not only the CER and Harbin but also employee services, such as a coeducational school system with required courses in Chinese. General D. L. Khorvat managed the CER from 1903 until 1920, extending Iugovich's constructions according to the gradualist colonial tactics espoused by Russia's masterful fin-de-siècle finance minister, S. Iu. Witte, and his successors. Witte only saw Harbin once, on an end-to-end inspection tour of the Trans-Siberian Railway in 1902. A brass band and local officials greeted him at Harbin Station, an imposing pistachio-green structure in the then-fashionable art nouveau style. Witte's commitment to a liberal Harbin allowed synagogues as well as churches to rise above the Manchurian plain.

In this tolerant environment, many Chinese and Russians tried to live across cultural boundaries. Some mixings were felicitous, others, cruelly chauvinistic. Even today, the Chinese remember this Russian presence, but the Russians are gone. *Do svidaniia, Kharbin.*

P. V. Shkurkin, one of the early graduates of the Eastern Institute active in the fledgling Society of Russian Orientologists. He emigrated to the United States in 1928. Here he is shown in his Russian official attire. (Courtesy of Vlad Shkurkin)

Shkurkin in his Chinese official attire. (Courtesy of Vlad Shkurkin)

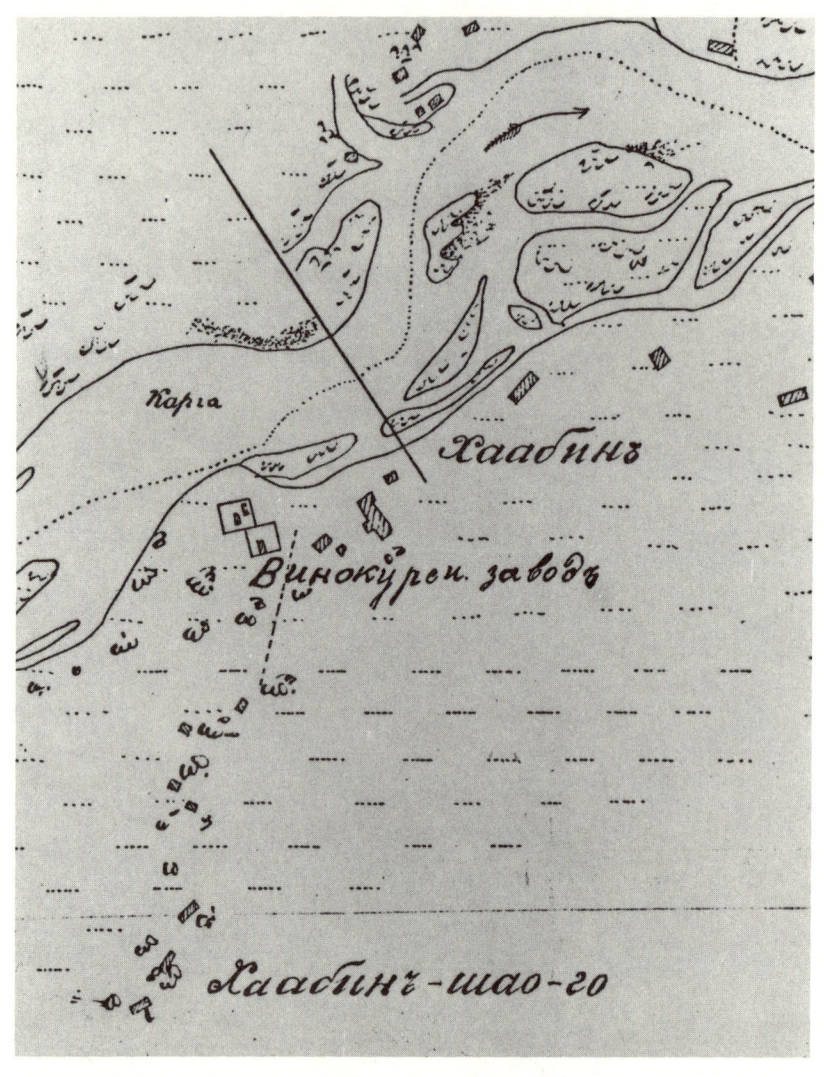

Map made by the *Telegraph* expedition of 1895. The arrow indicates "downstream" along the Sungari main channel. The dark, straight line traversing the river seems to be a later addition marking the position of the railway bridge that would be Harbin's raison d'être. This is probably the first rendering of the Chinese place-name Haerbin (in pinyin) into Russian ("Khaabin"). (Kokshaiskii, *Glazomernaia*)

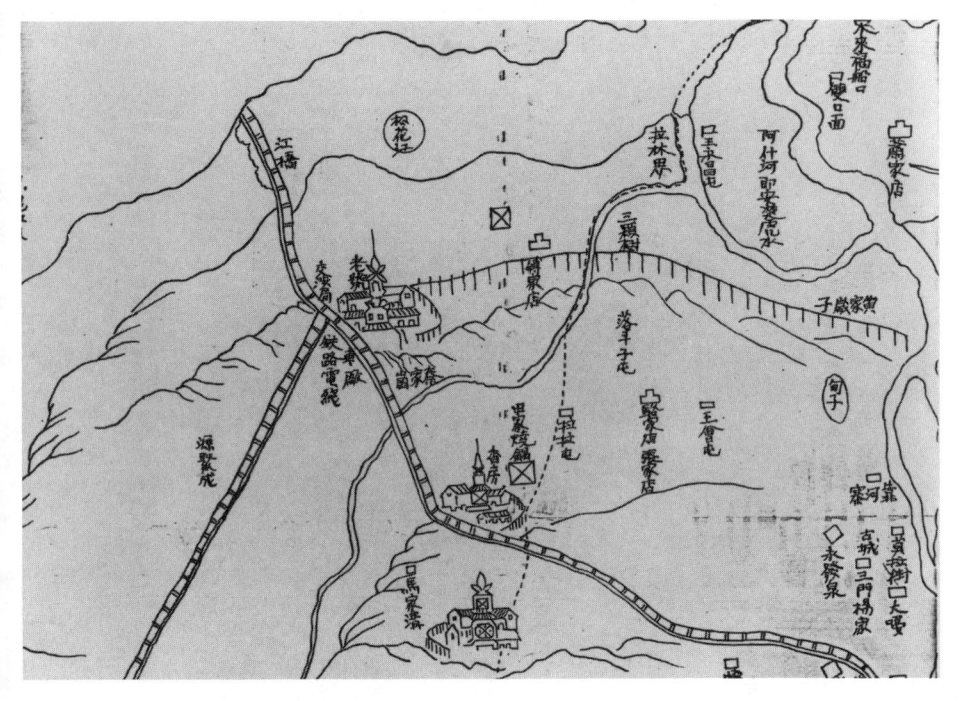

Chinese map of the railway juncture and bridge at Harbin, including Russianesque structures, 1901. (*Alabao sancheng yudi quantu*, 1901)

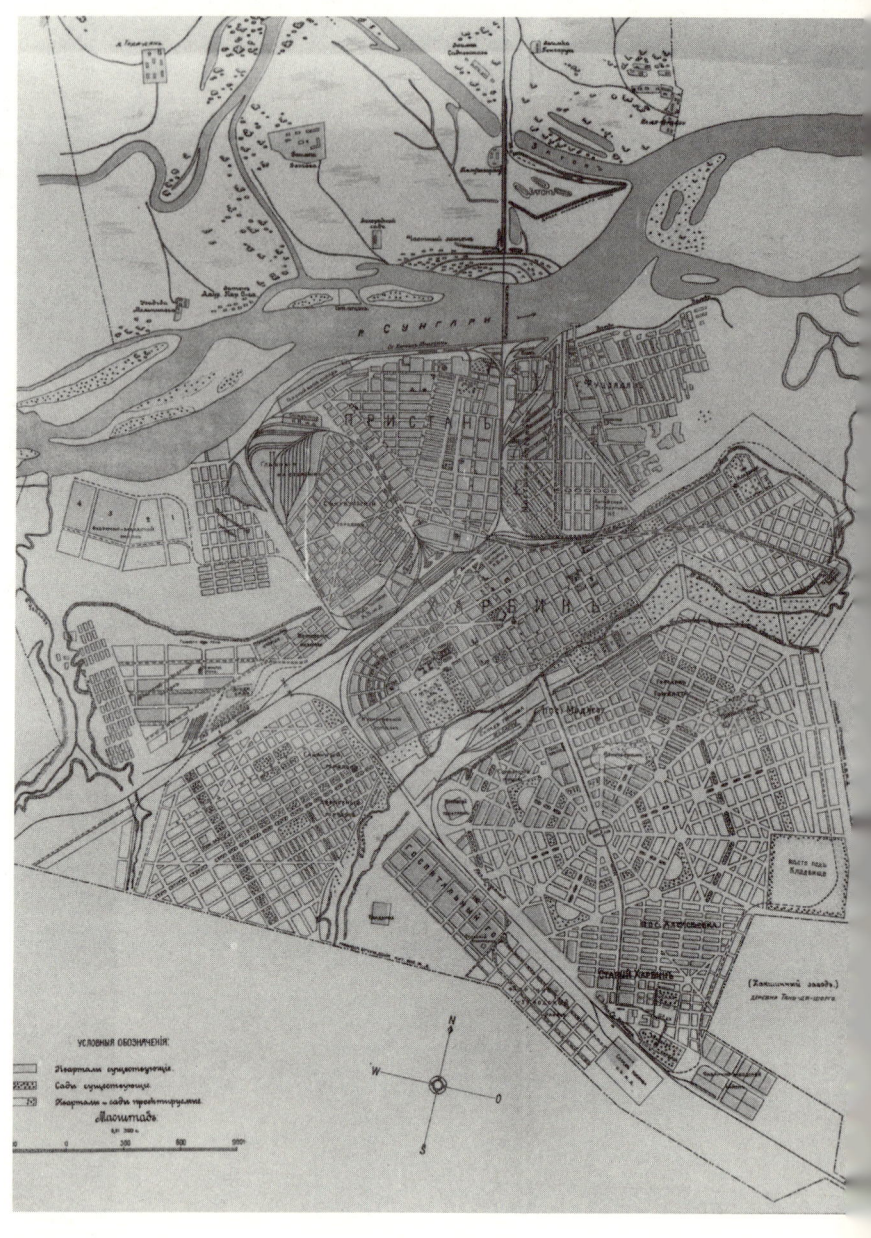

Greater Harbin, 1923. (Nilus, *Istoricheskii*)

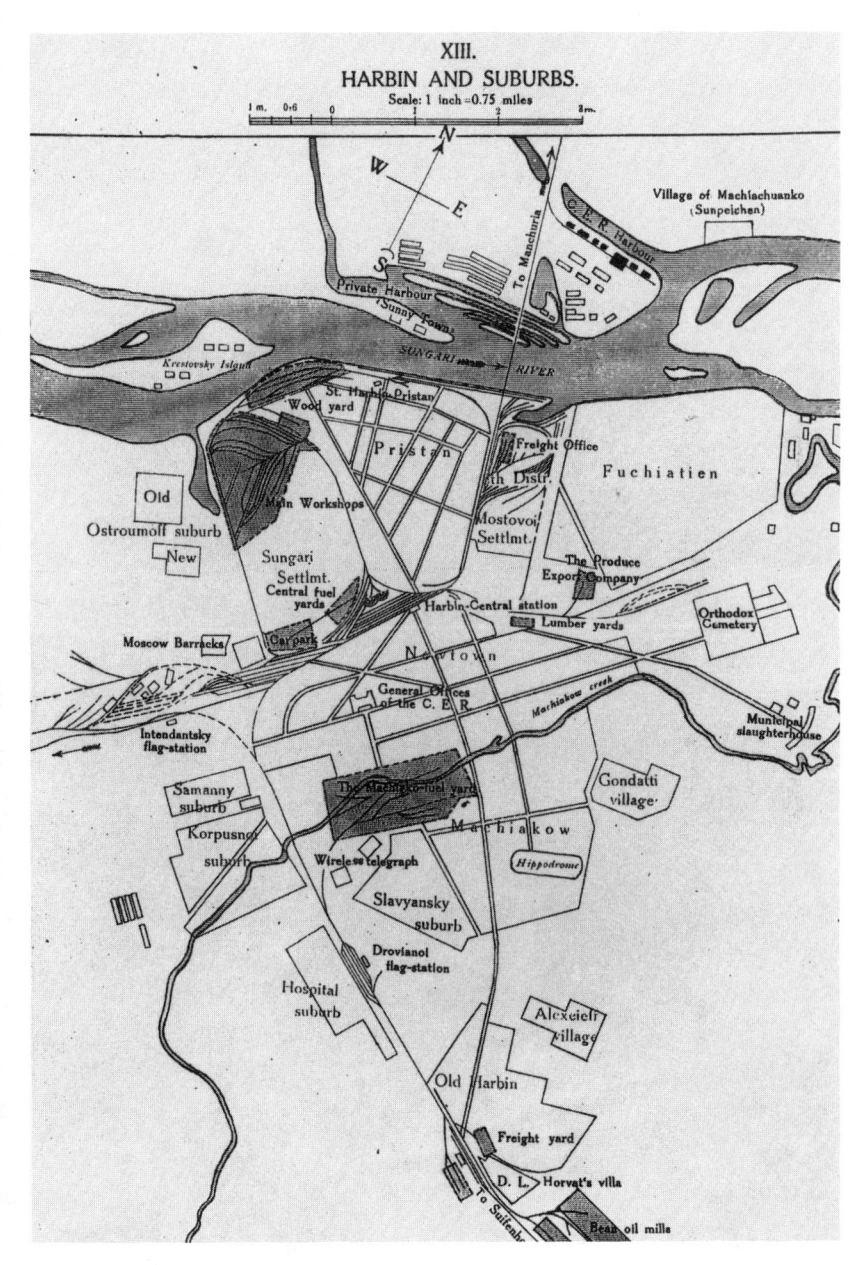

Schematic map of Harbin and suburbs (1921). (*The Chinese Eastern Railway and Northern Manchuria*, Harbin, 1923)

The Sungari Bridge under construction, ca. 1900. (*Al'bom sooruzheniia*)

Russian and Chinese officials assembled for the Chinese Eastern Railroad's groundbreaking, August 1897. (*Al'bom sooruzheniia*)

Pay day, ca. 1901. (*Al'bom sooruzheniia*)

A. I. Iugovich with schoolchildren, ca. 1902. On the CER chief engineer's return to Russia proper in 1903, scholarships were established in his name to honor his sponsorship of Harbin's school system. (*Al'bom sooruzheniia*)

Finance Minister S. Iu. Witte, ca. 1915. (Nilus, *Istoricheskii*)

D. L. Khorvat, general manager of the CER. Khorvat's tenure stretched from 1903 into the Soviet period; he was pressured into retirement at Beijing in 1920. (Nilus, *Istoricheskii*)

Chinese and Russian officials awaiting the arrival of Witte's train to the Harbin Station, October 1902. (*Al'bom sooruzheniia*)

The Plague of 1910-1911 at Harbin

LEGEND
- Locations of plague-killed corpses week 9
- Locations of plague-killed corpses week 13
- Locations of plague-killed corpses week 16
- Locations of plague-killed corpses weeks 18-20
- Plague checkpoints established week 13
- Blocks with greater than 70% Chinese population
- Blocks with 30-69% Chinese population

Chinese workers under quarantine for cholera, ca. 1901. (*Al'bom sooruzheniia*)

OPPOSITE: The plague of 1910 homed in on Harbin's Chinatown, and when the primary areas of Russian residence were sealed off, the disease destroyed the nearby Chinese villages. (Adapted from diagrams in *Chumnye epidemii na dal'nem vostoke*)

Many visitors to Harbin were impressed by its architecture, particularly the Vologda-style cathedral, consecrated in 1899 and dismantled by Red Guards in August 1966. (*Al'bom sooruzheniia*)

Like many of the city's early buildings, the pistachio-green Harbin Station was built in art nouveau style. It was replaced by a concrete slab in the 1960's. (Charov, *Kharbin Al'bom*)

Harbin's main synagogue, built in 1907. (Author's collection)

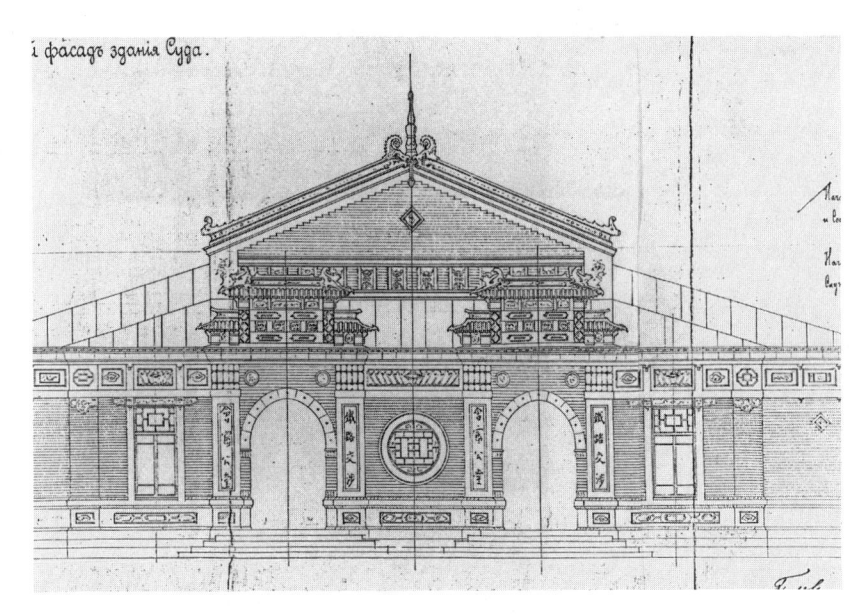

The plan for the Russo-Chinese mixed court also mixed architectural cultures. Note how the rooftop fishtails, to ward off fire, are perched on a classical pediment. (Author's collection)

Chinese merchant's stall in St. Sophia's courtyard, 1993. The church has lost its cross, but the emblem has retained it, testifying to memories of Russian culture among the contemporary inhabitants. (Author's collection)

The last of the Russians, 1995. (Author's collection)

CHAPTER 5

Know Thine Enemy, Know Thyself:
Russian Orientology in the Borderlands

> May our high-level breeding ground of Eastern science bloom everlastingly! May it succeed in all matters of real value for the Fatherland! May it be true to the basic behests [korennye zavety] of the Russian land and the historic tasks of education [prosveshchenie]! [May we] . . . with each passing year have greater cause to say that Russia owes its blossoming condition and might in the East, not so much to vastness of space and population as to knowledge of the East; and that in this development a considerable part was played by the zealous staff and alumni of the Eastern Institute—true servants of the White Tsar. —A. M. Pozdneev, 1903

AFTER 1896, the expanded Russian presence in Manchuria brought the acute need for qualified orientological support staff to the forefront of official and academic attention.* In the past, very limited opportunities had been available to men who chose to specialize in this field. For most, the climb into academia was a laborious, decade-long process that emphasized the elimination or attrition of would-be scholars rather than their production and placement. Suddenly confronted with new commitments in the military, administrative, transportation, and commercial spheres, the Petersburg authorities found themselves in desperate need of men with sufficient linguistic skills to handle immediate and wide-ranging tasks in Manchuria and China. Even before the Russo-Chinese War, well-publicized reports of the

---

*I have chosen throughout this chapter to translate *orientalist* as "orientologist." In part, this is because of the negative connotations associated with the English term orientalist ever since Edward Said's landmark book *Orientalism*. For similar reasons, I have translated the Russian *vostochnyi* as "eastern," rather than "oriental," resulting in the Eastern Institute. This institution pioneered the routine training of non-Chinese areas of "Eastern science," as Pozdneev called it, yet another reason why orientologist seemed appropriate in scope. The Appendix to this book deals with an earlier period, when the main thrust of Russian scholarship was overwhelmingly sinological, and is correspondingly titled.

dangerous, though occasionally amusing, consequences of unreliable translation brought the dearth of orientologists to public attention, making a speedy solution even more imperative.[1]

The founding of the Eastern Institute in Vladivostok in 1899 was the most important measure undertaken by the tsarist government to fill this gap. Two brothers, Aleksandr and Dmitrii Pozdneev, served as the first and second directors. Aleksandr was the foremost Mongolist of his generation, and Dmitrii held a similar reputation for the study of Manchuria. Both had been trained by V. P. Vasil'ev, the founder of the "practical school" of Russian orientology.

Between 1903 and 1916, more than 300 civilians and 200 military officers completed the Eastern Institute's four-year course. Many of these men became teachers, especially in the Far East, bringing the number of Russians with at least a rudimentary knowledge of a Far Eastern language into the thousands. Those numbers represented a quantum leap from the twenty-six students who graduated between 1887 and 1900 from the only institution in Russia offering a higher education in orientology at the time, the Chinese-Manchurian Section (*razriad*) of St. Petersburg University's Eastern Department.[2] Most of the Eastern Institute's alumni took up entry-level positions, both at home and abroad, in Russian institutions requiring a knowledge of Chinese, Japanese, Korean, Mongolian, Manchurian, or Tibetan. Additionally, many auditing and visiting students received some exposure to the new "practical" curriculum that was to have so profound an impact on the development of Russian and Soviet orientology.

On graduation, and sometimes even before, the Eastern Institute's students became pawns in the struggle between the competing visions of Imperial strategy discussed in the preceding chapters. Both visions aimed at Russian dominance, to be sure, but as we have seen, the methods for accomplishing it were quite different. The one camp, consisting largely of military men, drew inspiration from Prince E. E. Ukhtomskii's call to "reeducate" (*perevospitat'*) the Chinese and found an outlet in the policies adopted by the viceroy of the Far East at Port Arthur. A general commissar overseeing military commissars attached to each of Manchuria's three provincial governors was required to obtain "full influence" over the Chinese, both officials and subjects, so as "to gradually change them into true servants of our Fatherland."[3]

The other camp tended to see the Chinese as essential partners (though not necessarily equal ones) in a grand economic project linking a flourishing Manchuria to a revitalized Russian Far East. Witte was no less a believer in human engineering than Ukhtomskii, but for him the critical tools were technology and economics. The Finance Ministry, the most influential voice on the interministerial committee that discussed the establishment of the Eastern Institute, insisted that the main goal must be the promotion of "trade and industry in the Far East."[4]

Although some students graduated early enough to take part in the occupation of Manchuria and/or the Russo-Japanese War, thereby serving the more aggressive strategy, most alumni arrived on the scene after military defeat had left only one variant intact. This was the "Witte way," which until 1917 was promoted by the Finance Ministry and its subordinate organ in Manchuria, the CER.

This was also the strategy for which their education had prepared them, in terms of both skills and philosophy. "Practical" studies meant, first and foremost, mastery of the living language. When supported by area studies, the ability to communicate with the surrounding population offered much more sophisticated options for influence than the older methods of bribery, violence, and the threat of violence.[5] Also, the practical school's sympathy for the Chinese, passed down as Beijing Ecclesiastical Mission tradition (see Appendix), conditioned the new generation of orientologists to work with, rather than against the "natives," people who in fact had not been in Manchuria much longer than the Russian "invaders." But whether at war or at peace, the need for greater knowledge was clear. As a Beijing correspondent of *Novoe vremia* put it in 1909:

> If you look on China as a friend, then you need to know it in order to draw mutual advantage from this friendship; if you look on China as a potential enemy, as a yellow peril, then you must know it as one knows an enemy—a large step toward victory over it. The Japanese knew us and Manchuria thus during the last campaign, while we hardly knew them, or the Chinese, or the land in which we had to fight.[6]

As the geographic focus of Russian imperialist desires before the war and the central locus of Russian contact and competition with both the Japanese and the Chinese between 1905 and 1917, Harbin hosted the largest concentration of Eastern Institute alumni. In 1909, they formed the core of an amateur research society devoted to the same principles as their alma mater and sharing its schizophrenic tension between "pure" science and the application of their expertise in the service of Russian goals in the Far East. They also echoed *Novoe vremia*'s central perspective on orientology, claiming that "the results of this neglect of Eastern knowledge became clear on the Yalu, at Mukden, Tsushima, and the numberless multitude of 'tsushimas' in our daily political and economic relations with the peoples of the East."[7]

By loosening membership requirements, the Society of Russian Orientologists (SRO) drew in people from all branches of Russian activity in China and the Russian Far East. The CER, the consular service, the Russo-Chinese bank, the municipal council, and the stock exchange all contributed members, making the SRO into a sort of "union of unions," the effective successor to the radical organization Khorvat had shut down the year before. At a time of mounting pressure for the annexation of North Manchuria and rising fears of yellow peril, the SRO helped to mobilize support for the gradualist spirit in which Harbin had been constructed, and its orientological elite educated.

After 1917, the émigré Society of Russian Orientologists would share neither the principles nor the goals of Soviet orientology, but the pedagogical part of its program, aimed at educating both Russian and Chinese publics regarding the benefits of mutual understanding and cooperation, continued to play an important role in maintaining a continuity of Harbin identity in the face of political vicissitudes. The city on the Sungari's role in the history of Russian ties to and study of the East also represents the culmination of a distinct phase in Russia's millennium-old exploration cum self-exploration of the boundary between East and West, between Asia and Europe. Witte's fertile imagination and forceful leadership stretched beyond his innovations in colonization and local politics, though the seeds of his farsighted educational policies, which created the Eastern Institute, were not to bear fruit until after his fall from Imperial favor. Their ultimate result was a cultural intelligentsia uniquely qualified to appreciate and sustain the Harbin difference. The intellectual heritage of these men is explored more fully in the Appendix. In this chapter, we begin with their training in the Far East, at Vladivostok, one step prior to their deployment in Manchuria.

Training to Serve the White Tsar

At the Eastern Institute's opening ceremonies, timed to coincide with Coronation Day (Nov. 3/Oct. 21) 1899, Governor-General Grodekov presided over 27 speeches and the reading of 64 congratulatory telegrams. Highlights included addresses by the Chinese and Japanese commercial agents and a representative of the Korean community. The final act of the four-hour proceedings was a statement by Aleksandr Pozdneev, in which he pointed out the "purely utilitarian goals" of the institute. What made his institution distinctive, he suggested, was "the teaching of Far Eastern languages by the completely new method of practical linguistics." In the evening, Grodekov invited the cream of Vladivostok society to a banquet.[8]

The pedagogical novelties that Pozdneev hinted at involved both the linguistic curriculum and how it would be taught. Students could take only one other oriental language besides Chinese, which was required for the full four years of the program. Second-year students could choose their language of specialization from among Japanese, Korean, Manchurian, and

Mongolian. In recognition of the preeminent role of English both for foreign relations in Asia and for research on Asia, daily English courses were also obligatory.

Freshmen faced ten hours a week of classroom instruction in Chinese. In the second year, this dropped to six, with the introduction to the second language demanding the lion's share of time (ten hours). In 1900, in response to the Russian occupation of Manchuria, the perceived need for strengthening Chinese speakers caused Grodekov to propose a reduction in Manchurian and Mongolian to "secondary" status. The concomitant schedule change had majors in these two languages taking no more than six hours even at the introductory level. The time savings were allotted to more intensive work on Chinese. The specialization names soon reflected this conversion of "majors" to "minors." On September 13, 1900, the faculty council confirmed the distribution of the first entering class of eighteen students into the following groups: "Korean-Chinese" (5) and "Japanese-Chinese" (6), but "Sino-Mongolian" (3) and "Sino-Manchurian" (4). In the third and fourth years, both oriental languages were taught at a steady clip of six to eight hours a week.[9]

Pragmatism went beyond concentration on only two oriental languages and a willingness to let current events mold course offerings. In the methodology of language study, the Eastern Institute would make an even more durable contribution: its students spent two hours a day honing their conversational skills. For the first year, in accord with the schedule described above, this meant an hour of practice each on English and Chinese. After that, the language of specialization took over most of the English time. Dmitrii Pozdneev had identified the lack of full-time, native born *lektors* as an important reason why students of St. Petersburg University's Chinese Section could not speak the languages they studied, and his brother Aleksandr had no intention of reproducing this deficiency. The institute's original budget included salaries for twelve full-time lektors. Nine of these positions were occupied in 1909, with care being taken to hire well-educated men.[10]

The very location of the institute in Vladivostok can be considered an inherent part of the practical approach. The local press and visitors from abroad kept staff and students fully abreast of developments that could or would affect Russian interests in a rapidly changing region. Living in a city with large populations of Chinese, Japanese, and Korean speakers opened opportunities for casual exposure to and observation of oriental culture, as well as for the application of newly learned skills. But on the whole, the students had little time for socializing during the academic year, trapped as they were between a demanding schedule and their disciplinarian director. It was during the summer vacation that they were expected to justify their breeding in the "scientific nursery [*nauchnyi rassadnik*] of information on contemporary China at the point of contact between the two races."[11]

During the spring semester of 1900, A. M. Pozdneev sent letters to the largest Russian enterprises in China asking them to host Eastern Institute students during the summer months. According to Article 8 of the institute's official regulations, such stays were an essential part of perfecting language and area-study skills. The institute had originally intended to send first-year students to all the points where Russians were present in order to "cover" as much of China as possible, to allow first-hand exposure to "the interests and needs of Russo-Chinese affairs," and to provide the youths with a supportive environment during their first experience with independent research, self-teaching, and an exotic foreign lifestyle. In the second year, ran the plan, they would explore virgin territory, never visited by Russians before. In the summer of 1900, limited funds precluded such grandiose undertakings. The only affordable alternative was to take advantage of a 50-percent discount offered by the CER Steamship Company and organize a group trip under the leadership of Professor A. V. Rudakov. But that venture was ill-starred from start to finish, beginning with an accident requiring rescue at sea and ending with a premature return to Vladivostok as the Boxer uprising gathered steam.[12]

By the following summer, the situation had changed significantly. Russian troops under the command of Governor-General Grodekov had occupied all of Manchuria and had begun the military-topographical reconnaissance of the region. Since the soldiers needed translators and the students needed practical experience, Grodekov matched them up. Thirteen students joined survey parties, four were attached to Russian garrisons, and three others accompanied Professors Rudakov and Shmidt to Mukden to examine the palace library. Four students also worked for the CER. One student, the *Eastern Institute News* reported, even came under rifle fire by Chinese bandits. The only casualties, however, were the five students who were stricken with typhus and sent back to Vladivostok to recover. Because most of the first-year students had spent an exciting summer in Russian Manchuria, it is not surprising that a disproportionate number of them decided to major in Sino-Manchurian studies. Those who did well in first-year Chinese were also inclined to choose the Sino-Manchurian path, since this allowed them the widest latitude to focus on Chinese studies. These parallel trends in *komandirovki* (official business trips) and specialization continued in 1902 and 1903.[13]

From the start, the Russian authorities in the Far East recognized the value of the new resource at hand. For example, when Grodekov needed expert advice on matters as varied as a plague in Mongolia or Buriat views on obligatory military service, he turned to the institute. During the Russian invasion of Manchuria in 1900, Professors Rudakov and P. P. Shmidt translated personal letters intercepted on their way to the Chinese community of Vladivostok. It was claimed that this helped the Russians ferret out the disposition of Chinese border troops. Later, after the army occupied Manchuria, the two professors were invited to Qiqihar to examine the yamen archive. Their analysis of recent correspondence proved conclusively that orders to support the Boxer uprising had been sent from Beijing, implicating the Qing court in the attacks on the Russian railway. As a reward for "services to science and state," Grodekov presented the yamen archive to the Eastern Institute's library, instantly making the Vladivostok collection world class, especially in Manchurian materials. Director Pozdneev had been counting on just such riches from the moment the army moved in. Indeed, he had gone so far as to venture that "future Manchurian studies will owe both their successes and their materials to the present Russian [troop] movement through Manchuria." In the summer of 1901, Rudakov and Shmidt again crossed into Manchuria, this time to work with student helpers on a descriptive catalog of the Imperial library in the Manchu palace at Mukden. Once again, Manchuria's loss was Vladivostok's gain.[14]

At home in Vladivostok, other members of the institute's professoriate set an example of service to country by doing censorship work for the Interior Ministry. This turned into a monstrous burden, with over 40,000 foreign-language items arriving for evaluation in 1903 alone. In order of frequency, these included Japanese, English, Chinese, German, Korean, and French materials. Seventeen other languages were represented, though sparingly.[15] Publication aid from Grodekov permitted the academic censors to present the fruits of their wide reading to a broader public. Between July 1900 and December 1904, the institute issued *A Contemporary Chronology of the Far East* (*Sovremennaia letopis' dal'niago vostoka*), a trimonthly selection of translated excerpts from the Far Eastern press. With the institute's relocation from the blockaded city to Verkhneudinsk in January 1905, publication was suspended, never to be resumed.

Important as these services were, the real test of orientology as a support of the Fatherland came during the Russo-Japanese War. Immediately following the Japanese surprise attack on Port Arthur and the declarations of war, the thirty-four officers studying at the institute were recalled to their units. During February and early March, requests for Chinese, Japanese, and Korean translators led to the gradual depletion of upperclassmen. Within days of the first Japanese bombardment of Vladivostok, on March 6, lecture attendance fell off so drastically that the school was shut down. Most of the students specializing in Japanese and Korean became translators and interrogators in army and navy frontline units. Chinese and Mongolian speakers joined units attached to the commissars of the three Manchurian provinces or aided the quartermaster corps in the task of provisioning the Russian army with local products.[16]

From the glowing praise of the Mukden military commissar in Harbin at the end of the war, it appears that the military appreciated the contribution of the young orientologists. As he was preparing to leave Manchuria, he wrote to the institute that he considered it "an especially pleasant duty to send greetings to an institution that has produced such outstanding and talented alumni as Blonskii, Spitsyn, Tishenko, Dobrolovskii et al., whom I am proud to count among my collaborators and of whom the Eastern Institute should also be proud."

Not all students lived to experience such flattering evaluations. B. A. Khrushchov survived the sinking of the *Enisei*, but died of exposure after floating ashore on driftwood. His comrades saw fit to relay his last words to the *Eastern Institute News*: "It's cold. Oh, it's so cold." Institute participation in the war even had one delayed casualty: the lektor Z. A. Maeda, a Russian citizen of Japanese descent, who was assassinated in Tokyo during a 1907 komandirovka. After his fluency in Japanese, Russian, and English had prompted his nomination to the Sakhalin Boundary Commission, ultranationalist elements in the Japanese press had accused him of race treason and promised revenge. The institute mourned him as "an educated man not only in the Eastern, but even in the European sense of the word," noting, in particular, his aid to Professor E. G. Spal'vin in preparing Japanese textbooks.[17]

After the disruptions of the war, the Eastern Institute's enrollment spurted to 182 in 1909, a better than fivefold increase over the first class of thirty-five in 1899. During this ten-year span, the space allotted to the institute had grown slowly, with the library alone filling twelve rooms. The institute's printing press, the only one in Russia fitted for Japanese and Korean, was producing the *Eastern Institute News* at a steady clip of three a year. It had also by then filled the eight chairs promised by the joint commission that founded it in 1898.

That had turned out to be more difficult than the new director had anticipated. On November 13, 1900, A. M. Pozdneev had written to I. V. Pomialovskii, a member of the Education Ministry's Council (Sovet), evaluating the institute's first year as the distance "from nonexistence to disorder," and bemoaning his exile among "so-called professors" like Shmidt and Rudakov. He found the one a "most obtuse, though very hard-working, German, barely capable of writing Russian," and the other a "most complete child ... without any conception of life." Only two more men were on staff by then, E. G. Spal'vin and G. V. Podstavin, Russia's first professors of Japanese and Korean studies, respectively. Until 1902, Pozdneev personally covered both Manchurian and Mongolian.

With the arrival of N. V. Kiuner and G. Ts. Tsybikov in 1902–3, the institute set out in new directions. Kiuner's courses in physical geography, commercial geography, modern history, and ethnography tied Northeast Asia together into a conceptual whole. Although the focus was on China, Japan, and Korea, the "periphery" (Mongolia, Manchuria, the Russian Far East, and Tibet) received extensive treatment. Previously, each area had been covered as a separate unit by the specialist in the field. Now Kiuner took over all of these "area studies," allowing others to concentrate on language training and their own research interests. Tsybikov, a Buriat and native speaker of Mongolian, had just returned to Russia from two and a half years of traveling on his own in remote parts of Mongolia and Tibet. His arrival at Lhasa in August 1900 apparently made him the first Russian ever to visit that isolated capital. As a Buddhist, he was permitted to remain in Tibet for over a year, the first European scholar so favored. The death of Vasil'ev left Tsybikov and Aleksandr Pozdneev as the sole Russians capable of reading Tibetan.[18]

The Eastern Institute had clearly set itself the tasks of broadening and deepening the curriculum traditionally taught under the heading orientology. In 1907, the institute's academic conference, in acknowledgment of the proven value of allowing students to narrow their focus, proposed to reshape and expand the areas of specialization. Some changes were intended to reflect the new postwar realities in the region. The suggested conversion of the Sino-Korean major to Japanese-Korean would recognize the consolidation of Tokyo's influence on the Korean peninsula (just as the drastic drop in Korean majors had already testified to the contraction of Russian ambitions). And with Witte no longer an obstacle, a Tibetan-Mongolian combination under Tsybikov should be installed.

On the other hand, the proposal to establish separate majors for Chinese and Japanese studies was simply the natural extension of the logic with which Dmitrii Pozdneev had argued for reducing the original three to two languages. In fact, Dmitrii, who had briefly succeeded his brother as director in 1904 (after thanking Witte for making him "a man capable of working in the Far East"), believed that even a two-language program would make the institute into "a monastery, where the students have taken a vow for the attainment of a goal that they themselves have freely set." This kind of reclusive atmosphere could not be the appropriate breeding ground for pragmatic men of action. Similarly, the conference proposed that students concentrate on either legal/administrative studies or trade/industrial matters, but not both as previously taught.*

*IVI, 1907, p. 3; 1908, p. 14; RGIA 632: 1, 1, p. 197; GPB 590: d. 3, p. 4. This program had not been enacted by 1909 and possibly never was. Dmitrii's monastic analogy evokes the ecclesiastical mission heritage.

Not only did the Eastern Institute see the need to accommodate to the changes in the region (though some years later than Dmitrii Pozdneev, to whom, in 1904, "what happened five years ago ... already [seemed] of such antiquity as if it took place several generations ago"). It also had to adapt to changes back home. Specifically, this meant strengthening local ties to replace Petersburg's withering interest in a Far Eastern empire. Fortunately, by 1904, the institute had accumulated over 40,000 rubles in scholarship funds donated by local organizations and individuals, often in honor of the high-ranking visitors who had graced the podium at speech-days and graduations. These had included Finance Minister Witte, Minister of War Kuropatkin, Viceroy Alekseev, and Governor-General Grodekov.

Ultimately, however, hopes for long-term support of the institute both in the Far East and in Petersburg hung on the budding careers of the alumni, who by the end of 1908 numbered 60 civilians. Of the 54 the institute could locate for its *Tenth Anniversary Guidebook*, forty-one were working east of Lake Baikal and nine held positions in St. Petersburg. The only city to equal the capital's concentration was Harbin, where in 1909, institute graduates founded an organization, the Society of Russian Orientologists (Obshchestvo russkikh orientalistov), dedicated to furthering the same principles as their alma mater. The practical school of Russian orientology had returned to its source in China.[19]

The Society of Russian Orientologists

With the 1904 calling to arms of the Eastern Institute, Harbin saw the influx of dozens of young specialists prepared to serve the Russian war effort. Some of them remained behind in Manchuria afterward, but not enough to allow the Russo-Chinese Gathering (Russko-kitaiskoe Sobranie) in 1906 or the Eastern Club (Vostochnyi Klub) in 1908 to sustain themselves. What appeared to be a promising start in 1908 toward a formal orientological society also floundered. It was not for a lack of interested members this time—eighty or so graduates of the institute and St. Petersburg University's Chinese Section were enthusiastic enough to assemble in Beijing on June 25—but though they endorsed the concept, "disagreements and lack of solidarity" prevented further organization. Unhappy with that outcome, five of the institute's alumni in Harbin met nine days later and decided to proceed independently of the Beijing group. Three of them, I. A. Dobrolovskii, A. V. Spitsyn, and P. S. Tishenko, all from the class of 1905, were commissioned to draw up articles of incorporation for their proposed Society of Easterners (*Obshchestvo Vostochnikov*).[20]

The first articles identified the new society's primary task as "service to the state interests of Russia in the Asian East." But the intermediate goals set out in the next article softened this chauvinism, revealing the heritage of the Vasil'ev school (see Appendix). The multifaceted "study of Eastern and Central Asia," and the "rapprochement of Russia and the peoples of Eastern and Central Asia on the basis of mutual interests stemming from cultural exchange" emphasized propaganda for those goals "in the press and in society" without clarifying whether Chinese or Russians would be the target of this campaign. Mutual aid among members was encouraged. By the time these statutes were adopted in October, the organization's name had changed to the Society of Russian Orientologists (SRO). The cream of Harbin society greeted the SRO warmly, and membership grew quickly as soon as the requirement of an orientological higher education was modified to admit all those "individuals evincing an active interest in the study of the East and contributing to the realization of the Society's goals by their practical activities." From July 1909, the publication of *The Herald of Asia* (*Vestnik Azii*) attracted even more attention and members.[21]

Throughout 1909, the SRO shared the scene with a similar organization, whose name was almost identical. This was a branch of the Orientology Society (Obshchestvo Vostokovedeniia) of St. Petersburg, formed on the initiative of two leading officers in the Trans-Amur Border Guard, Colonel N. G. Volodchenko, the unit's chief of staff, and Lieutenant A. M. Baranov. Spitsyn, Dobrolovskii, and Tishenko served on its board of directors, but when the military men suggested that the existence of parallel organizations was "undesirable," the trio promptly quit. After subsequent merger negotiations broke down, the two groups parted company acrimoniously, at least on the military group's side. Baranov accused the SRO of stealing the Orientology Society's name (*vostokoved* = *orientalist*) and unpatriotically endowing it with a foreign connotation. He mocked the Eastern Institute graduates for setting themselves up as "a separate corporation in the manner of general staff officers."[22]

This whole affair may best be understood as a reprise of the civil-military tensions discussed in the preceding pages. Here too a common aim was not sufficient to reconcile divergent means and loyalties. A secret memorandum Baranov sent to Finance Minister Kokovtsov on January 13, 1907, illustrates the point. Baranov had traveled extensively in Mongolia during the Russo-Japanese War and believed that Russia should increase its involvement there. In this, he was prescient. The ten measures he recommended to Kokovtsov began with diplomatic, military, and political aid, before tapering off into economic and cultural proposals. The last items on the list were a "Russo-Mongolian school" at Harbin and a newspaper "on the model of the [Russian Chinese-language] paper *Yuandongbao*." In a similar memorandum, Volodchenko seconded the idea of a publication simply as a tool "for simplifying and broadening the collection of intelligence." In contrast, for the SRO, as well as the CER, economic and cultural means of suasion came first. We will come to the *Yuandongbao* in due course. For now, it is enough to observe that Spitsyn, its editor, and Dobrolovskii, his assistant, could hardly have appreciated the position to which their life's work had been relegated.[23]

The same distinction in attitudes toward the Chinese that characterized the civil-military split separated the two orientological societies. When asked their opinions on the establishment of a trade museum at Harbin, both groups endorsed the idea. But where the military men thought that it should be an "exclusively Russian institution," displaying only Russian goods, the SRO believed that the museum should promote Russo-Chinese trade in the fullest sense. Increasing Russian exports helped Russian manufacturers, of course, but Chinese exports, whether to Russia or other destinations, would also help the manufacturers by increasing the buying power of the local population of Manchuria. The SRO was ready to wager on inclusion, since the "guarantee of success" was the participation of all interested parties. This meant public organizations at Harbin, the CER, and official administrative organs, as well as the Chinese.[24]

Civil-military tensions were not the only ones reenacted in the field of orientology. Center-periphery rivalries also resurfaced with the establishment in St. Petersburg in early 1911 of an organization bearing the same name as the SRO, but boasting more illustrious supporters, including the Grand Princess Militsa Nikolaevna. Despite being both younger and smaller, the capital organization persuaded the Harbin SRO to become "the Harbin branch of the SRO" in November 1911. But when St. Petersburg decided that Harbin's *Herald of Asia* should be transferred to the capital, since that was where the SRO's "main activities [were] concentrated," the union evaporated. Of the 138 members of the Harbin branch listed in the St. Petersburg group's 1911 annual report, only six remained in 1912. Four of these were Eastern Institute professors whose national prestige (and pretensions) drew them toward the capital.[25] For most of their colleagues, however, loyalty to their students and the Far East was a stronger bond. The faculty of the Eastern Institute lent their intellectual authority to their former students' brainchild by joining the Harbin SRO en masse. The previously mentioned Professors Kiuner, Podstavin, Rudakov, Spal'vin, Shmidt, and Tsybikov all became members, as did junior faculty such as A. V. Grebenshchikov, P. K. Gol'denshtedt and V. M. Mendrin. The willingness to accept nonscholars as full members based on their "practical activities" can be taken as evidence that the SRO saw itself as the continuation of the pragmatic line in Russian orientology. An editorial in the second number of *The Herald of Asia*, celebrating the tenth anniversary of the Eastern Institute, reinforces this impression by its self-congratulatory tone and the explicit statement of paternity that "alumni of the Eastern Institute [had] the honor" of forming the SRO. The author's only recommendation for the Eastern Institute was "greater sensitivity to the interests of Russian society" in the Far East, exactly the tack taken by the SRO in admitting the pillars of the Harbin community to full membership.[26]

Strengthened orientological skills was one of the few positive developments in Russia's Far Eastern affairs in this period. Boris Arsen'ev, who had served in the Tokyo embassy just before the war and had been posted to Beijing in 1908, was in a position to make the comparison. Even though the Russo-Japanese treaty of 1907 had brought Japanese support for CER rights, Arsen'ev noted, in a shrewd memo to the Foreign Ministry in 1909, the two countries' long-term goals diverged. From Tokyo's point of view, every Russian victory over the Chinese would bring a further breakdown in Russo-Chinese relations; every loss would bring an ultimate Russian withdrawal from Manchuria a bit closer. The Japanese shadow on the continent had lengthened immeasurably, and the Chinese military had modernized since the defeats of 1900. Even more important, since the Russo-Japanese War, the reform movement in China had strengthened an anti-Russian nationalism dating back to the occupation of Manchuria in 1900, if not to that of Port Arthur in 1897. Arsen'ev considered the long-term implications: "Would it be cautious right now, while a 400-million-man China is shaping its political structure, to neglect the enmity toward us that has already begun to penetrate Chinese public opinion, and that, in connection with our activities in northern Manchuria, grows with every day?"[27]

Fears of a forced Russian retreat from Manchuria were complemented by a xenophobic panic over the possibility of Chinese penetration into all of eastern Siberia. For example, on April 13, 1908, Stolypin, trying to get Duma funding for the Amur railway, delivered a statement worthy of *Dr. Strangelove*: "If we sleep our lethargic dreams, this [Far Eastern] territory will become saturated with foreign juices, and when we awake perhaps it will be Russian only in name." The appropriation passed on the following day. Both external threat and domestic paranoia contributed to a shortsighted policy-making environment, where a sense of dire urgency precluded gradualism. It fell to the SRO to remind both Harbin and St. Petersburg that 70,000 Russians in Manchuria were not a negligible force, especially when mobilized by the CER's "encouragement of initiative" into "social organizations and institutions." Russians who knew China and the Chinese could still attain Witte's goals, given time and support.[28]

The potential usefulness of the society was not lost on the local authorities in Harbin, for influence through rapprochement rather than force had been a basic tenet of the Manchurian enterprise from its inception. Besides, the CER needed men with a knowledge of oriental languages. A study conducted in September 1909 showed twenty-eight employees with a command of oriental tongues (twenty-three Chinese speakers, four Japanese, and one Korean) but demand for over 100 more.[29] In early 1910, the CER Land Department gave the SRO a plot of land on which to build its headquarters. Later in the year, General Manager Khorvat spoke of the "tireless activity of the Society in support of Russian interests in the Far East" in a letter to the Finance Ministry requesting a 6,000-ruble construction subsidy. His request was granted. When this proved insufficient, an agreement was worked out with the Railroad Employees' Association to add a second story onto its building. Additional aid from the CER came in the form of permission to use the railroad's printing press for *The Herald of Asia*.

The willingness of I. Ia. Korostovets, the Russian ambassador at Beijing, and then Khorvat to serve as honorary chairmen of the SRO and of E. V. Daniel, the CER's plenipotentiary for relations with the Chinese, to serve as its chairman from 1911 to 1915 made it clear to all that the society enjoyed the patronage of those responsible for carrying out Russia's Far Eastern policies. N. L. Gondatti, the Priamur governor-general, became a member in 1911. That act underlined the shared agenda of the Russian Far East and Manchuria, already made abundantly clear through the Eastern Institute connection. All these ties did not escape the Chinese, who identified the SRO (as they do even today) as nothing more than an imperialist tool. In 1911, Dobrolovskii translated and debunked an article from the *Beijing Daily News* (*Beijing ribao*) claiming the SRO had just recommended to its new member Governor-General Gondatti that North Manchuria be annexed. In fact, from 1909 until 1925, the SRO did serve as a semiofficial umbrella organization not only for spreading Russia's cultural message to the Chinese, but also for strengthening the Russian population's belief that their presence in Manchuria was necessary and beneficial.[30]

Harbin Orientologists and the Peaceful Penetration of China

The SRO's major activities fell into three categories: research, propaganda, and pedagogy. In examining them, we will find significant overlap not only among these areas of activity, but also between them and the professional activities of the SRO's leaders, the Eastern Institute's corps of alumni. In a sense, the SRO's full membership simply served as a receptive sounding board for the leadership's gospel of cooperative cultural imperialism. As an influential elite drawn from local society, the members would then spread these views further among the inhabitants of Harbin. The Russo-Chinese interactions undertaken by the possessors of intercultural capital could only be sustained in the long run if they were valued by Russians. In Harbin, where the state had chosen the path of cooperation with society as the best means for pursuing its expansionist goals, the "service of state interests" of necessity meant "sensitivity to the interests of Russian society."

The 53 issues of *The Herald of Asia* (1909 to 1926) highlight the research activities of the SRO. A glance at a cumulative index makes it immediately clear that the SRO strove for the same breadth as the Eastern Institute. Mongolia, Japan, and Russian Asia were all well represented.[31] Nonetheless, in line with the practical needs of a membership that, in largest part, lived and worked in Manchuria and North China, those areas received the most coverage. For example, the first three issues each contained a long piece by an SRO founding member that reflected both a professional interest in northern Manchuria and the point of view of the Vasil'ev school of orientology.

A. P. Boloban (class of 1907, Japanese-Chinese major), a grain expert in the Commercial Bureau of the CER, wrote on colonization, a matter of continuing concern in a staple economy like Manchuria, where the production of grain (primarily soybeans) was a direct function of rural population.[32] Although many publicists had argued that Chinese migration to Manchuria would endanger the Russian presence there, Boloban, in keeping with the Vasil'ev school's sympathy, gave no credence to these "Yellow Peril" theses. Hewing to the Witte line, he argued that increased production meant more freight for the railroad and, consequently, prosperity for both races sharing Manchuria. Since the Commercial Bureau doubled as a research organ on the economy of northern Manchuria, and almost all of its staff became members of the SRO, this point of view soon became an implicit assumption in both organizations' publications.[33]

The second issue of *The Herald* featured an article by A. V. Spitsyn on "The Administrative Structure of Manchuria," in which the first chairman of the SRO traced the changes involved in demilitarizing the government of China's three eastern provinces. His positive evaluations of these regional reforms ("important and praiseworthy") and what they portended for national renovation were fully consonant with the optimistic vision of China's future espoused by the practical school ever since its founding. The topic was a long way from Spitsyn's student research on the difficult lives of Chinese coal miners in southern Manchurian, but the implicit populist and reformist sympathies came from the same intellectual tradition.[34]

For Spitsyn, who had edited the Chinese-language paper (*Shengjingbao*) that the Russian army had published in Mukden until the 1905 evacuation, the removal of the printing press to Harbin in 1906 turned into an opportunity not to be missed. With Dobrolovskii as his assistant (replacing Tishenko, who had been his assistant at Mukden), Spitsyn immediately launched *The Far Eastern Paper* (*Yuandongbao*), the first Chinese-language paper in northern Manchuria. By the time the thousandth issue came out on May 19, 1910, the *FEP* was still the largest of its kind (3,000 copies), drawing respect and 70 congratulatory telegrams from all over China. Even the strongly nationalist Chinese International Student Federation picked this wholly foreign-owned and -operated publication (all its employees were paid by the CER) as one of the five Chinese-language papers "worthy of an intelligent reader." For the Russians, however, it was the *FEP*'s ability to "clarify and explain events from a point of view favorable to us," while contributing to the "rapprochement [*sblizhenie*] of two great Empires, the Russian and Chinese," that justified the large subsidies.[35]

All this flattering press was especially important, since the expense was making the Finance Ministry nervous. In 1909–10, it briefly flirted with the idea of passing the venture to the Foreign Ministry, which clearly understood the need to compensate "by all peaceful means" for the precipitous drop in "military prestige" caused by the Russo-Japanese War. The diplomats were particularly disturbed by the growth of the Japanese-owned press in East Asia, reported at this point to have reached eighteen papers in Manchuria (of which eight were in Chinese) and forty throughout China. The CER's Khorvat tried to forestall the move by arguing that the *FEP*'s value in bringing Chinese customers to the railroad and in improving local relations with both government and populace went beyond mere "rubles and kopecks," and that in any case, subsidies had dropped every year since the paper had opened.

Under the pressure of these discussions, Spitsyn undertook a series of innovations. To reach even poorer Chinese without much formal education, he suggested in 1910 that a one-page supplement be issued in the spoken language (*baihua*). To disarm accusations of bias, he also began to include news items showing Russia in a negative light, culled from Reuters. Toned-down criticism of Chinese and Japanese officials was meant to avoid personal animosities. The paper's appearance closely resembled that of Shanghai's *Shibao*, China's most widely circulating newspaper, the better to pass as a "truly" Chinese publication. In the course of the next year, the *FEP* went from two to twelve pages, half of which were filled with paid advertisements. Administrative complaints evaporated along with the deficits.[36]

Whether as researcher or editor, Spitsyn certainly saw himself as serving Russia's goals in the East, but his means were in accord with his education and his social vision. The confidential information he received from Russian contacts in Beijing helped Spitsyn make sure the *FEP*'s editorial "course" would not contradict the general thrust of Russian Far Eastern policy, but the rest was in his hands. The decision to broaden circulation, for example, rested on populist assumptions of the need to draw, in Khorvat's words, "the sympathy of the most varied circles of the local population." Spitsyn's optimistic belief that acquainting the Chinese with Russia would naturally lead to rapprochement revealed the heritage of the practical school.[37]

Spitsyn's hopes for a reformed China helped him find able Chinese editors of a progressive bent. His first editor-in-chief (*zhubi*) was the novelist Lian Mengqing, who had worked as a journalist for several Shanghai newspapers in the three years after fleeing Beijing under a political cloud. As a member of the anti-Manchu Tongmenghui, he was forced to seek political asylum in the treaty ports. But in early 1911, as tempers flared over the Russians' proposed plague prevention measures in Fujiadian, Lian came under attack as a collaborator (*maishen toukao*). The *FEP*'s only competitor, *Dongchui gongbao* (Eastern Frontier), published an account of his checkered past, making clear the essential unity of his antigovernment activities, both domestic and foreign, at the level of unpatriotic ill-intent. Lian soon resigned his position. This kind of ad hominem attack, however, was considered out of bounds, and as soon as the plague crisis died down, the Russian and Chinese authorities agreed to close down *Eastern Frontier* and exile the editor from Harbin. Lian's replacement at the *FEP*, Yang Kai, did not see anything inherently treasonous in his work either and claimed to have worked out an agreement on how to avoid chauvinistic quarrels.[38]

Whatever agreement Yang thought he had fashioned, not all local Chinese subscribed to it. Xi Tingfu, an official in the Russian-dominated Diplomatic Bureau of Jilin, for example, tried to establish a newspaper at Harbin, *Dongfang xiaobao* (Eastern Dawn), precisely to contest the *FEP*'s perceived desire "to confound right and wrong, to confuse black and white" (*diandao shifei, hunxiao heibai*) when nothing came of his repeated protests in 1906–7 at Harbin's having become "the center of Russian enterprise in the Far East and a sacrifice [lit., 'meat offering,' *fu*] to the whole world's covetousness." The project seemed doomed from the start. A fire destroyed the press even before the first issue; and despite Chinese government aid, the paper folded after a few months.

Xi, angered by the *FEP*'s mocking references to his journalistic failure, continued to petition both local and provincial officials. Meanwhile, at the end of 1908, a successor and longer-lived publication, the *Binjiang ribao* (Harbin Daily), was founded by Yao Xiuyun to again "raise the banner of opposition to *The Far Eastern Paper*." It was this publication, renamed *Dongchui gongbao* in 1910, whose vitriol drove the *FEP* Chinese editor-in-chief from his position. Although Yao was reputed to owe the *FEP* favors dating back to his days on the Pristan Chamber of Commerce, his resistance to *FEP*-supported CER proposals during the plague outbreak were just as virulent as Xi's during the municipal self-government crisis in 1909. As noted above, the authorities clamped down on *Dongchui gongbao* as soon as the outbreak was over.[39]

When Baranov's suggestion for a Mongolian publication finally bore fruit, its approval was motivated by the same kind of competitive reaction. The suggestion had been rejected just a year earlier, but when the Chinese launched the *Mongolian Newspaper* (*Menghuabao*) in the summer of 1908 with a first issue that described Japan and Russia as watching Mongolia "like a tiger watches its prey," the Russians had second thoughts. *Mongolun Sonin Bichik* (*Mongol News*) appeared bimonthly starting in the spring of 1909 and was distributed without charge by Russian consulates in Mongolia. To keep costs down, the printing was entrusted to the *FEP*. When the Russians backed the Khalkha Mongolians in their bid for independence in 1913, a boycott organized by patriotic societies cost the *FEP* a third of its sales, and Spitsyn was the object of death threats.[40]

In 1911, Spitsyn was considered for a job as the Priamur governor-general's top expert on Chinese affairs, but the opportunity fell through. In 1914, ironically, he became the Heilongjiang governor's adviser on Russian affairs. In January 1917, Khorvat nominated Spitsyn to head up the CER Chinese Relations Section, but the regime fell before he could be confirmed. From his position at the *FEP*, Spitsyn continued to support Khorvat until March 1920, when the CER's general manager was forced to resign to an advisory sinecure in Beijing. Contemporary PRC sources that see Bolshevism and the May Fourth Movement as part of the same global process have difficulty reconciling Spitsyn's editorial resistance to the former and exuberant support of the latter.[41]

A more refined understanding of Spitsyn's academic background and political orientation within the Russian context resolves this false contradiction. As an intellectual descendant of Vasil'ev, Spitsyn wished China's progressive forces well. As a "Harbin liberal," he was obligated to support the authorities, Khorvat at their head, who had allowed the city so much more freedom and tolerance than were available in the metropole. In any event, his politics did not prevent him from taking Soviet citizenship in 1923 and serving as the head of the CER's International Communications Bureau throughout the period of Sino-Soviet co-management.[42]

Harbin Orientologists and Russo-Chinese Education

In the third issue of the *Herald of Asia*, Spitsyn's second in command, I. A. Dobrolovskii, published an article entitled "Extraterritoriality of Foreigners in China: Regarding the Question of Municipal Government in Harbin." In addition to praising the CER for wagering on self-government for the Russian community as the best guarantee of the settlement's future development, he had kind words for the way in which the new order of things gave the Chinese privileges they did not enjoy in other foreign concessions.[43] Liberality and tolerance went hand in hand in ensuring Harbin's intercultural success. Dobrolovskii also blasted the Russian central press for its ignorance in condemning the regulations of self-government, singling out *Novoe vremia* for ridicule, when it misidentified the Diplomatic Board (Jiaosheju), an organ of local diplomacy, as the name of a Chinese official.[44]

This article is particularly noteworthy as an example of a personal credo molded by training in the practical tradition at the Eastern Institute and service on the CER. Before and during the war, Dobrolovskii had worked under the military commissar of Heilongjiang province researching the localities closest to Mongolia. On graduation, he returned to Manchuria to work under Spitsyn as assistant editor of the *FEP*. Since he moonlighted as Chinese-, Japanese-, and Korean-materials censor for Harbin, Dobrolovskii was especially well informed on events in the Far East and was therefore able to keep the *FEP* abreast of all regional developments. A firm believer in direct influence, he also ran study groups for his Chinese employees at the *FEP*. In 1909, the Chinese press reported that the *FEP* was on the list of ten daily papers read by the Prince-Regent.[45]

Dobrolovskii was equally diligent in spreading the message of mutual understanding and benefit to the Russian population of Harbin.[46] As a founding member of the SRO, he served in various capacities, including chairman, vice-chairman, and secretary. Several issues of the *Herald* also came out under his editorship. Although the SRO may have been the focal point of orientological interests in Harbin, Dobrolovskii believed that wider popularization was necessary. As head of the municipal council's school commission, Dobrolovskii strove for the inclusion of both English and Chinese in the public school curriculum. English did indeed become a subject of universal instruction, but Chinese had a more checkered career. Originally offered at the CER's prestigious Commercial High School as options requiring additional payment, Chinese and Japanese between them attracted only thirty-six students in 1906-7. Even so, the following year, the board of guardians approved making Chinese a required course, and the number of students rose to 111 in 1907-8 and 236 in 1908-9 as the new rule was phased in. The parents' committee requested that Chinese be returned to "optional" status in 1909, but the CER refused. By 1911, 323 pupils were enrolled for three hours a week in the six-year program. The older students could already read stories and retell them in the vernacular. The teacher, N. K. Novikov (Far Eastern Institute class of 1907), used the same methods as his alma mater, including employing a Chinese lektor for conversational classes. By 1910-11, the commercial school's three-year vocational program added an additional 75 students to Novikov's teaching load. Since these youths were usually poor and often from other stations on the CER, they lived with Chinese families and progressed quickly.

Russian Orientology in the Borderlands   165

Nor were the younger students neglected. Both of the two-class primary schools, opened in 1908 under the newly formed municipality, required their 480 students to take Chinese, as well as English and Far Eastern area studies. This gradual move toward mandatory universal education in Chinese began to spill over into Russia in August 1909, when a conference of CER and Ussuri railroad teachers (the two lines had been united under Khorvat since 1906) called for the introduction of Chinese in all railway schools. By then the pedagogical norms of Harbin had already made their mark on public education in the Russian Far East. Vladivostok opened courses at the elementary school level in 1908; Irkutsk and Khabarovsk were preparing to follow suit in 1909. Although the SRO's attempt to found a two-year night school of orientological studies (modeled on the Eastern Institute) failed for lack of funding and interest, Dobrolovskii and his fellow members did organize a series of lectures designed especially for teachers. Russo-Chinese harmony was clearly envisioned not only as a cultural task, but as a multigenerational goal.[47]

But cross-cultural communication is a two-way street, and the training of Russians was only one of the directions. As Ambassador Korostovets argued to Foreign Minister Izvol'skii in 1909, "We cannot deny the importance of Chinese being taught the fundamentals of Russian by experienced Russian teachers; this is undoubtably one means of cultural influence over our big neighbor." Izvol'skii was also being told that Japanese efforts in this direction represented "the most reliable means of strengthening Japan's influence in the Middle Kingdom," but that many Chinese officials, including the influential Zhang Zhidong, were seeking a Russian alternative.

The Foreign Ministry passed the message on to the Finance Ministry and the CER, which with a pool of competent teachers at hand were now ready to mount a major campaign. The CER at this point had some ten years' experience in this department, having opened a Russo-Chinese school in Beijing in 1899 (the same year as the Eastern Institute). After a year's shutdown during the Boxer uprising, the school flourished. Over the next several years, despite Russia's declining role in the Far East, enrollment nearly doubled, from 60 to 110. The fact that one of the Chinese teachers had become ambassador to Russia probably helped attract students. By 1911, Eastern Institute graduates were represented on the staff. The renewed emphasis on making the Russian language a tool of influence sent other institute alumni to staff schools in Tianjin, Zhifu, Wuchang, and Jilin. The same motive caused Harbin's Commercial High School to step up its admittance of Chinese students from four in 1906 to twenty in 1911. In 1909, a proposal was even made to establish a Chinese section of the Eastern Institute on the model of Hong Kong University, but the idea went no further.

A plan presented in 1909 by the Russian consul at Jilin, Sokovkin, suggested a variant on the mixed school, while also illustrating the perception that training Russians was a better investment than teaching Chinese. Sokovkin was motivated to present his plan by the recent firing of a 1903 institute graduate, P. V. Shkurkin, as Russian teacher at a Chinese school in Jilin. There he had applied the "practical method," while serving as his own *lektor*. Despite the speed with which his charges learned Russian, the Chinese administrators considered the salary too high and the foreign influence too strong. So Shkurkin was let go after a year.[48] Shkurkin's pedagogical successes suggested to Sokovkin that Jilin—unlike Harbin, which he described as "rich in temptations and not known for its enviable morals"— was a favorable study environment, where students' "minds and souls" could be kept pure. Therefore, he proposed that the CER establish a translators' school on the railroad's land next to the consulate. As he envisioned it, a qualified director and two *lektors* could handle twenty-five Russian and five Chinese boys—a suitable mix, he thought, for a true "exchange of thoughts" and "comprehension of the vernacular." In return for providing these youths four years of schooling (from ages thirteen to seventeen) the CER would receive six years of service from a corps of bilingual cashiers, office workers, etc. Instead of poorly educated and unreliable Chinese translators, the CER would hire its own; as mostly employees' children, they were sure to show far greater company loyalty.*

Tishenko, the last of the SRO's founding triumvirate, had also come to Harbin after graduation. There his experience as Spitsyn's assistant on the army's paper, *Shengjingbao*, landed him the position of editor of *The Harbin Herald* (*Kharbinskii vestnik*), the official organ of the CER. Tishenko kept the paper firmly on the course it had taken since its 1903 founding, preaching pragmatic tolerance, even pacifism, as the key to Russian success in Manchuria. This stance sometimes even brought *The Harbin Herald* into conflict with the SRO's *Herald of Asia*, itself a proponent of accommodation. For example, in 1909, when concerns were being voiced about the accelerated pace and strategic orientation of Chinese colonization, *The Harbin Herald* declared Boloban's demographic estimates "extremely exaggerated." The SRO responded with a letter declaring the newspaper "poorly informed on the economy of Manchuria." As editor of one of the largest foreign-language papers in China, Tishenko had an appropriate forum in which to express his views.[49]

In 1917, when Russian power began to wane along the CER, improved communication with the Chinese became a necessity. To this end, all three

*RGIA 323: 1, 684, pp. 1, 30–31, 61–77 passim. Sokovkin's proposal was rejected as redundant, since Chinese students were already in the Commercial School, whose vocational section provided similar training. RGIA 323: 1. 937, p. 116.

of the SRO founding fathers were elected to the municipal council.* In July, Tishenko presented a report on the deteriorating food supply and was asked to manage the matter full time. With his knowledge of the Harbin community and orientological skills, he was able to investigate not only Russian and Chinese, but even Japanese sources of supply, as shown by his discussion of the comparative benefits of procuring coal from the Fushun, Zhalainuoer, and Cheremkhovskii mines. As the city fell deeper and deeper into economic and political crisis, Tishenko's penchant for accommodation made him the perfect compromise candidate. In September 1917, he was elected mayor. When he took up this post, his editorial duties were taken over by Dobrolovskii.[50] Once again, what was good enough for the Chinese reader was good enough for the Russians. Three months later, when the Chinese began to roll back Russian privileges in Manchuria, the presence of a sinologist at the municipality's helm would help Harbin to negotiate the first step in the transition to émigré status. The tie between orientologists and the governance of the local community persisted until 1926, when the Chinese, realizing the close connection, closed down *The Herald of Asia*, the SRO, and the municipal council all at the same time.

---

*It must have saddened them to take part in the decision to lift the ban on rickshaws in Harbin because all the cabbies had left for the front. Even though the repeal lasted only two years, the councilmen had grave reservations about the effect on the "moral development of children." TsGADV 577: 1, 21, pp. 94–95.

Conclusion

THE CITY OF Harbin clearly occupied a central place in the history of twentieth-century Manchuria. This study will have accomplished a good part of its purpose by simply demonstrating the uniqueness of this Russian colony in Northeast China. For a brief time, strategic tolerance found support, even among the intolerant, and political freedoms were granted to encourage municipal participation and intercultural cooperation. Social and political experiments unveiled at Harbin influenced policies and personages in both late Imperial Russia and its Soviet successor. The pre-1917 experience also defined the contours and ethos of the three-way competition among Russians, Chinese, and Japanese that would continue to contest Manchuria. Local affairs telescoped into regional and even global concerns as Harbin became the measure of Russia's role in Northeast Asia.

The international struggle for regional hegemony predates Harbin just slightly. In 1895, Russia, with a new Tsar, switched from a passive to an active Far Eastern policy, mobilizing Germany and France for the Triple Intervention. Japan's victorious occupation and then embarrassing retrocession of the Liaodong peninsula adumbrated the continental drift of things to come and indicated the future battlefield on which the stigma of diplomatic defeat would be washed clean. China's rout by Japan was an open invitation for any and all to demand port and railroad concessions. It also made clear that, whatever the Trans-Siberian's original thrust may have been, its completion would be seen in terms of anti-Japanese consequences. Even local events took on the aura of geopolitics. Trade may have been at the heart of the 1895 expedition that first put Harbin's future site on Russian maps, but for St. Petersburg it was also a move against "our dangerous rival," and the aggressive designs of its Yokohama merchants. Fifty years of competition had begun.[1]

With China prostrate and Japan biding its time, Russia would lead the way. An eastward twist on slavophilism identified Russia's unique historic destiny in the geographic and spiritual ability to link Europe and Asia. This ideology was then reified as a railroad and a city. The construction of Harbin and of the Trans-Siberian's final leg across Manchuria took place in an atmosphere of imperialist fantasy, one of the last bright moments of the tsarist regime. Apparent success produced interministerial rivalries, both personal and policy-driven, as many strove to be a part of the "triumph." Some of these dynamics were transmitted to the local level and would continue in force even when times changed. Abroad, Russian accomplishments inspired admiration and fear.

The Crimean War had convinced Europe that Russia was a giant with feet of clay. The Russo-Japanese War brought the same lesson eastward. After 1905, Russia, chastened by military defeat, turned away from its Far Eastern domains, leaving development to the region itself. Government financial support no longer made its way east, and all new initiatives were rejected for fear of Japanese retaliation. Harbin, at first economically and psychologically depressed by this abandonment, soon returned to prosperity as the hub of North Manchurian transport. Regional development radiated "from the Harbin Station," the point at which local, national, and world economies intersected.

Harbin owed its key role in regional integration to the growth of a great intercontinental trade in soybeans. By 1910, only silk had greater export value for China, with tea a close third. The soybean, accounting for nearly 80 percent of Manchuria's total exports, deserved the title bestowed on it by British consular intelligence: "the wealth of Manchuria." The financing, purchase, storage, processing, transportation, and marketing of soybeans quickly became the central functions of the Northeast Asian economy. As one scholar puts it: "New towns like Harbin sprang up to serve as the economic ganglia of a burgeoning industrial and commercial economy closely tied to the world market in soybeans, that miracle crop that provided man with bean curd and soy sauce for his table, fodder for his cattle, explosives for his wars, and varnish for his coffins."[2] Aside from its importance as a multibillion dollar item on the world commodity market, the soybean allows us to trace the progress of competing influences in the region by comparing the export volumes via Japanese-controlled Dairen (Dal'nii, Dalian) with those from Russian/Soviet Vladivostok.[3]

The post-1905 economic recovery and accelerating export competition in Manchuria provided the local context for an editorial in the January 1910 issue of *The Herald of Asia*. (We can take the short piece, entitled "On the Present Moment" and signed only with the initial "M," as an articulation of the SRO's views.)[4] The writer began by denouncing the groundless

170 *Conclusion*

rumors of imminent war with Japan that had circulated in both the Russian Far East and Petersburg during the preceding months. How could the "Russian pioneers" of North Manchuria, the CER at their head, advance trade and industry in such a tense atmosphere? Had not military measures and annexationist plans already proved their bankruptcy during the occupation of 1900–1903 and the war of 1904–5, showing that "our tasks here were never able to go beyond the limits of commercial interests?" And still the other (non-Finance) ministries continued to work at cross-purposes to the CER. The prognosis drawn from this state of affairs was of

> a sad result, until there is unified Russian rule in the Far East, acting according to a plan, and resting not on one department [*vedomstvo*], but on the whole Russian government, with all the means and forces at its disposal, as well as on the healthy social forces of our representative institutions. The cooperation and checks [*kontrol'*] of these latter will serve as a guarantee that the defense and fulfillment of our state interests in the Far East will be carried out according to plan and safe from the irresponsible influences in which the sad memory of Admiral Alekseev's viceroyalty is so rich.

One of the most repeated words in the article is "border" (*granitsa*), used in both its literal and its figurative meaning. In calling for "clearly defined borders on our tasks" in Manchuria, the author unconsciously put his finger on the irreducible tension of local identity. What "borders" can possibly provide a sense of security in a borderland, whose very essence is its freedom from clear limits and guarantees dictated by the state? Conceptually, borderland and borderline stand at loggerheads in the geographic and psychological space where risk and liberty are contradictory evaluations of the same situation. There are no family names beginning with "M" at the apex of the SRO organization, and it is tempting to conclude that the foregoing statement, capturing many of the dynamics described in this book, issues from the self-styled voice of Russian Manchuria.

The prominent place allotted in the editorial to the Viceroyalty of the Far East contrasts with how little historical work has been done on that institution. The brevity of its existence, its association with the loss of Port Arthur, and the inaccessibility of the pertinent archives go far to explain this neglect. The examination of its activities in Chapter Two illuminated important questions of foreign policy and interministerial dynamics, but also showed how close attention to the viceroyalty's plans, many of which never went beyond the drawing board, reveals the extent to which there really were two sharply conflicting options for Russian policy in the Far East.

Viceroy Alekseev's system of Russian commissars micromanaging Chinese officials in Manchuria diverged sharply from the CER's web of influence and propaganda. The latter was designed to encourage a positive interpretation of events and a belief in a cooperative future; the former would force the adoption of policies perceived as directly opposed to China's national interests. Some results might well have been the same, but the long-term legacies in interethnic relations would be diametrically opposed. The viceroyalty's desire to convert the Chinese "into true servants of our Fatherland" ran counter to the CER's (and later the SRO's) anti-missionary bias. Witte's belief that Chinese colonization in Manchuria signaled the arrival of the CER's future customers clashed with the military's fears of demographic Yellow Peril.

Local conflicts reflected such differences. In 1911, E. I. Martynov, commander of the guard, accused the CER's general manager of endangering the railway by providing plans of its bridges to a German engineering professor at Tianjin University for teaching purposes. The Harbin military judge, K. K. Miller, sided with Martynov and recommended that the case be investigated. Khorvat countered by labeling Martynov "insubordinate and inclined to act independently and in a chauvinistic way." Specifically, Martynov had meddled in Chinese-Mongolian relations and mounted expeditions far from the CER right-of-way, ostensibly in search of bandits. When the case reached St. Petersburg, Kokovtsov (now Prime Minister as well as Finance Minister) quashed it immediately. Martynov was recalled, Miller was demoted to a position in Plotsk, and Khorvat was exonerated. This all might seem like a harmless bureaucratic spat, unless one notes that 1911 was the year in which Russia began its eighty-year sway in Mongolia. The foreign policy consequences of this incident may have been more long-lasting than originally supposed.[5]

In turn, Manchurian tensions interacted with policy disagreements in St. Petersburg. The link between interministerial rivalry and foreign policy was never clearer than on December 2, 1910, when the army recommended the immediate annexation of northern Manchuria at an extraordinary meeting of the Council of Ministers. The Foreign Minister, S. D. Sazonov, presented his view that such a move was, indeed, an "imperative necessity," but not yet. Kokovtsov supported Sazonov. "Naturally, it would be impossible to declare that northern Manchuria will never be annexed by Russia," he said. "Political events in the future might make it necessary for us to do so, should the political situation be favorable at the time. By safeguarding at present all our treaty privileges in Manchuria, we can best prepare for the possibility just referred to." Kokovtsov grounded his caution in "legal considerations," as well as the fear that the "violent separation of a province from China" might be "misunderstood in Russia." Of course, though unmentioned, maintaining the status quo also continued to guarantee Finance and CER dominance in Manchuria.[6]

Under the Finance Ministry's direction, the Russian expansion into Manchuria took on a new form. In contrast to the military conquest and occupation of Central Asia and the Pacific littoral, in Harbin the railroad displaced the army as the standard-bearer of empire. As Boris Demchinskii wrote in 1908:

Until recently, Russia's gigantic size/growth [*ispolinskii rost*] depended almost exclusively on her armed might, and only the intervention in Manchuria opened up the new road to the cultural-economic conquest of a foreign country. . . . Here, for the first time and in embryonic form were revealed several new qualities, new indications of Russia as a nation debuting in the role of peaceful, cultural-economic fighter.[7]

Russia was still to be a conqueror pursuing its imperial destiny, but the means would be more subtle. Witte's new "principles" in 1902 would soon spawn Kokovtsov's "other forms" of 1911. Freedoms unknown in Russia would be introduced in order to draw colonists to Russian Manchuria. With intelligence and initiative, this human capital would outperform the dregs of peasant society, the usual recruits for state-sponsored settlement. This wager on individual talent must have been an experiment with personal meaning for Witte, a self-made man himself. Although Manchuria, fenced off from the Empire, offered the best opportunity to realize his vision of colonialism, Witte thought the people of Turkestan too should have "full equality of rights with other subjects, freedom of conduct of their religious needs, and nonintervention in their private lives."[8]

Khorvat's execution of Witte's plans was notable not only for his strict adherence to the spirit of the undertaking, but for his discretion in preventing Harbin's departure from the Imperial order from drawing unwonted attention. For example, in 1913, when Baroness Meiendorff asked Kokovtsov if she could open a branch of the Russian Society for the Protection of Animals (Rossiiskoe obshchestvo pokrovitel'stva zhivotnym), the request was referred to Khorvat. The general manager, sensitive to the bruised sensibilities that could result from rough intercultural mixing, begged leave to deny permission, merely noting that the presence of such an organization in a city where half the population was Chinese could lead to a "whole series of complications."[9]

The eventual results of the Finance Ministry plans, the construction of a liberal alternative in Russian Manchuria, were far different from what was contemplated in the measures passed by the Council of Ministers and an apprehensive Tsar. The same ministers who were bent on protecting the helpless Russian peasants from the Jewish "bloodsuckers" were ready enough to offer up the Chinese masses to exploitation.[10] Other anti-Semites were simply happy to see the Jews leave the country. Political tolerance, as well as religious equality, was exercised in the name of social unity, the surest or at least the cheapest method of defending the government's interest in the survival and prosperity of Russian Harbin. Under international pressure, it was hoped, all Russian subjects, regardless of race, creed, or political persuasion, would feel the need to let their Russian-ness become a primary identity. But tolerance would only go so far. Even as the radical Left was being infiltrated and crushed by the gendarmerie, the municipal council, the seat of more moderate sentiments, continued to enjoy the fruits of a cooperative relationship between state and society that Russia proper would never attain.

The anti-Chinese rationales with which even comparatively liberal policies mustered support in St. Petersburg found no outlet in Harbin itself. In Manchuria, competition took the form of integration. The SRO, the spearhead of local cultural life, united the members of Harbin institutions involved in Chinese affairs with orientological specialists. Those specialists, the leadership behind initiatives in newspaper publication, education, and intellectual life for the Russian and Chinese communities alike, endorsed the ideology of cooperation, both state-society and Russo-Chinese. Tolerance toward Jews and Chinese went together.

Harbin's Chinese residents obtained the right to vote in the elections to both their own and the Russo-Chinese assembly in the same year, 1909. Shortly thereafter, A. V. Spitsyn, the SRO's first chairman, commented on that reform and its effect on Chinese society in a *Herald of Asia* article:

Such public organizations as self-education circles, native-place groups with a political coloring, societies pursuing strictly *natsional'nye* [national or ethnic] goals, political circles, and various committees are no longer rarities in Manchuria.... At the necessary moment, public organizations unite in joint endeavor and come forward as the concentrated power of united public opinion, which, one way or another, the government and administration will have to take into account. Often local protests and demonstrations will find echoes in similar organizations in other provinces or even abroad, [which like the local groups] have maintained unbroken and active contact with the motherland.[11]

Most interesting is Spitsyn's lauding of certain forms of public activity that were permitted in Harbin but forbidden in Russia proper. Thus, his comments in a journal that sent most of its run back to Imperial Russia could be read as Aesopian language, exhorting his countrymen to admire and emulate the advanced liberties of both the Russians and the Chinese in distant Manchuria.[12]

At bottom, Witte and his successors regarded the Russian venture in Manchuria with optimism. As the difficult conditions for China's premature repurchase of the railway set out in Article 12 of the CER construction contract make clear, the Finance Ministry was convinced that eighty years of unimpeded development for both the CER and the social organism attached to it at Harbin would lead to Russian dominance in Northeast Asia. At the February 7, 1903 ministerial meeting where Witte clashed with Kuropatkin over limiting Chinese migration to Manchuria, he argued that the future of the Russian position in the Far East depended on the "peaceful and steady flow of events." As Minister of Finance, Witte believed that the shares of CER, Inc., secure in the ministry's vaults, would, given time, pay dividends on the gargantuan investment. He was right, but would not live to see who indeed would reap the whirlwind of regional development and international conflict.[13]

The policies implemented in Harbin had far-reaching effects. In Chapter Three, we saw how the results of Manchurian experiments in colonization made their way into Siberian and all-Russian legislation. Stolypin's "wager on the strong" was exactly what Witte had undertaken in Manchuria a decade earlier. A. V. Krivoshein and A. A. Rittikh, both men with extensive exposure to Siberian and Far Eastern resettlement, would take responsibility for implementing the reforms that, for posterity, would bear Stolypin's name.

In the Soviet period, personnel transfers would again bring men with Far Eastern experience to influential positions at the center. By an integrative process of promotion from the provinces, fairly common in the waning years of the New Economic Policy, M. N. Riutin and B. Z. Shumiatskii, both former residents of Harbin, arrived in Moscow. Shumiatskii, an experienced diplomat and, for a while, the Far Eastern Republic's chief negotiator with China, Japan, and Mongolia, now became the dean of the Communist University of the Toilers of the East. Riutin, who had gained his reputation in Siberia by antagonizing colleagues, met his match when he went head-to-head with Stalin. Resourcefulness had brought both men close to the pinnacle of the *nomenklatura*. In the 1930's, however, the steadfastness and spirit of initiative essential for success on the Far Eastern frontiers would be their undoing at the center.

The "practical school" of orientology, which had achieved its fullest expression in the Far East, also had far-reaching effects. The most important was its impact on the future course of the field. By 1910, both of its first two directors, the brothers Pozdneev, had returned to St. Petersburg to promote the adoption of their pioneering work in Vladivostok as central policy. That year saw the founding, with a government subsidy, of the Practical Eastern Academy, whose goals had a familiar ring: "To prepare individuals with practical knowledge of Eastern languages and countries for administrative, consular, and trade-industrial service and activities in our Eastern borderlands and neighboring countries." Graduates of the school, split into Chinese, Japanese, Mongolian, Persian, and Balkan departments, would earn the right to bear the title "Easterner" (Vostochnik). Many students at St. Petersburg University attended in order to supplement their theoretical training. A branch in Tashkent was subsequently established. After 1917, Dmitrii Pozdneev helped to set up a similar program for the Red Army, and the Eastern Institute at Vladivostok kept the regime well furnished with translators for the promotion of revolution in China.[14]

With regard to international relations in Northeast Asia, the Harbin story can tell us much about the links between domestic and foreign politics in the first half of the twentieth century. For example, Russian and Chinese residents of Harbin, both elected and appointed, served side by side with representatives of the diplomatic corps on the municipal council. Not surprisingly, this body played an important part in Harbin's experience when, in 1917, the Soviets' ascent to power provoked an international response. The first discussions of "intervention" began in November 1917 and concerned, not Siberia, but Manchuria.

The municipal council was only one of the often quite creative ways in which competitors in Northeast Asia shared power in order to contain conflicting interests. Some of them, such as the diplomatic bureaus (*jiaosheju*), gave Chinese local representatives an unprecedented degree of participation in legal proceedings against Russians in exchange for the exclusion of Beijing from the process. In the 1930's, the Japanese puppet state of Manchukuo merely gave a cooperative gloss to unilateral dominance, but Japanese aid to White Russian, Russian Fascist, and Jewish organizations, in contrast, led to considerable influence without the loss of the recipient organizations' autonomous identities. Still, unlike the Sino-Soviet joint management of the CER, which was a fairly equal sharing of power, Japanese "co-dominion" could mean anything from cooperation as equals, to collaboration, to "puppetry," a spectrum that gives the researcher a handy tool with which to measure the changing balances of power in the region.

Sometimes, shifting borders simply converted domestic interactions into foreign affairs. Thus, the rivalry between Harbin and Dal'nii discussed in Chapter Two became, after 1905, an element in Russo-Japanese international competition. Similarly, the Soviet consulates in Manchuria and the Chinese consulates in the Soviet Far East exercised extensive authority over their citizens abroad to a degree reminiscent of domestic governance. Moreover, neither government ever fully accepted its nationals' renunciations of citizenship. All Russians, whether Red or White, would remain Soviet wards, and all Chinese, whether *guoren* (countrymen), *tongbao* (compatriots), or *huaqiao* (Chinese abroad), owed allegiance to China. The unity and tension between the Russian Far East and Manchuria is an important theme of this work, as is the tie between the "Eastern Provinces" and China proper. The changing locations and porosities of boundaries have been a key factor in these relationships. Once we acknowledge the socially constructed nature of state borders and their limited value in analyzing transnational phenomena, the path is open toward a regional history integrating the shared aspects of several national histories.

By focusing on the shared social histories of the countries and parts of countries that make up the transnational region of Northeast Asia, we begin to see the correlation between the broader and narrower versions of regionalism. The word itself provides no clues to whether subnational or transnational geographic units are in question. Thus, if unqualified, *dal'nii vostok* in Russian serves equally well to indicate the Russian Far East and the Far East as a whole. Where a regionalism of the first type would express centrifugal tendencies at the expense of the nation-state, region formation across national borders suggests an integrative, constructive process.

The case at hand serves as evidence that these two kinds of regionalism are mutually reinforcing. Regional integration in Northeast Asia was accompanied by Manchuria's gradual detachment from China. Simultaneously, an elite cohort formed in the Soviet Far East. But when Stalin suspected secessionist plans, a complete purge of Party, army, government, and NKVD cadres followed. At the same time, the forced exodus of all Orientals, both foreign and Soviet, from the Russian Far East removed the demographic telltales of the borderland. The kharbintsy, a large number of whom had promptly repatriated after the 1935 sale of the CER to Manchukuo, fared no better. As "honorary" foreigners, and therefore automatically Japanese spies, most were arrested and imprisoned or killed. With the fortifying of the Sino-Soviet border and Stalin's turn to autarchy, both kinds of regionalism died out, at least for a while.[15]

Increasing contact with competitor states and peoples in Northeast Asia required each of the countries involved to develop cross-cultural knowledge and skills. Japanese organizations such as the East Asia Common Culture Academy in Shanghai and the South Manchuria Railway Research Department headquartered at Dairen were just as insistent on language mastery and practical applications as the Eastern Institute in Vladivostok and the Society of Russian Orientologists in Harbin. Harbin was home to Chinese Sovietology and to the Japanese school that prepared diplomats, scholars, and spies for work in Russia. As Russia, China, and Japan each became increasingly educated about the others' moves in Northeast Asia, the study of the common tasks inherent in competitive colonialism made possible the adoption of policies that had proved successful in other hands. This promoted a distinct convergence of both cooperative and exploitative techniques, together with accelerated rates of regional development and conflict. Here, the linkages between international power and intercultural knowledge can be traced clearly.[16]

The experience of the Chinese, Japanese, and Russians in Northeast Asia has implications that transcend the regional. For the first time, large populations from East and West lived together without a clear racial hierarchy. At any given moment, one nation might be on top, but memory and imagination could easily supply counterexamples drawn from recent local and regional events. Similarly, but on the global level, the emergence of a powerful Japan made it clear that the turning points of world history would no longer take place exclusively in Europe. The triangular competition that underlay Harbin's development led to other events with global repercussions, including the collapse of the League of Nations and the victory of Chinese communism.

What is harder to track is the effect that this extensive cross-cultural exposure had on the individuals involved. The ghost of cosmopolitanism that was so much a part of Harbin's history still lingers nostalgically in the minds of its scattered exiles and perhaps in the suppressed memories of its current inhabitants. Even now, when Harbin has become almost exclusively Chinese, the writing of local history still provokes discomfort about the city's true identity. An emphasis on Harbin's unique characteristics will always draw a line (which conveniently falls at the Great Wall) between Beijing's unifying version of national history and the Northeast's historical identity as a zone of contact with non-Chinese. On account of this tension, Manchuria is not used in China as a place-name. But everyone knows where it is, not least those who live there.

Reference Matter

APPENDIX

Some Notes on Russian Sinology in Beijing, Kazan, St. Petersburg, and Vladivostok, 1715–1899

MUCH HAS BEEN made of Russia's "special position" in China, with explanations running the gamut from geographical to psychocultural.[1] As V. V. Bartold told the Eurasian geographer P. N. Savitskii, he had decided to subtitle his book *Histoire de l'Orientalisme en Europe et Russie* because "I imagined separating the study of the East in Russia completely from the question of whether one should place Russia in Europe. I was guided simply by the consideration that the Russian attitude toward the East and its study has followed a special path that would not lose its importance even after the subordination of Russian science to Western Europe."[2] The historical "originality" (*samobytnost'*) of Russian sinology can be linked to more general claims of uniqueness in Russo-Chinese relations through the institution of the Russian ecclesiastical mission.

Once a decade, beginning in 1715, between 10 and 15 men, both priests and lay students, were nominated by the Russian Foreign Ministry for a 10-year sojourn in Beijing. Upon arrival, they were officially employed by the Qing court to attend to the spiritual needs of the Albazinians (Russian Orthodox believers employed in Chinese service). Unofficially, the missions provided Petersburg with information, translations, and capable interpreters.[3] No other European country had an institution quite like it.

Living conditions were terrible. The decrepit Huitongguan inn that housed the mission gradually broke down the health of its occupants. Father Avakkum Chestnoi (11th mission, 1830–40) reported to the Foreign Ministry's Asiatic Department: "The students' rooms are narrow and cramped, unsuitable for studies with teachers and bad for one's health in the winter. One cannot lean against any wall, for then the dampness and cold will penetrate right through to the bones, and rheumatism, so common here, becomes inevitable. . . . During the winter one's feet suffer always from heat, and the shoulders and back from dampness and cold. . . . The regular stipend for food is not sufficient."[4] Until 1821, when a medical doctor was included in each mission, mortality ran between a third and a half.[5]

Once service in China was no longer so grave a risk, the opportunities for serious study increased. Better direction, both academic and administrative, allowed eight of the 10 members of the 10th mission (1821–30) to prove themselves as qualified orientologists. From that time, all mission leaders had to have previously served in Beijing. For lack of qualified clerical candidates to lead the 10th, P. E. Kamenskii, a career diplomat who had been a student in the 8th mission, agreed to pro forma ordination as Archimandrite Kamenskii and the mission veterans who followed him in office provided administrative experience, smoother transitions, and sympathetic monitoring for novices. Additionally, a new set of instructions for mission students, coauthored by the Ministry of Public Education and the Russian Academy of Sciences, clarified both the ideal course of study and the expected results.[6]

Meanwhile, the publication of E. F. Timkovskii's *A Voyage to China* in 1824 raised interest in and appreciation for China among the educated public back home. In 1820, Timkovskii, a Foreign Ministry official, had been chosen *pristav* (appointed overseer) for the 10th mission, a post whose responsibilities included outbound travel arrangements for the new mission and the organization of the relieved mission's return, diplomatic negotiations with the Qing court, and personal command of the overland voyage from Petersburg to Beijing and back. As successor to the trade and tribute caravans discontinued in 1754, the three-month trip to China was a major production. For example, in 1850, 10 wagons, 80 two-wheeled carts, 60 camels, and 500 horses were needed to carry the entourage and its baggage; and 60 bulls and 500 sheep were driven along to "feed" the travelers by both trade and slaughter.

Timkovskii's three-volume work was based on his personal observations during his year's tour (including six months in Beijing), extensive discussions on the return trip with the head of the relieved mission, N. Ia. Bichurin (Father Iakinf), and heavy borrowings from Bichurin's translations of Chinese works. Within three years, translations appeared in German, Dutch, French, English, and Polish. International recognition of Russian sinology and a nasty scholarly spat over translations soon focused the limelight on Bichurin, as well as Timkovskii. G. Iu. Klaprot, a German orientologist in Russian service, attacked Bichurin's translations in his notes to the French and English editions of Timkovskii's opus. Bichurin responded, as was his wont, with vitriol.[7]

The subsequent publicity attending Bichurin's passage from head of the 9th mission (1810-20) to prisoner to celebrity further increased the awareness of orientology's importance. Immediately on his return to Russia, Bichurin was charged with a range of abuses, from neglecting the spiritual needs of his Albazinian flock and not attending church himself for 12 years to providing poor oversight of the mission and selling church property. Bichurin responded ineffectively to the accusations by explaining that (1) the Albazinians were interested only in monetary support, and (2) since funds from Petersburg were stopped during the Napoleonic invasion, he had no choice but to sell off church property to support the mission. As for the general charges of dereliction of duty, we can safely assume that Bichurin was distracted by sinological studies. Sentenced to life imprisonment at the Valaam monastery in Karelia, he passed his time editing the manuscripts that he had prepared during his years in China. In 1826, Timkovskii finally arranged for his release and appointment to the Foreign Ministry. The next decade saw the publication of eight major works that completely revolutionized the fund of European knowledge on Central Asia and its ties to China. Both for showing Europe the superiority of Russian sinology and for his unjust imprisonment, the Russian educated public lionized Bichurin. He attended V. F. Odoevskii's "Saturdays," traded compliments with A. S. Pushkin, and was (and is) generally recognized as the first "great man" of Russian sinology.[8]

For orientology, the result of this higher visibility was an effort to solidify Russian strengths in the field by including it in university curriculums. Two universities, Kazan and St. Petersburg, already had courses for "Eastern" languages, but not Chinese, by this time. Kazan University had begun instruction in Arabic, Persian, Turkic, and Tartar in 1807. Mongolian was added in 1828. As the historic site of Russian victory over Tartary and the location of Russia's foremost missionary school, the city of Kazan's association with the Mongolian and Muslim East continued well into the nineteenth century.[9] In 1837, Kazan University again demonstrated its preeminence in Eastern studies by inviting D. P. Savillov, an alumnus of the 10th Mission, to head a Chinese department. With him came a part of the impressive library originally collected by the Jesuit mission in Beijing. A. I. Sosnitskii, whose mastery of spoken Chinese had set him apart from other members of the Kamenskii (10th) mission, was put in charge of conversation practice. The Chinese textbook was Bichurin's *Chinese Grammar*, a book prepared for use in the Kiakhta interpreters' school and intended as the basis on which to build conversational fluency. On Savillov's retirement in 1844, the Kamenskii mission's medical doctor, O. P. Voitsekhovskii, replaced him and became Russia's first university teacher of Manchu.[10]

It is clear from the choice of both faculty and teaching materials that, from its inception, the new department emphasized the living language and its practical application in contemporary China. O. M. Kovalevskii, the head of the Mongolian Department, identified this approach as specifically Russian in a speech made at the Chinese Department's opening ceremony. Western Europeans were derided for accepting Herder's description of China as "a mummy wrapped in silk and covered with hieroglyphs." The result of such views, according to Kovalevskii, was that unsympathetic Europeans became the "sellers of pernicious opium." The Russians, by contrast, appreciative of the attainments of Chinese culture and the Chinese people's historical industriousness, had a reputation as "peaceful, honorable neighbors and true friends." Out of an academic milieu focused on practical skills for serving Russia and understanding China, ostensibly without prejudice, would come the "First School" of Russian sinology and its patriarch, Vasilii Pavlovich Vasil'ev.[11]

Vasil'ev was born in Nizhnii-Novgorod in 1818. Although he graduated from high school (gimnaziia) in 1832, he was forced to wait two years before reaching the minimum age for university matriculation. After entering Kazan University to study under Kovalevskii, he quickly made up for lost time, completing both candidate (1837) and master (1839) dissertations on topics related to Buddhism. For most of this period, he shared quarters with a Buriat lama and so spoke Mongolian "like a Mongol." In 1840, he joined the 12th mission and left for Beijing.[12]

In the Huitongguan, Vasil'ev occupied the cell next to P. I. Kafarov (Father Palladii). With Bichurin, these two scholars make up the revered "Trinity" of early Russian sinology. Vasil'ev deeply resented the monastic discipline and in hindsight wrote: "Before my time in the Beijing Mission, even some less oppressed than I had hanged themselves or taken poison. . . . Of course, neither would I have endured, had I not found comfort in my fantasies."[13]

During his nine years in China, Vasil'ev never left Beijing. His "voyages" were all mental as he mastered Chinese, Manchurian, and Tibetan before moving on to Korean, Japanese, and Sanskrit. "Triumph of the scholarly polyglot," says Vasil'ev's biographer, V. M. Alekseev. For Vasil'ev, however, the languages were but the scholarly means with which to trace the historical spread and mutation of Buddhist ideas throughout North Asia. In order to map this "most amazing and colossal mystification ever seen by mankind," he opted for ever greater breadth, making major contributions to the West's religious, historical, philosophical, philological, and literary knowledge of China. His ultimate goal was the conversion of Western Europe's amateur fascination with Eastern religion into a true science of Buddhist studies. His 1857 work, *Buddhism: Its Dogmas, History and Literature*, created a sensation. A German specialist announced that before reading the German translation, he had written about Buddhism "like a blind man about colors."

Because of Vasil'ev's belief in Russia's "special position" in sinology, a belief he inherited from his mentor, Kovalevskii, he insisted on publishing his works in Russian first.[14] A formative decade at Kazan University, half as student (1834–39) and half as professor (1850–55), also made the future doyen of Russian sinology into a believer in his alma mater's tradition of practical training for service to both the state and the educated public. Afterward, for another quarter of a century, this sense of social responsibility led him to send a steady flow of articles and memorandums on contemporary affairs to various journals and ministries. "As a man and a citizen," he once declared, "I cannot but take an interest in all questions of state and public life." Vasil'ev's major contribution to the polemics of the Great Reforms was a treatise on "Contemporary Questions" repressed by the censor in 1873 for demanding solutions to important state and social questions in a fashion "not only contrary to the views of the government, but often beyond the realm of possibility." These impossibilities occasionally took on an egomaniacal twist: "I have a small pretension to being neither more nor less than Russia's reorganizer" and "through this to influence the fate of the whole world and humanity. Things are not the way I'd like them!" [*Vse ne po-moemu!*][15]

Vasil'ev also inherited his enlightened views on China from his mentor. In an echo of Kovalevskii's opening-day speech (a ceremony that Vasil'ev almost certainly attended), Vasil'ev began his 50-year-long teaching career on December 10, 1850, with a lecture highlighting the ignorance about China in educated and even scholarly circles. "Are we not ashamed," he asked, "of overlooking the colossus beside us, of denying her, not only in the present, but even in the future, the capacity to hold the light of enlightenment [*svet prosveshcheniia*], . . . to be a powerful engine of humanity?" Later, he specifically attacked the "false theory that attributes powers of intellect by race." Through the whole of his tenure, this sympathy for China and belief in its prospects dominated Vasil'ev's foreign policy views, causing him to publicly espouse such unpopular causes as the return of Kuldja in Central Asia and of Port Arthur in the Far East.

In 1865, Vasil'ev persuaded the Eastern Department to consider publication of his brainchild, *The Asian Review* (*Aziatskoe obozrenie*), aimed at both specialists and the general public. But nothing came of this plan until 1882, when several members of the department began to write for *The Eastern Review* (*Vostochnoe obozrenie*), published by the Siberian regionalist N. M. Iadrintsev. Not surprisingly, Iadrintsev's "guiding motto"—to remove the prejudicial view that Asia was "doomed to stagnation" and to inculcate the belief that the East had "its own culture, its own progress . . . and maybe, its own [future] role in the history of mankind,"—practically paraphrases Vasil'ev. For liberals, the capital's policies toward Siberia and the non-Russian East could be viewed in similar lights.[16]

In 1855, falling enrollments in Kazan and the stir created in the capital by Murav'ev's Amur activities led to the wholesale transfer of the Eastern Department to St. Petersburg University.[17] Vasil'ev was put in charge of the new department, and his unofficial memorandum on his new post made clear three of the policies that he hoped to pursue. First of all, he thought that language study should proceed simultaneously on the theoretical and practical fronts. Second, he believed that Sanskrit and Tibetan should be added to the curriculum. Finally, he pointed out the essential connection between providing appropriate employment for graduates and the ability to attract talented students to the field.

In practice, the first point represented a continuation of the pedagogical policies pursued at Kazan; and the second point merely highlighted Vasil'ev's love of breadth.[18] Ultimately, it was the final point, with its explicit concern for recruits and graduates alike, that inclines me to speak of a "Vasil'ev school."[19] The founder repeatedly made reference to his "family" and lavished paternal care both on those carrying on the scholarly part of his vision and on those involved with the equally important practical tasks. That they felt a reciprocal attachment is quite clear in a letter A. M. Pozdneev wrote to P. S. Popov in 1889: "Our old man has grown old, very old. Sometimes the old flame still flares up, but then it dies down. His previous sympathy for all that is good and the old desire to do good still remain, but there is already little activity."[20]

For the successors to Vasil'ev's scholarly mantle, the question of intellectual paternity was quickly submerged in the more mundane matter of filling the gap that Vasil'ev's impending retirement would open. The top candidate was S. M. Georgievskii, a professor in the Chinese Section since 1885, but with his untimely death in 1893, A. O. Ivanovskii became next in line. Ivanovskii unsparingly applied his talents in the attempt to follow where Vasil'ev had led: he not only learned Chinese, Manchurian, Mongolian, Tibetan, and Sanskrit in order to continue the tradition of Buddhist studies, but also collected and analyzed materials for the reconstruction of the aboriginal languages of Yunnan and Manchuria. Despite resistance from the professor of Mongolian studies, A. M. Pozdneev, it appeared that Ivanovskii's appointment would ensure a smooth succession, but again tragedy intervened. The death of his son in 1899 brought on a bout of alcoholism, and he was still in a sorry state when he was hit by the loss of Vasil'ev on May 10, 1900. Two days later, Ivanovskii was admitted to a mental hospital, never to leave.[21]

The Chinese Section was consequently placed in a difficult position, and the more so because the best of the recent student crop had already been committed to the newly founded Eastern Institute in Vladivostok. Ivanovskii's disappearance from the scene guaranteed that the legacy of Vasil'ev and the ecclesiastical mission would migrate to the Golden Horn of Vladivostok and then back to China, whence it had come.

The signing of the Russo-Chinese alliance and the CER construction contract in 1896 led to a run on Russia's limited sinological expertise. The sudden immediacy of Witte's plan to build a railroad across and a sphere of influence in Manchuria made the Ministry of Finance particularly needy in this respect. But the four students who made up the Chinese Section's class of 1896 were already promised to the university and the Foreign Ministry. The ministry had also succeeded in snatching up all three of the 1897 graduates. Although the exciting vision of Russian empire in Asia inspired many college-bound young men to look eastward, the record-breaking forty-nine matriculants to the Chinese Section in 1898 would be long years in the making.

Witte's needs were urgent, so his methods would be direct. He simply poached some qualified sinologists from among both the diplomats and the scholars. Chief among the diplomats was a man we met several times in the text, D. D. Pokotilov, whom Witte enticed to leave the Foreign Ministry for a position in his own "Foreign Ministry," the Third Section of the General Chancellery. As a director of the CER and head of the Russo-Chinese Bank's Beijing office from 1896, Pokotilov carried out a host of tasks that placed him at the very heart of Witte's financial diplomacy in Asia. The marriage of Pokotilov's sister to his immediate superior, P. M. Romanov, reinforced bureaucratic ties.[22]

Witte's fishing in scholarly waters landed him D. M. Pozdneev, Pokotilov's junior by several years. Young Dmitrii no sooner completed his training in Petersburg, London, and Paris, than he was recruited by Witte.[23] After the signing of the Russo-Chinese Treaty, Pozdneev became the editor of *A Description of Manchuria* (*Opisanie Manchzhurii*), a massive enterprise whose goal was to compile all available information on contemporary Manchuria for the benefit of both the general public and "future researchers." The two volumes that resulted were published in 1897 by the Ministry of Finance and became a standard reference work. In a short review, *Russian Thought* (*Russkaia mysl'*) greeted the books as "most timely in view of the animation of our relations with China and of the important, complicated tasks that lie ahead for our Fatherland in the Far East."[24]

Dmitrii Pozdneev's ability to straddle the academic world and government service made him a logical nominee to represent Witte's interests on a joint Finance and Education ministry committee formed in February 1898 to consider the establishment of a specialized school whose graduates would serve "in the administrative and trade-industrial (*torgovo-promyshlennyi*) institutions of East Asian Russia and adjoining countries." To maximize student exposure to an oriental milieu, the school was to be located in Vladivostok.[25] Witte's recruitment of Pokotilov and Pozdneev had successfully covered his short-term needs in Petersburg and Beijing, but only expanded educational opportunities could provide a steady flow of personnel to maintain Russian political and economic dominance in the larger sphere of influence envisioned by the Minister of Finance.[26]

Once the ministries agreed to the proposed school, the committee's experts turned to the curriculum and other important details.[27] B. R. Rosen, the Arabist dean of St. Petersburg University's Eastern Department, chaired this series of meetings. The dominant personalities were the director-to-be, Aleksandr Pozdneev, and his brother Dmitrii, who in the course of time would succeed him. Just as the 1897 publication of *A Description of Manchuria* had made Dmitrii Pozdneev Russia's foremost authority on that region, so the 1896 appearance of the first volume of *Mongolia and the Mongols* had brought his older brother Aleksandr similar kudos in his area of study. After graduating from the Eastern Department, Aleksandr accompanied the Potanin expedition of 1876–77 to Mongolia and stayed on until 1879, accumulating a collection of 1,700 books and manuscripts. His own leadership of a research trip in 1892–93 confirmed Aleksandr in the belief that in-country experience was essential practical training for orientologists. In addition, his knowledge of Mongolian, Kalmyk, Chinese, Manchu, and Tibetan suggests the influence of Vasil'ev's polyglotism. A strong interest in lamaism makes the intellectual genealogy even clearer.

Aleksandr was a proud and ambitious man. He found the potential successors to Vasil'ev unacceptable. The conflicts over the appointment of Ivanovskii ("who has never seen China") in 1887 soured relations in the department. Colleagues called Aleksandr "strict" but "straightforward." His students chose less charitable adjectives: "capricious" and "despotic." His four-year term as director of the Eastern Institute would be remembered as life under the "Mongolian yoke" (*mongol'skii ig*). Aleksandr had cultivated bureaucratic contacts for many years, and this paid off in 1898, when he was offered the opportunity to design and develop the Eastern Institute.[28]

By 1898, the need was urgent. Clamorous demands for "educated translators," instead of untrustworthy "uneducated, and expensive Chinese dragomans," were coming into the Finance Ministry from the CER construction crews in Manchuria. A Russian geologist described this linguistic bane as "a sort of educated Chinese proletarian who knows quite a few characters and has ambitions to be an official or a merchant." In a February 1898 memorial, the governor-general of Heilongjiang, En Ze, advised Beijing that "since the coming of the Russians, most of the cases of people being killed were caused by the ignorance of trouble-making interpreters."[29]

The position paper that Dmitrii brought to the joint commission laid out a few guidelines, probably motivated by both intraministerial discussions and CER complaints. First of all came the "strictly practical character" of the venture. Next in importance was the need to maximize the number of students in order to meet the CER need for translators, projected to reach the "hundreds" shortly. The inclusion of auditors and night students at the institute was one suggestion for how to attain this goal. Third, preference should be given to military men already serving in the Far East as a speedy and inexpensive solution to the problem. Although all of these points exhibit the Witte trademark, the "hothouse" approach to development, the counterpoint belief in initiative as the essential ingredient for success was also present. Students were to be allowed to choose their specialty, since only "love" would permit them to overcome the inherent difficulties of the subject matter.[30]

The great extent to which Finance Ministry views prevailed at the conference can be inferred from the final result. The original goal of the Eastern Institute approved in 1895–96 was "the satisfaction of the local need for individuals with both theoretical and practical familiarity with the languages of the peoples neighboring the Priamur, and the encouragement of the broadest and most multifaceted study of the regions adjoining the Empire's eastern outskirts [*okraina*]." The 1898 version eliminated "theoretical" perspectives and the centrifugal tendencies that might flow from "multifaceted study." As Dmitrii Pozdneev explained to the Russian ambassador in Beijing, M. N. Girs, practical and scientific goals were "often contradictory." In this contest, versatility lost out to an "exclusive" devotion to "practical" training for "administrative and trade-industrial institutions," with extra emphasis to be placed on the latter.[31]

Aleksandr's major achievement during the interministerial conference was permission to divert the most talented students from St. Petersburg University's Eastern Department. The first fruits of this decision were two professors of Chinese from the class of 1896, A. V. Rudakov and P. P. Schmidt, who had left for self-training in China after receiving the funds allocated in March 1896. They were to be followed in the next several years by what would become Russia's first professors of Japanese (E. G. Spal'vin), Korean (G. V. Podstavin), Tibetan (G. Ts. Tsybikov), and Far Eastern Area Studies (N. I. Kiuner). As a result, St. Petersburg University's Eastern Department was temporarily crippled by the inability to choose successors to Vasil'ev, Ivanovskii, and Aleksandr Pozdneev from among their last crop of students. Only in 1905 would the first of a new generation, brought up on

Western European orientology rather than the ecclesiastical mission tradition, begin teaching. Thus, during the boom years of Russian Far Eastern activity from 1900 to 1905, the center of academic gravity and the tradition of practical orientology passed from St. Petersburg to the large stone building on the hillside overlooking Vladivostok's Golden Horn harbor.

Notes

For complete authors' names, titles, and publication data on the works cited in short form in these Notes, see the Bibliography, pp. 239–49. Russian archival sources are cited in abbreviated form. I use RGIA 323: 1, 2, pp. 17, 23, for example, for fond 323, opis' 1, delo 2, ll. 17, 23. Other abbreviations used in the citations are:

AT	Archives de l'Armée de Terre
AVPR	Arkhiv vneshnei politiki Rossii
FO	British Foreign Office files, Public Record Office
GAIO	Gosudarstvennyi arkhiv Irkutskoi oblasti
GARF	Gosudarstvennyi arkhiv Rossiiskoi federatsii
GPB	Gosudarstvennaia publichnaia biblioteka, Rukopisnyi otdel
HLJ	Heilongjiangsheng danganguan
IVI	*Izvestiia vostochnogo instituta*
MAE	Ministère des Affaires Etrangères
NGB	Japanese Foreign Ministry, *Nihon gaiko bunsho*
Nilus ms	Papers of E. Kh. Nilus, Hoover Institution
PGM	Primorskii Gosudarstvennyi Muzei
RGIA	Rossiiskii gosudarstvennyi istoricheskii arkhiv
RTsKhIDNI	The Russian Center for the Storage and Study of Contemporary Historical Documentation
Stat. op.	G[orod] kharbin i ego prigorody po odnodnevnoi perepisi 24 fevralia 1913 g., vol. 1: *Statisticheskoe opisanie*
TsGADV	Tsentral'nyi gosudarstvennyi arkhiv dal'nego vostoka
TsKhSD	Tsentral'noe khranilishche sovremennoi dokumentatsii

BOOK EPIGRAPHS: Pushkin, *The Bronze Horseman*; Kokovtsov, *Otchet birzhevogo komiteta*.

INTRODUCTION

1. It is clear from the earliest maps that the Russians found an existing settlement on their arrival at the Harbin site. Just as clearly, what existed was not a city.

2. Brief English overviews of this process from an economic standpoint can be found in Chao; and Sun. Many specialized areas and industries were treated very

professionally in the publications of the Research Department of the South Manchurian Railway (1907–45) and the Economic Bureau of the Chinese Eastern Railway (1903–35). These books, pamphlets, and articles were issued in very small print runs and are therefore bibliographic rarities. An exhaustive catalog of the Research Department's output is *Kyushokuminchi kankeikikan kankobutsu sogomokuroku: Mantetsuhen* (Tokyo, 1979), published by the Institute of Developing Economies (Ajia Keizai Kenkyujo). Presumably, the National Diet Library, which carried out a project in the 1970's and 1980's to microfilm all items not already in its collection, possesses almost a full set. The Library of Congress in Washington, D.C., also houses a remarkable collection, expropriated in 1945 by the American Occupation forces from the Tokyo office of the South Manchurian Railway Company. John Young's catalog, *The Research Activities of the South Manchurian Railway, 1907–45*, indicates where volumes not located in Washington can be found. Further information, especially on the 1930's and early 1940's, when the Research Department housed many staff with Marxist leanings, is in Takeo Ito's memoirs, translated as *Life Along the South Manchurian Railway*, with an excellent introduction by Joshua Fogel. The Dairen (Dalian) head office's library, together with the company's archives, should make the Liaoning Provincial Archive the foremost repository for studies of Manchuria. Unfortunately, much of this archive is still not "open," especially for non-Chinese scholars.

The best collection of Economic Bureau publications was maintained by the Chinese Eastern Railway library, now located in the basement of Jilin University's library in Changchun. It was placed there for safekeeping during the Cultural Revolution and the Russian-language materials were cataloged in 1973. There are over 3,000 items.

3. The international relations of Northeast Asia have been treated mainly as the object of negotiations and conflict between the capitals of the powers involved. The local level has received remarkably little attention. Furthermore, not one of the field-shaping studies cited below has been based on open access to archival materials from all pertinent parties. The following list, in roughly chronological order by period treated, is not meant to be exhaustive, but should provide the reader with the diplomatic background on which Harbin's history would be etched. It should also be noted that the selection is more complete for Russo-Chinese relations, since that is the most apposite for an understanding of tsarist Harbin.

Myers and Peattie, *Japanese Colonial Empire*; Myers, Peattie, and Duus, *Japanese Informal Empire*; Malozemoff, *Russian Far Eastern Policy*; Romanov, *Russia in Manchuria*; McDonald, *United Government and Foreign Policy in Russia*; Tang, *Russian and Soviet Policy*; Seki, *Gendai higashi ajia kokusai kankyo no tanjo*; Hara, *Shiberia shuppei*; Chihiro Hosoya, *Shiberia shuppei*; Morley, *Japanese Thrust*; Iriye, *After Imperialism*; Leong, *Sino-Soviet Diplomatic Relations*; Tkachenko, *Sovetskie trudiashchiesia*; Lee, *Revolutionary Struggle*; Levine, *Anvil of Victory*.

A number of recent articles by Bruce Elleman touch on important but as yet poorly studied aspects of Northeast Asian international relations, in particular "secret diplomacy." See, e.g., "The Soviet Union's Secret Diplomacy Concerning the Chinese Eastern Railway." Sarah Paine's Ph.D. dissertation, "A History of the Sino-Soviet Border, 1858–1924," devotes Part 3 to "Manchuria, 1896–1905."

4. On the ideology of railway imperialism and its integration into geopolitical thought, see Hauner, especially pp. 98–112. In Japan, thinking that envisaged railroads as the sinews of geopolitical might was called *tetsudoron* and made the completion of the Trans-Siberian into a countdown to war between Russia and Japan. The paradigm endured into the nuclear age. In 1955, Chiang Kai-shek, who had learned his strategic doctrine when these ideas were still prevalent, predicted the outbreak of World War Three in 1956 to the *New York Times* correspondent C. L. Sulzberger. Chiang's reasoning ran as follows, starting from a misapprehension regarding the initiator of the Russo-Japanese War: "You will remember that as soon as the Russians had completed the Trans-Siberian Railway they started their disastrous war with Japan fifty years ago. Russian strategy depends upon railways. According to Communist planning, new railways linking China and Russia across Mongolia and Sinkiang will be ready. As soon as these roads are finished the Russians will figure that the moment has arrived for war." Sulzberger, p. 154.

5. Winnipeg's population, for example, rose from 38,500 in 1895 to 144,040 in 1911. Eagle, pp. 218–23. Berton's book on the building of the Canadian Pacific has a popular tone and style similar to Tupper's work on the Trans-Siberian. Regarding the Canadian Pacific Railway, the title of the collection edited by Hugh Dempsey, *The CPR West*, expresses well the attitude many Russians had regarding the CER company town, Harbin. For the ties between railroad building and regional development in the American Northwest, see Michelson; and Lewitz.

6. The role of competition as a goad to development lies at the ideological core of market capitalism. Since war is (to paraphrase) merely competition by other means, it should come as no surprise that violence can also be construed constructively. For arguments along this line, see Tilly; and Spruyt, p. 82.

7. The seminal work on "informal empire" (of which "railway imperialism" is a subcategory) is Gallagher and Robinson, "Imperialism of Free Trade"; for an update on the article's impact, see Louis. David Fieldhouse is generally credited with suggesting an increased emphasis on "periphery" dynamics, rather than "metropolitan" policies, thereby confusing the previously clear opposition between these two terms. See his article "Imperialism: An Historiographical Revision." Rosemary Quested, in the introduction to her important book on the Russians in Manchuria, cites both Gallagher/Robinson and Fieldhouse. I also favor a "periphery" emphasis that takes the actions and perceptions of both colonizer and colonized into account in defining the colonial experience.

8. In examining this problem for the Russian Far East, Stephan, pp. vii–viii, refers to multilateral "parochial historiography," with special attention to the Soviet Union's efforts to remake history. A clear illustration of such a fabrication can be found in Sahlins, p. 38, where nonexistent mountains are drawn onto a map to provide a "natural" borderline.

9. See Duara, *Rescuing History*. Even more exactly on this topic is Clausen and Thogersen, *Making of a Chinese City*. This collection of articles by Chinese scholars from Harbin about Harbin reveals general directions and levels of local scholarship; it illustrates very effectively the special importance that the nationalist project attaches to writing (and rewriting) history. State-of-the-art local scholarship on Harbin is represented by Ji Fenghui, *Haerbin xungen*. Ji works in the Heilongjiang

Provincial Archive and has therefore had unparalleled access. There is much new information here, unfortunately, without citations.

10. Davis and Wilburn, *Railway Imperialism*. R. Edward Glatfelter's contribution to this volume discusses the CER. See also Robinson's conclusion, which divides railway imperialism into several types.

11. Von Laue, pp. 188–92.

12. In Russian, it is easy to distinguish between the Russian Far East as the "Far Eastern part of the Russian state" (*Rossiiskii dal'nii vostok*) and "the parts of the Far East where Russians live" (*russkii dal'nii vostok*). This distinction is not made so succinctly in English.

13. "Za" means beyond or across in Russian.

14. Stephan, p. 2. See also pp. 7, 43, 90, 92, 98. The converse was also true. Roman Moiseevich Kabalkin, invited to Manchuria by Witte to develop a world market in soybeans (and thereby create sufficient freight revenue to support the CER), would appreciate the Harbin difference when the governor-general of Priamur, N. L. Gondatti, threatened him with expulsion from Vladivostok. Kabalkin needed to oversee the export of his soybeans, but Jews were not allowed in Vladivostok without special permission. As we will see, the case went all the way to the Council of Ministers.

15. Chow, p. 163. For more on the centennial controversy, see Lahusen, pp. 186–88.

16. I present preliminary views on this "problem-complex" in the Epilogue to Kotkin and Wolff, pp. 323–29. Chow probes these issues for the Hong Kong case with particular attention to cultural production. The opening three essays by Arif Dirlik, Alexander Woodside, and Bruce Cumings in Dirlik, *What Is in a Rim?*, pp. 1–47, also insightfully discuss the relationship between words and actions in the creation of geopolitical cultural constructions. I find Dirlik's argument for analysis that is both "deconstructive and reconstructive" quite persuasive (p. 3).

17. On Finland, see Polvinen. Virulent strains of racial prejudice and russification along late Imperial Russia's European frontier, especially in urban settings, are also discussed in Corrsin, *Warsaw*; Hamm, *Kiev*; Herlihy, *Odessa*; Rogger, *Jewish Policies*; Thaden, *Russia's Western Borderlands*; Thaden, *Russification*; Weeks, *Nationalism*; and Weinberg, *Revolution of 1905*.

18. The two were A. S. Ermolov, Minister of Agriculture and State Domains, and M. I. Khilkov, Minister of Communications. On Witte's dominance, see Von Laue, pp. 79, 115. Witte's centrality, even "omnipotence," is discussed and illustrated with quotations in Ford, p. 20.

19. Von Laue, p. 78.

20. For the history of the Trans-Siberian, see Sabler and Sosnovskii, a celebratory, contemporary account of the project's completion; and Tupper, a popular account filled with local color, good pictures, and information on the construction process. Marks, *Road to Power*, is the best work on this subject with the colonization aspects, supplemented by Marks's article on the tsarist bureaucrat responsible for implementing Witte's "inspiration," A. N. Kulomzin. See "Conquering the Great East: Kulomzin, Peasant Resettlement and the Creation of Modern Siberia" in Kotkin and Wolff, pp. 23–39. All of these works treat the CER as a part of a con-

tinuous whole with no discussion of the social and political differences entailed in crossing the border.

Marks's article briefly discusses tsarist plans for Siberian natives (pp. 33–34). This, and the policies' effects, are covered in greater chronological breadth and depth by Forsyth. Slezkine, p. 97, makes the point that the sale of Alaska to the United States and the Trans-Siberian's south Siberian location turned attention away from the northern reaches where most of the indigenous population lived. Railroad construction also brought a completely new population to Siberia, railway workers. The standard work on this group in late Imperial Russia is Reichman, *Railwaymen and Revolution*. Reichman extends this treatment to Siberia in "The 1905 Revolution on the Siberian Railroad." In my article "Between War and Revolution," I discuss the "railway brigade" as an intermediary organization between railway workers and soldiers in Russian Asia.

21. Romanov, p. 71.

22. Ibid., pp. 78–85; Malozemoff, pp. 79–81.

23. Quested, *Russo-Chinese Bank*. The French version of the treaty was considered binding; the text can be found in Romanov, pp. 400–402.

24. Romanov, pp. 32–33.

25. Polvinen, p. 114, states: "Witte of course held that unity was a desirable goal, but that it should be the result of a long-term process of slow historical development, during which the Finns would themselves become convinced of the benefits of integration." On the Baltics, see Thaden, *Russification*, p. 73, where Witte is labeled "moderate." Regarding the inhabitants of Turkestan, Witte called for their "full equality of rights with other subjects, freedom of conduct of their religious needs, and nonintervention in their private lives." RGIA 821: 150, 409, p. 5.

26. For example, see Ananich and Ganelin, pp. 298–374. In Chap. 2, I also catch Witte in a half-truth regarding land acquisition along the CER. What Witte said appeared to vary with the identity of his conversation partner.

27. Ambassador Kurino to Foreign Minister Komura, no. 775, Sept. 12, 1903, in NGB, 1903, 2: 793–96.

28. The first chapter of David McDonald's book is entitled "The Witte Kingdom in the Far East."

29. Several recent studies treat the importance of interministerial rivalries in shaping the politics of late Imperial Russia. The only one to focus on civil-military tensions is Fuller, *Civil-Military Conflict*. Others are McDonald; Marks; Orlovsky; Whelan; Yaney, *Systemization*; and Yaney, *Urge to Mobilize*.

30. The secret Imperial ukase extending Russian law into the CER zone is dated Aug. 2, 1901, and can be found in Nilus, p. 563. An English version is in MacMurray, pp. 88–90.

31. Robert Thurston has pointed out that "liberal" is a "slippery" word, and Charles Timberlake has also bewailed the terminological "lack of precision," but both historians include the qualities listed above in their minimum descriptions of "liberals." None of the kharbintsy or their supporters in St. Petersburg refer to themselves as liberals, but as Timberlake notes, no late Imperial Russian political figure chose this self-appellation. For more extensive discussions of the political and semantic intricacies, see Raeff, "Some Reflections"; Thurston, pp. 8–9; and

Timberlake, "Introduction," pp. 1–17. The Timberlake volume also contains a useful "Bibliographical Essay" (pp. 182–86).

32. Unfortunately, much of the necessary material is not yet accessible to either Chinese or foreign scholars. The most important locations are Beijing, Nanjing and, of course, Haerbin. Japanese "Harupin" also deserves a separate study.

33. Harbin had more than twice as many non-Chinese residents in the early 20th century as Shanghai (International and French settlements, including Pudong): 43,700 in March 1913, compared with Shanghai's 20,924 in Oct. 1915. Hong Kong's non-Chinese population was slightly lower than Shanghai's. Darwent, p. 177; Murphey, p. 23.

34. Although there is no overall analytical work on post-1917 Harbin, there is a fairly large body of memoirs, articles, and chapters, much of it about the cultural sphere, broadly defined. The extent and impact of the Soviet presence, Soviet-Chinese relations, and Japanese–Russian émigré relations are only some of the important areas that were previously inaccessible at the archival level. Much remains to be done. The following list is not meant to be exhaustive. Stone and Glenny, *The Other Russia*; and Raeff, *Russia Abroad*, give limited attention to Harbin. Stephan, *Russian Fascists*, has more on the Far East. Carefully culled demographic and social data can be found in Simpson, *Refugee Problem*, especially pp. 62–116, 495–513. Among retrospective descriptions by former citizens, Peter Balakshin's *Final v Kitae* stands out. The occasional journal *Politekhnik* (Sydney, 1969–92) reflects the historical interests of those former kharbintsy who ended up in Australia and contains much useful material, especially of a memoir nature. An index for vols. 1–12 can be found in vol. 12 (pp. 217–25). On Russian literary Harbin in the émigré period, see Karlinsky, "Memoirs of Harbin"; and from one of the central figures, Valerii Pereleshin, *Russian Poetry and Literary Life*. Harbin, in particular with regard to its intellectual ties to the Russian Far East, makes cameo appearances in Khisamutdinov, *Russian Far East*. Major bibliographic works are expected shortly from Patricia Polansky at Hawaii and Olga Bakich at Toronto.

In Russia, Harbin studies have undergone a kind of boom, underwritten by newly opened archives, post-Soviet angst about the locus of Russian true identity, and a vague sense that rich émigrés might respond to such interest with investments. A few books have appeared since 1991, notably Chernolutskaia, *Rossiiskaia emigratsiia*; Melikhov, *Manch'zhuriia*; and Taskina, *Neizvestnyi Kharbin*. Numerous articles have appeared in *Problemy Dal'nego Vostoka* and other central publications. In the Far East, scholarly journals, as well as popular literature, have produced a steady stream of Kharbinalia. This has been greatly facilitated by the declassification of the BREM (Biuro Rossiskikh Emigrantov v Man'chzhurii) archive, removed by the NKVD in 1945 from Harbin to Khabarovsk. Probably the widest impact was made by the Feb. 1995 issue of *Rodina*, which contained several articles on Harbin and the CER, and a photo essay (pp. 123–28).

35. My researches were simplified by the paucity of secondary literature on pre-1917 Harbin. One of the most important works is Nilus, *Istoricheskii obzor*, written at the behest of the CER's board of directors and intended as a 25th anniversary commemorative book for both the railroad and Harbin. Nilus, a military judge in Harbin from 1914 until 1920, and afterward a pillar of the émigré community, con-

ducted exhaustive document searches in the CER administration archives and numerous personal interviews. The result was a 600-page tome and three manuscript boxes containing draft chapters for a second volume. Although slightly rose-tinted in his perceptions of prerevolutionary Harbin, Nilus's account provides a range of detail and color that exists nowhere else. The lack of access to central government materials, however, made full evaluation of St. Petersburg policy decisions impossible for Nilus. Furthermore, his volume's status as an official history makes it a poor source for critical analysis of the CER or the larger imperialistic goals of which the railroad was a part.

In contrast to Nilus, other Soviet, Chinese, and Western historians have subsumed the treatment of Russian Manchuria in discussions of the origins of the Russo-Japanese War or the nature of Russian imperialism. The works of Harold Ford, Andrew Malozemoff, David McDonald, B. A. Romanov, and Peter Tang belong in the former category. Because of their lack of interest in local affairs, Harbin appears only rarely. Thus, Romanov's trailblazing work, the only one based on Finance Ministry archives, is correctly titled *Russia in Manchuria*, rather than "Russians in Manchuria." In addition, the work suffers from a certain imbalance because of the author's apparent dislike of Witte. Malozemoff was the first to recognize the importance of local documents, but he used them only to clarify affairs in the capital. A recent work by David McDonald is close to my own interpretation in its emphasis on the role of interministerial rivalry in derailing the foreign policy process, but here too a concentration on St. Petersburg tells us only half the story.

Rosemary Quested is a special case. Quested is the modern pioneer in this field. Without the benefit and example of the many years of patient research that went into her *"Matey" Imperialists*, I very much doubt that I would have ventured into such otherwise uncharted waters. Howard Spendelow's dissertation, "Russia's South Manchurian Adventure," adds to our knowledge of Russo-Chinese relations in South Manchuria but rarely touches on North Manchuria. I aim to complement the North Manchurian aspects of Quested's work by making use of newly released documents from Russian and mainland Chinese archives, both central and local.

36. For an extensive bibliography of publications on Russian urban history, almost all from the 1970's and 1980's, see Hamm, *City in Late Imperial Russia*, pp. 355–59.

37. Briefly, from Aug. 1903 until Feb. 1904, the presence of the viceroy in Port Arthur made that city the seat of power in Russian Manchuria and the Russian Far East in general.

38. MAE, 168: 184.

39. Geyer, p. 37.

40. *Izvestiia kharbinskogo obshchestvennogo upravleniia* 2 (1913): 75–77.

41. Starr, pp. 29–30, points out the role of the Empire's peripheral regions as "laboratories where innovations could be tested before being applied to Russia." He cites cases from the reigns of Catherine II (Odessa), Alexander I (Poland), and Alexander II (western provinces).

42. There is limited evidence from elsewhere in the Empire that the definition of "Russian" could be "broad and flexible" when strategically necessary. Livezeanu, p. 496.

43. The last two Priamur governor-generals, P. F. Unterberger (1905–10) and N. L. Gondatti (1911–17), believed in the "Yellow Peril," although they disagreed on which nationality represented the greatest danger to Russia. See Stephan, *Russian Far East*, pp. 79–80.

44. Lenin's first mention of Harbin is in a letter dated Feb. 26, 1902, a reference to his brother-in-law Mark's trip there. Rossiiskii tsentr khraneniia i izucheniia dokumentov noveishei istorii 2: 1, 725. (This archive's Lenin section has a handy and rather reliable geographic card catalog that makes it easy to access Lenin facts.)

CHAPTER ONE

EPIGRAPH: Beveridge, *Russian Advance*, p. 74.

1. Pozdneev, pp. 34–37; Kokshaiskii (from observations during his two trips up the Sungari in 1895); "Dnevnik Dmitriia Bogdanova po poezdke po Sungari na parakhod *Telegraph* v 1895 godu," in RGIA 1273: 1, 216, pp. 59–77. Reports by N. A. Zinov'ev (who made the same trip a few months later) and Capt. Grulev are in the same *delo*. In order to paint a clearer and more vital sociogeography of the Sungari basin in this period, I have interwoven materials taken from Sokolova's three-part article on her 1898 findings. Real jasmine does not grow in this region, but *chubushnik* ("wild jasmine"), whose smell is similar, is present in abundance. Bogdanov, p. 60, emphasizes the "striking" similarity of the Ussuri and Sungari rivers and their natural settings.

2. RGIA 1273: 1, 216, p. 80. Quested, *"Matey" Imperialists*, p. 21, states that permission was not granted, citing the Sept. 1, 1895, memorial of the acting Jilin governor, En Ze. Appointments in Manchuria were in transition in 1895, which may explain this confusion. In any case, the Siberian Railroad Committee archives show clearly that the Russians, in Petersburg, at Khabarovsk, and on the Sungari, thought themselves in order. See Quested, *"Matey" Imperialists*, p. 21.

3. The Manchu official at Lahasusu was also the commanding officer of the Gold border guard. The Gold, shamanists with a fierce respect for tigers, panthers, and bears, gained their livelihood from fishing the Ussuri and Sungari rivers. In exchange for minimal supplies of necessary commodities, they had traditionally paid local Chinese officials a tribute of one sable pelt per adult male each year. However, in 1880, the Ili crisis drove the Qing government to supplement the increasingly ineffective Manchu border guard. Overnight, the Gold, previously considered uncivilized, were given (according to Pozdneev) full rights and assigned to state service. In order to achieve the full integration of these new servitors, 50 Gold boys were studying Chinese and Manchu by 1888. Pozdneev pp. 229–32. The only internationally famous Gold personage was the hunter Dersu Uzala, whose friendship with V. K. Arsen'ev's narrator made him an object of literary and filmic interest. Hunting, however, was very much secondary to fishing in the Gold way of life, especially after the sable tribute was eliminated in 1880. Owen Lattimore, in his anthropological study of the Gold, states that they "were brought into the Manchu Banner organization" in the 17th century. See Lattimore, "Gold Tribe."

4. Details of Tifontai's earlier years and conversion are drawn from R.K.I.; Quested, *"Matey" Imperialists*, p. 134; and Shreider. Additional biographical data are

available in RGIA 1343: 40, 5077. Shreider's work is largely based on his travels in the Far East from 1891 to 1893. Tifontai was in many ways a unique case. Chinese were generally considered by the Russians to be the least adaptable of the Oriental nationalities present in the Russian Far East. (Tifontai's Chinese surname is sometimes given as Ji instead of Li.) The biography and career of Zhang Tingge stand in contrast to Tifontai's, since after 20 years of business in Vladivostok, Zhang transferred his headquarters to Harbin. See Jin Zonglin.

5. Pozdneev, pp. 182–83, quoting the renowned botanist K. I. Maksimovich's *Ocherk rastitel'nosti vostochnoi Azii*, p. 99. Grulev's presence could be seen as an intimation of railroading activities to come, since he had surveyed the route for the Transbaikal section a few years earlier. In his 1930 memoirs, he claims to have picked the site for Harbin during this trip, but his secret report in RGIA 1273: 1, 216, pp. 15–34, gives no hint at all that he was thinking about railroads and bridges, rather than tactics and logistics. Nor does his list of trip goals include such a choice. He does, however, mention the village "Khaabin," which matches one of the spellings on Kokshaiskii's map. If the line bridging the river on the map is contemporaneous with the map's production, then Grulev's claim may be true, though it strikes me as unlikely that he and Kokshaiskii would draw in such a line and then remain silent about its significance in their written commentary. See Grulev, pp. 144–45, 196–97. I am grateful to Boris Bresler and Gregory Grossman for pointing out this source to me.

6. Pozdneev, pp. 201–2.

7. Kokshaiskii gives 1878 as the date on which the left channel was dammed. Pozdneev, p. 111, gives 1879; and Bogdanov, l. 63, gives 1880. "Bayantu" is the romanization of the Russian transliteration. I have not been able to locate this site on a Chinese map.

8. Pozdneev, p. 296 (on the conflicting population estimates in 1895). Chinese official statistics for Sanxingcheng in 1892 from *Jilin tongzhi*, as reported in Rudakov "Pozemel'nyi vopros," p. 32, show a banner and statelands population of over 16,000. Once the Han Chinese and city outskirts are added in, the population total could easily rise to a number closer to the Chinese estimate than the Russian one.

9. RGIA 1273: 1, 216, pp. 63–66; Pozdneev, p. 37.

10. See Pozdneev's Bibliography for all citations except Dobrovidov, which I have not been able to locate. I include him in the list of authors based on Pozdneev's statement (p. 37) that Dobrovidov also published an "account."

11. Pozdneev, p. 290. How could Tifontai know that taking delivery on the return trip would be complicated by the fudutong's claim that Bogdanov's permission to trade in Jilin province was not valid for Hulan, since that left-bank city was located in Heilongjiang province? Possibly the fudutong also saw an economic threat in the decision to make livestock purchases in Bodune, the meat market for 100,000 Mongol herdsmen. In Hulan, the highest-ranking official held the meat monopoly; see ibid., p. 301 on Hulancheng; and pp. 536–37 on Tifontai's and Bogdanov's difficulties there. Bogdanov took all this in stride (at least in hindsight), commenting stoically that little could be expected of people who thought that all Europeans spoke the same language, that humans with dogs' heads existed, and that a kingdom populated solely by women was a reality. In the end, by threatening

the fudutong with the Chinese Foreign Ministry's wrath, Tifontai took delivery of his goods. His arrival in Khabarovsk, towing a barge and three Chinese junks filled with grain, livestock, wool, and tobacco, triggered three more voyages up the Sungari in 1895. RGIA 1273: 1, 216, pp. 57, 72, 82. The success of those trips led five prominent merchants to file applications to navigate the Sungari the next year. In the winter of 1895, the Siberian Railroad Committee voted 35,000 rubles in subsidies for Sungari voyages, at around 1.5 rubles per verst traveled.

12. Kokshaiskii, Map 18.

13. *Stat. op.*, 2: 1, 51–52. Population statistics for China are always open to question, but this claim is easy to make since no other foreign settlement was even close. MAE, 171: 79, gives Shanghai's foreign population in 1910 as 3,000. According to Murphey, p. 23, prior to the influx of Russian émigrés that began in 1919, Shanghai's non-Chinese population was 10,000–20,000. Kabuzan, p. 224, provides statistics on Russian cities.

14. Shteinfel'd, pp. 47, 50. See also *Otchet Kharbinskogo birzhevogo komiteta za 1913 god*, p. 52.

15. *Otchet Kharbinskogo birzhevogo komiteta za 1911 god*, p. 37; Zhao Dejiu, pp. 138–39.

16. FO371: Carton 845, f. 214, p. 228.

17. *Sbornik pamiati V. F. Komissarzhevskaia*, pp. 88–89; Melikhov, "Zarisovki starogo Kharbina," p. 114.

18. Malevskii-Malevich to Izvol'skii, Oct. 14, 1909, in AVPR, *Iaponskii stol*, 1909, d. 915, p. 156.

19. The description of Ito's assassination is based on Melikhov, "Zarisovki starogo Kharbina," p. 118; AVPR, *Iaponskii stol*, 1909, d. 915, pp. 156–58; Ji Fenghui, *Haerbin xungen*, 246–52; Wu Jinglin, pp. 168–70; and Shi Fang, pp. 49–50. See also Tsuru.

20. Marinov, pp. 92–98; Hara, "Korea Movement," pp. 3–4.

21. AVPR, *Iaponskii stol*, d. 206, p. 75, as cited in *Kitai*, p. 216.

22. Russian officials may have come to accept without giving much thought to it that a "renewed" Japanese attack would first involve Harbin, since the city had been the presumed next objective of the Japanese land armies just before the Russo-Japanese War ended in Sept. 1905.

23. Fomenko, p. 236.

24. Nilus, *Istoricheskii*, pp. 49, 51. Khilkov's men had hoped to complete their survey by the end of the summer, as shown by the fact that Iugovich found them adding warm clothes purchased from the local Chinese and Mongolians to the standard garb of the Russian explorer. "Has carnival [*maslianitsa*] already arrived in these parts?" he is reported to have joked.

25. Romanov, pp. 121–22. Iugovich attended the meeting in a purely advisory capacity.

26. Nilus, *Istoricheskii*, p. 42. The importance of a degree from one of these two institutions actually made Iugovich somewhat the outsider, since he had received his engineering degree in England. However, the need for this qualification was somewhat diluted by the large number of subordinates Iugovich brought with him to the CER and the broad geographic diffusion of the CER work sites, which made contact with the chief engineer a rare occasion. In fact, by 1899 the extremities of

the three lines were under the semiautonomous control of the engineers N. N. Bocharov (West), N. S. Sviagin (East), and F. O. Girshman (South). Only Harbin and the thousand or so versts of track nearest to it remained under Iugovich's direct authority. Nilus, *Istoricheskii*, p. 60. A more "mainstream" choice might have made the recruitment of other engineers easier, something that may have prompted Witte's preference for K. Ia. Mikhailovskii, one of Russia's most renowned railroad builders, to become chief engineer of the CER. However, L. Iu. Rothstein, the agent for the French investors who had, in large part, financed the whole enterprise, had insisted on Iugovich and got his way. Rothstein had also pushed for the selection of Kerbedz as vice-chairman of CER, Inc. Witte had previously worked with Kerbedz in the 1870's and 1880's on the Southwest Railroad. Nilus ms., "Ocherk deiatel'nostsi," p. 6; Witte, p. 21. Iugovich's annual salary, the largest of all, was 75,000 rubles. GARF 818: 1, 64, p. 10.

27. RGIA 632: 1, 72, pp. 86, 97.

28. For details on the statutes, see RGIA 1273: 1, 265, pp. 15–28. On the decision to postpone a definitive division of labor between board and administration, see Nilus ms., "Pravleniia KVZhD," p. 5.

29. The information in this paragraph and the one that follows is from Romanov, p. 125; and Ukhtomskii and Tsigler to Romanov n.d. (early June 1897), telegram 439, and Pokotilov to Romanov, June 8, 1897, in RGIA 632: 1, 1, pp. 60, 62.

30. Nilus, *Istoricheskii*, p. 40 (*Silach*); RGIA 1273: 1, 266, pp. 18–19 (Navy friction). Like Istanbul's famous natural harbor, Vladivostok's is called the "Golden Horn."

31. Nilus, *Istoricheskii*, pp. 32–34.

32. Ibid., p. 51; RGIA 632: 1, 1, p. 85; RGIA, 632: 1, 72, p. 95; Poletika, p. 7. The chief engineer stopped in Jilin province, where he met the jiangjun Yan Mo and learned of that official's establishment of a lumber and coal monopoly. Only by Beijing's intercession was the CER saved from rapacious squeeze in procuring these essential railroad-building commodities. Poletika, in tow, cured Yan Mo of a minor circulatory ailment by prescribing digitalis. There is a certain irony in this demonstration of Western medical "magic" by the prescription of an herbal remedy, an area in which Chinese knowledge was unquestionably superior.

33. Nilus, *Istoricheskii*, pp. 51–52; RGIA 1679: 1, 24, p. 20; Quested, "Local Sino-Russian Political Relations," p. 122. En Ze memorialized the throne on June 9, 1897, claiming that the most serious defect of the southern route was that it bypassed Qiqihar. In another memorial, of July 16, 1897, he suggested that if this route could not be prevented, and the Russians refused to build branch lines to Qiqihar, possibly the provincial capital should be moved to Bodune.

34. Nilus, *Istoricheskii*, p. 53; RGIA 632: 1, 72, p. 88; Poletika, p. 9. The guard contingent included the young A. I. Guchkov, who would make his mark in 1905 as a leader of the Octobrists.

35. Nilus, *Istoricheskii*, pp. 69, 75.

36. Lensen, *Russo-Chinese War*, p. 148.

37. I found the Shidlovskii story told in detail in five sources, four Russian, and one Polish. Whether attributed or not, they are all drawn from Veselovzorov, "Kak byl zalozhen Kharbin." V. M. Veselovzorov was a meteorologist who accompanied Shidlovskii. His modest laboratory, which began to accumulate observations

on May 8, 1898, was the predecessor of the large-scale Manchurian research ventures soon to follow. Since Nilus, *Istoricheskii*, pp. 126–291, quotes extensively from this work, I used that work as the main source for my narrative. The inclusion of a woman and child in the party is noted in Charov. The number and kind of buildings in the distillery are given in Gints; and *Politekhnik* (Sydney, Australia), 5 (1974), p. 41. The Polish work (*Polacy na dalekim wschodzie*) departs from the others in claiming that the purchase was made for 12,000 lan, but this is probably a confusion in currencies, since 8,000 lan in 1898 was worth about 12,000 rubles. Also, RGIA 560: 28, 83, p. 81, identifies *the* owner of the distillery as one En Sisan (according to the Russian transliteration). The second man may have been along to help with the haggling.

38. Nilus, *Istoricheskii*, pp. 130–31; Pozdneev, p. 433.

39. *Instruktsiia dlia proizvodstva izyskanii*, p. 5; RGIA 1273: 1, 265, p. 138 (map). In the late 1990's the question of Harbin's true birthday (or at least birth year) became more than academic. The intention of both Harbin municipality and Heilongjiang province, of which Harbin is now the capital, to fête the city's centenary triggered an acrimonious debate among local historians, with the result that at this writing (1998), a date had not yet been set. For more on the regional significance of this debate, see my concluding essay in Kotkin and Wolff, pp. 323–29.

40. Nilus ms, "Lands and Land Administration," annex 1A; Romanov, p. 84. On the conclusion of the Russo-Chinese treaty, D. D. Pokotilov, Witte's and the Russo-Chinese Bank's main agent in Beijing, immediately began studies of currency, land, and labor issues related to the CER's planned construction; on land, see Pokotilov's work cited in the Bibliography.

41. Nilus ms, "Lands and Land Administration," p. 11.

42. Nilus, *Istoricheskii*, pp. 64, 410–11.

43. Nilus ms, "Zemel'nyi konflikt," p. 168. The data on the Lukouqiao-Hankou railway are from Pokotilov, in RGIA 632: 1, 1, p. 72.

44. RGIA 1273: 1, 268, p. 84, breaks down the 2,435 figure into 2,235 desiatinas purchased at 55 rubles a piece and 200 desiatinas purchased at 60 rubles. Since the Chinese map of Harbin shows the Xiangfang (Old Harbin) plot to be roughly one-tenth the total area and since we know that Shidlovskii paid 12,000 rubles for the liquor factory, the separate purchase at 60 rubles was almost certainly for Old Harbin.

45. "Obshchii obzor," p. 4. This source is a documented report prepared for the Soviet negotiators at the 1930–31 Moscow Conference on the CER. The Chinese map probably dates to 1901, since the borderline is labeled: "The red line is where the ditches have all already been dug [to mark] the circumference of the Concession occupied last year." The fact that the bridge is shown incomplete suggests an earlier dating, but that would put the supplementary ditch-digging into the pre-Boxer period, which is not possible.

46. Nilus ms., "Zemel'nyi konflikt," pp. 156, 190–91, and "Lands and Land Administration," p. 6. A Chinese version of the May 28 contract is in my possession. For the sake of perimeter defense, the Russian negotiators wanted to round out the CER holdings in 1902. The Chinese, however, stubbornly refused to turn over the villages of Fujiadian and Tianjiashaogou. These "wedges" (*klin*), as the Russians

termed them, became a permanent feature of the Belt of Alienation. RGIA 560: 28, 414, p. 15.

47. Nilus ms, "Ocherki byta," p. 4, quoting the veteran builder E. P. Ia.

48. Bakich, "Origins," p. 6. Bakich states that A. A. Gershov, S. M. Vakhovskoi, K. I. Veber, and S. Ts. Offenberg, as well as Girshman, Shidlovskii, Ignatsius, and Khilkov, followed Iugovich from the Riazan-Ural'sk Railway. (It is not clear from her references where she got this information, and I cannot confirm all these names from my own research.) According to Nilus, *Istoricheskii*, pp. 36–37, at least three senior Ussuri engineers occupied key posts on the CER: N. S. Sviagin, N. N. Bocharov, and M. G. Amosov. See also Sokolova, 1: 81.

49. RGIA 632: 1, 72, p. 86.

50. Ibid., 1, 84, p. 11 (July 30, 1899).

51. Sokolova, 1: 82; Nilus, *Istoricheskii*, p. 67; Leroy-Beaulieu, p. 141. In 1897, the engineer S. M. Vakhovskii traveled to England and Belgium to order disassembled boats, including tugs with only two feet of displacement for use on the shallow Sungari. At Iman, where the Ussuri railway meets the Ussuri River, these boats were reassembled and put afloat. By late 1898, the CER fleet based at Krasnaia Rechka, outside of Khabarovsk, consisted of 18 steamers, 4 launches, and 60 barges.

52. Sokolova, 1: 82. Despite a misleading title and unreliable dating, this is a very informative version of life on the CER and in Harbin.

53. Nilus ms, "Ocherki byta," p. 4.

54. Sokolova, 1: 95–98; RGIA 1273: 1, 272, p. 7. According to Sokolova, Rozanov was soon fired, but because of the administrative independence of the three branches (East, West, and South), Bocharov was able to rehire him to the Xingan sector.

55. Borzunov, pp. 158–59 (data on the Trans-Siberian workforce). The CER percents are calculated from figures below in text.

56. Levitov, p. 25. For more details on Chinese lodgings, see Siviakov, p. 97. On Iugovich's office, see RGIA 1273: 1, 272, p. 8. One factor that kept food costs down was the CER's guarantee of a low, even unprofitable, price for rice in its labor contracts with the Chinese. See RGIA 1273: 1, 272, p. 7.

57. RGIA 323: 1, 1185, pp. 9–28. Iugovich recognized the importance of the Chinese contribution, citing the "industriousness" of coolies in his July 14, 1903, farewell message to all CER employees. See Nilus, *Istoricheskii*, p. 265; and RGIA 632: 1, 1, pp. 32, 35. Pokotilov later became the Russian minister in Beijing. The Third Department of the General Chancellery (Obshchaia Kantselariia) was Witte's "in-house" foreign affairs committee. See Romanov, pp. vii–viii.

58. RGIA 632: 1, 84, pp. 6–7.

59. RGIA 1273: 1, 272, p. 143; RGIA 323: 1, 1185, pp. 158–60.

60. CER newspaper advertisements in Beijing, Tianjin, and Zhifu also attracted workers, although it is unclear how many were recruited by this method. A copy of a CER ad entitled, "Daqing dongsheng tielu gongsi zhaomu tugong gaobai" can be found in RGIA 323: 1, 1185, p. 39.

61. The advances (*zadatki*) paid in China were suspected in St. Petersburg of being a source of financial malfeasance. CER officials responded with an anecdote about the Russian troops in China for the 1860 campaign who had been forced to

hitch rides with Japanese transport because their quartermaster would not authorize advances, and the Chinese would not work without them. RGIA 1273: 1, 272, 109.

62. Nilus, *Istoricheskii*, pp. 146, 184; Polatika, p. 15; Sokolova, 1: 94–100.

63. Nilus ms, S. Ts. fon-Offenberg, "Pervye opyty organizovat' zemlianye raboty na V [piatom] stroitel'nom uchastke," pp. 2, 5–7. Aside from this narrow escape from pogrom, working on the CER may have provided these "model" workers the economic opportunity to obviate a return to the Russian side of the border after the Boxer Rebellion had passed. For more on this point, see Siegelbaum, p. 319. On the Blagoveshchensk "Utopia," see Lensen, *Russo-Chinese War*, p. 68.

64. Siviakov, p. 120 and foldout.

65. The Harbin population estimate is from RGIA 323: 7, 1243, p. 10. The Fujiadian information is based on *Kitamanshu keizai chosashiryo*, pp. 154–55. Though it has often been assumed that the *dian* in Fujiadian refers to the many hostelries, the original reference seems to have been to a single Chinese medicine store run by Fu Baoshan (the *fu* in Fujiadian). His family had migrated from Shandong to Hulan county, just across the Sungari into Heilongjiang province, and he had moved on to set up his own store around 1890. As the only doctor/veterinarian in the area, he did well. When his brother (also Fu Baoshan, but with a different character and tone for the last syllable) joined him, they opened a hotel and a tavern. In 1904, when they split up, the doctor formed a real estate company controlling several hundred properties in Fujiadian. There are advantages to early arrival. See Zhao Tian, pp. 135–37. Zhao's article is based on interviews with Fu family descendants and former employees, as well as written sources.

66. On the price and wage increases, see RGIA 1273: 1, 267, p. 11. Migrant labor in the service of imperialistic construction is a factor that Joseph Esherick does not discuss in his sociogeographic hunt for the "Home of the Boxers." Large-scale employment and concomitant imperialist presence would certainly have been a factor in the Shandong peninsula's relative lack of agitation. How Northwest Shandong, Esherick's choice as the Boxer homeland, was affected by comprador hirings from Tianjin is still an open question. See Esherick, *Origins of the Boxer Uprising*, chap. 1.

67. Offenberg in Nilus ms (see n. 63 above), pp. 79–80. The only exception that Offenberg adds to this damning portrait is the Cossack Old Believers from Chikoi in the Transbaikal. Although their horse-drawn methods were unusual, their productivity and behavior drew praise. The size of the workforce is from RGIA 1273: 1, 268, p. 64.

68. RGIA 1273: 1, 272, p. 9.

69. The 4,100 figure comes from subtracting the 4,500 Transbaikal "derelicts" from the total figure for Russian "craftsmen and workers" in RGIA 1273: 1, 267, p. 114. On the paymasters, see Nilus ms, "Ocherki byta," pp. 14–22. The *artel*'s contract and relationship with the CER persisted into the Soviet period, when an unsuccessful attempt was made to reconstitute the Far Eastern affairs of the cooperative into a separate business entity.

70. Nilus, *Istoricheskii*, pp. 116, 140; RGIA 323: 1, 1185, p. 190. Russia's limited experience with tunnels led Iugovich to petition the Finance Ministry for permission to invite Italian specialists to build the Xingan tunnel. His request was granted.

71. RGIA 1273: 1, 269, p. 265.
72. Nilus, *Istoricheskii*, pp. 214-17; Lensen, pp. 145-51. When Iugovich was asked by Petersburg to explain why the Boxer danger had not been detected earlier, CER personnel all along the line generated extensive post facto reports; see RGIA 1273: 1, 267, pp. 29-106. For Chinese documents on this episode as translated by a Russian professor at Vladivostok's Eastern Institute, see Rudakov, *Obshchestvo i-khetuan*, p. 76. Although the engineers' wives arrived unharmed in Khabarovsk, their boat came under fire near the town of Sanxing. To evade incoming fire, the captain ordered an attached barge loaded with luggage cut loose, leaving the ladies "chut' ne golymi i bosymi" ("nearly naked and barefoot"). AT 7N1543, p. 13, newspaper clipping.
73. 1902 data from RGIA 323: 1, 481, p. 21; 1902 data from RGIA 1273, 1, 268, p. 121; Witte report cited in Nilus, *Istoricheskii*, p. 150 (complete version in RGIA 560: 28, 262). For Harbin residents by employment, see *Spravochnaia knizhka Kharbina*, pp. 6-7. Quested, *"Matey" Imperialists*, p. 100, presents Harbin population data, most of which fits the figures given above. Additionally, she includes a 1901 Harbin "civilian" total of 12,000. Her footnote (no. 73), although marred by a typesetting error, seems to indicate the source as A. Kokhanovskii's 1909 book on colonization. This work, as extracted in *Izvestiia vostochnogo instituta* 29 (1909), was thoroughly criticized on both demographic and orientological grounds in *VA* 2 (1909): 202-4.
74. RGIA 632: 1, 72, p. 100; RGIA 1273: 1, 260, p. 5.
75. RGIA 1273: 1, 272, p. 27; RGIA 1273: 1, 268, pp. 27-28. I have a copy of what appears to be the original 1899 planning map for New Town—labeled "A Plan for the Arrangement of the Sungari Settlement" (Plan raspolozheniia Poselka Sungari). Many of the features, including two "Chinese quarters" and multiple grand intersections, would never be built. No planning is shown for Pristan. The name Harbin does not even appear, since in this period it was used only to describe Xiangfang (Old Harbin). Koshizawa's "1899 map" (p. 40) is clearly from a later period, as shown by the inclusion of the expanded borders after the 1900 Boxer siege.
76. The church/cathedral has not survived. In August 1966, Harbin's Red Guards dismantled it as a manifestation of the "four olds" (old habits, old ideas, old customs, and old culture). Since the structure was a product of the joiner's art, no nails had been used, and its complete removal took only one day. See Qiao Gu, pp. 142-45.
77. RGIA 1273: 1, 268, p. 28; von Nottbeck, p. 41; Spaits, pp. 53-54. Though not quite as exuberant as Mackintosh's structures in Glasgow or Gaudi's in Barcelona, several of Harbin's Art Nouveau buildings were quite flamboyant. For a fuller discussion of architectural styles and many illustrations of Harbin buildings, see Koshizawa, especially pp. 49-53, 59, 85-103. The art nouveau station was not Harbin's first. Temporary stations in Pristan and Old Harbin were constructed in 1898. Only after it became clear where the east-west mainline would meet the Port Arthur branch could a central station be planned. On this process, see Zheng Changchun, "Haerbin huochezhande bianqian," pp. 90-96.
78. Sokolova, 1: 104-5 (wives' trading enterprises); RGIA 560: 28, 951, pp. 129-31 (Pozdneev report); *Amurskii krai*, July 24, 1901, clipping in AT 7N1543. Although Harbin prices generally ran between double and triple those of Khabarovsk, for

some bulk items the profits were much higher: for example, vodka at 300%, salmon and rice (!) at 400%, onions at 700%, and potatoes at 1,100%. "Haerbinde zhifenye," *Haerbin wenshi ziliao,* 4 (1984): 67.

79. RGIA, 560: 28, 951, p. 130.

80. Hundred-year floods were another matter. In July 1932, when over a half meter of water fell in 27 consecutive days of rain, the river breached the dikes, making boats into Pristan the only means of transport. The head of the flood committee (Haerbin Shuizai Shanhou Fuxing Weiyuanhui), Bao Guancheng, reported nearly 100,000 refugees; later counts climbed to over double that number. For details on Harbin's weather and a chronology of natural disasters, see *Haerbin shizhi: dilijuan,* pp. 166–69, 404–6.

81. AT 7N1543; RGIA 1273: 1, 266, p. 41; 1, 268, p. 10; 1, 269, pp. 57, 65, 328–30; 1, 272, p. 103. Total CER expenditures in Harbin are estimated variously at 30,000,000 rubles (Miller, p. 114), 100,000,000 rubles (Sokolsky, p. 26), and 260,000,000 rubles (Koshizawa, p. 313, n. 13, citing Manzhouguo publications claiming to be based on an unnamed Russian source). The first figure seems reasonable until 1903, although some of the items Miller includes were never constructed. He clearly had access to some of the CER's city planning materials. The second figure also appears reasonable as a grand total for both Russian government and private investment in Harbin until 1917, not just government until 1903, as Sokolsky suggests. The final number is simply absurd, possibly an exaggerated conversion into 1930's rubles as the USSR prepared to negotiate the sale of the CER to Manzhouguo.

82. AT 7N1521, cahier 5, p. 58 (quarry 82 versts downstream from Harbin); RGIA 1273: 1, 268, p. 11 (sawmill); and 1, 269, p. 335 (brick factory becoming self-supporting with private orders; see a description of CER sponsorship of the factory in Sokolova, 1: 100–101); *Kharbinskii vestnik,* June 10, 1903, p. 4, (Nobel Bros.).

83. HLJ 78.1, *juan* 638 (this is the archive of the CER Land Dept., which was confiscated by the Chinese in 1924). The inequalities between the two "towns" persisted. A 1909 Harbin taxation committee found the average value of a property in New Town to be 9,491 rubles, compared with only 1,936 for Pristan. Fo371, carton 845, file 214, pp. 225–28.

84. Golovachev, p. 131, 171. There are several layers of meaning to this *poslovitsa,* whose main thrust is the affirmation of difference as in the original: *rak ne ryba, i zhenshchina ne chelovek.* The "100 rubles" refers to both the gargantuan budget of the CER and the colossal opportunities for personal, often immoral, profit. The "50 versts" works as a flattering reference to the 1,500-mile length of the Promethean task, but in addition may hint at the 50-verst duty-free zone established on both sides of the Manchurian border between Russia and China. The creation of this strip made the interception of contraband almost impossible. Smuggling proliferated. The final term not only gives the whole saying a racist flavor, but testifies to the devaluation of human life common along the frontier of civilization.

85. Sokolova, 1: 105–6; RGIA 560: 28.951, 131; Miller, p. 118. The serious smuggling of alcohol, however, was not into but out of Manchuria, to subvert the 1898 Russian state liquor monopoly. One of the most innovative methods was filling hollow eggshells with vodka. Stozh, p. 202. Possibly, Witte had Manchuria in mind when he wrote: "By 1903 . . . the vodka monopoly had been established nearly

throughout the extent of Russia, except some of the distant border provinces."
Memoirs, p. 55.

The Russian *khanshin* probably derives from the Chinese *hanxing* meaning "the exhilaration of liquor" (*Mathews' Chinese-English Dictionary*, p. 302). The first edition of *Kharbinskii vestnik* (June 10, 1903) would advertise an unidentified khanshin casualty. If Miller's estimate is correct (and we assume that the Chinese did not imbibe *à la Russe*), on the average every Russian man, woman, and child drank a pint of vodka a day. In 1908, when the municipal council took over the supervision of distilleries, 486 enterprises were registered. TsGADV 577: 1c, 3, p. 7. Finally, it may be more than coincidence that the most famous Russian-émigré vodka producers of the present day have the same names as the two Russian firms whose experience in distilling and marketing outside of Russia began before 1917.

86. Golovachev, p. 135; *Spravochnaia knizhka Kharbina*, p. 10. Quested, *"Matey" Imperialists*, p. 103, cites a more substantial representation of females among the Russians than I calculated, putting the ratio at 44: 100. She also puts the females' overall representation slightly higher, at 14% (p. 101).

87. Poletika, pp. 22–23, 53–54, 57, 59. Japanese prostitution in Harbin is discussed in more detail in Chap. 3. For an amusing account of the Russians' adoption of Japanese wives at Nagasaki, see Alexander, pp. 103–9.

88. RGIA 632: 1, 72, p. 100; RGIA 1273: 1, 269, p. 50, and 1, 266, pp. 47–51; Nilus, *Istoricheskii*, pp. 140–41.

89. Quested, *"Matey" Imperialists*, pp. 65–66; Poletika, p. 32; Ukhtomskii, *K sobytiiam*, p. 77 (many sections of this book, especially portions related to racial "philosophy," are taken verbatim from Ukhtomskii's *Puteshestvie gosudaria imperatora Nikolaia II na Vostok*).

90. RGIA 1273: 1, 266, p. 206; 1, 269, p. 51; 1, 272, pp. 46–48; Avtonomov, pp. 7–8; Nilus, *Istoricheskii*, pp. 289–91.

91. Avtonomov, pp. 37–38, 123.

92. *Kharbinskii vestnik*, June 10, 1903 (o.s.).

93. Ibid., June 12, 1903 (o.s.). The *Herald* replaced the *Kharbin listok* (*Harbin Broadsheet*), which had been coming out since the fall of 1902 under the editorship of P. V. Rovenskii, (a former revolutionary to whom we will return). Pleve's request to Witte to have Rovenskii's collection of telegrams and ads closed down was the first case of sparring over Harbin's reputation as a safe haven for the politically unreliable. RGIA 560: 28, 1009, pp. 1–5.

94. Malozemoff, p. 154.

95. *North American Review*, May 1904, pp. 683–84, as cited in Asakawa, pp. 43–44.

96. Ukhtomskii cited in Malozemoff, pp. 43–44.

97. Leroy-Beaulieu, p. 135; Pierre Leroy-Beaulieu, *Awakening of the East*, tr. Henry Norman (New York, 1900), p. viii. On the Paris exposition, see Daniel Brower, "Siberia in Paris: Russia at the 1900 Paris World's Fair" (Paper presented at the American Association of Asian Studies annual meeting, Chicago, 1989). After serialization in the *Revue des Deux Mondes* and the *Economiste français*, the book sold out four editions between 1900 and 1904.

98. RGIA 1273: 1, 272, p. 230 (Grodekov); Romanov, p. 42 (Witte).

99. Whigham, p. 58.

100. The CER justified the astronomical 328,000,000-ruble outlay (Romanov, p. 33) by, first, subtracting nonconstruction "special expenses" paid out of CER funds (e.g., the Guard, bribes to Chinese officials), and then arguing that since the difference between the CER and the Transbaikal Kaidalovo branch costs was approximately equal to the summed differences of rolling stock and station buildings, the CER's actual per-verst construction rate was no greater than that of the Kaidalovo branch. Witte and his aides were always good at "financial logic." *Kitaiskaia*, pp. 122–23, 285–94.

101. Levitov, *Zheltaia Rossiia*, p. 36. It is important to note that the two points of view, separated only by an antagonistic polarization of the slippery racial concept, were so close that the same author could preach both versions with apparent sincerity. For example, Levitov is less sanguine about the Orientals in his earlier pamphlet *Zheltaia rasa* (1900), as cited in Malozemoff, pp. 190, 302. (Possibly because Malozemoff's book was posthumously edited, there are occasional glaring errors in factual material. I have never seen the pamphlet *Zheltaia rasa*. Is it simply an editorial distortion of *Zheltaia Rossiia*?) Hermann Brunnhofer, a follower of Prince E. E. Ukhtomskii, also betrays ambivalence when considering the meeting and merging of the white and yellow races. See Hauner, p. 58. All the pre–Russo-Japanese War "Yellow Peril" tracts are comparatively mild. On the intensified racism that followed, see Siegelbaum, pp. 319–23. For more on pre-Petrine Russia's fear of the East, see Riasanovsky, pp. 6–7.

102. NGB, 1903, 1: 41–45 (cabinet decision no. 50, Dec. 30, 1903). In this resolution, the cabinet also explores the logic by which the alliance system that Tokyo had recently joined could escalate regional conflict into "a great total world war" (*sekai zenkyoku no daisenran*). I am grateful to Nakachi Mie for drawing my attention to this point.

103. This composite of Ukhtomskii's Eurasianism, which he drew in large part from V. S. Solov'ev, comes from his book *Puteshestvie gosudaria imperatora Nikolaia II na Vostoke* (1897), in which the chapter "Our Asia" is followed by "Through Siberia," suggesting a clear division between two areas that have often been united under the headings "Russian Asia," "Asian Russia" or "Siberia." In addition, see his subsequent books *K sobytiiam v Kitae* (1900), pp. 74–87; *Iz kitaiskikh pisem'* (1901), p. 24; and *Pered groznym budushchem* (1904). In the last, issued just after the outbreak of the Russo-Japanese War, he claimed that because Russia had failed to take care of Japan like a "younger brother," the Japanese had learned from "a different race" (Europeans) to hate Russia (p. 7).

104. U.S. State Dept., *Consular Reports*, Feb. 15, 1904.

105. *Kitaiskaia*, pp. 190–91. Malozemoff, p. 190, comes to the conclusion that private freight carriage was disappointing because of a rabid anti-CER pamphlet, but he casts doubt on his own figures on p. 302, n. 94. The source's anonymous author is mislabeled S. Khabarovskii; in fact, the source is St. (for *stantsiia*) Kharbinskii, *Chto takoe Kitaiskaia Vostochnaia zh. d. i kuda idut eia milliony* (St. Petersburg, 1908). In any case, one year is hardly the measure of success or failure for an enterprise of this size. This questionable judgment has been passed on as an illustration of the weak "relation between internal economic expansion and imperialist expansion" by Geyer, p. 149; see also pp. 210–11.

106. *Tsusho Isan*, Sept. 18, 1903, and Nov. 23, 1903, as cited in Asakawa, p. 44 (the "laborious process of obtaining permits to carry on business only for short terms in these great sites for future cities"). On bribes, see Valliant, p. 275.

107. Hackett, pp. 138–39; Valliant, pp. 234–35, 264–65, 282–86, 295–96. Japanese diplomatic correspondence shows great attention to all details of the construction, carriage capacity, and actual usage of the CER and Trans-Siberian. The main reporters were the Japanese consul at Niuzhuang and the trade representative at Vladivostok, who ran a whole network of informers, both for pay and for country. Examples can be found in NGB, 1901, pp. 682–83; 1903, 1: 826–27, 874–75, 877–883; and 1904, 1: 642–47.

108. Weale, pp. 139, 141, 143, 149, 169, 401. But the author did find something to like in Harbin after being too long in the Far East. "What bread! It is so sweet and pure and light that you can eat on for ever, blessing the generous soil which can grow such crops. If the railway would only learn sense and forget that it is a strategic line, all the Far East might eat of this finest of flour, and suffer less from dyspepsia" (pp. 143–44).

109. Rudakov, *Obshchestvo i-khe-tuan*, p. 76.

110. Nilus, *Istoricheskii*, p. 137; HLJ, archive of the CER Land Dept. (Zemel'nyi otdel), 78.1.638; *Spravochnaia knizhka Kharbina*, p. 6 (example of auction action, plot 1237, between Politseiskaia and Prodovol'stvennaia streets).

111. Bakich, "Russian City," pp. 129–31; Valliant, p. 279; Asakawa, p. 43; Brooke, p. 10; Baring, pp. 33–37; Whigham, pp. 76–77; Weale, p. 148; Repington, p. 197; Japanese consul Segawa, Niuzhuang, to Foreign Minister Komura, Oct. 19, 1903, in NGB, 1903, 2: 891.

112. Baring, p. 33; Whigham, p. 77.

113. Nilus, *Istoricheskii*, p. 58; Beveridge, pp. 63, 86–87, 438, 460.

114. *Sovremennaia letopis' Dal'nego Vostoka*, July 1, 1903–Dec. 31, 1904, p. 62. This *Chronicle* was issued as a regular appendix to *Izvestiia vostochnogo instituta*.

115. Kuropatkin, *Russian Army*, pp. 185–86; Romanov, p. 32. Witte commanded an effective "financial intelligence" network to match his in-house "foreign ministry." Thanks to it, for example, he was supposedly the first in St. Petersburg to know of the attack on Port Arthur. Kuropatkin, "Dnevnik A. N. Kuropatkina," p. 109.

CHAPTER TWO

EPIGRAPH: Kuropatkin, "Dnevnik," pp. 48–49.

1. For example, in 1906, N. I. Grodekov (then commander of the Priamur military district) tried but failed to have the CER placed under the Ministry of War. Meanwhile, the CER practiced "reverse colonization" by taking over the operation of the Ussuri railway inside Russian borders. In 1910, the Finance and Foreign ministers headed off an army plan to annex northern Manchuria, and in 1915, the Foreign Ministry sold a portion of the CER to the Japanese, despite the Finance Minister's loud protests.

2. Japanese ambassador Kurino, St. Petersburg, to Foreign Minister Komura, Sept. 12, 1903, no. 775, and Kurino to Komura, Aug. 20, 1903, no. 13, in NGB, 1903, 1: 15, 795; Nish, p. 162.

3. Recently, a number of books have appeared that stress the importance of interministerial rivalry in understanding the final years of Imperial Russia. (For a partial list, see Introduction n. 29.) Yaney, *Urge*, p. 205, observes, of the Stolypin reforms, the autocratic government's last great initiative: "The enactment process evolved out of an interministerial conflict, not an ideological one. The main issue in the enactors' minds was not the nature of the reform but who was to control it." Possibly historians of late Imperial Russia will find convincing explanations for the contradictions that gradually whittled down the viability of the tsarist regime only when they sift more carefully through the "elaborate rhetorical exercises" of the policy-making process. Then they will have to compare the statutory results arrived at in Petersburg with implementation at the local level. In this chapter, I place special emphasis on the period immediately preceding the Russo-Japanese War in order to highlight previously neglected connections between domestic and foreign affairs. Even so excellent a study as McDonald's *United Government*, for example, dwells on the process in the capital, and therefore the influence of local dynamics is underestimated. Much of this bias can be traced to the sources McDonald used, all of central provenance. Ministerial memoirs are not likely to admit that sometimes the tail wags the dog. Lieven, p. 62, holds that "the woeful lack of co-ordination between the Emperor, Foreign Ministry, armed forces, civilian government and Far Eastern Viceroy" in 1904 "played a major role" in the coming of war.

4. Fuller, p. 74.

5. Cited in ibid., p. 95.

6. Ibid.

7. Ukhtomskii, *K sobytiiam*, p. 85. This was also Lenin's generation, and he shared the prevalent belief in technology. The first record we have of his mentioning Harbin is in this context. His brother-in-law made a business trip to Harbin in 1902, and Lenin wrote: "Well, I think Harbin is already not so unusually far, and soon it will be even nearer; as soon as the railway reaches it." RTsKhIDNI 2: 1, 725.

8. MAE, 166: 159–60.

9. Cited in Lensen, *Russo-Chinese War*, pp. 253–54.

10. B. A. Romanov's rich archival study, *Rossiia v Man'chzhurii* (1928), is largely concerned with proving that Witte's imperialism was no different from any other brand. This confuses ends and means. Geyer, pp. 1–3, explicitly focuses on causes rather than methods, and therefore also dismisses Witte's conceptual distinction between political and economic conquest. Geyer's attempt (pp. 210–11) to discredit the viability of "peaceful penetration" is based on the financial performance of the CER between 1901 and 1903, a dubious line of argument, since the CER was not opened to regular traffic until July 14, 1903, and even then was not completely constructed. Geyer (following Malozemoff, p. 190), mistakenly uses Witte's ceremonial opening to "temporary" traffic, planned to flatter the Tsar by coinciding with Coronation Day in November 1901, as an actual starting point for his economic analysis. The Japanese, however, were not fooled. See trade representative Kawakami, Vladivostok, to Foreign Minister Komura, Nov. 8, 1901, no. 534, in NGB, 1901. Even before Alekseev became viceroy and, as such, diplomatic plenipotentiary in the Far East, his influence was significant, especially in late 1902 and early 1903, when his

chief foreign policy agent at Port Arthur, I. Ia. Korostovets, was transferred to Beijing as a fill-in during the Russian ambassador, Lessar's, extended trip to St. Petersburg for medical treatment and consultations. See MAE, 167: letter of Nov. 21, 1902.

11. Alexander, p. 169; Kuropatkin, "Dnevnik."

12. Von Laue, p. 147 (it is worth noting that Von Laue often concludes that events are "driven" by either "the logic of industrialization" or a related abstraction, "the logic of modernization").

13. MAE, 169: 34. Much of the false modesty is lost in translation. The original reads: "Quoique les affaires très variées et compliquées qui se trouvent sous la direction du Ministère des Finances, et l'étendue nouvelle et toujours croissante de son activité, présentent une charge considérable pour le Ministre des Finances et ne correspondent pas entièrement à ses vues, cependant, vu la gravité des considerations ci-dessus mentionnées, le secrétaire d'État Witte ne croit pas pouvoir s'opposer à l'agrandissement de l'activité du Ministère des Finances, si le comité du chemin de fer Transibérien le trouve indispensable." The CER statutes are found in RGIA 1273: 1, 265, 15–30. Because of government-backed financial ties with the Russo-Chinese Bank, French diplomatic materials are often taken verbatim from secret Russian sources. The same is true of the French military archives at the Château de Vincennes. Close ties and intelligence sharing between the Russian and French general staffs predate the Franco-Russian Alliance of 1894 by at least a decade and continue until 1917.

14. Kuropatkin, "Dnevnik," p. 55; McDonald, p. 63; Malozemoff, p. 226. In a provocative analogy, the Soviet historian M. N. Pokrovskii likens Witte's powers to those of the post-1917 Supreme Economic Council. Cited in Von Laue, p. 164.

15. Kuropatkin, "Dnevnik," pp. 49, 59.

16. Khorvat, "Memoirs," chap. 2, p. 6; MAE, 166: 17.

17. Kuropatkin, "Dnevnik," p. 31; Romanov, p. 283. In May 1904, at a conference on Far Eastern enterprises, A. M. Abaza, chairman of the Far Eastern Committee, specifically stated that the purpose of the viceroyalty was administrative unity, to be attained by removing Far Eastern affairs from the hands of the ministries. RGIA 1237: 1, 1, 88.

18. RGIA 1273: 1, 265, p. 65.

19. Amburger, pp. 407–8. Additional detail on military dominance in the Russian Far East can be found in Stephan, pp. 55–56. Only after 1910 were top administrative posts occupied by civilians.

20. Malozemoff, pp. 1–3; Landgraf, pp. 289–94, 300–304, 308–11. Of course, some settlements did receive favorable locations and prospered. This was particularly true of the upper Amur.

21. Kabuzan, pp. 162–64; *Priamur'e*, p. 90.

22. *Vladivostok: Sbornik istoricheskikh dokumentov, 1860–1907 gg.*, pp. 53–54.

23. Wolff, "Russia Finds Its Limits," p. 43. Instead, after a branch line from Novonikolaevsk (later Novosibirsk) to Tomsk was constructed, the new city swiftly grew to become the "capital" of Siberia.

24. "Pervye shagi russkogo imperializma," pp. 85, 87–88. As a compromise, Dukhovskoi suggested a 500-verst detour through northernmost Manchuria from Sretensk to Blagoveshchensk via Mergen.

25. Dukhovskoi, pp. 5, 92–95. Note that the population figure given in *Priamur'e* is less than half the number Dukhovskoi claimed as "based on official data" (p. 530).
26. Romanov, p. 119.
27. Ibid., pp. 125, 127–28. This is the same visit referred to earlier that overlapped with Iugovich's stop in Beijing on his way to Vladivostok.
28. Malozemoff, p. 100; Romanov, p. 138.
29. Harcave, pp. 227, 274.
30. Romanov, p. 140.
31. Ibid., pp. 141, 148; Harcave, p. 277.
32. Romanov, pp. 149–50, 417; Malozemoff, p. 110. The memoirs of Baron R. R. Rosen (Rozen), the Russian ambassador to Japan at this time, suggest that the Japanese were aware of Witte's discomfiture. According to him, the Japanese ambassador to Petersburg informed Tokyo that Russia was willing to yield the financial adviser position to a Japanese national in exchange for retaining control of the military adviser's appointment. Rosen, p. 159.
33. Romanov, pp. 158, 167; Malozemoff, pp. 115–16. An additional factor, which neither Romanov nor Malozemoff mentions, is that after the creation of the CER commercial fleet in 1898, Witte's plan of choice was to attack the British market share via the Yangtse River, not by a rail line to Hankou. In 1901, CER officials reported that they had 15 ships poised to take over the downriver transport of tea from the British. RGIA 560: 28, 816.
34. Later on, after Witte had left the stage, Mongolia entered into the picture. Many of the dynamics were similar to the Manchurian case, but that is another long story, outside the bounds of this study.
35. Romanov, p. 83.
36. Witte claimed credit for baptizing the city. See Harcave, p. 278.
37. Nilus, *Istoricheskii*, pp. 157–60; RGIA 1273: 1, 265, pp. 108–10.
38. This paragraph and the two that follow are based on RGIA 1273: 1, 265, pp. 119–23, 152–53.
39. RGIA 632: 1, 1, pp. 137–38.
40. RGIA 1273: 1, 266, pp. 12–13; RGIA 632: 1, 84, pp. 6–7; Nilus, *Istoricheskii*, p. 118.
41. RGIA 1273: 1, 266, p. 67; Glinskii, p. 235.
42. Bompard, St. Petersburg, to Foreign Minister Delcassé, Oct. 30, 1902, in MAE, vol. 167.
43. Nilus, *Istoricheskii*, pp. 161–66; RGIA 1273: 1, 266, p. 67; RGIA 1273: 1, 272, p. 125.
44. Nilus ms, "Ocherk deiatel'nosti," pp. 7–8; Nilus, *Istoricheskii*, p. 54.
45. Romanov, p. 401; Nilus ms, "Lands and Land Administration," Annex 1/A, pp. 3–4; Tang, p. 93; MAE, 169: 29–37.
46. Nilus, *Istoricheskii*, p. 503; RGIA 632: 1, 72, p. 92; Gelicen, p. 21. The last is a Chinese translation of a rare jubilee volume, *Ocherk uchastiia okhrannoi strazhi kitaiskoi vostochnoi zheleznoi dorogi v sobytiiakh 1900 goda v Man'chzhurii* (Harbin, 1910). I have never seen a Russian copy, nor was George Lensen able to find one for his work specifically on the 1900 suppression of the Boxer uprising in Manchuria. Unfortunately, Li Shuxiao, the Chinese translator, lent his copy to a student who never returned it.

47. Nilus, *Istoricheskii*, pp. 504–5; RGIA 632: 1, 72, pp. 93–94; Gelicen, p. 13.
48. Nilus, *Istoricheskii*, pp. 508–10, 551; Gelicen, p. 19; *Kitaiskaia*, p. 26; TsGADV 542: 1, 8, pp. 1–3. On the attitude of the officer corps, see Fuller.
49. RGIA 632: 1, 72, p. 94; Gelicen, pp. 13–14.
50. Gelicen, pp. 13–14. These outbreaks of superstition among the guards make nonsense of the condescending air with which the Russians regarded the Chinese fear that locomotives ran on human grease. Kazarkin later served as Harbin's first chief of police. For a while I was not sure what the Russian original of the Chinese phoneticization was until I read in Nilus, *Istoricheskii*, p. 538, that the Ural Cossack Kazarkin, who "by the will of the fates" became *politseimeister*, had been wounded in the right hand in 1900. That enabled me to match them. Not everyone is so fortunate in the search for corroboration. Tang, p. 92, has poor, underpaid General Diterikhs down as "General Gidilikhs."
51. Bushnell, p. 14; Gelicen, pp. 15–16; Nilus, *Istoricheskii*, pp. 507, 521. According to Fuller, p. 15, many men also "fled to better paying posts in the Frontier Guard, the Gendarmes, or the Ministry of the Interior."
52. *Kitaiskaia*, pp. 26–27, 99–100; Gelicen, pp. 19–20. Various sources give the Guandong troop strength as 12,500 in the Port Arthur garrison in late 1898 (Quested, *"Matey" Imperialists*, p. 36, citing MAE, 165: Dec. 9, 1898); 12,000 in that garrison in May 1900 (Romanov, p. 178); and 13,500 in the Guandong leasehold (Gelicen, p. 11).
53. This bloody, xenophobic, anti-Christian secret-society uprising, which eventually garnered the support of the Qing Court, delayed and derailed many projects throughout North China in the summer of 1900. For further information, see Esherick; and Purcell.
54. Quested and Tsuji, pp. 476–77, 486. It has been claimed that the Guandong authorities took advantage of Iugovich's ignorance of military matters to "advise" him to call for help. But this claim must be treated with caution. The source is Glinskii, a Witte apologist. Blaming the army for all the aggressions that culminated in the Russo-Japanese War is a stock argument in Witte's memoirs and the works of publicists under his sway.
55. Lensen, *Russo-Chinese War*, p. 136.
56. RGIA 1273: 1, 267, p. 56; Lensen, *Russo-Chinese War*, pp. 136–37, 145–51. Approximately 3,000 CER employees were formed into a supplementary militia. During the retreat from Mukden, the CER engineer Verkhovskii and an army lieutenant named Valevskii argued over the correct course of action. The group split up, and Verkhovskii ended up with his head stuck on a stake. Lensen, *Russo-Chinese War*, pp. 49–54. At the local level, interministerial rivalry could have a dramatic impact. Chang Shun's handling of the Boxers is his own description as communicated to E. V. Daniel, the head of the CER's Dept. of Chinese Relations. Chang also claimed that Cheng Xun, the officially appointed leader of the Boxer movement in Jilin, betrayed his subordinates to him. RGIA 1273: 1, 267, pp. 60ff.
57. Romanov, p. 192. Romanov gives only a synopsis (pp. 191–93). The full text can be found in GARF 818: 1, 69.
58. RGIA 323: 1, 1243, p. 4.
59. Romanov, p. 193; Quested, *"Matey" Imperialists*, p. 99.

60. RGIA 1273: 1, 268, pp. 150, 258; *Obshchestvo KVZhD* (1903), p. 55.
61. RGIA 1273: 1, 268, p. 150; Glinskii, pp. 217–19; Kuropatkin, "Dnevnik," p. 60; letter from Ambassador Bompard, Sept. 10, 1903, in MAE, vol. 168.
62. Romanov, p. 429.
63. *Kharbinskaia starina*, p. 77; Lensen, *Russo-Chinese War*, p. 157; RGIA 1273: 1, 268, p. 3; RGIA 560: 28, 244, pp. 1–2.
64. RGIA 323: 1, 1243, pp. 1, 11, 13, 44–45.
65. Iugovich's extensive reports on the Boxer devastation are in RGIA 1273: 1, 267. The write-off total is on p. 12.
66. Romanov, pp. 260, 266, 448–49.
67. Nilus ms, "Deiatel'nost' tserkovnogo otdela upravleniia KVZhD," p. 5; Romanov, p. 287; Nish, p. 147.
68. Japanese consul Segawa, Niuzhuang, to Foreign Minister Komura, Aug. 2, 1902, no. 811, app. 3, in NGB, 1903, 1: 827.
69. Kuropatkin, "Dnevnik," pp. 60, 83. McDonald's first chapter (p. 9) is titled "The Witte Kingdom in the Far East."
70. Ibid., pp. 23, 31. Malozemoff and Romanov, both relying on Kuropatkin's diary entry for April 23, 1903, argue that Witte and Foreign Minister Lamsdorff had already abandoned their position on the evacuation, but this is hard to reconcile with their later memorandums (July) in favor of honoring the letter, if not the spirit, of the withdrawal convention. Possibly, Kuropatkin's reference is to Witte's agreement to allow troops to evacuate into the CER right-of-way. Exactly what their status would be had yet to be discussed. Romanov, pp. 294, 304.
71. RGIA 560: 28, 138, p. 23.
72. Kuropatkin, "Dnevnik," p. 41; RGIA 1273: 1, 269, p. 316. As hybrid organizations, railway battalions throughout Siberia and the Far East not only bound railroad officials and military officers contentiously together in the fulfillment of their duties, but also, in the heat of the 1905 revolution, served as a social catalyst uniting railroad workers and homesick soldiers into mutiny and strikes, Siberia's first glimmer of Soviet power. For more on this point, see Wolff, "Between War and Revolution."
73. RGIA 560: 28, 244, pp. 22, 62; 560: 28, 280, pp. 66–68.
74. Romanov, pp. 256, 294, 459, 464; MAE, 166: 159–60.
75. Romanov, p. 464. Lamsdorff's conversation with the Tsar is based on Kuropatkin, "Dnevnik," p. 85. Alekseev, concerned that the Chinese might not take his plenipotentiary powers seriously enough, requested that the Beijing embassy find him an appropriate title in Chinese. Given three choices, he rejected those modeled on Chinese officialdom and the Chinese translation for the British viceroy of India, in favor of the literal rendition of "Regent, Namestnik Ego Imperatorskogo Velichestva Gosudaria vserossiiskogo na Dal'nem Vostoke" as "Daeguo dahuangdi qinming liushou yuandong dachen." The Sept. 18, 1903, memorandum on the choice of title is in GARF 818: 1, 60. The Japanese ambassador to China reported that the Chinese government did not in fact know what to make of the appointment but looked on it with "concern and alarm." See NGB, 1903, 1: 336.
76. Malozemoff, p. 224; Kuropatkin, "Dnevnik," pp. 76, 80, 85, 87.

77. Ambassador Kurino, Beijing, to Foreign Minister Komura, Oct. 7, 1903, no. 337, in NGB, 1903, 1: 399; Malozemoff, p. 242.

78. Ambassador Honno, Paris, to Foreign Minister Komura, Jan. 8, 1903, no. 769, in NGB, 1903, 1: 778–88; Ambassador Kurino, Petersburg, to Komura, Sept. 12, 1903, no. 775, ibid., pp. 793–96; Kurino to Komura, Aug. 20, 1903, no. 13, ibid., p. 15 (quote). In the embassy's reports on pp. 817–18, Bezobrazov is made out to be more bellicose than Alekseev.

79. Ambassador Kurino, Petersburg, to Komura, Sept. 12, 1903, no. 775, ibid., p. 796; Ambassador Uchida, Beijing, to Foreign Minister Komura, Sept. 9, 1903, no. 197, ibid., p. 358; Nish, p. 149, citing Japanese difficulties with the viceroyalty diplomat G. A. Planson. Kurino believed that time was also working against Japan's edge in naval power. In his report of Sept. 12, he noted that by Aug. 7, the Japanese advantage in tonnage had shrunk to a ratio of 4: 3. Malozemoff, pp. 239–40, describes the convoluted diplomatic channel as "the result of the creation of the viceroyalty."

80. Ambassador Uchida, Beijing, to Foreign Minister Komura, Sept. 9, 1903, no. 198, in NGB, 1903, 1: 359. The Japanese consul at Niuzhuang reported war rumors in Harbin on Oct. 10, 1903.

81. RGIA 323: 1, 1357, pp. 13–14, 27.

82. Ambassador Uchida, Beijing, to Foreign Minister Komura, Nov. 2, 1903, no. 361, in NGB, 1903, 1: 420.

83. RGIA 323: 1, 1357, pp. 43–44.

84. GARF 818: 1, 64, pp. 1–2, 5. The jiangjun's attempt to play on Russian interministerial rivalries, reported in Khorvat, "Memoirs," chap. 4, p. 8, is a classic example of Chinese "barbarian management" (*yiyizhiyi*). For further information on military commissars in the period 1900–1903, see Quested, *"Matey" Imperialists*, pp. 55, 69–88; and Malozemoff, p. 224.

85. The Japanese had by this time presciently prepared guidelines to cover a rupture in negotiations. See cabinet decision of Dec. 30, 1903, no. 50, in NGB, 1903, 1: 41–45.

CHAPTER THREE

EPIGRAPH: "Sinim" may refer to China, since China in Hebrew is "Sin" and its general direction from Israel is south and east. Or it may refer to an area near Sinai.

1. Colonization was the second-most-important activity of the Siberian Railway Committee, after railway construction. It consumed over 80% of the funds allotted for "auxiliary enterprises." See Sabler and Sosnovskii, App. table 2.

2. Frankel, pp. 338–41.

3. Nilus ms, "Russkie konsul'stva," p. 15.

4. RGIA 560: 28, 164, p. 8. After a series of clashes with the tsarist government, primarily over military service, 7,500 members of the "Large Party" left for Canada in 1898–99. For more information on fin-de-siècle Dukhoboria, see Klibanov, pp. 125–40. Earlier in the 19th century, various sectarians had flowed into Odessa in search of frontier freedoms. Herlihy, pp. 25–26.

5. RGIA 560: 28, 164, pp. 1–7. CER diplomatic bureaus (*jiaosheju*), located in Harbin, were created for all three Manchurian provinces. The first agreement was with Jilin in late May 1899. These mixed Russo-Chinese commissions had been organized by Iugovich to prevent excessively careful Chinese local officials from referring all matters to Beijing, thereby hampering completion of railway construction. Instead "all cases that directly or indirectly [touched] the interests of the CER and also the interests of contractors of every sort of labor and of artisans" would be decided by the provincial bureaus. These institutions could also be interpreted as a substitution for Russia's Foreign Ministry personnel and did indeed lose most of their importance after 1907, when Russian consulates opened in Manchuria; I know of no incident in northern Manchuria in early 1899. However, there were several bloody moments in the south following the Russian arrival at Port Arthur. The worst involved Russian soldiers firing into a crowd at Piziwo in February. See Quested, "Local Sino-Russian Political Relations," p. 130.

6. Gunji Yoshio, the CER expert in the Harbin office of the South Manchurian Railway Research Bureau, disagrees with my contention that there was no concerted colonization planning before the Boxer Rebellion. Working with CER archives inherited after the sale of the CER to Manzhouguo, Gunji, pp. 80–81, states that various "preparatory plans" existed, the first of which called for the settlement of reservists in the belt. He adds that no attempt was made to hide this matter, and it appeared in the newspapers. Unfortunately, the only example he gives, cited as "Manchuria Colonization Plan for Russians" (Rokokujin niyoru manshu shokumin keikaku), is undated. Gunji estimates early or mid-1900, which might or might not be post-Boxer. Moreover, the fact that he does not even describe the contents, let alone provide copious details and quotes as he tends to do in such cases, suggests that he never actually saw that document. Further doubts regarding Gunji's pre-Boxer claims are created by the contradiction between the blatant settlement intentions that Gunji suggests and the generally conciliatory tone of Russian Far Eastern policy from 1898 until 1900. Gunji's first concrete example of the colonization policy-making process is the December 1900 Harbin conference. This is also my first instance on the *local* level. Without access to Petersburg materials, Gunji was at a disadvantage in trying to elucidate the central-local dialectic that so laboriously generated policy. It is also possible that his materials were less than complete because of a fire in 1905 that gutted the CER administration building. This caveat aside, Gunji's work is extremely important, providing as it does unique, well-documented access to materials whose fate is unknown.

7. MAE, 166: 26. Kuropatkin also spoke out "energetically" against missionaries, from which one might infer a lack of interest in a Russian cultural mission in the East.

8. Grodekov's report and the responses to it in Petersburg and Harbin discussed in the following paragraphs are based on RGIA 560: 28, 867, pp. 1–9.

9. I have not been able to discover any direct link between Grodekov's suggestion of, and Witte's 1899 flirtation with the idea of, Dukhobor settlement. Certainly, there is no reason why Grodekov's knowledge of the important role that exiled sectarians had played in settling Siberia should not have led him to this idea independently. The only semantic link between Witte's *spravka* and Grodekov's

otchet is the characterization of the Dukhobors as *stoikii* ("steadfast"). The Dukhobors' destination, the Canadian transcontinental railway, may also have sparked the thought of analogous applications, since the Trans-Siberian was often compared to the long, cold Canadian trunkline.

10. Romanov, pp. 258, 447.
11. Romanov, pp. 257–59. Romanov, p. 287, believes that Iugovich's real estate "idea" was the germ of Witte's later colonization plans. The land amount is from RGIA 1273: 1, 268, p. 20.
12. RGIA 560: 28, 867, pp. 84–86.
13. Grodekov stated that this information came from Chinese officials.
14. Art. 2 of the CER construction contract divided the purchase of necessary lands into two categories. Chinese state lands were to be transferred to the CER gratis. Private property would be sold at "current prices." Nilus ms, "Lands and Land Administration," Annex 1.
15. On Dukhovskoi, see "Pervye shagi russkogo imperializma," pp. 88–89. On Bogdanov, see RGIA 560: 28, 867, p. 164; and Gunji, p. 82.
16. Iugovich had expressed similar pessimism to an American visitor, Sen. Albert Beveridge, in the summer of 1901. Beveridge left a flattering description of the chief engineer, marred only by the unfortunate misspelling of his subject's name: "Engineer-in-Chief Tugovitch is, perhaps, sixty years of age, of powerful physical frame, face glowing with intelligence, an eye dull in lustre but keen in suggestions of quick mentality, . . . a planner of empire, a moulder of the future, a suggester of material schemes for the seizure of power and opportunity by the Russian government." *Russian Advance*, pp. 53–54.
17. RGIA 560: 28, 867, pp. 84–94. This fear of Chinese "elemental" (*stikhiinyi*) colonization had motivated the inclusion of a prohibition against settlement near the right-of-way in Russian ambassador to China Lessar's wish-list of additional conditions for Russian withdrawal. It was not included in the final text presented to and rejected by Beijing in April 1902. GARF 818: 1, 47, p. 12.
18. RGIA 560: 28, 867, pp. 73–77; Gunji, pp. 82–85; GARF 818: 1, 49, p. 6.
19. RGIA 560: 28, 867, p. 146. Manakin later became military governor of the Maritime district (1911–14). Stephan, pp. 67–68 and appendix C.
20. Quested, *"Matey" Imperialists*, p. 103 (apparently based on British Foreign Office intelligence), implies that the sectarian option was Pleve's idea. Manakin's words indicate that he was under the same impression. But they are both mistaken. The idea originated with either Grodekov or Witte. It was simply that Pleve's strong backing transferred the Dukhobor plan's apparent "affiliation" to the Interior Ministry. (At a guess, I favor Grodekov, who would certainly have been aware that sectarians, particularly Dukhobors and Molokans, had been an important element in the agricultural colonization of the middle Amur.) The results of the February/March 1903 joint conference testify to Pleve's active support, as does the fact that, in much the same spirit, he "embraced emigration" under Zionist auspices. But Pleve's views on Siberian migration in general suggest that, for him, the needs of European Russia outweighed those of Siberian development. See Rogger, *Jewish Policies*, pp. 80–83; and Treadgold, p. 128.
21. Witte's report is cited in Glinskii, pp. 190–242. See especially pp. 220 and

222–24 for his claims regarding land acquisition and colonization. Attacks on Witte's veracity date back to his ministerial colleagues' memoirs and diaries. In the Soviet and post-Soviet periods, the well-documented vitriolic attacks in B. A. Romanov's *Russia in Manchuria* have spawned a tradition of Witte bashing centered in the Academy of Science's Institute of History in Leningrad. For example, see Ananich and Ganelin. But debunking Witte's self-serving *Memoirs* does not detract from his fundamental importance in the history of this period.

22. "Pervye shagi russkogo imperializma," pp. 115, 118.

23. My discussion of the February 1903 joint conference is based on Gunji, pp. 85–91 (which includes the complete final project in Japanese translation); RGIA 1273: 1, 269, pp. 317–18; and Nilus, *Istoricheskii*, p. 540.

24. "Obshchii obzor," p. 5; RGIA 1273: 1, 269, p. 319; *Kitaiskaia*, p. 199.

25. RGIA 1273: 1, 269, pp. 318–19.

26. RGIA 560: 28, 164, pp. 194–204.

27. Ibid., pp. 221, 242. A sensationalist article appeared in 1930 under the title "Soldier Cantonments in Yellow Russia." Although it is clear from the contents that the author had access to the materials from the CER archive that Nilus collected for his 1923 book, the general context of the colonization plan is misconstrued. See Skvirskii, "Soldatskie slobodki v zheltorossii."

28. RGIA 560: 28, 165, p. 190; RGIA 1273: 1, 269, pp. 319–20; Gunji, p. 82. Exactly what caused the delay Chichagov complains of is unclear. Civil-military rivalry is one possibility. The August 1903 arrival of the Transamur Railway Battalion, which was then settled at Handaohezi, Liaoyang, and Harbin, three of the four sites that had previously been designated for the soldier colonies, is another. And the "normal" sluggishness of the Russian bureaucracy cannot be excluded. The settlements were built in late 1903 and came in very handy after war broke out. Freiherr von Tettau, the German military observer with the Russian army, who arrived in Manchuria in mid-1904, praised the "new city" Buchatu (Bohedu) with its numerous houses, churches, hospitals, and barracks. He was especially impressed with the thousand-man mess hall used for feeding whole trainloads of soldiers in transit to the front. Tettau, 1: 38.

29. The one-day census of May 1903 was the first in Harbin. The original data were destroyed in 1905 by a series of fires that gutted the CER administration building. Fragmentary statistics can be found in *Spravochnaia knizhka Kharbina*, pp. 6–7. Since 7,500 Russian men were employed by the CER in Harbin in 1902 (5,500 on the railroad and 2,000 as guards), I am assuming that the accelerating urgency of the task would mean an increase in 1903. Therefore, at least three-quarters of the male inhabitants were working for the railroad. RGIA 1273: 1, 272, p. 27. Though Bakich, "Russian City," pp. 141–42, is inclined to believe there was another census in October, based on a 1904 *National Geographic* article written by Henry Miller, the U.S. consul at Niuzhuang, the lack of an exact date and the round numbers cited (40,000 Chinese, 20,000 Russians) do not inspire confidence. In Russian materials, I found numerous references to the May census but no mention of one in October.

30. Tettau, 2: 383; Brooke, p. 10.

31. Quested, *"Matey" Imperialists*, p. 143.

32. Ibid., p. 221.

33. Renewed faith in Russian Harbin can be traced by the sell-off of real estate. Whereas 164, 189, and 185 parcels changed hands in 1904, 1905, and 1906, respectively, the pace slowed to 138 in 1907 and 109 in 1908. RGIA 560: 28, 167, p. 40.

34. *Stat. op.*, pp. 63–64. On Japanese prostitution in Harbin, see Quested, *"Matey" Imperialists*, pp. 101, 275; and Sanbo honbu, pp. 29–31. For a more general picture covering the Kyushu origins of the *tairiku joshigun*, see Hara, *Shiberia shuppei*, pp. 8–12. Imamura Shohei's film "Zegen" can also be recommended as an introduction to this topic.

35. Glinskii, pp. 221–22; *Stat. op.*, p. 60. Zheng Changchun, p. 139, gives the Chinese names and the present locations of the sections of Russian Harbin mentioned in this chapter. If neighboring Fujiadian (which was not part of the Harbin municipal area) is included, Chinese accounted for slightly more than half the population of Greater Harbin.

36. Jin Shuangping, p. 124; *Stat. op.*, pp. 55, 4; *Spravochnaia knizhka Kharbina*, p. 7.

37. *Stat. op.*, pp. 8, 55, 57; *Chumnye epidemii*, table 5b. The last work was edited by F. A. Iasenskii, the CER's head doctor during the plague epidemic of 1910–11; the results of the 1911 population survey can be found in the appendixes. In fact, only 5% of the land in New Town was privately held by Russians, softening some of the impact of the Chinese figure. The CER held on to the balance, 40% of which was still undeveloped. The landholding data are from FO371, carton 845, f. 214, p. 227.

38. *Stat. op.*, pp. 55–56; FO371, carton 845, f. 214, p. 228; *Chumnye epidemii*, tables 5b (professions) and 3 (street-by-street racial breakdown). 6,299 (59.7%) of the 10,548 Chinese in Pristan in the 1911 survey (table 8) lived inside the rectangle formed by Kitaiskaia, Vodoprovodnaia, Politseiskaia, and Diagonal'naia streets. A substantial number of others lived on the seven streets that crossed through this Chinese "ghetto." To calculate the ghetto population of three of the seven (Mostavaia, Birzhevaia, and Kommercheskaia), I averaged the number of Chinese living in the streets immediately to the north and south to obtain an approximate population for the relevant section. Thus, for Birzhevaia, I used an average of Bazarnaia and Iaponskaia. For another, Skvoznaia, I used the figure for Shkol'naia, since the two streets are parallel, adjacent, and of equal length within the "ghetto." These four approximations added 1,081 Chinese, bringing the percentage to exactly 70%. Failing any appropriate geographic analogy for the other three streets—Politseiskaia, Polevaia, and Zavodskaia—I decided to err on the side of statistical safety and simply leave them out. Their total Chinese resident population was 915. At least, several hundred Chinese must have lived in the "ghetto," raising the final percentage to "over 70%."

39. The density figures for Harbin are from *Stat. op.*, pp. 3, 5, 7; those for Petersburg are from Bater, pp. 318–21. In 1910, according to Bater, the average building in the Imperial capital contained 15 apartments. In a compactly built area, this suggests an average of three to five stories.

40. Soldatov, "Smertnost' naseleniia," pp. 26–27.

41. *Chumnye epidemii*, pp. 4, 257; Quested, *"Matey" Imperialists*, p. 199. A Chinese source awards all credit for the suppression of the plague to Dr. Liande Wu. See

Si Yuanyi, pp. 151–54. For a more balanced account, relying heavily on American diplomatic correspondence and emphasizing the international aspects of the fight against the plague, see Carl Nathan.

42. See diagram in photo section adapted from *Chumnye epidemii*.

43. *Stat. op.*, p. 1; *Chumnye epidemii*, pp. 330–31; Soldatov, *K perepisi*, p. 20.

44. Though the counts are not complete enough for a seasonal analysis of traffic flow, partial data indicate about a 30% drop in the winter months. Maximum figures show almost 73,000 daily "crossings." Soldatov, "Smertnost' naseleniia," inside cover.

45. *Stat. op.*, pp. 37, 78, 97. For the best information on the dating of the placename Haerbin, see Ji Fenghui "Heilongjiang yutu," pp. 142–43. In this article, Ji discusses a reference to Haerbin he found in a Heilongjiang yamen document of 1862 (Tongzhi 1). Thus the fishing village Haerbin predated Russian Harbin by at least 35 years.

46. G. *Kharbin*, 2: table 15 (Harbin births), table 21 (place of origin—the survey did not include enlisted men and those living in dormitories); Soldatov, "Smertnost' naseleniia," p. 24.

47. *Stat. op.*, pp. 1–2; Soldatov, *K perepisi*, p. 6.

48. The final version of the Harbin questionnaire is in *Stat. op.*, pp. 113–15. For a copy, see Wolff, "To the Harbin Station: City Building in Russian Manchuria, 1898–1914" (Ph.D. dissertation, Univ. of California—Berkeley, 1991), pp. 218–19. A preliminary list of questions to be included is in Soldatov, *K perepisi*, p. 15. The "program" for the 1897 census is given in Litvak, p. 117. Disease and sanitary needs were often the motivation for local censuses in Siberia. For example, in 1895, the city of Barnaul cited cholera and generally unsanitary conditions as grounds for a census. Similarly, though in a preventive vein, Irkutsk undertook a census in 1909 as part of a study for the installation of a sewage system. Tsepliaev and Shipilov, pp. 225–30; Soldatov, *K perepisi*, p. 7.

49. Soldatov, "Smertnost' naseleniia," pp. 75, 77.

50. Ibid., p. 50.

51. Ibid., pp. 79, 88–91; *Stat. op.*, pp. iii–iv; Soldatov, *K perepisi*, pp. 20–21. Whether or not the Chinese questionnaire was actually used during the census is unknown. In any case, the differences between the two texts were minimal.

52. *Encyclopaedia Judaica*, "Irkutsk"; *Stat. op.*, pp. 51, 63.

53. After 1905, there were, of course, representatives of many other Russian Imperial "nationalities," of which at least three had registered *Landsmanschaft*. Aside from the Jews and Poles, I have discovered national organizations for the Georgians and Latvians. Their bylaws, approved on Jan. 12, 1909, and March 8, 1912, respectively, are in RGIA 323: 1, 937, pp. 121, 134. The Ukrainians also had a club, as one would expect in a city not far from the Maritime province's *zelenyi klin* (green, i.e., Ukrainian, wedge). TsGADV 577: 1, 2, p. 126.

54. 1903 protocols 1–2, 5–7, in HLJ 83.1, juan 1.

55. Protocol 8, in HLJ 83.1, juan 489.

56. *Politekhnik*, 10 (1979), p. 142. According to Shillony, pp. 144–45, some 33,000 Russian Jews were under arms in Manchuria by late 1904, including a majority of the medical corps. This dominance of the healing arts in Harbin would continue.

A December 1917 list of doctors employed by the municipality in TsGADV 577: 1, 24, p. 170, shows four of the five to be Jewish, including the leader of the Jewish community at that time, Dr. A. I. Kaufman. The most famous Jewish veteran of the Russo-Japanese War was Joseph Trumpeldor, who, after losing an arm at Port Arthur and spending a year in Japanese internment, was repatriated, decorated, and promoted. A Zionist, he later moved to Palestine to take up the fight there.

57. RGIA 323: 1, 937, pp. 79, 99; HLJ 83.1, juan 6, 184, 487; Dicker, p. 24.

58. RGIA 632: 1, 293, pp. 5, 8, 50 (lists of postwar debts of Jewish community leaders I. S. Fride, B. L. Berkevich, and G. B. Drizin); *Encyclopaedia Judaica*, "Siberia" (1899 ban); Dicker, p. 22 (arrival of servicemen and families; see also Karlinsky, p. 284).

59. *Kharbinskaia starina*, pp. 63–67. Natanson and Co. was initially represented in Harbin by David Grigor'evich Vul'f. Myth or not, Kabalkin was right: soybeans were to dominate the economy of Manchuria until the early 1930's.

60. RGIA 560: 28, 290, pp. 63–75; *Zheleznodorozhnaia zhizn' na Dal'nem Vostoke*, 40 (Oct. 22, 1913): 4–5. Kabalkin opened his oil mill at Old Harbin in 1914. *Iubileinyi sbornik*, p. 190. Even if his petition had been approved by Gondatti, he would probably have lost the factory after the Soviet takeover in 1922. In 1923, Gondatti, in exile at Harbin, was nominated as a candidate for mayor, but the seven Jewish members of the municipal council revenged past slights by voting en bloc to help defeat him. A. I. Kaufman, "Poselok Kharbin," p. 18.

61. Quested, *"Matey" Imperialists*, pp. 267–68. The family orientation of these anecdotes may be indicative of the values held by Harbin Jewry. The statistics below also support this supposition. In all fairness, it should be added that Skidel'skii, in his 1916 will, left all of his employees a month's salary for each year they had been with the firm. Leshko, p. 18.

62. *Otchet birzhevogo komiteta*, pp. ix–xii; *Otchet kharbinskogo obshchestvennogo upravleniia* p. 2. I made most of my determinations of Jewishness by a person's known adherence to the community. Some 10–20% more people were added where an examination of the full name revealed a personal name or patronymic based on an Old Testament figure and a German family name. Although not positive identification, this combination is very strong circumstantial evidence.

63. RGIA 1068: 1, 19, pp. 22–27.

64. Lembergskaia, pp. 298, 317. This source claims only that Nadarov agreed to arm the Jews. Whether he actually did so is another matter. The information on the Jewish self-defense measures is contained in the protocol of the CER Employee Strike Committee's Dec. 9 session. GARF 211: 1, 3/905.

65. *VA*, 9 (May 1911): 186.

66. Gosudarstvennyi arkhiv Irkutskoi 600: 1, 908, p. 5.

67. Rogger, *Jewish Policies*, p. 96; Pinkus, p. 26.

68. G. *Kharbin*, 2: table 28, pp. 300–301; Quested, *"Matey" Imperialists*, p. 267. Nonetheless, emotional ties to the Pale were still strong. Dr. A. I. Kaufman's speech about the Beilis trial on Kol Nidre night (Yom Kippur eve) in 1912 helped to catapult him to the head of the community he would lead until his arrest and internment by Soviet occupation forces in 1945. See *Igud yotsei sin* Archives, box 3, file 25. Kaufman, educated in Bern, died in Israel in 1971. His biography (contained in

the memorial issue of *Biulleten' iguda yotsei sin*, 1972) covers many of the peripaties of Zionism in Eurasia during the 20th century.

69. G. *Kharbin*, table 14, p. 5 (Harbin statistics); *Stat. op.*, p. 113 (question 13: "Na kakom iazyke vy obychno razgovarivaete v sem'e?"); Pinkus, p. 36 (1897 Yiddish figure). The most telling evidence of the trend toward Russian in Harbin is the fact that children in the 9–17 age group were 97.1% literate in the language. G. *Kharbin*, 2: table 24, p. 246. The use of the *ivrit beivrit* (Hebrew-in-Hebrew) teaching method in the Jewish elementary school opened in 1907 suggests underlying Zionist sympathies on the part of the Jewish mainstream. RGIA 323: 1, 937, p. 79.

70. *Stat. op.*, p. 54; Soldatov, "Smertnost' naseleniia," p. 25.

71. *Stat. op.*, pp. 3, 56; *Otchet kharbinskogo obshchestvennogo upravleniia*, pp. 12–14.

72. The mortality statistics in Table 3 suggest that between 1911 and 1913 the Jewish female population of Harbin nearly doubled. This growth can be ascribed to the arrival of wives and families to join the men who had gone ahead to establish themselves and to an influx of women who, hearing of the shortage of females, migrated to Harbin in search of husbands. Interviews with former kharbintsy show that both phenomena existed, although there is no way to measure what part each played.

73. The community's bylaws are in RGIA 323: 1, 937, pp. 100–103.

74. Romanov, pp. 273–74.

75. Gosudarstvennyi arkhiv Irkutskoi 245: 1, 252, p. 45; RGIA 560: 28, 224, pp. 90–91, 106; Quested, *"Matey" Imperialists*, p. 266; Rogger, *Jewish Policies*, p. 86. It is Quested who states that the CER did not hire Jews. Her source is not clear from fn. 7 on p. 364, but there is other evidence to suggest that both Jews and Poles were pushed out of nationalized railroad companies. Since the CER was a semi-state enterprise, it seems likely that hiring practices might have followed this precedent. There does not seem to have been any legal basis for these actions. At least, the closest student of railroad labor, Henry Reichman, makes no mention of such a law in his book. See also Westwood, p. 162. By 1915, however, the situation had changed, as can be seen in the CER's publication *Spravochnaia khizhka po lichnomy sostavu sluzhashchikh KVZhD na 1-e Ianvaria 1915 goda*, pp. 131–35, 168–71, 204, 218 and passim, where employees' professed religions are listed.

76. Quested, *"Matey" Imperialists*, p. 269; RGIA 560: 28, 165, p. 312; RGIA 323: 1, 977, pp. 21–24; *Otchet kharbinskogo obshchestvennogo upravleniia*, p. 3. In addition to Witte's desires, Khorvat may have based his policies on a higher authority, active even after Witte's fall. In 1902, before his first visit to the CER, Khorvat was granted an Imperial audience at which he asked Nikolai if he "should encourage Russian immigration into the leased territory of the railway and particularly into the interior of Manchuria." According to Khorvat, the Tsar replied that "the latter was absolutely undesirable." This could well be taken as an endorsement of the urban over the agricultural variant. Khorvat, "Memoirs," chap. 1, p. 6.

77. Von Laue, pp. 239–40, 252–53.

78. Romanov, pp. 318–21; RGIA 1237: 1, 1.

79. A thorough discussion of ministerial views on Jews can be found in Hans Roggers's essay "Russian Ministers and the Jewish Question" in *Jewish Policies*. The relevant passages on Witte and Kokovtsov are on pp. 84–89 and 91–93, respectively.

But there is nothing in their statements as important figures in the central government to suggest that they would take up a pro-Jewish stance in Harbin (though Hamm, *Kiev*, p. 133, credits Kokovtsov with preventing a pogrom in the wake of the Beilis acquittal). Deductions from central policy to local implementation can be misleading.

80. For example, on Nov. 9, 1906, the Interior Ministry queried Kokovtsov's Ministry of Finance on the procedures for opening a Jewish charitable society in Harbin. The very short reply said that the request should go directly to the CER manager, General Khorvat. RGIA 323: 1, 936, p. 62. Witte also discouraged the discussion of local Jewish questions in central forums, possibly with similar motivation. See Rogger, *Jewish Policies*, pp. 78–79.

81. The reason why all these attacks on CER heterodoxy came at this time was the "Lepeshinskii case," in progress throughout 1910, although only decided against the CER and the Ministry of Finance in November. This victory bolstered the hopes of men within the Interior Ministry that they might further roll back the Finance Ministry's prerogatives in Manchuria. We will return to a full exposition of the Lepeshinskii case in Chap. 4. It should also be noted that the question of international competition central to Kokovtsov's defense was tied to the ongoing formation and implementation of elected municipal government with foreign participation at Harbin.

82. RGIA 323: 1, 937, pp. 42, 47 (quote), 153–57 (society's bylaws). I choose to discuss the Society of Voters in this context, though it could just as appropriately be discussed in connection with Harbin's emerging politics (the subject of Chap. 4), since the organization was meant to strengthen Russian participation in the municipal council. The "Voters" set of bylaws is followed immediately in the archives by the municipal bylaws, where suffrage was open to all who could meet the property requirement regardless of "citizenship, nationality, caste, or religion" (pp. 158ff).

83. I found copies of Kurlov's letter in the archives of both ministries. It is clear from the Interior file that a September denunciation by the so-called Union of the Russian People (Soiuz russkogo naroda) had put the police on the scent of Polish sympathies within the CER. The anonymous attack was on a certain Oksakovskaia, whose secondary school, with 500 students and official accreditation, had made her, according to General Afanas'ev, "an educational pioneer" in Manchuria. For a while, she had rented the Polish Association space for its meetings. Kurlov saw this connection, although secondary in the denunciation, as his main chance. It is interesting to note that an educational institution was also what brought Interior to focus on the Harbin Jewish community. The Kurlov letter is in RGIA 323: 1, 937, pp. 50–52; and GARF 102: 119, 281, chast' 5, pp. 4–6. For the Afanas'ev quote and more information on Oksakovskaia, see the same GARF file, pp. 7–8.

84. RGIA 323: 1, 937, pp. 60–61.

85. See, for example, Rogger, *Russia*, p. 182; and Starr.

86. RGIA 323: 1, 937, pp. 79–80. *Rassvet* had a very extensive network for collecting and distributing information. By 1914, it had 665 subscribers in Siberia, including 64 in Harbin. Slutskiï, pp. 251–54. I thank Takao Chizuko for bringing this source to my attention.

87. RGIA 323: 1, 937, pp. 66–68 (internal memorandum), 82–83 (letter to Stolypin).
88. RGIA 323: 1, 937, pp. 84, 112; GARF 102: 119, 281, chast' 5, p. 25.
89. Macey, chaps. 2–4.
90. Glinskii, pp. 197–203.
91. Macey, pp. 56–62, 68.
92. Treadgold, pp. 128–29; A. A. Kaufman, *Pereselenie*, pp. 132–50.
93. Treadgold, p. 128.
94. Kabuzan, p. 153; *Aziatskaia Rossiia*, 1: 87. For example, in the period 1897–1910, the population of Siberia and the Far East increased 57%. Urban areas grew 125%.
95. Kabuzan, pp. 137, 205.
96. Macey, pp. 8 (quote), 62–63; Yaney, pp. 207, 225–26; *Kitaiskaia*, p. 199.
97. Yaney, pp. 5, 205, 215.
98. Von Laue, p. 78. Translation Von Laue's.
99. Macey, p. 245.

CHAPTER FOUR

EPIGRAPHS: *Na voinu*, pp. 109–10; Lembergskaia, pp. 306–7.
 1. Nilus, *Istoricheskii*, pp. 556–57. The consuls were Ia. P. Shishmarev, stationed at Urga; V. M. Uspenskii, in transit from Kuldja to Turfan; and a certain Pokrovskii who does not appear in Lensen's compilation of Russian diplomatic personnel (1968).
 2. Nilus ms, "Russkie konsul'stva v Man'chzhurii," p. 11.
 3. Nilus, *Istoricheskii*, p. 538.
 4. Ibid., pp. 557, 559.
 5. Nilus ms, "Russkie konsul'stva," pp. 2–4; RGIA 565: 7, 29178, pp. 1–20.
 6. The complete Russian text of the ukase is in Nilus, *Istoricheskii*, pp. 562–64. An English translation is in MacMurray, pp. 88–90.
 7. RGIA 323: 1, 481, p. 31; GARF 818: 1, 49, pp. 13–18.
 8. RGIA 1273: 1, 269, p. 264; RGIA 323: 1, 482, pp. 27–42 (fond 323 gives the same caseload for just the first half of 1902, but this seems unlikely to me, especially in comparison to the 1903 and 1904 figures cited below); RGIA 565: 7, 29178, p. 62. The war intervened and the Harbin court was not opened until sometime between 1905 and 1907.
 9. RGIA 323: 1, 482, p. 82.
 10. Nilus, *Istoricheskii*, p. 564;
 11. Sikorskii, pp. 76–77.
 12. Quested, *"Matey" Imperialists*, p. 146; Baring, pp. 34–35. Quested, n. 43, chap. 8, cites Nilus, *Istoricheskii*, p. 555, but she does not mention the Russo-Japanese War period on that page.
 13. See Jin Zonglin on the successes of one Zhang Tingge; and Wu Xuejian, pp. 95–99, on Wu Baixiang.
 14. Nemirovich-Danchenko, pp. 109–10, 118.

15. Quested, *"Matey" Imperialists*, p. 143; AT 7N1520, pp. 1–11, 54. Interestingly, sidings laid in the swamp between Pristan and Fujiadian for storage space helped reshape what had once been only a hunting ground for residents into Harbin's industrial core, the Eighth District (Vos'moi uchastok).

16. *Kharbinskaia starina*, p. 60; AT 7N1517, "Rapport d'ensemble du Général Sylvestre."

17. AT 7N1521, pp. 62–63; Golovachev, p. 135; *Kharbinskaia starina*, p. 59; Brooke, p. 12; Nemirovich-Danchenko, p. 117; Veresaev, p. 64.

18. *Spravochnaia knizhka Kharbina*, pp. 106–17; U.S. War Dept., *Reports*, Part 2: p. 55 cites 30,000 but p. 162 speaks of a "nearly 40,000 patient" capacity for Harbin.

19. Ossendowski, pp. 92–93.

20. AT 7N1517, pp. 10a–11a; AT 7N1520 (Boucé on Harbin fortifications); Nilus, *Istoricheskii*, p. 303; *Politekhnik*, 10 (1979): 66.

21. Nilus, *Istoricheskii*, p. 308; Baring, p. 34; *Kitaiskaia*, p. 227, 261, 275, 279–80; *Politekhnik*, 10 (1979): 66.

22. RGIA 323: 1, 936, p. 42; Nilus ms, "Ocherki byta," pp. 9, 22.

23. *Kitaiskaia*, pp. 272–84; Quested, *"Matey" Imperialists*, p. 146; AT 7N1517, p. 12; Khorvat, "Memoirs," chaps. 3, p. 6, and 5, p. 14. Ossendowski, pp. 118–19, claims that the telegram condemning the army's conduct of the war was provoked by a "passionate arraignment" that he delivered.

24. *Kitaiskaia*, p. 281.

25. RGIA 560: 28, 1009, p. 17; Lembergskaia, pp. 316–17; Pankratova, p. 1090. "Unheard-of proportions" is General Linevich's term.

26. The million figure is from Koniaev, p. 93. Pankratova, p. 1095, places 80,000 of the 600,000 army reserves in Harbin. A 1-to-4 ratio of regulars to reserves is a not unreasonable minimum, especially since Harbin was Rear Headquarters. Hence my total of "over 100,000."

27. Lembergskaia, p. 308.

28. Pankratova, pp. 1084, 1091; Nilus, *Istoricheskii*, p. 338. Nilus says the evacuation began in early October and was delayed for 12 days by the strike. The fact that Linevich had time to send an expedition headed by Colonel Zakharov to Transbaikalia to explore the possibility of reopening the line does indeed suggest a longer delay than four days.

29. Nilus, *Istoricheskii*, p. 339.

30. Ibid., pp. 354–55; Vetoshkin, p. 160.

31. RGIA 323: 1, 886, p. 32, as cited in Andreev, p. 123. The details on Lepechinskii's life are from GARF 102: 119, 281, *chast'* 11, p. 21.

32. The article, "Otkrytoe pis'mo gen. leit. Ivanovu, glavnomy nachal'niku tyla voisk Dal'nego Vostoka," ran in *Dvadtsatyi vek* on May 25, 1906. A clipping is in RGIA 1068: 1, 19, pp. 22–27.

33. Harbin was not granted Duma representation, but in 1917, elections to the Constituent Assembly were held on the CER.

34. Bushnell, pp. 86–87; Pankratova, pp. 1084–1086.

35. Lembergskaia, pp. 306–7, 323; Weressaiew, pp. 350, 352, 363–64 (quote). The CER futilely complained about vandalism and fights with station employees by

soldiers camped out in and around railroad stations. The army simply responded that there was no space available in Harbin for these units.

36. Nilus, *Istoricheskii*, pp. 341, 355–56; RGIA 560: 28, 1009, pp. 1–9, 26–28; Nilus ms. "Pressa," pp. 3–7. In 1906, Rovenskii was sentenced to eight years (eventually reduced to two) of penal servitude for his political activities. Artem'ev, by contrast, was given a warm welcome in Petersburg: he was not only received by the Tsar but recompensed for his Port Arthur losses. More on Rovenskii (alias Serbin) can be found in GARF 533: 1, 318, pp. 1–20.

37. RGIA 1068: 1, 12, pp. 1, 2, 7.

38. GARF 211: 1, 7/905, p. 5. The stillbirth of this telegraph union corroborates Henry Reichman's characterization of the profession as "volatile" and conscious of its own unique "strategic position in communications." *Railwaymen*, p. 58.

39. Vetoshkin, pp. 158–59. Almost all the information about Vetoshkin's (aliases Ivanov and Orlov) activities in Harbin comes from materials he himself wrote or assembled. The underground organization that had ostensibly sent him to Harbin was obliterated by the Rennenkampf punitive expedition. Since Vetoshkin says he was the sole survivor, we are left to take his word for it that he was dispatched to Manchuria on the Siberian Union's orders. In the protocol of the Harbin Worker Congress, which he published in Chita in 1906, he very flatteringly portrays himself as the founder of the Soviet of Workers and Soldiers. His 1929 version of events in *Sibirskie ogni* shows him valiantly waging intraparty war against a group whose elective principles gave off a "Menshevik odor" (*men'shevistskii dushok*; p. 161). By 1955, 50 years after the fact, the 77-year-old memory managed to eliminate almost everything from the earlier version except the fire-breathing Ivanov and the reactionary generals' fear of him. In his contribution to Pankratova, *Revoliutsiia 1905–1907*, the middle of the political spectrum vanishes completely: the Bolsheviks are credited with taking over the CER. We should be wary of Ossendowski's claim that Ivanov was an agent for the tsarist gendarmerie, for in that case, it is hard to imagine Vetoshkin's living through the 1930's to such a ripe old age.

40. Nilus, *Istoricheskii*, pp. 340, 343–45. The torching of the CER administration building provided further identification with events in Russia proper, since the railway administration building at Tomsk had gone up in flames just weeks before, on November 3. The key difference was that hundreds of liberal and left-leaning *intelligenty* had died in the Tomsk fire and the ensuing pogrom. The Harbin fires did not claim any victims.

41. Cited in Poleshchuk, p. 327.

42. Reichman, *Railwaymen*, pp. 262–63; RGIA 1068: 1, 14, p. 22; GARF 211: 1, 3/905, telegram 4330.

43. GARF 211: 1, 3/905, p. 94, telegrams 4178, 4181.

44. Ibid., pp. 94–96, telegrams 263, 3830, 4343; RGIA 1068: 1, 14, p. 21.

45. RGIA 1068: 1, 14, pp. 25–30. Undated and not always identical lists of ESC delegates can be found in RGIA 1068: 1, 13, pp. 9–13. On Ossendowski, see his entry in the *Modern Encyclopedia of Russian and Soviet History*. The bibliography there lists more detailed debunkings of Ossendowski's literary efforts, including Sven Hedin, *Ossendowski und die Wahrheit*; and George Montandon, "Ossendowski, le menteur

sans honneur." Ossendowski was most notorious for his involvement with the Sisson documents that purported to prove the Bolsheviks were German agents. Ossendowski presents his own version of life on the CER and in Harbin during 1905 in *From President to Prison*.

46. GARF 211: 1, d. 3/905, p. 94, telegram 4180; Lembergskaia, p. 300.
47. RGIA 1068: 1, d. 14, pp. 47, 52; Lembergskaia, p. 300.
48. GARF 211: 1, 3/905, p. 95, telegram 4343.
49. Ibid., pp. 91–98.
50. Ibid., pp. 94–96, telegrams 4178, 4344, 115; RGIA 1068: 1, 14, p. 25 (minutes of Nov. 25 ESC session); Vetoshkin, p. 159; Lembergskaia, p. 297.
51. RGIA 1068: 1, 14, pp. 22–23, 43; ibid., 1, 19, p. 22; Lembergskaia, p. 298; Vetoshkin, p. 167; Ossendowski, p. 143.
52. Bushnell, p. 87; Koniaev, pp. 95, 104–5; RGIA 1068: 1, 14, p. 63.
53. Pankratova, p. 1106; Ossendowski, p. 137.
54. RGIA 1068: 1, 19, pp. 22–27.
55. Weressaiew, p. 351.
56. Lembergskaia, p. 299.
57. Ibid., pp. 299–300; GARF 211: 1, 4, p. 64.
58. GARF 211: 1, 3/905, p. 3. In still another version of the speech, Rovenskii quotes Nadarov as saying: "With revolvers in hand and a dagger between my teeth, sparing neither women, nor children, nor the aged, I will make my way [*prolozhu sebe put'*] to Russia." GARF 533: 1, 318. p. 18.
59. RGIA 1068: 1, 17, p. 33.
60. Poleshchuk, p. 327; Lembergskaia, p. 315; Pankratova, pp. 1090, 1098; GARF 533: 1, 318, p. 19 (Rovenskii meeting).
61. Poleshchuk, p. 337; Nilus, *Istoricheskii*, p. 345.
62. GARF 211: 1, 3/905, pp. 40, 58–63; Maksakov, p. 98.
63. Vetoshkin, pp. 167, 173; Maksakov, pp. 112–13.
64. GARF 211: 1, 3/905, pp. 74–78; Vetoshkin, p. 173; Maksakov, p. 113. Makasov, p. 218, quotes Rennenkampf as stating that General Ivanov began the destruction of the strike organizations "at my request and on his own initiative. . . . Clearly, he did not receive any support." This suggests that Linevich may not have known in advance of the January 23 raid. Rennenkampf's plenipotentiary powers may have been enough to persuade Ivanov to take matters into his own hands. The generals' meeting in Harbin before Rennenkampf's departure probably decided the ex-strikers' fate.
65. RGIA 1068: 1, 19, pp. 22–27; Ossendowski, pp. 176–78; Khorvat, "Memoirs," chap. 6, p. 6.
66. Andreev, p. 124; Pankratova, p. 1108.
67. Ossendowski, pp. 198–200.
68. Ibid., pp. 203–4; *Kharbinskaia starina*, p. 61; GARF 533: 1, 318, p. 20; "Otchet o deiatel'nosti Obshchestva," pp. 7–9 (strangely, Ossendowski's patronymic is given here as Martinovich); Nilus ms, "Pressa," p. 10.
69. GARF 533: 1, 173, pp. 15–17.
70. Ibid., pp. 8, 13–20 passim. The escapees were Pavel Iordan and Ivan Klark.

71. GAIO 245: 3, 513, pp. 14–17; ibid., 3, 51, p. 161; TsGADV 577: 1c, 3.
72. GARF 102: 119, 281, *chast.* 11, pp. 32, 71, 74–75 (Kokovtsov-Stolypin correspondence); *Zheleznodorozhnaia zhizn' na Dal'nem Vostoke*, 40 (Oct. 22, 1913): 4 (Denisov visit). The gendarmerie's local chief, Fedorenko, had approved Lepeshinskii's reappointment. Fedorenko later insisted he did not know exactly what position the CER was planning to appoint him to, but he was still reprimanded for "lack of firmness." This probably explains why Fedorenko took the cautious road a year later in recommending that Gospoda Polska be closed without any grounds other than that some "politically unreliable" people were involved. GARF 102: 119, 281, *chast.* 5, p. 14.
73. RGIA 323: 1, 483, p. 133; Shumiatskii, p. 137.
74. GAIO, 245: 3, 963, pp. 5–10.
75. GARF 102: year 1908, *delo* 118, pp. 2–23.
76. Perhaps anticipating this sort of interministerial squall, Khorvat moved to reestablish his antirevolutionary credentials. On May 27, he "discovered" that he at least had the powers necessary to close the Harbin Society of Commercial and Industrial Employees. It seems the general had just noticed that, for quite some time, he had been granting permission to that group and 10 other professional organizations to meet in different rooms of the same building on the same day at the same time. The resulting "picture of a general meeting of the representatives of various societies" reminded him of the Union of Unions and might well represent an "antigovernment" movement. RGIA 323: 1, 936, p. 80.
77. GARF 102: year 1908, *delo* 118, pp. 2–23. A series of radical abuses of Harbin's liberal environment finally forced a crackdown, starting that very year. The embarrassing events consisted of a minor mutiny in the railroad battalion, escapes from the prison, the appearance of an anarchist band specializing in assassination, bombings and expropriations, and, finally, the murder of Ito Hirobumi. In addition to closing down Rovenskii's bookstore, which had served as a front for the Social Revolutionaries after the old man's release from prison, and tightening the checkpoint procedures at the border stations into Manchuria, the Irkutsk gendarmerie began to run a group of provocateurs in Harbin, who quickly put an end to Harbin's reputation as a safe house for illegals on the run. GARF 533: 1, 522, pp. 10–11; GARF 102: 253, 40, pp. 185–86; Wolff, "Between War and Revolution"; Zhukovskii-Zhuk; *Katorga i ssylka*, 4 (1922): 69–79.
78. Shumiatskii, pp. 163–64.
79. Andreev, p. 125.

CHAPTER FIVE

EPIGRAPH: "Godichnyi akt Vostochnogo Instituta 21 oktiabria 1903 goda" in *IVI*, 1903–4, p. 38. The quote is from Director A. M. Pozdneev's final speech to the Institute before returning to St. Petersburg in December 1903 to take up a position on the Council of the Ministry of Public Education.
1. According to *VA*, 2 (1910): 16, for example, military topographers asking for the names of Manchurian villages had often received the answer "Budongde," mean-

ing "I don't understand." This useless information made its way onto the map as "Butunda One," "Butunda Two," etc. This story, which may be apocryphal for I have never seen such a map, can also be found in Ossendowski, p. 11; and Poppe, p. 15.

2. Skachkov, pp. 259, 252. Skachkov's detailed history of Russian sinology was completed posthumously by his student the academician V. S. Miasnikov.

3. Ukhtomskii, *Iz kitaiskikh pisem'*; Malozemoff, p. 224; RGIA 323: 1, 1357, pp. 13–14, 27, 43–44; GARF 818: 1, 64, 1–2, 5. For further information on military commissars in the period 1900–1903, see Quested, *"Matey" Imperialists*, pp. 55, 69–88.

4. RGIA 565: 8, 29365, pp. 12–13.

5. In Beijing, all of these methods were used by all parties, Witte and the CER included; but in this period, such practices were the very core of interstate relations among unequal powers. In Manchuria, the question was one of influence over local elites and a local population in a direction often at odds with Beijing's unenforceable wishes.

6. RGIA 323: 1, 684, p. 67 (*Novoe vremia*, Feb. 25, 1909). The very first issue of *Vestnik Azii*, the organ of the Society of Russian Orientologists, discussed the Toa Dobunkai, the educational institution in Shanghai whose alumni gave the Japanese an advantage in China. For more on the influence of that institution, see Reynolds, *China*; and Reynolds, "Training Young China Hands."

7. *VA*, 1 (1909): 271–72. "Tsushima" refers to the place where, on May 14–15, 1905, the Russian Baltic fleet was routed by the Japanese navy. After that debacle, the Russians felt themselves constrained to negotiate an end to the lost war.

8. *Priamurskie vedomosti*, 1899, no. 304, p. 5.

9. *Spravochnaia knizhka po Vostochnomu Institutu*, pp. 12, 15; *IVI*, 1900–1901, pp. 46–49, 283–86, 1901–2, pp. 284–88, 1909–10, pp. 118–32. Although small doses of French were included in the schedule during the institute's early years, it became an optional "early-bird" course after 1905.

10. RGIA 560: 28, 813, 41; *Spravochnaia knizhka po Vostochnomu Institutu*, pp. 11, ii–iv, lxv–lxxix. Furthermore, as teaching aids for the study of contemporary Far Eastern languages, the institute printed 40 textbooks between 1899 and 1908. Most were original works by its professors; a few were translations from publications in English (Wade, Lay) and Japanese (Korean-study materials). Many were conversation guides, collections of recent official documents, or calligraphic compendiums to be used in conjunction with the "hands-on" training in speech and composition provided by the native-speaking lektor. As such, these texts provided the link between the tasks of professor and lektor, the team whose cooperative efforts were the heart of the practical methodology.

11. "Zapiska o Vostochnom Institute" (probably by Dmitrii Pozdneev), in GPB 590: d. 113, pp. 87–88. The final quote is from Rudakov, *Obshchestvo i-khe-tuan*, p. 68.

12. *Spravochnaia knizhka po Vostochnomu Institutu*, pp. 2, 8; *IVI*, 1900, pp. 110–13; RGIA 565: 8, 29365, p. 80. When Pozdneev's correspondence yielded only one affirmative reply, he turned to the institute's board of guardians, which under Art. 50 was obliged to aid in the organization and funding of *komandirovki*. Since Vladivostok had enthusiastically welcomed the opening of the Far East's first institution of higher education, the board consisted of important government and business

figures. Three of Vladivostok's wealthiest men, M. G. Shevelev, A. V. Dattan, and M. I. Suvorov, stepped in and supplemented the insufficient government allocation of 3,500 rubles. The Russo-Chinese Bank appears to have directly aided Rudakov and his charges as well through its employees Liuss in Port Arthur and Pokotilov in Beijing. It was also, of course, the owner of the CER Steamship Line. For more on the board of guardians, see Fedorkina.

13. *IVI*, 1901, pp. 73-75, 180; 1902, pp. 86, 149-50, 154; 1903, p. 66. In 1903, 37 of the 46 students spent the summer in China, primarily Manchuria (29).

14. "Avtobiografiia prof. Rudakova A. V.," in PGM; GPB 590: *delo* 113, pp. 89-90; *IVI*, 1900, p. 25, 1902, p. 42; Rudakov, p. 76. The "Manchurian archive" was returned to China in the late 1950's and is now divided between the No. One Ming-Qing Archive in Beijing and the Heilongjiang Provincial Archive in Harbin. On the return, see TsKhSD 4: 15, 549, p. 16.

15. *IVI*, 1903, pp. 105, 108-9. In fact, censorship work became so burdensome that foreign lektors "under observation" were drafted into helping out. *Spravochnaia knizhka po Vostochnomu Institutu*, pp. lviii-lix.

16. According to a short, laudatory biography of the Pozdneev brothers, 70 students served as translators, although it is unclear if all of them were civilian students. GPB 590: d. 116, p. 19. The history of officer-students at the Eastern Institute is a separate story in its own right. Some of the complexities are treated in Shkurkin.

17. *IVI*, 1903, pp. 176-79; 1905, pp. 104, 119, 299-300; 1907, p. 5. Spal'vin married Maeda's widow.

18. Pozdneev had taken care to see that "the clarification of the meaning of lamaism" for Mongolia would be among the tasks allotted to the institute by adding that to the founding regulations in 1898. A few years later, in 1901, he applied to the Ministry of Education for the establishment of a chair in Tibetan. The area needed to be studied for purely practical reasons, he argued: to counter aggressive British movements northward from India; to ensure Russian dominance in Mongolian studies (and, by implication, Mongolia); and to fully comprehend the religious impact of lamaism both outside Russian borders and within (Buriats, Tungus, Kalmyks). The Education Ministry referred the matter to Witte, a move that suggests the Finance Ministry's continued dominance of institute affairs. Witte's reply took the form of a categorical no on the ground that the value of Tibetan studies was largely in the academic realm rather than the practical. But it may be that this was something of a pretext to disguise his fear that P. A. Badmaev, a Buriat Mongol, graduate of the Eastern Dept., doctor of Tibetan medicine, royal confidant, and confirmed adventurer, might thereby be brought back into the picture. GBP 608: 1, 1132, p. 14; *Spravochnaia knizhka po Vostochnomu Institutu*, pp. 2, xxxvii; *IVI*, 1902, pp. 34-39, 1903, p. 15. On Badmaev, see Malozemoff, pp. 48-49; and *Modern Encyclopedia of Russian and Soviet History*, 2: 234-36. See also Tsybikov, *Izbrannye trudy*, vol. 1 (a republication of the edited "diary" of his wanderings in Tibet, which first appeared in 1918 as *Buddist-palomnik u sviatyn' tibeta: po dnevnikam vedennym v 1899-1902 gg.*).

19. *IVI*, 1904, pp. 16-18, 1909, pp. 28-32, 47-50. Data on alumni are from *Spravochnaia knizhka po Vostochnomu Institutu*, app. 2, pp. xxii-xxix; and *Otchet za 1909* (Vladivostok, 1910), pp. 28-32. Eight graduates served in Vladivostok. The institute also began to draw an increasing proportion of its students from secondary

schools in Siberia and the Far East. By 1909, their share was 47%. The Vladivostok gimnaziia singlehandedly accounted for 20%. This was a measure of both the institute's reputation in its area of greatest activity and the recovery of St. Petersburg University's Eastern Dept. from its turn-of-the-century doldrums. For more on Russian sinology's roots in Beijing, see the Appendix.

20. *VA*, 1 (1909): 272–77. I have not been able to determine what the "disagreements" in Beijing were about.

21. The information on the society's founding and first years is drawn from *ibid.*; and *VA*, 53 (1925): 413–15. By January 1911, there were 125 members in Harbin. To increase exposure throughout the city, members gave numerous public lectures in the spring of 1909 at schools, clubs, and libraries in both New Town and Pristan.

22. RGIA 323: 5, 134, pp. 10, 42–43, 75, 169–75. It should come as no surprise that Baranov had no formal training in oriental languages.

23. RGIA 560: 28, 370, pp. 1–15.

24. RGIA 23: 8, 20, pp. 4–5.

25. RGIA 560: 28, 1126, pp. 32, 59, 98.

26. RGIA 560: 28, 1126, p. 73 (1911 membership list); "K desiatiletiiu vostochnogo instituta," *VA*, 2 (1909): 5–19.

27. GARF 818: 1, 179, pp. 3, 5, 7. On Arsen'ev's career, see Lensen, *Russian Diplomatic and Consular Officers*, p. 21. The Tsar, in his usually dithering way, wrote this comment on the memorandum: "We will soon have to make a definite decision on this important question. Excellent memo."

28. Stolypin as cited in Merkulov, p. 55; Dobrolovskii, chairman of the SRO, to Venttsel, chairman of CER, Inc., in RGIA 560: 28, 1126. Many still had little faith in Russia's orientological prowess. On Jan. 23, 1909, Ambassador Korostovets in Beijing wrote to Foreign Minister Izvol'skii wondering why St. Petersburg University's Eastern Dept. still produced students with "insignificant . . . knowledge." He did grant that Eastern Institute students were a little better, since they "lived in constant contact with Chinese." RGIA 323: 1, 684, p. 62.

29. RGIA 323: 1, 684, pp. 79–86. Many of these new jobs were in the Telegraph Section, however, and might not have been considered appropriate by graduates of an institute of higher learning.

30. *VA*, 53 (1925): 427, 429, 444–45; RGIA 560: 28, 1126, pp. 12–14; RGIA 323: 1, 937, p. 87.

31. *The Herald* has now become a rarity. The Hoover Institution at Stanford University has a complete run. *VA*, 52 (1924): 469–73, contains an index for all the issues except the last (no. 53, published in 1926). Probably in deference to the sensitivities of Russia's Japanese allies, there were no feature articles on Korea after Japan annexed it in 1910.

32. See Melville H. Watkins, "A Staple Theory of Growth," *Canadian Journal of Economics and Political Science*, 29 (May 1963). On soybeans, see Wolff, "Kitchen Imperialism"; and the Conclusion, below.

33. *VA*, 3 (1910): 88–103. As commercial attaché at the embassy in Urga, Mongolia, from 1913 to 1916, Boloban would have the opportunity to spread his ideas even further. Lensen, *Russian Diplomatic and Consular Officials*, p. 21. In 1917, as the devaluation of the Russian ruble plunged Harbin into economic chaos, Boloban

chaired a meeting that called on Khorvat to seek advice from local experts in Harbin society in order to stave off a crisis. The resolution also called on Khorvat to honor all agreements with the Chinese. The Vasil'ev school's values of social participation and cross-cultural cooperation were principles that were familiar to kharbintsy too.

34. *VA*, 2 (1909): 26–55. Spitsyn's student research paper is listed in the Bibliography.

35. This paragraph and the two that follow are based on RGIA 323: 1, 878, pp. 7, 17, 34, 46–47, 65; RGIA 323: 1, 591, p. 11; RGIA 323: 4, 1304, pp. 95, 113; and *Heilongjiang shengzhi*, p. 19. Despite the *FEP*'s large print runs, I have been unable to find a full set of it anywhere. Partial collections are in Harbin and Shanghai. A list of lead articles published between 1914 and 1919 can be found in RGIA 323: 4, 1304, pp. 123–352. The wartime publication at Fengtian (Mukden) is an even greater rarity. I do not know of any extant copies.

36. Imitating *Shibao*'s success was common among Chinese political newspapers in this period. See Judge, p. 36.

37. RGIA 323: 1, 591, p. 11; RGIA 323: 4, 1304, pp. 2, 95, 113.

38. *Heilongjiang shengzhi*, pp. 19, 20, 27; "Dongchuigongbao," in *Heilongjiang baikequanshu*. The number of Russian intellectuals in Harbin was small, but their Chinese counterparts were even rarer. Yang's wife, one of the few educated women in Harbin, became a teacher at Fujiadian's first public primary school (1912). Her students were initiators of the women's movement in Harbin. Yang's progressiveness can be inferred from his willingness to marry such a "modern" woman. His *zi* ("pen name") was Moxuan. See Kong Fanzhen, p. 13. The role of the treaty port as political asylum has been discussed elsewhere for other Chinese cities. See, Elvin, p. 144.

39. "Dongfang xiaobao" and "Dongchui gongbao," in *Heilongjiang baikequanshu*; *Haerbin baokanshi*, pp. 23–28; *Heilongjiang baokan*, pp. 149–50, 160–62 (protests). In 1908, the editor of Harbin's first Chinese daily, the *Binjiang ribao*, requested government support as the only way to compete with the Russian-subsidized *FEP*. He got it. HLJ 13.1–3.

40. RGIA 323: 1, 880, pp. 17, 15, 32, 37, 51; RGIA 323: 1, 878, pp. 65, 109; RGIA 560: 28. 370, p. 70; *Zheleznodorozhnaia zhizn' na Dal'nem Vostoke*, 46 (Dec. 1913): 11–12. What appears to be a copy of the *Menghuabao* can be found attached to HLJ 21.5, juan 78, a Chinese memorial describing the paper as a *response* to the Russian *Mongolun Sonin Bichik*, which it labeled "transparent villainy" (*Zi Mazhao zhixin, lurujiezhi*). This illustrates nicely the cycle of accelerating competition so visible in the many contested spheres of Manchuria's history. The links between Russian and Chinese involvement in Manchuria and Mongolia are explored in Tang.

41. RGIA 323: 1, 591, pp. 8, 14; RGIA 323: 9, 4987 (Spitsyn's CER personnel file).

42. Already financially independent from the railway, the *FEP* continued in business until the Chinese authorities closed it down in 1924 as part of "rights' recovery." The CER's Russian-language paper was shut down at the same time, all part of redefining the CER as a purely commercial enterprise. Established two weeks after the *FEP* closed, with a similar profile (including coverage of the Russian Far East), the *Binjiang Shibao* (*Binjiang Times*) seems to have picked up most of the liberated subscribers. See *Harbin baokanshi*, p. 21; and "Binjiang shibao" and "Haerbin xinwen," in *Heilongjiang baikequanshu*.

43. The same argument is made in *VA*, 9 (1910): 42-43.
44. Lieven, p. 132, states: "Whereas most of the Russian press was liberal in sympathy, *Novoe vremia* was conservative." Such a political bent may well have made the newspaper anathema to the orientologist descendants of Vasil'ev.
45. Dobrolovskii's article is in *VA*, 1 (1909): 136-88. The following information on him is based on his obituary in *VA*, 48 (1922): 3-5; and his personnel file in RGIA 323: 1, 669.
46. N. M. Iadrintsev, the Siberian regionalist, had also insisted that the first step in helping the indigenous population must be reeducating the Russians. Iadrintsev's cooperation with Vasil'ev on the *Vostochnoe obozrenie* explains this convergence between the opinions of the Vasil'ev school and the Siberian regionalists. On Iadrintsev, see Slezkine, p. 117.
47. On orientological education, see RGIA 323: 1, 684, pp. 87-91, 127, 129-30; TsGADV 577: 1c, 3, pp. 7-8; and *VA*, 53 (1925): 424, 432.
48. On Shkurkin, see *VA*, 1 (1909): 262. Shkurkin's personal archive is in the keeping of his grandson; an extremely useful finding aid has been prepared by Olga Bakich.
49. Davidov, pp. 52, 57.
50. TsGADV 277: 1c, 24, pp. 1, 104-12, 129-30; Dobrolovskii in RGIA 323: 1, 669, p. 1. The employment record of I. N. Verevkin (class of 1907) is another case of the revolving door between Russian- and Chinese-language publishing and pedagogy. Different sources have him serving at *Kharbinskii vestnik* (Davidov, p. vi), *Yuandongbao* (*Haerbin baokanshi*, p. 19), and the CER's Russian-Chinese school in Beijing (RGIA 560: 28, 1126, p. 73), all at about the same time. For all three of these jobs, he would have remained an employee of the CER.

CONCLUSION

1. Malozemoff, pp. 55-67; Marks, pp. 29, 34-44; RGIA 1273: 1, 216, p. 2.
2. Levine, p. 16. Shipments to China and Japan from South Manchuria dated back to the 18th century, but only in 1908 did Mitsui Bussan and Natanson and Co., a Russian-Jewish firm active in Harbin since 1903, pioneer the export of beans to Europe as an alternative seed oil and cattle feed.
3. For example, during the Japanese occupation of Vladivostok as part of the Siberian intervention, all beans moved southward to Dairen. Later, with the revival of Sino-Soviet joint management on the CER, Vladivostok recovered a portion of its prerevolutionary position, although a decade of deterioration had taken a toll on the port facilities. For the Japanese, control of the bean trade not only made its colonies in Northeast China self-supporting, but also provided a new staple source of protein for the home islands. At the level of consumer taste, a vast expansion in bean-based (tofu, soya sauce, misoshiru, etc.) food production and sales addicted Japan to Manchuria and its soybeans. The populations of the three cities mirrored the multiethnicity of the bean trade. In 1913, 40% of Harbin's inhabitants were Russians; Chinese made up nearly all of the rest. In the same period, Vladivostok's ethnic mix was almost exactly the reverse. By 1934, Dairen's Japanese population had reached 39%. The international division of labor that underlay these statistics

provided ample opportunity for economically as well as racially motivated strife, but a host of local councils, native-place associations, and émigré organizations were generally successful in repressing and channeling such tensions.

4. *VA*, 3 (1910): 5-10.
5. Khorvat, "Memoirs," chap. 2, p. 11; Martynov; RGIA 560: 28, 138, p. 34.
6. Tang, pp. 102-3 (ministers' quotes); Price, pp. 62-63.
7. Demchinskii. p. 82.
8. RGIA 821: 150, 409, p. 5. I am grateful to Dan Brower for pointing out this similarity.
9. RGIA 323: 1, 937, pp. 174, 195. Like all long-term residents of China, Khorvat knew that finding different ways to skin a cat was no mere figure of speech there, but he also knew better than to disclose this unpleasant truth to the Baroness.
10. For P. Kh. Shvanebakh, a member of the State Council and the holder of numerous high offices, including assistant minister of Agriculture, the Jews in the Pale were like a nest of fleas: "If one were to uncover it, the fleas would spread out over the whole country, and the peasant population would be . . . surrendered to the bloodsuckers." Cited in Rogger, *Jewish Policies*, p. 111.
11. *VA*, 2 (1909). On Chinese voting rights in the elections for the provincial assemblies (*ziyiju*) and the municipal council, see Brunnert and Hagelstrom, pp. 56-57; and *VA* 3 (1910): 156, respectively.
12. Following Vasil'ev's advice, Russian sinologists portrayed China as capable of carrying the "light of enlightenment" (see Appendix). This symbolic use of China as an Aesopian device for discussing reforms in Russia has been explored for a more recent period by Rozman.
13. Romanov, pp. 89-93 (repurchase rights); GARF 818: 1, 49, p. 10 (Witte quote). For a Chinese account of Russian government and private investment in Manchuria until 1907, see Zhu Xianping, pp. 47-49.
14. RGIA 323: 1, 684, pp. 55-56, 94, 147-49.
15. Stephan, "Far Eastern Conspiracies." The NKVD issued orders to deport all Koreans and arrest kharbintsky on Aug. 29 and Sept. 20, 1937, respectively. For the texts of these orders, see Tsentralnyi gosudarstvennyi arkhiv Sovetskoi Armii (Central State Archive of the Soviet Army) 33879: 1, 115, pp. 1-2; and *Biulleten' igud yotsei sin*, May-June 1994: 36-37.
16. For an example of the competitive convergence of China, Japan, and Russia in Manchuria, see Wolff, "Russia Finds Its Limits," pp. 48-52.

APPENDIX

1. The topic of Russia's "special position" in China would make a good book in its own right. Here are but a few references to show the variety of approaches to that theme: Panskaia, p. 14; Lattimore, *Manchuria*, pp. 244-46; Quested, *"Matey" Imperialists* (the title says it all); Mancall, p. 76; Urufu; and Beveridge, pp. 29-32. The last deserves a quote: "Russian peasant and Chinese working-man and Korean laborer mingle together as though they were all of one race, one blood, one faith, and even of one nationality."

2. Bartold, p. 11.
3. For an analysis of the functions and shortcomings of the mission in its early years, see Widmer.
4. Panskaia, pp. 12, 15.
5. I have calculated a mortality rate for each mission from the list of members and their dates in Skachkov, pp. 358–61. The 7th mission (1781–94) was the most deadly, losing six of its 10 members.
6. Ibid., pp. 127–30. N. Ia. Bichurin's suggestion in 1816 to increase the educational prerequisites for nomination to a mission was probably taken into account in choosing members of the 10th mission. In 1821, however, Bichurin's name was under a cloud, and no direct credit was attributed to him. See ibid., p. 95.
7. Ibid., pp. 181–82, 331.
8. Ibid., pp. 97–101, 123.
9. Bartold, p. 302; Skachkov, pp. 132–42, 190–91, 333. In 1816, Petersburg's Main Pedagogical Institute (after 1819, St. Petersburg University) followed suit by establishing an Arabic-Persian department under the direction of Professor O. I. Senkovskii, the sole Arabist with a mastery of the spoken language. In 1829, he submitted a proposal for the inclusion of Chinese and Manchurian to be taught by Bichurin and S. V. Lipovtsov, a veteran of the 8th mission and the Asiatic Dept. Nothing came of Senkovskii's suggestion. Lipovtsov was the first translator of the King James Bible into Manchu for the English Bible Society.
10. Bartold, p. 305. Although the exact role of M. N. Musin-Pushkin is unclear, his interest in Oriental studies seems to have been a key factor in the development of academic sinology in Russia. As warden (*popechitel'*) of the Kazan Educational District, he oversaw the initiation of Mongolian, Chinese, Sanskrit, and Armenian studies. Afterward, as warden of the St. Petersburg Educational District (1845–56), he was instrumental in the wholesale transfer of the Eastern Dept. to the capital. See "Musin-Pushkin," in Brokkhaus-Efron, 1897 ed.
11. Skachkov, pp. 111, 138, 192–97; Alekseev, p. 160.
12. Skachkov, pp. 204–5.
13. Ibid., p. 227.
14. Vasil'ev's insistence on publishing in Russian led to constant friction with the "German-dominated" Academy of Sciences, which demanded endless editorial revisions. As a result, 10 volumes of his Buddhist studies remain even today "almost ready for publication." Alekseev, pp. 38, 63, 66, 165; Skachkov, pp. 208–9. Bartold, pp. 543–44, writes of the "slavish submission of Russian scholars . . . to their West European colleagues and German priority in fields of knowledge that it seems should first of all be at home (*naiti sebe mesto*) in Russia." Bartold accuses the Russian government of fostering this attitude, citing Interior Minister A. A. Makarov's (1912) statement: "If we need anything scientific, we'll find it in foreign publications."
15. Skachkov, p. 227; Alekseev, pp. 67, 395; Dobrovel'skii, p. 111.
16. Skachkov, pp. 198, 227, 229, 239; Bartold, p. 542; "Vostochnoe Obozrenie," in Brokkhaus-Efron, 1892 ed., 7: 301–2. On "race," see Bartol'd, *Sochineniia*, 9: 626. Malozemoff, p. 42, presents a distorted view of Vasil'ev in order to classify him

with the *vostochniki*. Although recognizing Vasil'ev as a "world-renowned Sinologue," Malozemoff adduces his views on the Far East using excerpts from a speech about the Caucasus and Trans-Caspian.

17. The Imperial ukase ordering the creation of the St. Petersburg Eastern Dept. and the closure of all other departments was issued on Nov. 3, 1854. RGIA 323: 1, 684.

18. Skachkov, pp. 201–4; Alekseev, p. 168. Bichurin's grammar and Vasil'ev's introduction to Chinese characters remained the backbone of Chinese-language studies until the turn of the century. Ismail Abu-Karimov, a Muslim from Northwest China and the lektor at Kazan, eventually moved to Petersburg, where he continued to teach conversational Chinese until his death in 1868. Afterward, as at Kazan, returnees from ecclesiastical missions were brought on staff: I. I. Zakharov (12th mission) taught Manchurian; and K. A. Skachkov (13th) and then D. A. Peshchurov (14th) took over spoken Chinese after Abu-Karimov's death. Vasil'ev would later speak out in favor of Korean, Japanese, and Hindi, but, as with his campaign for Sanskrit and Tibetan, it was to no avail. During his lifetime, only Chinese, Mongolian, and Manchurian were part of the regular program of instruction in the Eastern Dept. More successful were efforts to expand the department's definition of "Chinese area studies." The list of courses grew to include history, literature, religion, geography, and Russo-Chinese relations. Skachkov, pp. 220–21, 224, 226.

19. Others disagree. Bartold, p. 306, for example, argues that Vasil'ev's extreme scientific scepticism prevented a school from forming around him, but Alekseev, p. 64, while wondering how one could possibly transmit an insistence on "self-teaching" and "originality," concurs: "no shkola Vasil'eva—fakt!" I maintain that the fraternal associations and intellectual orientations Vasil'ev encouraged left their mark into the Soviet period.

20. Skachkov, pp. 228 (Pozdneev letter), 236, 238. Over half the Chinese Section's graduates served in the Russian Foreign Ministry; many became consuls in China, but only one (D. D. Pokotilov) rose to the ambassadorial level. In honor of the pater familias's 70th birthday, his students in China raised 6,000 rubles for a scholarship.

21. Skachkov, pp. 231–35, 341; Alekseev, pp. 65, 423. Georgievskii paralleled his teacher's interest in Buddhism with his historical and philosophical study of Confucianism. The practical tendency was reflected in his courses on the contemporary political organization of China and a "pragmatic history of China." Georgievskii's attack on Western European sinology for declaring China a "historical fossil" echoed the views of Vasil'ev and Kovalevskii. But his unfamiliarity with any Eastern language other than Chinese raised doubts about his scholarly breadth.

22. Harcave, pp. 100, 277, 425. Pokotilov's fall from grace, together with the Finance Minister, in 1903 did not prevent his glorious return to public service, in a supporting role at Portsmouth, and then as ambassador to China from 1905 to 1908. Although Lensen, *Russian Diplomatic and Consular Officials*, p. 120, lists Pokotilov's tenure as 1906–7, French diplomatic correspondence clearly shows him in the ambassadorial post in September 1905. (MAE 169: 185). He died in office on Feb. 1, 1908. Nilus, *Istoricheskii*, pp. 34–35. As the report of his death made the rounds in the Foreign Office in London, a flattering collective obituary accumulated in the

margins, including such phrases as "faithful servant," "attractive personality," and "clever financier." See FO371, carton 426, pp. 757–59. Details of Pokotilov's services as head of the Russo-Chinese Bank's Beijing branch can be found in RGIA 632: 1, 8 and 1, 72. See also Quested, *Russo-Chinese Bank*, p. 59. P. M. Romanov was Witte's trusted aide from the late 1880's on, when he served as head of the Dept. of Railway Affairs. He ultimately became director of Witte's "Foreign Ministry" within the General Chancellery of the Finance Ministry.

23. Dmitrii Pozdneev's solid mastery of his specialty, historico-geographic compilations, was reflected in his receipt of three gold medals in the departmental competition—for papers on eastern Turkestan, southeast Mongolia, and the Uigurs. Upon his graduation in 1893, the university sent him abroad for further training at the British Museum and the Bibliothèque Nationale. That resulted in another paper, on the English and French schools of sinology; it was published in the Russian Ministry of Public Education's official organ the following year.

24. Skachkov, pp. 231, 271, 343; "Otchet za 1904," *IVI*, 14: 5–6; *VA*, 3 (1910): 213; Pozdneev, p. i (for intended audience); *Russkaia mysl'*, June 1897: 202–3. Even as Pozdneev was editing his massive work, he was collecting information on the "commercial geography of the Far East" and the teaching of that subject in Russia. Discovering a pedagogical vacuum, he filled the gap by offering a course of the same title at the St. Petersburg Commercial College. In 1897–88, Pozdneev took the marriage of the practical and the academic preached by his teacher Vasil'ev one step further by adding a Chinese history course at St. Petersburg University to his Finance Ministry workload. Pozdneev taught at the university for only one year, before his commitment to Witte and practical tasks took him to China and Manchuria.

25. The need for qualified orientologists in the Russian Far East had been raised as early as 1891, during the Tsar's visit to China. At Hankou, the firm of Tokmakov, Molotkov and Co. had presented him with 10,000 rubles as a donation to the Chinese-Manchurian section of St. Petersburg University's Eastern Dept. Ukhtomskii, *Puteshestvie*, 2: 241. But it was only several years later that Vladivostok began to receive attention. On Nov. 8, 1895, the Ministry of Public Education suggested the conversion of Vladivostok's *progimnaziia* into an "Eastern Institute." The Finance Ministry immediately provided 6,000 rubles for the training of Chinese-language professors, and the Tsar approved the measure on March 10, 1896. Later in 1896, however, the Education Ministry had a change of heart. It now thought that Vladivostok's population growth and social development warranted replacing the six-year progimnaziia with a gimnaziia (eight years of schooling with the right to take university entry exams). The Ministry of Finance, whose prospects in the Far East had just improved, sent back a counterproposal, suggesting that the new Eastern Institute be elevated still further, to become eastern Siberia's first institution of higher education. The Ministry of Public Education demurred, but in the negotiations that followed, the gimnaziia and the Eastern Institute emerged as Siamese twins, sharing a single director and a single building. The gimnaziia opened in 1897, the institute in 1899. Skachkov, pp. 252–53, conflates some of these steps by simply attributing the initiative for "a special lycée for the study of Eastern languages" to the Finance Ministry. The archives are clearer; see RGIA 565: 8, 29365, p. 1. See also "Otchet za 1904," *IVI*, 14: 6; and Dukhovskoi, p. 10.

26. The tenth-anniversary report of the Eastern Institute states that the institute owed its establishment to Witte's initiative. See *VA*, 7 (1911): 79.

27. In his 1896–97 report, the Priamur Governor-General, Dukhovskoi, indicated that though the Eastern Institute had been decided on, it had not yet opened. His mention of a three-year course instead of the four it came to have and other differences confirm that the programmatic changes came out of the 1898 commission.

28. Skachkov, pp. 234–35; Alekseev, p. 268; Bartold, p. 453; "A. M. Pozdneev," in Brokkhaus-Efron, 1898 ed.; *VA*, 2 (1909): 10.

29. RGIA 1273: 1, 266, p. 16; Quested, *"Matey" Imperialists*, p. 31.

30. RGIA 560: 28, 813, pp. 12–16.

31. The true path of pragmatism, however, was open to interpretation. The Priamur governor-general Grodekov, for example, was convinced that since the Chinese Emperor was a Manchu and Russian affairs were centered in Manchuria, Manchurian-language courses should be offered. The Ministry of Finance made clear that its main concern was the CER when it told Dmitrii Pozdneev to seek the advice of Iugovich, "whose relations with the population of Manchuria are at present so widespread that he will be able to decide unerringly the question regarding the practical necessity of the Manchurian language in Manchuria." Iugovich replied that the use of Manchurian was limited to official correspondence "mainly with Russian authorities," and that all "without exception" spoke Chinese. Tifontai (mentioned in Chap. 1) added that all of his firm's business was conducted in Chinese. Nonetheless, Grodekov's viewpoint, which meant an additional chair for the institute, received strong enough backing from Aleksandr Pozdneev and the Education Ministry to be adopted. RGIA 560: 28, 813, p. 14; RGIA 565: 8, 29365, pp. 2, 12–13, 63, 73, 80–82.

Bibliography

I. UNPUBLISHED WORKS

I found two collections of manuscripts at the Hoover Institution, Stanford University, to be invaluable. The first consists of the writings of E. Kh. Nilus, the embryonic chapters of a second volume of *Istoricheskii obzor*. The most useful papers were:
"Deiatel'nost' tserkovnogo otdela Upravleniia KVZhD"
"Kitaiskaia Vostochnaia Zheleznaia Doroga: eia polozhenie i nuzhda"
"Kratkii ocherk istoricheskogo razvitiia mestnogo kontrolia KVZhD"
"Kratkii ocherk organizatsii i deiatel'nosti kommercheskoi chasti i tarifnoi politiki KVZhD"
"The Lands and Land Administration of the C.E.R. Co., and the Incident of August 1, 1923."
"Ocherk deiatel'nosti Pravleniia KVZhD"
"Ocherki byta i pravovogo polozheniia sluzhashchikh KVZhD"
"Pressa"
"Russkie konsul'stva v Man'chzhurii"
"Uchebnyi otdel KVZhD"
"Upravlenie dorogi kak tsentral'nyi organ tekhnicheskogo i administrativnogo nadzora"
The second Hoover collection is the Khorvat Collection, from which I have used one work, D. L. Khorvat's "Memoirs."
Other archives and the most important files I consulted are:
Archives de l'Armée de Terre (Vincennes), Paris: Attachés militaires 7N1517, 7N1520, 7N1521, 7N1543
Gosudarstvennaia publichnaia biblioteka imeni Saltykova-Schedrina, St. Petersburg: Rukopisnyi otdel, f. 590, A. M. and D. M. Pozdneev; f. 608, I. V. Pomialovskii
Gosudarstvennyi arkhiv Irkutskoi oblasti, Irkutsk: f. 245, Irkutsk Appellate Court, f. 600, Irkutsk Public Prosecutor
Gosudarstvennyi arkhiv Rossiskoi federatsii (formerly Tsentral'nyi gosudarstvennyi arkhiv oktiabr'skoi revolutsii), Moscow:
   f. 102, Police Department
   f. 211, Harbin Social Democrat Archive

f. 533, Society of Political Exiles
f. 818, G. A. Planson
Heilongjiangsheng danganguan, Harbin: quanzonghao 21, Heilongjiang Yamen; q. 78, CER Land Department; q. 83, Jewish Community
Igud Yotsei Sin Archives, Tel Aviv
Ministère des Affaires Étrangères, Paris: Chine—Politique étrangère— Relations avec la Russie, vols. 166–71
Primorskii gosudarstvennyi muzei imeni V. K. Arsen'eva, Vladivostok: "Avtobiografiia prof. Rudakova A. V. im samym sostavlennaia" (June 22, 1941)
Public Record Office, London. Foreign Office files
Rossiiskii (formerly Tsentral'nyi) gosudarstvennyi istoricheskii arkhiv, St. Petersburg:
    f. 23, Ministry of Trade and Industry
    f. 323, Chinese Eastern Railway
    f. 560, Finance Ministry
    f. 565, State Treasury
    f. 632, Russo-Chinese Bank
    f. 1068, N. N. Tychino
    f. 1237, Preliminary Conference on Russian Financial, Industrial, and Economic Undertakings in the Far East
    f. 1273, Trans-Siberian Railway Committee
    f. 1343, Heraldry Department
Rossiiski tsentr khraneniia i izucheniia dokumentov noveishei istorii, Moscow: f. 2, Lenin; f. 17, Tsk KPSS
Tsentral'noe khranilishche sovremmenoi dokumentatsii, Moscow: f. 4, Sekretariat
Tsentral'nyi gosudarstvennyi arkhiv Sovetskoi armii, Moscow: f. 33879, Far Eastern Army
Tsentral'nyi gosudarstvennyi arkhiv dal'nego vostoka, Tomsk: f. 542, CER Gendarmerie; f. 577, Harbin Municipal Government
For the abbreviations and form of citation used on these archival materials, see Notes, p. 191.

II. PUBLISHED WORKS

Al'bom sooruzheniia KVZhD, 1897–1903. St. Petersburg, 1903.
Alekseev, V. M. Nauka o Vostoke. Moscow, 1982.
Alexander, Grand Duke of Russia [Mikhailovich Romanov]. Once a Grand Duke. New York, 1932.
Amburger, Erik. Geschichte der Behördenorganisation Russlands von Peter dem Grossen bis 1917. Leiden, 1966.
Ananich, B. V., and P. Sh. Ganelin. "Opyt kritiki memuarov S. Iu. Vitte." In Voprosy istoriografii i istochnikovedeniia istorii SSSR, pp. 298–374. Leningrad, 1963.
Andreev, G. I. "1905 god na KVZhD," Izvestiia sibirskogo otdeleniia AN SSSR, 6.2 (May 1976).

Asakawa, Kanichi. *The Russo-Japanese Conflict.* Boston, 1904.
Avtonomov, N. P. *Istoricheskii obzor kharbinskikh kommercheskikh uchilishch za 15 let.* Harbin, 1921.
Aziatskaia Rossiia. Comp. Migration Administration of Ministry of Agriculture, St. Petersburg, 1914. 3 vols.
Bakich, Olga. *Arkhiv Pavla Vasil'evicha Shkurkina: Predvaritel'naia opis'.* San Pablo, Calif., 1996.
———. "Origins of the Russian Community on the Chinese Eastern Railway," *Canadian Slavonic Papers,* 25.1 (March 1985).
———. "Russian City in China: Harbin before 1917," *Canadian Slavonic Papers,* 28.2 (June 1986).
Balakshin, Petr. *Final v Kitae: vozniknovenie, razvitie i ischeznovenie beloi emigratsii na Dal'nem Vostoke.* San Francisco, 1958–59.
Baring, Maurice. *With Russians in Manchuria.* London, 1905.
Bartold, V. V. *La Découverte de l'Asie: Histoire de l'Orientalisme en Europe et en Russie.* Paris, 1947.
Bartol'd, V. V. *Sochineniia.* Moscow, 1977.
Bater, James. *St. Petersburg: Industrialization and Change.* Montreal, 1976.
Berton, Pierre. *The Impossible Railway: The Building of the Canadian Pacific.* New York, 1972.
Beveridge, Albert. *The Russian Advance.* New York, 1904.
Bogdanov, Dmitrii. *Dnevnik Dmitriia Bogdanova po poezdke po Sungari na parakhode 'Telegraf' v 1895 godu.* n.p., n.d.
Borzunov, V. F. "Rabochaia sila na stroitel'stve sibirskoi magistrali," *Istoricheskie zapiski,* 70 (1961).
Brooke, Guy. *An Eye-witness in Manchuria.* London, 1905.
Brunnert, H. S., and V. V. Hagelstrom. *Present Day Political Organization of China.* Beijing, 1910.
Bushnell, John. *Mutiny Amid Repression: Russian Soldiers in the Revolution of 1905–1906.* Bloomington, Ind., 1985.
Chao, Kang. *The Economic Development of Manchuria: The Rise of a Frontier Economy.* Ann Arbor, Mich., 1982.
Charov, Innokentii. *Kharbin Al'bom.* Harbin, 1930.
Chernolutskaia, E. N. *Rossiiskaia emigratsiia v Manchzhurii: voenno-politicheskaia deiatel'nost, 1920–1945: sbornik dokumentov.* Iuzhno-Sakhalinsk, 1994.
Chow, Rey. "Between Colonizers: Hong Kong's Postcolonial Self-Writing in the 1990s," *Diaspora* 2.2 (Winter 1992): 151–70.
Chumnye epidemii na dal'nem vostoke. Ed. F. A. Iasenskii. Harbin, 1912.
Clausen, Soren, and Stig Thogersen. *The Making of a Chinese City: History and Historiography in Harbin.* Armonk, N.Y., 1995.
Corrsin, Stephen. *Warsaw Before the First World War: Poles and Jews in the Third City of the Russian Empire, 1880–1914.* Boulder, Colo., 1989.
Darwent, C. E. *Shanghai: A Handbook for Travellers and Residents.* Shanghai, 1920.
Davidov, D. A. *Kolonizatsiia Man'chzhurii i S.[everno]—V.[ostochnoi] Mongolii.* Vladivostok, 1911.
Davis, Clarence, and Kenneth Wilburn, eds. *Railway Imperialism.* New York, 1991.

Demchinskii, Boris. *Rossiia v Manchzhurii*. St. Petersburg, 1904.
Dempsey, Hugh, ed. *The CPR West*. Vancouver, 1984.
Dicker, Herman. *Wanderers and Settlers in the Far East*. New York, 1962.
Dirlik, Arif, ed. *What Is in a Rim?: Critical Perspectives on the Pacific Region Idea*. Boulder, Colo., 1993.
Dobrovol'skii, L. I. *Zapreshchennaia kniga v Rossii, 1825–1904*. Moscow, 1962.
Duara, Prasenjit. *Rescuing History from the Nation: Questioning Narratives of Modern China*. Chicago, 1995.
Dukhovskoi, S. M. *Vsepoddaneishii otchet priamurskogo general-gubernatora Generala-Leitenanta Dukhovskogo, 1896–1897*. St. Petersburg, 1898.
Eagle, John. *The Canadian Pacific Railway and the Development of Western Canada, 1896–1914*. Montreal, 1989.
Elleman, Bruce. "The Soviet Union's Secret Diplomacy Concerning the Chinese Eastern Railway," *Journal of Asian Studies*, 53.2 (May 1994): 459–86.
Elvin, Mark. "The Mixed Court of the International Settlement at Shanghai (Until 1911)," *Papers on China*, 17 (1963).
Esherick, Joseph. *The Origins of the Boxer Uprising*. Berkeley, Calif., 1987.
Fedorkina, E. A. "Dal'nevostochnye metsenaty vostochnogo instituta," *Dal'nevostochnaia panorama*, 1 (1991): 23–26.
Fieldhouse, David. "Imperialism: An Historiographical Revision," *Economic History Review*, 14 (1961): 187–209.
Fomenko, S. M. *Putevoditel' po portam Dal'nego Vostoka, 1909–10*. Harbin, n.d.
Ford, Harold. "Russian Far Eastern Diplomacy, Count Witte and the Penetration of China, 1895–1904." Ph.D. diss., University of Chicago, 1950.
Forsyth, James. *A History of the Peoples of Siberia: Russia's North Asian Colony, 1581–1990*. Cambridge, Eng., 1992.
Frankel, Jonathan. *Prophecy and Politics*. Cambridge, Eng., 1981.
Fuller, William. *Civil-Military Conflict in Late Imperial Russia, 1881–1914*. Princeton, N.J., 1985.
Gallagher, John, and Ronald Robinson. "The Imperialism of Free Trade," *Economic History Review*, 6 (1953): 1–15.
Gelicen [Golitsyn], V. V. *Zhongdong tielu huludui canjia 1900-nian manzhou shijian jilue*. Tr. Li Shuxiao. Harbin, n.d. A Chinese version of *Ocherk uchastiia okhrannoi strazhi kitaiskoi vostochnoi zheleznoi dorogi v sobytiiakh 1900 goda v Man'chzhurii*. Harbin, 1910.
Geyer, Dietrich. *Russian Imperialism*. Leamington Spa, Eng. 1987.
Gints, M. A. *Russkaia sem'ia doma i v Man'chzhurii*. Sydney, Australia. 1986.
Glatfelter, R. Edward. "Russia, the Soviet Union and the Chinese Eastern Railway." In Clarence Davis and Kenneth Wilburn, eds., *Railway Imperialism*. New York, 1991: 137–54.
Glinskii, B. B. *Prolog russko-iaponskoi voiny: materialy iz arkhiva Grafa S. Iu. Witte*. Petrograd, 1916.
Golovachev, P. M. *Rossiia na Dal'nem Vostoke*. St. Petersburg, 1904.
G[orod] *Kharbin i ego prigorody po odnodnevnoi perepisi 24 fevralia 1913 g.*, vol. 1: *statisticheskoe opisanie*; vol. 2: *Itogovye tablitsy*. Harbin, 1913.
Grulev, M. V. *Zapiski generala-evreia*. Paris, 1930.

Gunji Yoshio. *Toshitetsudo unchin seisakushi*. Dairen, 1943.
Hackett, Roger. *Yamagata Aritomo in the Rise of Modern Japan*. Cambridge, Mass., 1971.
Haerbin shizhi: dilijuan. Harbin, 1993.
Hamm, Michael. *Kiev: A Portrait, 1800–1917*. Princeton, N.J., 1993.
———, ed. *The City in Late Imperial Russia*. Bloomington, Ind. 1986.
Hara Teruyuki. "The Korea Movement in the Russian Maritime Province, 1905–1922." In Dae-sook Suh, ed., *Koreans in the Soviet Union*, Honolulu, 1987.
———. *Shiberia shuppei*. Tokyo, 1989.
Harcave, Sidney, tr. and ed., *The Memoirs of Count Witte*. Armonk, N.Y., 1990.
Hauner, Milan. *What Is Asia to Us?* Boston, 1990.
Heilongjiang baokan. Harbin, 1985.
Heilongjiang baikequanshu. Beijing, 1990.
Heilongjiang shengzhi: baoyezhi. Harbin, 1993.
Herlihy, Patricia. *Odessa: A History, 1794–1914*. Cambridge, Mass., 1986.
Hosoya Chihiro. *Shiberia shuppei no shiteki kenkyu*. Tokyo, 1955.
Instruktsiia nachal'nikam uchastkov dlia proizvodstva izyskanii i sostavleniia proekta Kitaiskoi vostochnoi zheleznoi dorogi. St. Petersburg, 1897.
Iriye, Akira. *After Imperialism: The Search for a New Order in the Far East*. Cambridge, Mass., 1965.
Ito Takeo. *Life Along the South Manchurian Railway: The Memoirs of Ito Takeo*. Tr. Joshua Fogel. Armonk, N.Y., 1988.
Iubileinyi sbornik Kharbinskogo birzhevogo komiteta, 1907–1932. Harbin, 1934.
Japan, Foreign Ministry. *Nihon gaiko bunsho*. Tokyo, [1903–4].
Ji Fenghui. *Haerbin xungen*. Harbin, 1996.
———. "'Heilongjiang yutu' yu Haerbin diming," *Xuexi yu tansuo* 4 (1990).
Jin Shuangping. "Nangangqu zaoqi bufen jianzhu fengge suotan," *Nangang wenshi* 1 (1989).
Jin Zonglin. "Zhang Tingge qiren qishi," *Haerbin wenshi ziliao* 2 (1983): 17–25.
Judge, Joan. *Print and Politics: "Shibao" and the Culture of Reform in Late Qing China*. Stanford, Calif., 1996.
Kabuzan, V. M. *Dal'nevostochnyi krai v 17-nachale 20 vv. 1640–1917: Istoriko-demograficheskii ocherk*. Moscow, 1985.
Karlinsky, Simon. "Memoirs of Harbin," *Slavic Review*, 48.2 (Summer 1989).
Kaufman, A. A. *Pereselenie i kolonizatsiia*. St. Petersburg, 1905.
Kaufman, A. I. "Poselok Kharbin," *Biulleten' iguda yotsei sin*, 250 (Feb. 1981).
Kharbinskaia starina. Harbin, 1938.
Khisamutdinov, Amir. *The Russian Far East: Historical Essays*. Honolulu, 1993.
Kitai. Iaponiia: Istoriia i filologiia. Moscow, 1961.
Kitaiskaia Vostochnaia Zheleznaia Doroga: Istoricheskii ocherk, 1896–1905. Comp. CER Chancellery. St. Petersburg, 1914.
Kitamanshu keizai chosashiryo. Ed. South Manchurian Railway Research Bureau. n.p. 1910.
Klibanov, A. I. *History of Religious Sectarianism in Russia, 1860's–1917*. Oxford, 1982.
Kokshaiskii. *Glazomernaia s'emka reki Sungari*. n.p., 1896.
Kong Fanzhen. "Haerbin funu xiejinhui chengli shimo," *Haerbin wenshi ziliao*, 2 (1983).

Koniaev, A. T. "Bor'ba bol'shevikov Sibiri za revoliutsionnuiu evakuatsiiu soldat Man'chzhurskoi Armiiv 1905 g." In *Bol'sheviki Sibiri i Dal'nego Vostoka v bor'be za massy (1903–1917 gg.)*. Tomsk, 1976.

Koshizawa Akira. *Harubin no toshikeikaku*. Tokyo, 1989.

Kotkin, Stephen, and David Wolff, eds. *Rediscovering Russia in Asia: Siberia and the Russian Far East*. Armonk, N.Y., 1995.

Kuropatkin, A. N. "Dnevnik A. N. Kuropatkina," *Krasnyi arkhiv* 2 (1922): 5–112.

———. *The Russian Army and the Japanese War*. New York, 1909.

Lahusen, Thomas. "A Place Called Harbin: Reflections on a Centennial," *China Quarterly*, June 1998: 181–90.

Landgraf, Dieter. *Amur. Ussuri. Sachalin, 1847–1917*. Neuried, 1989.

Lattimore, Owen. "The Gold Tribe: 'Fishkin Tatars' of the Lower Sungari." In *Memoirs of the American Anthropological Association*. 1932.

———. *Manchuria, Cradle of Conflict*. New York, 1932.

Lee, Chong-sik. *Revolutionary Struggle in Manchuria: Chinese Communism and Soviet Interest, 1922–1945*. Berkeley, Calif., 1983.

Lembergsksaia, V., ed. "Dvizhenie v voiskakh na Dal'nem Vostoke," *Krasnyi arkhiv*, 11–12 (1925).

Lensen, George. *Russian Diplomatic and Consular Officials in East Asia*. Tokyo, 1968.

———. *The Russo-Chinese War*. Tallahassee, Fla., 1967.

Leong, Sow-theng. *Sino-Soviet Diplomatic Relations, 1917–1926*. Honolulu, 1976.

Leroy-Beaulieu, Anatole. *La Renovation de l'Asie*. Paris, 1900.

Leshko, O. "Skidel'skie," *Biulleten' iguda yotsei sin*, Jan. 1992: 18.

Levine, Steven. *Anvil of Victory: The Communist Revolution in Manchuria, 1945–1948*. New York, 1987.

Levitov, I. *Zheltaia Rossiia*. St. Petersburg, 1901.

Lewitz, Peter. *To the Columbia Gateway: The Oregon Railway and the Northern Pacific, 1879–1884*. Pullman, Wash., 1987.

Li Shuxiao. *Haerbin lishi biannian, 1896–1949*. Harbin, 1986.

Lieven, D.C.B. *Russia and the Origins of the First World War*. New York, 1983.

Litvak, K. B. "Perepis' naseleniia 1897 goda o krest'ianstve Rossii," *Istoriia SSSR*, 1 (1990).

Livezeanu, Irina. "Defining Russia at the Margins," *Russian Review*, 54.4 (Oct. 1995): 495–99.

Louis, William, ed. *Imperialism: The Robinson and Gallagher Controversy*. New York, 1976.

Macey, David. *Government and Peasant in Russia, 1861–1906*. Dekalb, Ill., 1987.

MacMurray, John. *Treaties and Agreements With and Concerning China, 1894–1919*, vol. 1. New York, 1921.

Maksakov, V., ed. *Karatel'nye ekspeditsii v Sibiri v 1905–6 gg*. Moscow, 1932.

Malozemoff, Andrew. *Russian Far Eastern Policy, 1881–1904*. Berkeley, Calif., 1958.

Mancall, Mark. *China at the Center: 300 Years of Foreign Policy*. New York, 1984.

"Man'chzhurets." *Russkaia kazna na Kitaiskoi doroge*. St. Petersburg, 1910.

Marinov, V. A. *Rossiia i Iaponiia pered pervoi mirovoi voinoi, 1905–1914*. Moscow, 1974.

Marks, Steven. *Road to Power: The Trans-Siberian Railroad and the Colonization of Asian Russia, 1850–1917*. London, 1991.

Martynov, E. I. *Vydacha kitaitsam chertezhei zheleznodorozhnykh mostov.* Moscow, 1913.
McDonald, David. *United Government and Foreign Policy in Russia, 1900–1914.* Cambridge, Mass., 1992.
Melikhov, G. *Manch'zhuriia: dalekaia i blizkaia.* Moscow, 1991.
———. "Zarisovki starogo Kharbina," *Problemy dal'nego vostoka,* 4 (1990).
Merkulov, S. *Russkoe delo na Dal'nem Vostoke.* St. Petersburg, 1912.
Michelson, Sig. *The North Pacific Railroad and the Selling of the West.* Sioux Falls, S.D., 1993.
Miller, Henry B. "Russian Development of Manchuria," *National Geographic,* 15.3 (1904).
Morley, James. *The Japanese Thrust into Siberia, 1918.* New York, 1957.
Murphey, Rhoads. *Shanghai: Key to Modern China.* Cambridge, Mass., 1953.
Myers, Ramon, and Mark Peattie, eds. *The Japanese Colonial Empire, 1895–1945.* Princeton, N.J., 1984.
Myers, Ramon, Mark Peattie, and Peter Duus, eds. *The Japanese Informal Empire in China, 1895–1937.* Princeton, N.J., 1989.
Nathan, Carl. *Plague Prevention and Politics in Manchuria, 1910–31.* Cambridge, Mass., 1967.
Nemirovich-Danchenko, V. I. *Na voinu.* Moscow, 1904.
Nicholas II [Romanov]. *The Secret Letters of the Last Tsar.* New York, 1938.
Nilus, E. Kh. *Istoricheskii obzor: Kitaiskoi vostochnoi zheleznoi dorogi, 1896–1923 gg.* Harbin, 1923.
Nish, Ian. *The Origins of the Russo-Japanese War.* London, 1985.
Nottbeck, Friedrich von. *Erlebnisse und Erinnerungen aus dem russisch-japanischen Kriege.* Berlin, 1906.
Obshchestvo KVZhD. Smeta dokhodov i raskhodov na 1903 god. St. Petersburg, 1903.
Obshchestvo KVZhD. Smeta dokhodov i raskhodov na 1904 god. St. Petersburg, 1904.
"Obshchii obzor k otchetu po otchuzhdeniiu zemel' sushchestvuiushchei linii KVZh dorogi, 1897–1918 gg." (1930–31).
Orlovsky, Daniel. *The Limits of Reform: The Ministry of Internal Affairs in Imperial Russia, 1802–1881.* Cambridge, Mass., 1981.
Ossendowski, Ferdynand. *From President to Prison.* New York, 1926.
Otchet birzhevogo komiteta. Harbin, 1911.
Otchet Kharbinskogo obshchestvennogo upravleniia. Harbin, 1908.
Otchet Kharbinskogo birzhevogo komiteta za 1911 god. Harbin, 1913.
Otchet Kharbinskogo birzhevogo komiteta za 1913 god. Harbin, 1914.
"Otchet o deiatel'nosti Obshchestva za 1907 g.," *Russkoe geograficheskoe obshchestvo. Vladivostokskoe otdelenie,* 12 (1908).
Paine, Sarah. "A History of the Sino-Soviet Border, 1858–1924." Ph.D. diss., Columbia University, 1993.
Pankratova, A. M., ed. *Revoliutsiia 1905–1907 gg. v Rossii: Dokumenty i materialy, Noiabr–Dekabr 1905 goda,* vol. 2. Moscow, 1955.
Panskaia, Ludmilla. *Introduction to Palladii's Chinese Literature of the Muslims.* 1979.
Pereleshin, Valerii. *Russian Poetry and Literary Life in Harbin and Shanghai, 1930–50: The Memoirs of Valerij Pereleshin.* Amsterdam, 1987.
"Pervye shagi russkogo imperializma na Dal'nem Vostoke," *Krasnyi arkhiv,* 52 (1932).

Pinkus, Benjamin. *The Jews of the Soviet Union*. Cambridge, Eng., 1988.
Pokotilov, D. D. *Nekotorye dopolnitel'nye dannye po voprosu ob otchuzhdenii zemel' pod zheleznoi dorogoi v Kitae*. St. Petersburg, 1897.
Polacy na dalekim wschodzie. Harbin, 1928.
Poleshchuk, V. E. "Revoliutsionnoe dvizhenie v Man'chzhurskoi armii v 1905 godu," *Istoricheskie zapiski*, 49 (1954).
Poletika, M. I. *Obshchii meditsinskii otchet po postroike VKZhD*. St. Petersburg, 1904.
Polvinen, Tuomo. *Imperial Borderland: Bobrikov and the Attempted Russification of Finland, 1898-1904*. Durham, N.C., 1995.
Poppe, Nicholas. *Reminiscences*. Ed. Henry Schwarz. Bellingham, Wash., 1983.
Pozdneev, Dmitrii. *Opisanie Man'chzurii*. St. Petersburg, 1897.
Priamur'e: fakty, tsifry, nabliudeniia. Comp. Obshchezemskaia Organizatsiia. Moscow, 1909.
Price, Ernest. *The Russo-Japanese Treaties of 1907-16 Concerning Manchuria and Mongolia*. Baltimore, Md., 1933.
Purcell, Victor. *The Boxer Uprising, a Background Study*. New York, 1963.
Qiao Gu. "Lamatai beihui mujiji," *Nangang wenshi*, 1 (1989).
Quested, Rosemary. "Local Sino-Russian Political Relations in Manchuria, 1895-1900," *Journal of Oriental Studies*, 10.2 (July 1972).
———. *"Matey" Imperialists?* Hong Kong, 1982.
———. *The Russo-Chinese Bank*. Birmingham, Eng., 1977.
Quested, Rosemary, and N. Tsuji. "A Fresh Look at the Sino-Russian Conflict of 1900 in Manchuria," *Journal of the Institute of Chinese Studies of the Chinese University of Hong Kong*, 9.2 (1978).
Raeff, Marc. *Russia Abroad: A Cultural History of the Russian Emigration, 1919-1939*. New York, 1990.
———. "Some Reflections on Russian Liberalism," *Russian Review*, 18 (1959).
Reichman, Henry. "The 1905 Revolution on the Siberian Railroad," *Russian Review*, 47 (1988).
———. *Railwaymen and Revolution: Russia, 1905*. Berkeley, Calif., 1987.
Repington, Charles. *The War in the Far East, 1904-1905*. New York, 1905.
Reynolds, Douglas. *China, 1898-1912: The Xinzheng Revolution and Japan*. Cambridge, Mass., 1993.
———. "Training Young China Hands: Toa Dobun Shoin and Its Precursors, 1886-1945." In Ramon Myers, Mark Peattie, and Peter Duus, eds., *The Japanese Informal Empire in China, 1895-1937*. Princeton, N.J., 1989, pp. 210-71.
Riasanovsky, Nicholas. "Asia Through Russian Eyes." In Wayne Vucinich, ed., *Russia and Asia*. Stanford, Calif., 1972.
Rogger, Hans. *Jewish Policies and Right-wing Politics in Imperial Russia*. London, 1986.
———. *Russia in the Age of Modernisation and Revolution, 1881-1917*. London, 1983.
Romanov, B. A. *Russia in Manchuria*. Tr. Susan Mann Jones. Ann Arbor, Mich. 1952. Originally published in 1928 as *Rossiia v Man'chzhurii*. All quotations in the text and notes are from the English translation unless otherwise noted.
Rosen, Baron [R. R. Rozen]. *Forty Years of Diplomacy*. London, 1922.
Rozman, Gilbert. *A Mirror for Socialism*. Princeton, N.J., 1985.
Rudakov, A. *Obshchestvo i-khe-tuan i ego znachenie*. Vladivostok, 1901.

———. "Pozemel'nyi vopros v Girin'skoi provintsii v sviazi s eia zaseleniem," *Izvestiia vostochnogo instituta*, 3 (1902).
Rybakovskii, L. L. *Naselenie dal'nego vostoka za 150 let*. Moscow, 1990.
Sabler, S. V., and I. V. Sosnovskii. *Sibirskaia zheleznaia doroga*. St. Petersburg, 1903.
Sahlins, Peter. *Boundaries: The Making of France and Spain in the Pyrenees*. Berkeley, Calif., 1989.
Sanbo honbu. *Keizaijo yori mitaru Haerbin*. n.p., 1925.
Sbornik pamiati V. F. Komissarzhevskaia. Moscow, 1931.
Seki Hiroharu. *Gendai higashi ajia kokusai kankyo no tanjo*. Tokyo, 1969.
Shi Fang. "Chaoxian minzu yingxiong An Zhongren," *Haerbin Yanjiu*, 6 (1986).
Shillony, Ben-Ami. *The Jews and the Japanese*. Rutland, Vt., 1991.
Shkurkin, P. V. "Perevodchik ili orientalist?," *Vestnik Azii*. 9 (1911): 1–13.
Shprintsin, A. G. "O russko-kitaiskom dialekte na dal'nem vostoke," *Strany i narodi vostoka*, 6 (1968): 86–100.
Shreider, D. I. *Nash Dal'nii Vostok: Tri goda v Ussuriskom krae*. St. Petersburg, 1897.
Shteinfel'd, N. P. "Rol' i znachenie goroda Kharbina v ekonomicheskoi zhizni Russkoi Man'chzhurii," *Byt i kul'tura Vostoka*, 3 (May 8, 1910).
Shumiatskii, B. Z. *V sibirskom podpol'e: ocherki, 1903–8*. Moscow, 1926.
Si Yuanyi. "Fangyi gongzuode xianquzhe—Wu Liande boshi," *Haerbin wenshi ziliao*, 3 (1984).
Siegelbaum, Lewis. "Another 'Yellow Peril': Chinese Migrants in the Russian Far East and the Russian Reaction Before 1917," *Modern Asian Studies* 12.2 (April 1978).
Sikorskii, F. Iu. "Russkii sud v Man'chzhurii," *Zhurnal ministerstva iustitsii*, March 1915: 49–83.
Simpson, John Hope. *The Refugee Problem: Report of a Survey*. London, 1939.
Siviakov, P. "Chzhi-fu," *Izvestiia vostochnogo instituta*, 3.4 (1902).
Skachkov, P. E. *Ocherki istorii russkogo kitaevedeniia*. Moscow, 1977.
Skvirskii, F. B. "Soldatskie slobodki v zheltorossii: tsarskii plan voennoi kolonizatsii Man'chzhurii," *Vestnik Man'chzhurii*, April 1930: 14–16.
Slezkine, Yuri. *Arctic Mirrors: Russia and the Small Peoples of the North*. Ithaca, N.Y., 1994.
Slutskii, Yehuda. *Haitonut hayehudit-rusit bamea haesrim (1900–1918)*. Tel Aviv, 1978.
Sokolova, A. "Vospominaniia o pogrome v Man'chzhurii po linii KVZhD v 1898," *Istoricheskii vestnik*, 1906, 3 parts, 10: 81–106; 11: 424–46; 12: 810–28.
Sokolsky, George. *The Story of the Chinese Eastern Railway*. Shanghai, 1929.
Soldatov, V. V. *K perepisi naseleniia goroda Kharbina*. Harbin, 1912.
———. "Smertnost' naseleniia g. Kharbina v 1909 g. v sviazi s rozhdaemost'iu," *Izvestiia kharbinskogo obshchestvennogo upravleniia*, 7 (1913).
Spaits, Alexander. *Mit Kosaken durch die Mandschurei*. Vienna, 1906.
Spendelow, Howard. "Russia's South Manchurian Adventure: The Liaodong Leasehold and China's Resistance to Imperialism, 1898–1905." Ph.D. diss., Harvard University, 1979.
Spitsyn, Alexander. "Rabochii vopros na kamenno-ugol'nykh kopiakh Mukdenskoi provintsii," *Izvestia vostochnogo instituta*, 9 (1903).
Spravochnaia knizhka Kharbina. Harbin, 1904.

Spravochnaia knizhka po lichnomu sostavu sluzhashchikh KVZhD na 1-e Ianvaria 1915 goda. Comp. Chinese Eastern Railway. Harbin, 1915.
Spravochnaia knizhka po Vostochnomu Institutu v g. Vladivostoke na 1909 god. Vladivostok, 1909.
Spruyt, Hendrik. *The Sovereign State and Its Competitors*. Princeton, N.J., 1994.
Starr, S. F. "Tsarist Government: The Imperial Dimension." In J. Azrael, ed., *Soviet Nationality Policies and Practices*. New York, 1978.
Stephan, John. "Far Eastern Conspiracies? Russian Separatism on the Pacific," *Australian Slavonic and East European Studies*, 4.1–2 (1990): 135–52.
———. *The Russian Far East: A History*. Stanford, Calif., 1994.
———. *The Russian Fascists*. New York, 1978.
Stone, Norman, and Michael Glenny. *The Other Russia*. London, 1990.
Stozh, M. E. *Sputnik po Sibiri i Dal'nemu Vostoku*. n.p., 1916.
Sulzberger, C. L. *The Last of the Giants*. New York, 1970.
Sun, Kungtu (assisted by Ralph W. Huenemann). *The Economic Development of Manchuria in the First Half of the Twentieth Century*. Cambridge, Mass., 1969.
Tang, Peter. *Russian and Soviet Policy in Manchuria and Outer Mongolia, 1911–1931*. Durham, N.C., 1959.
Taskina, Elena. *Neizvestnyi Kharbin*. Moscow, 1994.
Tettau, Freiherr von. *Achtzehn Monate mit Russlands Heeren in der Mandschurei*, vols. 1–2. Berlin, 1907.
Thaden, Edward. *Russia's Western Borderlands, 1710–1870*. Princeton, N.J., 1984.
———, ed. *Russification in the Baltic Provinces and Finland, 1855–1914*. Princeton, N.J., 1981.
Thurston, Robert. *Liberal City, Conservative State*. New York, 1987.
Tilly, Charles. *Coercion, Capital, and European States, AD 990–1990*. Cambridge, Mass., 1990.
Timberlake, Charles. "Introduction: The Concept of Liberalism in Russia." In Timberlake, *Essays on Russian Liberalism*. Columbia, Mo., 1972, pp. 1–17.
Tkachenko, Gennadii. *Sovetskie trudiashchiesia na KVZhD, 1924–35*. Moscow, 1988.
Treadgold, Donald. *The Great Siberian Migration*. Princeton, N.J., 1957.
Tsepliaev, L. N., and B. P. Shipilov. "Odnodnevnye perepisi kak istoricheskii istochnik dlia izucheniia gorodov zapadnoi Sibiri v epokhu kapitalizma," *Iz istorii Sibiri*, 17 (1975).
Tsuru Kesatoshi. *Tenshukyoto An Jukon*. Tokyo, 1996.
Tsybikov, G. Ts. *Izbrannye trudy*, vol. 1. Moscow, 1991.
Tupper, Harmon. *To the Great Ocean*. Boston, 1965.
Ukhtomskii, E. E. *Iz kitaiskikh pisem'*. St. Petersburg, 1901.
———. *K sobytiiam v Kitae*. St. Petersburg, 1900.
———. *Pered groznym budushchem*. St. Petersburg, 1904.
———. *Puteshestvie gosudaria imperatora Nikolaia II na Vostok (v 1890–1891)*, vol. 2. St. Petersburg, 1897.
United States, State Department. *Consular Reports*. Washington, D.C.
———. War Department. *Reports of Military Observers Attached to the Armies in Manchuria During the Russo-Japanese War*. Washington, D.C., 1906.

Urufu, D. "Shiberia to Manshu o meguru Roshia to Chugoku." In *Shuen kara no rekishi*. Tokyo, 1994.
Valliant, Robert. "Japan and the Trans-Siberian Railroad, 1885-1905." Ph.D. diss., University of Hawaii, 1974.
Veresaev, V. *In the War: Memoirs of V. Veresaev*. New York, 1917.
Veselovzorov, V. N. "Kak byl zalozhen Kharbin," *Izvestiia obshchestva izucheniia Man'chzhurskogo kraia*, 1 (Nov. 1922).
Vetoshkin, M. K. "1905 g. v Manchzhurii," *Sibirskie ogni*, 1 (1929).
Von Laue, Theodore. *Sergei Witte and the Industrialization of Russia*. New York, 1963.
Weale, B. L. Putnam. *Manchu and Muscovite*. London, 1907.
Weeks, Theodore. *Nationalism and Russification on the Western Frontier, 1863-1914*. DeKalb, Ill., 1996.
Weinberg, Robert. *The Revolution of 1905 in Odessa: Blood on the Steps*. Bloomington, Ind., 1993.
Weressaiew, W. *Meine Erlebnisse im russisch-japanischen Krieg*. Stuttgart, 1909.
Westwood, J. N. *A History of Russian Railways*. London, 1964.
Whelan, Heide. *Alexander III and the State Council*. New Brunswick, N.J., 1982.
Whigham, Henry. *Manchuria and Korea*. London, 1904.
Widmer, Eric. *The Russian Ecclesiastical Mission in Peking During the Eighteenth Century*. Cambridge, Mass., 1976.
Witte, Sergei Iulevich. *Memoirs*. New York, 1921.
Wolff, David. "Between War and Revolution: Railway Brigades in Siberia, 1905-7," *Russian Review*, 55.4 (1996).
———. "Kitchen Imperialism: Soybeans and the Making of Northeast Asia." Unpublished manuscript.
———. "Russia Finds Its Limits: Crossing Borders into Manchuria." In Stephen Kotkin and David Wolff, eds., *Rediscovering Russia in Asia*. Armonk, N.Y., 1995.
Wu Jinglin. "An Zhongren cisha Iteng Bowen (Ito Hirobumi)," *Nangang wenshi*, 1 (1989).
Wu Xuejian. "Wosuo zhidaode Wu Baixiang," *Haerbin wenshi ziliao*, 1 (1982).
Yaney, George. *The Systemization of Russian Government*. Urbana, Ill., 1973.
———. *The Urge to Mobilize*. Urbana, Ill., 1982.
Young, John. *The Research Activities of the South Manchurian Railway, 1907-45*. New York, 1966.
Zhang Fushan. "Shae he Sulian zhu Haerbin zonglingshiguan," *Haerbin wenshi ziliao*, 6 (1985).
Zhang Xiaohong. "Eguo he Sulian zhu Haerbin zonglingshiguan shimo," *Nangang wenshi*, 1 (1989).
Zhao Dejiu. "Jiefangqian haerbin zuowei beiman jingji zhongxinde yixie lishi ziliao," *Haerbin yanjiu*, 5 (1985).
Zhao Tian. "Fujiadiande lailongqumai," *Haerbin wenshi ziliao*, 5 (1984).
Zheng Changchun. "Haerbin huochezhande bianqian," *Nangang wenshi*, 1 (1989).
———. "Haerbin nangangde youlai," *Nangang wenshi*, 1 (1989).
Zhu Xianping. "Lun diyici shijie dazhanqian dongbei beibude waiguo ziben," *Haerbin yanjiu*, 5 (1986).
Zhukovskii-Zhuk, I. "Provokator Richard Frank," *Puti revoliutsii* 1 (1927): 169-93.

Index

In this index an "f" after a number indicates a separate reference on the next page, and an "ff" indicates separate references on the next two pages. A continuous discussion over two or more pages is indicated by a span of page numbers, e.g., "57–59." *Passim* is used for a cluster of references in close but not consecutive sequence. References to the illustration section following p. 145 are given as "plate."

Aleksandr III, Tsar, 56
Aleksandr Mikhailovich, Grand Duke, 53, 73
Alekseev, E. I., 74–77, 89, 97, 124f, 155, 214; and interministerial rivalry, 48f, 52, 54, 70, 72. See also viceroyalty
Amur, 3–5, 14, 67, 140. See also Blagoveshchensk; Russian Far East
An Chonggun, 20. See also Korea
Angola, 79
architecture, 18f, 34, plate
archives, viif, 4, 27, 48, 152, 192, 194, 216, 230
area studies, 4, 41, 160, 176. See also Eastern Institute; language learning
Armenians, 115
Ashehe, 21, 24–29 *passim*

bandits, 26, 35, 69, 151
Baranov, A. M., 156, 163
Bat'ianov, M. I., 135f, 138
Beijing, 12, 23, 155, 161, 165
Beijing Ecclesiastical Mission, 40, 148, 181–84
Beveridge, Albert, 14, 32, 47
Bezobrazov, A. M., 49, 51, 73, 75, 103, 105
Blagoveshchensk, 33, 38, 81
Bodune, 21f, 24
Borokhov, Ber, 79

Boxer uprising and suppression, 40, 43, 56, 66ff, 70, 118, 146, 148, 151f; and Harbin, 29, 33f, 46, 81
British, see England
Buriat, 34, 151, 154

Canada, 1, 3, 79f
Cassini, A. P., 15, 42
Caucasus, 80, 94
censorship, 129, 132, 152, 164
CER, see Chinese Eastern Railroad
Chang Shun, 68
Changchun, 19f
Chichagov, N. M., 89, 139
Chinese Eastern Railroad (CER):
—commercial section, 99, 142, 160
—construction, 9, 21–41; perceptions of, 41–48, 208, plate
—Employee Strike Committee (ESC), 116, 131–39 *passim*
—guard, 25, 35, 39, 51, 65–69 *passim*, 80. See also frontier (border) guards
—Railway Club, 124, 126f, 131, 137
—strike, 11, 126, 131–36, 139f
—workshops, 126, 130, 134, 138f
Chinese life in Harbin, 7f, 33, 38f, 41, 84f, 91–94 *passim*, 219, plate
Chinese migration, 78, 81, 84–87 *passim*, 158, 160, 174. See also *under* labor: Chinese

Chita, 34, 117, 120, 130
civil-military conflict, 10f, 50–77, 81, 137, 156f. *See also* interministerial rivalry
colonialism (colonization), 2, 4, 6–12 *passim*, 41, 52, 78–114, 146–67, 170–74, 193. *See also* Cossacks; Jewish community; sectarians
Cossacks, 14, 38, 48f, 52, 54, 65, 70, 138; and colonialism, 56, 78, 83, 89, 108

Dairen (Dalian; Dal'nii), 19f, 32f, 47, 54, 62–65, 99, 120, 169
Daniel, E. V., 159
Denikin, A. I., 67
Diterikhs, 69
Dobrolovskii, I. A., 153, 155f, 160, 163ff, 167
Dubasov, F. N., 62
Dukhobors, 78, 80, 82, 86f
Dukhovskoi, S. M., 15, 57f, 83f
Duma, 107, 144, 158, 225

Eastern Institute, 12, 146–55, 157, 159, 164f, 188ff, 237f, plate
education, 35, 40f, 88f, 96, 98, 101, 103, 105ff, 146–66. *See also* Eastern Institute
émigrés, vii, 8, 100, 149, 167, 175, 196, plate
En Ze, 24, 201
engineers, 9, 30–33 *passim*, 40, 200–201
England, 7, 32, 43, 45, 59ff, 74f, 80, 150, 152, 164f
extraterritoriality, 117, 163

Far Eastern Committee, 74, 76, 105, 211
Far Eastern Paper (*Yuandongbao*), 156, 160–64 *passim*, 232
Finland, 4, 7
food, 31, 34, 36f, 56, 91, 97, 121ff, 153
France, 5f, 74f, 81, 122, 152
frontier (border) guards, 87, 89, 118f, 137, 143; and interministerial rivalry, 51, 54, 69, 71–77 *passim*. *See also under* Chinese Eastern Railroad: guard
Fujiadian, 18, 33, 93f, 96, 162, 204

gendarmerie, 66, 101, 116, 139, 142f, 228
general commissar, 76, 170f
Georgians, 78, 115
Germany, 5, 28, 47, 59f, 115, 152
Gerngross, A. A., 65, 69, 118
Gondatti, N. L., 99, 159

grain, 18, 91, 108, 160
Grodekov, N. I., 69f, 81–85 *passim*, 141, 149–52 *passim*, 155, 209
Grulev, M. V., 16, 199
Guandong Leasehold, *see* Port Arthur
Guchkov, A. I., 51, 67

Hailar, 89, 119
Handaohezi, 89
Harbin census of 1913, 93–96 *passim*
Harbin identity, vii, 4, 10ff, 18–21 *passim*, 25, 28, 41, 46, 96, 107, 137, 149, 158f
Harbin population, 9f, 18, 33, 35, 38f, 85, 89–103, 118
Harbin press, 12, 41, 133. *See also* publishing
Harbin Station, 19–21, 29, 36, 45, 128, plate
Herald of Asia (*Vestnik Azii*), 100, 156f, 159f, 163, 167, 231. *See also* Society of Russian Orientologists
Hong Kong, 4, 64
housing, 26f, 31, 35–38, 70, 89, 120, 123, 141
Hulan, 17, 21, 24

Iadrintsev, N. M., 233
Ignatsius, S. V., 22ff, 27, 29
India, 32
interministerial rivalry, 8, 10, 25, 47, 49–78, 81, 118ff, 170–71, 210. *See also* civil-military conflict
Irkutsk, 18f, 37, 56, 96, 141f, 165
Ito Hirobumi, 19ff
Iugovich, A. I., 62, 64, 66–70 *passim*, 80–89 *passim*, 117f, 217; and CER construction, 21–25 *passim*, 27, 29, 31, 40, plate
Ivanov, N. I., 138f
Izvol'skii, A. P., 20, 165

Japan, 1f, 5, 19–23 *passim*, 39, 54, 56, 60f, 69, 80, 99, 123, 131, 164, 167–70, 174–77; views on Russian expansion, 7f, 10, 42–47 *passim*, 49, 52, 73–78; Japanese in Harbin, 19–20, 91, 102f, 175–76; Japanese studies in Russia, 146–54 *passim*, 158f, 209. *See also* Russo-Japanese war
Jewish community, 10f, 53, 78f, 96–109, 115, 134f, 143, 172f, 175, plate
Jiaosheju, 29, 80, 93, 119, 164, 175, 216
Jilin, 18, 21, 68, 138, 165f

Kabalkin, R. M., 99
Kamchatka, 99

Index

Kaufman, A. I., 221f
Kawakami Toshitsune, 20
Kazan, 12, 183–86 passim
Kerbedz, S. I., 22f, 29, 52, 58, 62ff, 66, 81f, 85, 140
Khabarovsk, 14, 21, 23, 30, 34ff, 43
Khilkov, S. N., 21, 23–27 passim, 84
Khodorovskii, I. I., 29, 64, 81
Khorvat, D. L., 20, 24, 54, 159, 161, 163, 165, 171; on Manchurian colonization, 77, 88, 90, 99, 103f; and Harbin politics, 116, 124f, 129, 131, 133, 136, 139–44 passim, 228, plate
Kiuner, N. V., 154, 157
Kokovtsov, N. I., xix, 11, 19, 71, 125, 134, 142ff, 156, 171; and Manchurian colonization, 105–8 passim, 113f
Komissarzhevskaia, 19
Komura Jutaro, 50, 75
Korea, 5, 19–20, 31, 44f, 47, 59ff, 80, 85, 146–54 passim, 159
Korf, A. N., 15
Kornilov, L. G., 67
Korostovets, I. Ia., 20, 159, 165, 231
Krivoshein, A. V., 87f, 111ff, 174
Kuropatkin, A. N., 7, 100, 115, 124f, 136, 155; and interministerial rivalry, 47, 49, 52ff, 62f, 68, 70, 73f, 80–87 passim, 119

labor, 30–35 passim, 39f, 58, 66, 74, 78, 90, 94f, 114, 166, plate; Chinese, 26, 31–33, 43, 102, 164. See also Chinese migration
Lake Baikal, 43
Lamsdorff, 49, 54, 74f, 118
land, 9, 26–29, 37, 46, 74, 82–88 passim, 92f, 104, 127, 159
language learning, 32, 95f, 102, 146–54, 158–59, 176, 229, 236. See also Eastern Institute
Latvians, 78
Lazarev, K. P., 99
legal system, 28, 117–20, 195, plate
lektors, 150, 153, 164
Lenin, V. I., 12
Lepeshinskii, V. P., 126, 136–42 passim, 223
Li Hongzhang, 5f, 23, 28, 58, 61, 82f
liberalism, 4, 7–12 passim, 41, 78–79, 85–90 passim, 104–8 passim, 114, 142–45, 195–96. See also colonialism; Khorvat, D. L.; religion; Witte, S. Iu.

Linevich, N. P., 124f, 128, 135–40 passim
liquor, 18, 26, 38, 92, 122, 128, 207
Lobanov-Rostovskii, A. B., 6, 59
Lobko, P. L., 70

Maeda, Z. A., 153
Malevskii-Malevich, N. A., 19
Manchu language, 147–54 passim, 184, 238
Manchuria Station, 9, 91, 135
Maritime province, 9, 67, 91, 111, 121
Martynov, E. I., 51, 171
May Fourth movement, 163
medicine, 23, 30, 38ff, 103, 113, 122f, 136
migration, 6, 32, 57, 78–114
Mishchenko, P. I., 67
Mitsui Bussan, 99
Mojiagou, 92, 123
Mongolia, 44, 60, 121, 147, 150–56 passim, 163f, 171, 231f
Moscow, 3, 34
Mudanjiang, 17
Mukden, 18, 42, 116, 123–27 passim, 148; and Russian occupation, 68, 72, 76f, 151ff, 160
municipal council, 100f, 104, 128f, 142, 148, 163, 167
Murav'ev, M. N., 58–61 passim
Murav'ev (-Amurskii), N. N., 56, 186
Muslims, 17

Nadarov, I. P., 76, 100, 127, 131, 136ff
Nagasaki, 25
Nemirovich-Danchenko, V. I., 115, 121
Nesmelov, Arsenii, 14
New Town (nangang), 18, 29, 36ff, 92ff, 119, 122, 137
Nikolai II, Tsar, 5, 44, 67, 82f, 86, 88, 109, 113, 127; and interministerial rivalry, 48–57 passim, 59, 61, 73f
Ninguta, 24f
Nishi-Rosen agreement (1898), 60, 80

Odessa, 30, 34, 56, 65, 97, 126
Old Harbin (xiangfang), 26, 29, 36ff, 92, 94, 122
opium, 27, 67
Ossendowski, A. F., 116, 122, 124, 132, 135, 139ff, 144, 226

Palestine, 78f, 98
Paris, see World's Fair

plague, 92–95, 162, plate
Pleve, V. K., 48, 73, 76, 83, 86, 88f, 109, 111, 217
Pobedonostsev, K. P., 47, 50
Podstavin, G. V., 153, 157
Pogranichnaia (Suifenhe), 9, 84, 89, 91
Pokotilov, D. D., 32, 37, 82
Poletika, M. I., 23, 33
Polish community, 4, 10, 78, 96f, 102–8, 141, 223
Port Arthur, 25, 32f, 38, 42, 54, 58–77 passim, 81, 90, 104, 129, 158; Japanese attack on, 20, 44, 77, 120, 122, 152
Port Said, 90
Portsmouth peace treaty (1905), 11, 90, 115, 125
Pozdneev, Aleksandr, 146–54 passim, 174f, 186–89 passim, 230
Pozdneev, Dmitrii, 17, 27, 32, 147, 150, 154f, 174f, 187ff, 236
Prison El Dorado, 12, 116, 140f
Pristan (daoli), 11, 29, 36ff, 46, 92ff, 103, 119, 134, 137
prostitution, 38f, 103, 122, 125, 134
publishing, 41, 129, 133, 140f, 152f, 156, 159–66, 235. See also censorship; Harbin press

Qiqihar, 18, 21, 24, 26, 33, 80, 83, 88; in Boxer uprising, 35, 46, 152

railroads, 1ff, 5–11 passim, 20–21, 28–31 passim, 42–47 passim, 56, 112f, 193. See also Chinese Eastern Railroad; Trans-Siberian Railway
regions, regionalism, 3f, 16, 40f, 57, 168–77, 197
religion, 34–40 passim, 66, 72, 85f, 88f, 122, 154, plate. See also Jewish community; sectarians
Rennenkampf, P. K., 12, 138
Revolution of 1905, 125–39 passim. See also labor; Lepeshinskii, V. P.; Ossendowski, A. F.; Rovenskii, P. V.; Vetoshkin, M. K.
Riazan-Ural'sk, 21f, 30, 99
Rittikh, A. A., 88, 109, 111f, 174
Riutin, M. N., 174
Romanov, B. A. vii, 6, 49, 51f, 59, 61, 68, 74
Romanov, P. M., 23, 58, 62, 65, 80, 117

Romanov Commission (1903), 87–89, 104, 109, 111. See also colonialism
Rothstein, L. Iu., 28, 201
Rovenskii, P. V., 129, 135, 140
Rudakov, A. V., 151ff, 157
Russian Far East, 3, 9–14 passim, 20f, 30–39 passim, 67, 83f, 87, 111, 116f, 144; governors general, 54–58, 70, 99, 159. See also Maritime province; Transbaikal; Ussuri; Vladivostok
Russian sinology, 7f, 147–67 passim, 181–90, plate
Russian "specialness," 12, 44, 234. See also Ukhtomskii, E. E.
Russo-Chinese Bank, 6, 28, 53, 58, 60–63 passim, 105; activities in China, 23f, 32, 37, 63, 72, 82, 90f, 99
Russo-Chinese local relations, 33, 41, 91, 107f, 172, plate. See also Jiaosheju; Jilin; Qiqihar
Russo-Chinese trade, 15–18, 90–94 passim, 98, 101, 108f, 157, 206; prior to Russo-Japanese war, 40f, 57f, 85, 147f, 208, 210
Russo-Japanese war, 6–11 passim, 16, 35, 112, 116, 152f, 155f, 161, 169; and interministerial rivalry, 50f, 55, 74–77; and Harbin, 90, 97, 120–26. See also Japan
Russo-Korean Bank, 60

St. Petersburg, vii, 3, 12, 93, 106, 133, 155
St. Petersburg University, Chinese section, 147, 155, 186–89 passim, 231
Sakhalin, 153
Sakharov, V. V., 63
Sanxing, 17
Sazonov, S. D., 171
sectarians, 66, 85, 87ff, 111
Shandong, 15, 59, 94
Shanghai, 23, 122, 161f
Shcheglovitov, I. G., 142
Shidlovskii, A. I., 23–29 passim, 35
Shkurkin, P. V., 166, plate
Shmidt, P. P., 151ff, 157
Shou Shan, 68
Shumiatskii, B. Z., 144, 174
Siberian Railway Committee, 27, 35, 54f, 62ff, 70, 110
Skidel'skii, L. S., 99

Social Democrats, 11, 130, 136, 144
Society of Russian Orientologists (SRO), 148f, 155–60, 173, 231. *See also Herald of Asia*
Soldatov, V. V., 91, 93f, 96
Sol'skii, D. M., 55, 70
South Manchurian Railway, 19
Soviet era, 7f, 163
soybeans, 18, 91f, 98f, 160, 169, 233
Spal'vin, E. G., 153, 157
Spitsyn, A. V., 153, 155f, 160–66 *passim*, 173
Stolypin, Peter, 101, 106, 108, 142ff, 158
Stolypin reforms, 6, 79, 109–13 *passim*
Suez Canal, 43, 62
Sungari River, 1, 14–18, 24–29 *passim*, 34–37 *passim*, 75, 123, plate

telegraph, 126, 130f
Tianjin, 31ff, 165
Tibet, 147, 154
Tifontai, N. I. (Li Fengtai), 14–17 *passim*, 199f
Tishenko, P. S., 153, 155f, 160, 166f
Tolstoi, L. N., 80
Tomsk, 18, 57, 136
Trans-Amur Railway Brigade, 73f, 119, 195, 214, 218
Transbaikal, 9, 24, 44, 56, 83, 88, 104; railroad, 31, 33, 124, 126, 133, 138
Trans-Siberian Railway, 56–59 *passim*, 78, 86, 115, 126, 128, 135f; construction, 1, 5, 9, 28, 31, 53, 194f; perceptions of, 42f, 45, 62, 75, 168f. *See also* Transbaikal; Ussuri; *and under* Chinese Eastern Railroad: construction
treaties, 42f, 58–61 *passim*, 72, 80, 94, 101, 117, 158; 1896 Russo-Chinese, 6, 65, 70
Tsybikov, G. Ts., 154, 157
Turkestan, 2, 7, 156
Tychino, N. N., 140f

Uganda, 79
Ukhtomskii, E. E., 5, 23, 28, 40, 42, 44, 52, 58ff, 147
Ukraine, 78, 106

United States of America, 1, 4, 20, 23, 42–47 *passim*, 62, 64, 75, 104
Ussuri, 3, 14f, 22, 56, 58, 83; railroad, 24, 30–33 *passim*, 43, 54, 133, 165

Vannovskii, P. S., 50, 59, 65
Vasil'ev, V. P., 12, 147, 154, 156, 160, 163, 184–88
Venttsel, A. N., 20, 28, 65, 82
Veresaev, V. V., 128, 136
Vetoshkin, M. K., 116, 126, 130, 134–40 *passim*, 226
viceroyalty, 51, 54f, 72, 74–77, 120, 123, 147, 170f, 215. *See also* Alekseev, E. I.
Vladivostok, viii, 43f, 56, 59, 62f, 65, 117, 119f, 127, 165, 169; and CER construction, 5, 24–27 *passim*, 30, 32f, 39, 99; orientology at, 12, 138, 149–52 *passim*, 174f, 188, 190
Volodchenko, N. G., 67, 156
Volunteer Shipping Fleet, 63, 65

Witte, S. Iu., 23, 35, 40, 43, 134, 136f, 140, 147ff, 154f, 187ff; and colonialism, 3, 5ff, 10, 160, 172ff, 195, plate; and interministerial conflict, 47–54 *passim*, 58–74 *passim*, 80–91 *passim*, 104f, 109–14, 118f
World's Fair (Paris), 42–43

Xingan mountains, 9, 31, 83
Xu Jingcheng, 22, 28

Yamagata Aritomo, 45
Yangtse (Changjiang), 60, 212
Yellow Peril, 12, 20, 43f, 81, 148f, 158, 160, 198
Yellow Russia, 43
Yellow Sea, 22, 43, 58
Yingkou, 32
Yokohama, 20

Zhailainuoer coal mines, 133, 167
Zhanguangcailing Range, 21f, 24f
Zhifu, 14, 31ff, 40, 165
Zionists, 79, 107

Library of Congress Cataloging-in-Publication Data
Wolff, David
  To the Harbin Station : the liberal alternative in
Russian Manchuria, 1898–1914 / David Wolff.
    p. cm.
  Includes bibliographical references and index.
  ISBN 0-8047-3266-3
  1. Harbin (China) — History. 2. China — History — 20th
century. 3. Russians — China — Harbin. I. Title.
DS796.H4W64   1999
951'.84 — dc21   98-29100
                                                        CIP
                                                        Rev.

⊚   This book is printed on acid-free, recycled paper.

Original printing 1999
Last figure below indicates year of this printing:
08   07   06   05   04   03   02   01   00   99